AF844672

Witnesses and Evidence in Ancient Greek Literature

Trends in Classics – Supplementary Volumes

Edited by
Franco Montanari and Antonios Rengakos

Associate Editors
Stavros Frangoulidis · Fausto Montana · Lara Pagani
Serena Perrone · Evina Sistakou · Christos Tsagalis

Scientific Committee
Alberto Bernabé · Margarethe Billerbeck
Claude Calame · Kathleen Coleman · Jonas Grethlein
Philip R. Hardie · Stephen J. Harrison · Stephen Hinds
Richard Hunter · Giuseppe Mastromarco
Gregory Nagy · Theodore D. Papanghelis
Giusto Picone · Alessandro Schiesaro
Tim Whitmarsh · Bernhard Zimmermann

Volume 123

Witnesses and Evidence in Ancient Greek Literature

Edited by
Andreas Markantonatos, Vasileios Liotsakis
and Andreas Serafim

DE GRUYTER

ISBN 978-3-11-075116-1
e-ISBN (PDF) 978-3-11-075197-0
e-ISBN (EPUB) 978-3-11-075207-6
ISSN 1868-4785

Library of Congress Control Number: 2021946982

Bibliographic information published by the Deutsche Nationalbibliothek
The Deutsche Nationalbibliothek lists this publication in the Deutsche Nationalbibliografie; detailed bibliographic data are available on the Internet at http://dnb.dnb.de.

© 2021 Walter de Gruyter GmbH, Berlin/Boston
Editorial Office: Alessia Ferreccio and Katerina Zianna
Logo: Christopher Schneider, Laufen
Printing and binding: CPI books GmbH, Leck

MIX
Papier aus verantwortungsvollen Quellen
FSC® C083411

www.degruyter.com

Contents

Part III: Scripting Witnesses and Evidence: Prose and Verse Texts

Part IV: The Cultural Workings of Witnesses and Evidence

Acknowledgements

The editors would like to acknowledge a number of individuals and institutions, whose help and support have been invaluable in the conception and completion of this volume. We would like to thank, first and foremost, the two senior editors of *Trends in Classics* at De Gruyter, Professors Antonios Rengakos (Aristotle University of Thessaloniki/Member of the Academy of Athens) and Franco Montanari (University of Genova), for believing in the value of the work at hand and wholeheartedly supporting its publication.

The editors would also like to thank most warmly the contributors, who have been very patient and helpful throughout the process of putting together this volume, in the face of many rounds of revisions and demands on their time. Indeed, we have been fortunate to work alongside the contributors from our initial inquiries and theoretical meanderings, and we have been delighted to see how those exchanges of initial ideas and outlines have led to the formulation of chapters that will enhance our knowledge and understanding of the features, purposes, texts and contexts of witnesses and evidence in antiquity. It is fair to say that this fruitful and fascinating result of our admirably harmonious cooperation smooths our path and lightens our labours.

Andreas Serafim would like, finally, to thank the Research Centre for Greek and Latin Literature of the Academy of Athens for providing excellent research facilities that make the timely completion of this volume possible; and Millie Gall for reading and commenting on several drafts of the Introduction and of other chapters within the volume.

Abbreviations throughout this volume follow those in *L'Année philologique* or the *Oxford Classical Dictionary*. A certain level of formatting standardisation has been imposed to ensure consistency across the volume, but individual stylistic distinctiveness has been respected. The volume is intended for the specialist scholars and graduate students of prose (oratory, philosophy and historiography) and verse (drama) texts. All long quotations of ancient Greek (and Latin) are accompanied by English translation.

Andreas Markantonatos, Vasileios Liotsakis and Andreas Serafim
Kalamata and Athens, June 2021

Andreas Markantonatos, Vasileios Liotsakis and Andreas Serafim

Introduction: Witness and Evidence in Legal, Oratorical and Other Literary Contexts in Antiquity

In March 2018 the Centre for Ancient Rhetoric and Drama (C.A.R.D.) at the University of the Peloponnese organised the Second Attic Drama and Oratory International Kalamata Conference with the theme *Witnesses and Evidence: Information and Decision in Drama and Oratory. From Antiquity to Byzantium*, which gave rise to many highly interesting and thought-provoking papers. In particular, these fourteen selected chapters that began life at the Second Kalamata Conference aim to examine an important interdisciplinary, intertextual and intercultural topic: witnesses and a wide range of ways and means of collecting evidence.

This is of great significance in varied legal systems across cultures and ages, but also in the texts and contexts which provide us with information about these systems. Classics, anthropology, sociology and studies of comparative law, among a plethora of contemporary disciplines, and several texts that present the mindset, folklore and cultural identity of ancient populations, provide details about the degree to which legal systems of the past valued the importance of witnesses. Chanakya, who was, among other qualities, an ancient Indian jurist, points out, in his political treatise *Arthashastra* (book J, chapter 11, verse 50), that "the parties shall themselves produce witnesses who are not far removed either by time or place. Witnesses who are far away, or who will not stir out, shall be made to present themselves by the order of the judge".[1] In the ancient Hindu legal system, "the king, cognizant of laws, and in consideration of the duties of the (four) several tribunal, shall ascertain the truth and determine the correctness of the allegation, description, time and place of the transaction, giving rise to the case, as well as its usages, and pronounce the true judgment".[2]

The quintessence of legal systems across cultures and ages has always been the ability to deliver justice that is based on provable truth and impartiality. This makes the ways and means of collecting, constructing and using witnesses

1 Sharan 1978, 65.
2 Dutt 1979, 258.

https://doi.org/10.1515/9783110751970-001

and evidence as important as to be protected, diachronically and interculturally, by the gods and the divine. The Quran, for example, pays much attention to the god-protected and -favoured character of witnesses; "O true believers, observe justice when you appear as witnesses before God, and let not hatred towards any induce you to do wrong, but act justly; this will approach nearer unto piety, and fear God, for God is fully acquainted with what you do" (Volume 1, page 74). The divine character of witnesses is also a matter of importance in the ancient Athenian legal system, since the gods are summoned by litigants as witnesses, who can testify the validity and factuality of their arguments.[3]

The references in ancient Indian and Hindu legal systems, as well as in the Islamic sacred text, to the value and importance of witnesses and evidence point to an intriguing topic that deserves, and thus calls for, further scholarly investigation: namely, that there is a universal intercultural model of gathering or constructing witnesses and other pieces of evidence. Ancient systems of justice use them, at least in principle, to reveal the truth. In theory, this applies to the function of witnesses in the ancient Greek (the classical Athenian) legal system, since the declared purpose of all speakers is to reveal, tell, present and defend the truth. In practice, however, the purpose of witnesses and evidence that is presented through speech is to corroborate the arguments of the speakers regardless of whether or not these are true. The highest principle in the mind of speech-writers, their clients and the speakers themselves was to win the case whatever the arguments and techniques they used; that is why Todd says that "cases in Athens are won or lost... on the quality of speech".[4]

Beyond truthfulness, or what we may call "convenient truthfulness" (i.e. the presentation of arguments and witnesses for the purpose of supporting a speaker's arguments, despite these being not fully compatible with factual

3 Dinarchus 1.64: "I summon as my witnesses (μαρτύρομαι), Athenians, the awful goddesses and their abode, the heroes of the land, Athena Polias, and those other gods who have obtained our city and countryside as their home, to show that when the people has consigned to you for punishment one who, against his country's interests, has accepted a part of the <imported money>, one who has defiled and ruined the city's prosperity and betrayed that country". Demosthenes 25.11: "before you cast your votes, each of the judges must reflect that he is being watched by hallowed and inexorable Justice (τὴν ἀπαραίτητον καὶ σεμνὴν Δίκην), who, as Orpheus, that prophet of our most sacred mysteries, tells us, sits beside the throne of Zeus and oversees all the works of men. Each must keep watch and ward lest he shame that goddess". On the techniques of calling upon the gods to act as witnesses in classical Athenian lawcourt, see Polinskaya 2012, 23–37; Martin 2009; Serafim 2020a, Chapters 1 and 2 on the role of the divinised *phēmē* in providing evidence for the validity of Aeschines' accusations against Timarchos of being a prostitute (1.127–129).

4 Todd 1990, 23; Martin 2009; Serafim 2020b.

events and actions), the Attic legal system also converges with other ancients in the fact that the act of witnessing or evidence-gathering relates to divinity. It was customary for the Athenian speakers to call upon the gods (cf. Demosthenes, *Philippic* 3.54)[5] and the divine (including divinised entities or agents, such as Earth and Sun, as, for example, in Aeschines 3.260, Demosthenes 22.78, 23.61, 34.29, 40.5), and use their witnesses to achieve strategic purposes in the context of the deliberative decision-making art of the Athenian public speaking. References to omniscient and omnipresent divinised entities can also be found in Solon's fr. 36: "the great mother of the Olympian gods, the Black Earth, from whom I drew up the boundary stones stuck in everywhere, witnesses these things in the court of time". As argued in Serafim's book on the use of religious discourse in Attic oratory, "the Sun, an important generator of life, is personified and deified and, together with Earth, they are considered 'all-seeing' divine witnesses of past events, especially wrongdoing. References to Earth that the Athenians revere are an attempt to appeal to the audience's emotions and to inculcate into the people the impression that their decision affects their land and, by extension, their civic community. The invocations to Earth and Sun demonstrate the way Attic orators use fear to manipulate the emotional reaction of the audience, whose members are subtly invited to envisage themselves as being inspected and punishable by the divine audience, should they decide to vote in favour of the speakers".[6] There is, in other words, an incessant game of control, power and manipulation that lies behind the use of divine-like witnesses for the purpose of winning over the audiences in the settings for public speaking.

To mention the omnipresent and omniscient gods or divine agents as witnesses for the speakers' arguments in oration is, in fact, to offer an implicit but still masterful substitute for the process of examining accounts (the so-called *euthynai* or *euthyna*), aiming to control the judges and reduce the extent of making arbitrary decisions in legal and political, or politicised, cases. References to the gods as being witnesses in secular legal contexts also point to the value that religion had in harmonising the world, keeping factions of the society together,

5 *Philippic* 3.54: "and that, as all Heaven is my witness, you will never be able to do; but you have reached such a height of folly or of madness or—I know not what to call it, for this fear too has often haunted me, that some demon is driving you to your doom, that from love of calumny or envy or ribaldry, or whatever your motive may be, you clamour for a speech from these hirelings, some of whom would not even disclaim that title, and you derive amusement from their vituperations".

6 Serafim 2020a, 98–99. On the use of oaths to summon divine witnesses, see Sommerstein and Torrance 2014, esp. 1–2, 28, 41–44.

determining the function of the institutions in the ancient *polis*, and intervening in the lives of humans. To call upon the divine witnesses becomes, then, a matter of interpreting life, understanding human behaviour and shedding further light on the anthropological, sociological and spiritual construction of ancient societies – in short, divine witnesses become a powerful heuristic tool of (re)discovering aspects of ancient culture.

The importance of witnesses and the other means and forms of evidence for the ancient Greek legal, political and cultural system is also underlined by the fact that they were used in all the steps and processes of legality, from the right of litigants to call upon witnesses during pre-legal procedures (as the *anakrisis* was, the preliminary hearing of a case before an *archōn* of the city-state)[7] to the use of legal statutes, oaths, slave statements (mostly obtained through torture – a topic of controversial character in classical scholarship on the Greek orators, which is discussed below), contracts, wills etc. – all the "artless" or "inartistic" proofs, as Aristotle calls them, i.e. evidence that orators do not invent on their own but rather find already in existence (*Rh.* 1355b35–39). There are also, according to Aristotle, the "artful" or "artistic" proofs (*Rh.* 1356a1–4), which fall largely into three categories: the presentation of the speaker's character (*ēthos*),[8] the arousal of an emotional response of the audience (*pathos*)[9] and the construction and presentation of arguments (*logos*).[10] The strategies that relate to these three categories of "artful"/"artistic" proofs and corroborate the speaker's arguments, with the purpose of enabling him to win over and persuade the audience (e.g. narrative and lively picturing of past events and actions; references to the gods and the divine; and the use of the language of persuasion

7 On *anakrisis*, see Serafim in this volume.

8 Aristotle notes that "the orator persuades by moral character when his speech is delivered in such a manner as to render him worthy of confidence" (1356a4–6); and "character has almost, so to speak, the greatest authority in winning belief" (1356a13; cf. 1377b20–24; 1378a6–15). The *ēthos of sympathy* succinctly underlines the potential of the description of the speaker's character, and that of his opponents, to persuade the audience: as Bruss 2013, 37 points out, "to create trustworthy speaker–centred *ēthos* through reasonable thoughts, standard style and artless composition". Further on the same matter: Wisse 1989, 34, 58–59; Amossy 2001, 6–7; Riggsby 2004, 181.

9 The importance of emotions is also highlighted in several works before Aristotle, as he himself points out (*Rhetoric* 1354a11–24): from Gorgias' *Encomium of Helen* 9–10 and Homeric epics to Hesiod, Thucydides, the lost work of Thrasymachus, *Eleoi*, several tragic plays and, of course, orators. Cf. Carey 1994, 26–34; Konstan 2006, 3–40, 125–133; 2010, 411–425; Rubinstein 2004, 189–190; Fortenbaugh 2007, 117–120.

10 On a comprehensive discussion of all three sorts of "artful" proofs, with suggestions about further readings, see Serafim 2017, Chapter 1.

when depicting the speaker's *ēthos*, or interrogating and receiving information from the opponents, in order to refute accusations, confirm allegations and influence decision-making), are of paramount importance for the quality of the speech which determines the outcome of an oration in the Athenian institutional contexts of public speaking.

There is booming bibliography in the classical scholarship on the role, the features, the purposes and the means of collecting or constructing witnesses and other forms of evidence.[11] Much discussion has been devoted, for example, to the use of violence to receive witnesses from slaves through the process of *basanos*, which took place out of the court.[12] Not many scholars believe that this process was actually used in antiquity: the speakers never miss the opportunity to ask for the opponents' slaves to be tortured under the law, but the receivers of this request are highly likely to deny it. The speakers were able to anticipate the rejection of their request, so they claim in speeches that this is an indication of their opponents being guilty of error and trying to hide the truth.[13] There are some scholars, however, who leave open the possibility that violence was at times actually used as a means of gathering information; as Mirhady argues, "the rhetorical effectiveness [of evidentiary *basanos*] had to rely on a reality in which violence and torture against slaves was common practice. Otherwise, the fiction would have been utterly transparent".[14] A dispute is also provoked by the ambiguous character of *basanos*: does it include violence, even to death, or does it only include verbal cornering of the opponents? Or is it perhaps a bit of both, as it seems to be indicated in Isocrates 17.15, where Pasion is presented as being agreed a verbal *basanos* to be used on his slave, while deciding to withdraw him when torture was demanded?[15] It seems that the reference by Isocrates points to the twofold nature of *basanos*: verbal questioning changes gradually,

---

11 Thür 2005, 146–169 offers a succinct, comprehensive and usefully informative recent overview of the importance of witnesses in the Athenian legal system, helping us to better and more fully understand the processes and outcomes in the law-court. Further on proofs in Attic oratory: Thür 1977; Gagarin 1990; Todd 1990, 19–39.

12 Thür 1977, 214–232; Mirhady 1996.

13 Thür 1977, 1996; Todd 1990; Gagarin 1996.

14 Mirhady 2000, 72; cf. Hunter 1994, 91–95; Johnstone 1999.

15 Isocrates 17.15: "After he had acted in this way, men of the jury, Pasion, believing that his past conduct had clearly been in error and thinking he could rectify the situation by his subsequent acts, came to us and asserted that he was ready to surrender the slave for torture. We chose questioners and met in the temple of Hephaestus. And I demanded that they flog and rack the slave, who had been surrendered, until they were of opinion that he was telling the truth. But Pasion here asserted that they had not been chosen as torturers, and bade them make oral interrogation of the slave if they wished any information".

under conditions, into torture – a combination that makes *basanos* effective in releasing the truth (cf. Dem. 30.37).[16]

Another topic that has received the interest of the scholarly community is the use of witnesses in genres other than oratory. Todd, for example, in a recently published chapter in the volume *The Ancient Art of Persuasion across Genres and Topics*, offers a detailed account of the use of the language of witnesses (*marturía/martúrion*) in the context of historiography, examining the role witnesses have to play in validating the historicity and factuality of the histories that writers describe.[17] It is this kind of multi-genre approach to the ways and means of constructing witnesses and collecting evidence that enhances our knowledge and understanding of the limits between (prose and verse) genres and the etiquette of literary techniques, which, as argued, provides the writer with the restrictive framework within which he needs to compose a work.[18]

These aspects of witnesses and evidence that put them in the centre of the institutional and cultural (e.g. religious, literary) construction of ancient societies indicate that it is important to keep offering nuanced approaches to the topic of this volume. To advance knowledge of the processes of presenting witnesses and gathering or constructing evidence is, in fact, to better and more fully understand the ways in which deliberative Athenian democracy functions, what the core elements of political life and civic identity are, and how they relate to the system of using *logos* to make decisions. For, witnesses and evidence were important prerequisites of getting the Athenian citizenship and exerting the civic/political identity as a member of the community. We should not forget that having steady evidence and providing witnesses was an important part of the process of *dokimasia*, formally used when an Athenian sought to become a member of the *Boulē*. He should provide information and witnesses about matters of political importance, such as his family tombs, payment of taxes and

16 Dem. 30.37: "Therefore you believe that in private and in public torture is the most accurate of all proofs, and when both slaves and free men are present, and it is necessary to find out what is being investigated, you don't use the testimony of the freemen, but torture the slaves in order to discover the truth. And rightly so, men of the jury. For in the past some witnesses seem not to have sworn truthfully, whereas none of those who have been tortured have ever been convicted of not speaking the truth under torture".

17 Todd 2017, 281–298.

18 It has been argued, for example, that the use of techniques of arousing emotions is different from context to context; Rubinstein 2004, 187–203; 2005, 129–145. It has also been argued that the public or private legal character of the cases affects the use of religious discourse in speeches; cf. Martin 2009; Serafim 2020a.

military services (cf. Aristotle, *Ath. Pol.* 55.3–5).[19] It is important, therefore, all the matters that relate to information-gathering and decision-making to be examined anew. Emphasis should be placed on a variety of genres to allow scholars to recreate the fullest and clearest possible image about witnessing and evidencing in antiquity. Prose genres (especially, oratory and historiography), together with verse genres (mostly, but not exclusively, drama), point to the impact of witnesses and evidence in constructing the quality of public orations and, thus, in influencing the cultural workings of the society (as reflected, for example, upon social institutions such as marriage, and matters of interpersonal relations such as gender relations and communication between individuals). Chapters in this volume include considerations of social, political, literary and moral theory, alongside studies of the impact of information-gathering and decision-making in oratory and drama, with a steady focus on the application of key ideas and values in social and political justice and issues of ethical concern.

The interdisciplinary and multi-contextual character of the analysis of witnesses and evidence in the chapters of this volume is developed across four themed parts, each examining a specific aspect or feature of information-gathering. Part I, "Written and Oral Evidence", comprises two chapters that revolve around several matters of the oral and written character of witnesses. In the first chapter of this part, "The Role of Written Documents in Athenian Trials", Edward M. Harris discusses the claim of several scholars that written records played hardly any role in trials at Athens. This chapter examines the use of written documents in trials for public cases and questions this assumption. It is shown that laws, decrees, letters of kings and officials, catalogues, plaints and other records are frequently cited, quoted and discussed in trials starting in the late fifth century. The reliability of these documents is almost never questioned, and written records are often preferred to the testimony of witnesses.

In the second and last chapter of Part I, "Rumour and Hearsay Evidence in the Athenian Law-Courts", Asako Kurihara aims to examine the usage of hearsay information in the Athenian legal system. Hearsay evidence (*akoē*) was accepted in the Athenian courts more widely than what usually believed. Athenian law imposed restrictions on the use of hearsay witness. For example, Dem. 57 indicates that the hearsay evidence is regarded as an unreliable source of information. However, re-examination of forensic speeches that make use of hearsay witnesses shows that these are often presented as eligible sources of information, even though it ranks second to testimony provided by eye witness-

19 Further on *dokimasia* and identity construction: Todd 1993, 288; 2010, 73–98.

es. The reliance on hearsay is further attested in the litigants' use of rumour. One prominent example is Aeschines, who had succeeded in prosecuting Timarchus without presenting any direct evidence for his prostitution. For him, the rumours served as testimony confirming common knowledge in the Athenian community. Demosthenes, who had criticised Aeschines' use of rumour at that time, later reemphasised the force of rumour as a form of evidence. Rumour, as common knowledge based on hearsay, does not have to be confirmed by individual witnesses. Here lies the democratic feature of the Athenian courts, as well as the danger. The Athenian courts distinguished between direct evidence and hearsay evidence, privileging the former over the latter.

Part II, "The Rhetoric of Information-Gathering and Decision-Making", consists of four chapters that discuss a variety of techniques, pertaining to the Aristotelian "artful"/"artistic" proofs. The chapters in Part II examine, specifically, the ways in which rhetorical techniques that draw on *ēthos*, *pathos* and *logos* are used to influence decision-making in the institutional contexts of public speaking in Athens. The first chapter of this part by Guy Westwood has the title "Audience Memory as Evidence in the Trial *on the Crown*". Although we are accustomed to seeing plenty of use of witness testimony in the surviving speeches from fourth-century Athenian public trials – for example in Aeschines' and Demosthenes' speeches from the trial on the Embassy in 343 BC – the speeches from the trial on the Crown in 330 BC (Aeschines' *Against Ctesiphon* and Demosthenes' *On the Crown*) present an intriguingly different picture. Although both orators make ample use of other familiar types of documentary evidence, Demosthenes only calls witnesses twice (18.135, 137), and Aeschines never calls any. Analysing a series of significant passages, Westwood argues in this chapter that Demosthenes' near-avoidance of witnesses is part of a concerted strategy to co-opt the judges (and the citizens in the informal trial audience) as the most significant "witnesses" to his own career (and Aeschines'), and part of a wide-ranging effort to capitalize on Aeschines' failure (at least judging by *Against Ctesiphon* as we have it) to build explicit meaningful connection with the judges based on their past shared experiences and on their recollection of how the *dēmos* – many of the listeners included – had personally endorsed Demosthenes' policies, especially in the critical years 341–338 BC.

The second chapter, "Additional Information in Witness Testimonies in Classical Athens", by Noboru Sato, has two purposes: the first is to show that a litigant gives detailed information on his own liturgical services or on the opponent's wrongdoings other than the main issue through witness testimonies, without telling anything concrete about himself. In other words, witness testimony with additional information gives credibility to the character portraiture either of the litigant himself or of his opponents. The second purpose of the chapter is to argue that Athenian litigants could bring to the attention of the court a wide range of personal supporters by making use of this type of witness testimonies. Although litigants usually presented those who were thought to have the best knowledge about the fact to be testified, they could presumably produce many supporters as witnesses of matters such as their own liturgical services or their opponents' bad conduct.

The next chapter, "Self-Quotations as Witnesses and Evidence: The Case of Isocrates' *Antidosis*", by Pasquale Massimo Pinto, aims to address the role of these quotations in the complex structure of the *Antidosis*, in relation to Isocrates' past experience as a logographer and as part of his effort to transform oratory into a new kind of prose. The speech has nothing to do with the *antidosis* case, except for the telling title: in fact, Isocrates imagined defending himself, like a new Socrates, from the charge, brought by a fictitious prosecutor, of corrupting youth through his teaching. In this imaginary trial, extensive quotations from his previous works are read by a clerk as if they were key evidence and, at the same time, the most reliable witnesses to his honourable conduct towards the *polis*. However, this set of extracts also functions as an auto-anthology, thus merging fictional court speech and literary criticism.

The chapter of Robert Sullivan, "Antiphon's Witnesses: Extending the Earliest Greek Theories of Argumentation", aims to advance our understanding of how argumentation was conceived in the earliest Greek rhetorical theory. It does so by examining a body of arguments, and the paratextual statements made about those arguments, as they are found in the works of the Attic orator Antiphon (480–411 BC), in situations where he attempts to either qualify or disqualify witnesses and their testimony. Though there is already a robust literature on Antiphon's use of *eikos* in argumentation, scholarship has rarely extended itself to note the reliance of sophistic argumentation on premises related to "probability". This chapter seeks to give nuance to our understanding of Antiphonic argument by examining the author's paratextual statements about matters of argument at stake. Taken together, Antiphon's paratextual statements give us the fullest sense of how argument theory was understood by him, and how the criteria used in the judgement of argumentation might be imagined. This chapter, then, gives shape to some general conclusions about Antiphon's conceptions of two related matters; the practical need to either qualify or disqualify the testimony of witness at trial and the contribution of such testimony to a more general theory of argumentation. These findings point to a nascent, quasi-technical vocabulary and conceptual structure, and support for a position that sophistic argumentation in the 5th century was becoming more sophisticated than the standard account would lead one to expect.

Part III, entitled "Scripting Witnesses and Evidence: Prose and Verse Texts", comprises five chapters, the first and the second of which explore Plato's *Apology of Socrates*. The first chapter, "The Questions in (Answering the Question about the Historicity of) Plato's *Apology of Socrates*", by Andreas Serafim, has two interrelated purposes: the first is to discuss the content, place and use of questions that are inserted into the transmitted Platonic text, with the aim of providing rhetorical and, in some cases non-verbal, evidence for Socrates' innocence and the lies of his accusers. The second purpose is to use questions as evidence about the historicity and factuality of the speech that Plato attributes to his teacher. It has been argued that questions are used in a rhetorically skilful way, being *introductory* or *explanatory* – enabling the speaker to present rhetorical evidence for his innocence and for Meletus' lies (19b–23d); *ēthos-depicting* for both the defendant and his accuser(s) (24c–34d); and *investigatory* – aiming to convey a message to the audience about the verdict Socrates thinks the judges should cast about him (36b–41c). The use of questions in the *Apology*, combined with our knowledge and understanding of oratorical practice and performance, may also point to this text being a reliable source of Socrates' law-court speech.

In the second chapter of Part III, "Plato's *Apology of Socrates*: The Rhetoric of Socrates' Defence and the Foundation of the Ancient Quarrel between Philosophy and Poetry", Ioannis N. Perysinakis examines the ancient quarrel between philosophy and poetry, as this is presented in the conversation between Socrates and Glaucon in *Republic* 607b. The ancient quarrel is a self-defence of philosophy against poetry and, as argued, it is a second-round defence of Socrates after the *Apology of Socrates*. Counteracting the prejudicial attack, Socrates uses arguments that might refute the unpleasant suspicion; he contests the disputed points by denying the fact and its harmfulness, and substitutes one motive for another not only denying the charges but arguing for the services done to the Athenians. Socrates also adopts elements of *eikos* and *ēthopoiia* to provide rhetorical evidence for his defence strategy and exploit his philosophical programme.

Vasileios Liotsakis, in the third chapter of Part III, "Witnesses and Evidence in Thucydides: The Institutional and Rhetorical Context of the Digression on the Tyrannicides", focuses on three levels of Thucydides' style, i.e. vocabulary, content and arrangement of the material, aiming to discuss two specific issues: the first is about the description of a period of uncertainty (in 415 BC), during which Alcibiades was accused and proved guilty of the sacrilege of mutilating the busts of Hermes. The second issue relates to the authorial ways in which Thucydides is presented as defending Alcibiades, mostly by neutralising the validity of the witnesses and evidence that Alcibiades' prosecutors used against him. The chapter comprises three parts: in the first, Liotsakis examines forensic vocabulary and themes of Thucydides 6.27–29 and 53–61; in the second, he explores the vocabulary Thucydides uses to highlight the fact that the *exemplum* of the tyrant slayers was presented in a misleading way by speakers in the law-court and the Assembly. It has been argued, in these two sections, that both forensic and political vocabulary indicate Thucydides' intention to accuse the Athenian orators of falsifying witnesses, testimonies and evidence (including the story of the tyrannicides) in Alcibiades' trial. In the third and last section of this chapter, reading Thucydides' digression on the tyrannicides through the prism of fourth-century oratory which includes references to Harmodius and Aristogeiton, Liotsakis concludes that Thucydides chose to narrate the tyrant slayers' story in a way that moves beyond the communicative etiquette of the Athenian court and the Assembly, in order to stress the superiority of historiography over oratory.

David Mirhady, in his chapter "The Torture of Prometheus", discusses torture, which is recognised by Aristotle, as argued earlier in this Introduction, as one of "inartistic" proofs. In *Prometheus Bound*, the god Prometheus is cast as an avatar, a divine incarnation embodying an idea of the free man bravely resisting tyrannical oppression. He is tortured at the beginning of the play as punishment, at the end in an attempt to elicit information from him. The play suggests connections between this torture and the "democratic" account of the torture of Aristogeiton, the Athenian tyrannicide, who was likewise tortured before being executed.

A similar analysis of witnessing and evidence-gathering that takes into consideration verse genres is also presented in the chapter of Margarita Sotiriou, "Poet, Patron, Message: Witness-Roles and the Game of Truth in Epinician *Eidography*". The victory Odes of Bacchylides and Pindar do not belong either to the masterpieces of the narrative genre or to the great speeches of classical Athens; *epinikion* is a "communal drama" (Kurke 1991), which celebrates an athletic victory in order to preserve the fame of the addressee in perpetuity. However, as Carey has indicated, the poet's task, his diction and the strategy he displays in order to persuade his audience, provide affinities not only with epideictic oratory, but also with the Athenian dramatic scene. Sotiriou attempts to examine this association by using Bacchylides' *Epinician* 10 as a test case. This Ode deserves closer examination: being the only poem of Bacchylides for an Athenian victory in the Isthmian games, the poem presents, through its rhetorical means of persuasion (the priamel etc.), an eloquent example for the political contextualisation of classical encomiastic poetry modelled, in a way, on the Old Elegy of Solon.

The final part of the volume, Part IV, has the title "The Cultural Workings of Witnesses and Evidence" and consists of two chapters which discuss two matters of culture: marriage and sexuality in the form of stories about sexual scandals. The first chapter, "Information and Decision in Sophocles' *Trachiniae* and Euripides' *Medea* and *Ino*", by Smaro Nikolaidou, is about marriage. In Sophocles' and Euripides' plays, there is awareness about monogamous marriage, which is expressed through the theme of female jealousy, tragically combined with kin-killing. In all three tragedies a central heroine, after having received the information of her husband's infidelity, makes her decision by organising a plan. In *Trachiniae*, Deianeira attempts to deter Heracles from loving his young captive, Iole, but unwillingly causes his death. In Euripides' *Ino* (according to Hyginus' *Fabula* 4), jealous Themis plans to kill Athamas' children born by his previous wife, Ino, but she unconsciously kills her own children because of Ino's plot against them. And Medea consciously kills her own children at the culminating point of her jealous agency against the unfaithful Jason. What is interesting for the themes and topics the volume at hand discusses is that in all three plays the dramatic heroines fight for their aim with witness and evidence. Euripides' *Ino* combines the role of a witness (as Themisto's devoted servant) with that of a central heroine, who plans her plot after having been informed by her mistress (and rival) Themisto. But, unfortunately, Ino's exceptional paradigm belongs to a lost play.

The second and last chapter of Part IV, and in fact the last of the whole volume, belongs to Rosalia Hatzilambrou and has the title "Scandals as Evidence in Attic Forensic Oratory: The Case of Aeschines' *Against Timarchus*". In this chapter, Hatzilambrou explores the inclusion of sexually scandalous incidents in the narrative of forensic speeches. Aeschines' *Against Timarchus* provides a case study, whereby the author argues that the narration of scandalous stories compensates for Aeschines' lack of factual evidence, mainly regarding his claim that Timarchus had prostituted himself, and contributes to the success of the action that Aeschines brought against Timarchus. Hatzilambrou calls attention to the tactics employed with reference to the narration of such incidents, which reveal the understanding on the part of the orator of the rhetorical importance and the potential persuasive power of the skilled construction and presentation within a narrative of scandalous stories, which could, and actually in Aeschines' speech did, function as pieces of evidence.

Bibliography

Amossy, R. (2001), 'Ethos at the Crossroads of Disciplines: Rhetoric, Pragmatics, Sociology', in: *Poetics Today* 22, 1–23.
Bruss, K.S. (2013), 'Persuasive *Ethopoeia* in Dionysius's Lysias', in: *Journal of the History of Rhetoric* 31, 34–57.
Carey, C. (1994), 'Rhetorical Means of Persuasion', in: I. Worthington (ed.), *Persuasion: Greek Rhetoric in Action*, London, 26–45.
Dutt, M.N. (1979), *The Dharma Shastra: Hindu Religious Codes*, New Delhi.
Fortenbaugh, W.W. (2007), 'Aristotle's *Art of Rhetoric*', in: I. Worthington (ed.), *A Companion to Greek Rhetoric*, London, 107–123.
Gagarin, M. (1990), 'The Nature of Proofs in Antiphon', in: *CPh* 85, 22–32.
Gagarin, M. (1996), 'The Torture of Slaves in Athenian Law', in: *CPh* 91, 1–18.
Hunter, V.J. (1994), *Policing Athens: Social Control in the Attic Lawsuits, 420-320 BC*, Princeton.
Johnstone, S. (1999), *Disputes and Democracy. The Consequences of Litigation in Ancient Athens*, Austin.
Konstan, D. (2006), *The Emotions of the Ancient Greeks: Studies in Aristotle and Classical Literature*, Toronto/Buffalo/London.
Konstan, D. (2010), 'Rhetoric and Emotion', in: I. Worthington (ed.), *A Companion to Greek Rhetoric*, Malden, MA, 411–425.
Martin, G. (2009), *Divine Talk: Religious Argumentation in Demosthenes*, Oxford.
Mirhady, D.C. (1996), 'Torture and Rhetoric in Athens', in: *JHS* 116, 119–131.
Mirhady, D.C. (2000), 'The Athenian Rationale for Torture', in: V. Hunter/J. Edmondson (eds.), *Law and Social Status*, Oxford, 53–74.
Polinskaya, I. (2012), 'Calling upon Gods as Witnesses in Ancient Greece', in: *Mètis* 10, 23–37.
Riggsby, A.M. (2004), 'The Rhetoric of Character in the Roman Courts', in: J. Powell/J. Paterson (eds.), *Cicero the Advocate*, Oxford, 165–185.
Rubinstein, L. (2004), 'Stirring up Dicastic Anger', in: D.L. Cairns/R.A. Knox (eds.), *Law, Rhetoric and Comedy in Classical Athens: Essays in Honour of Douglas M. MacDowell*, Swansea, 187–203.
Rubinstein, L. (2005), 'Dangerous Liaisons? Litigants and Witnesses in the Athenian Courts', in: R.W. Wallace/M. Gagarin (eds.), *Symposion 2001: Vorträge zur griechischen und hellenistischen Rechtsgeschichte*, Vienna, 99–120.
Serafim, A. (2017), *Attic Oratory and Performance*, London/New York.
Serafim, A. (2020a), *Religious Discourse in Attic Oratory and Politics*, London/New York.
Serafim, A. (2020b), *A Commentary on Lysias' Olympic Oration: Introduction, Translation, Comments*, Athens.
Sharan, M.K. (1978), *Court Procedure in Ancient India*, New Delhi.
Sommerstein, A.H./Torrance, I.C. (2014), *Oaths and Swearing in Ancient Greece*, Berlin/Boston.
Thür, G. (1977), *Beweisführung vor den Schwurgerichtshöfen Athens. Die Proklesis zur Basanos*, Wien.
Thür, G. (2005), 'The Role of the Witness in Athenian Law', in: M. Gagarin/D. Cohen (eds.), *The Cambridge Companion to Ancient Greek Law*, Cambridge, 146–169.
Todd, S.C. (1990), 'The Purpose of Evidence in Athenian Courts', in: P.A. Cartledge/P.C. Millett/S.C. Todd (eds.), *Nomos: Essays in Athenian Law, Politics and Society*, Cambridge, 19–39.
Todd, S.C. (1993), *The Shape of Athenian Law*, Oxford.

Todd, S.C. (2010), 'The Athenian Procedure(s) of *Dokimasia*', in: G. Thür (ed.), *Symposion 2009: Vorträge zur griechischen und hellenistischen Rechtsgeschichte*, Vienna, 73–99.

Todd, S.C. (2017), 'The Language of Rhetorical Proof in Greek Historical Writers: Witness Terminology', in: S. Papaioannou/A. Serafim/K. Demetriou (eds.), *The Ancient Art of Persuasion across Genres and Topics*, Leiden, 281–298.

Wisse, J. (1989), *Ethos and Pathos from Aristotle to Cicero*, Amsterdam.

Part I: **Written and Oral Evidence**

Edward M. Harris

The Role of Written Documents in Athenian Trials

Abstract: In his *Against Ctesiphon* (3.73) Aeschines observes that politicians may change their stories in their oral statements and try to cover up their crimes, but public records kept by public officials allow the people to discover those who have been corrupt in the past. This chapter studies the role of written documents in public cases in classical Athens. It reviews the kinds of written documents available in the Metroon (laws and decrees of the Council and Assembly, honorary decrees from other states, records of trials, letters from officials and foreign kings, records of import and export duties, leases of mines and sales of property, lists of citizens). These documents were used extensively in public cases starting in the late fifth century (Andocides' *On the Mysteries*, Lysias' *Against Agoratus*) down the late fourth century (Aeschines' *Against Ctesiphon*, Demosthenes' *On the Crown*) and are often used more than the testimony of witnesses.

In the speech he delivered in response to Demosthenes' accusation of treason at his trial in 343 BC, Aeschines (2.89) claims that he has been slandered. Fortunately, he says, the Athenians have provided the victims of slander with a powerful way to defend themselves: the preservation of written records in the public archives. Aeschines (3.73) returns to this theme in the speech he delivered against Ctesiphon in 330 BC. Politicians may change their stories in their oral statements and try to cover up their crimes, but public records kept by public officials allow the people to discover those who have been corrupt in the past. In both passages Aeschines draws a strong contrast between the oral statements made by accusers and politicians, and written records. While oral statements are often false or unreliable, written records can be trusted to preserve accurate information about the actions of politicians. It is striking that Aeschines does not mention the oral testimony of witnesses in these two passages. For him the most reliable source of information about political activity are written public records. A passage from Euripides' play *Palamedes* (fr. 578 Collard/Cropp) also praises the role of written records in litigation: "for the troubles that afflict men when they fall to quarrelling - a written tablet does away with these and prevents the telling of lies".

Even though these authors state that written records played an important role in Athenian trials, some scholars have recently claimed that most legal business in Athens was conducted without the use of documents. According to W.V.

https://doi.org/10.1515/9783110751970-002

Harris, "legal practice like the administration of large-scale business, remained to a considerable extent oral and independent of documents".[1] M. Gagarin believes that "it seems that the Athenians restricted the amount of writing in the legal process as far as was practical (...) the exclusion of writing from trials was a feature of Greek law in general (...) Athenian litigants participated in this ambivalence [i.e. about writing], sometimes praising, at other times questioning the value of written documents of all sorts".[2] According to Gagarin, "Athenian Law also displays from the beginning a reluctance to use writing for procedural matters or to insert writing into the traditionally oral trial process".[3] A similar view is taken by D. Cohen: "the social and legal appreciation of the role that writing might assume was circumscribed and emergent rather than general and complete".[4] R. Thomas notes Aeschines' statements about the role of public documents but claims that his attitude was new and unusual at the time.[5]

In this chapter, I will examine the use of written documents vs. witness statements in cases delivered in public cases to see what kind of evidence litigants present. It is important to start with two early speeches, Lysias' *Against Agoratus* and Andocides' *On the Mysteries* to see whether there was a change in the use of written documents between the late fifth century and the second half of the fourth century. We will then turn to Demosthenes' speeches public cases in the late 350s *Against Leptines, Against Timocrates, Against Aristocrates* and *Against Androtion*, his two speeches in the 340s *On the False Embassy* and *Against Meidias*, and his *On the Crown* delivered in 330. I will also discuss Aeschines' two speeches *On the False Embassy* and *On the Crown*, and Dinarchus' speech *Against Demosthenes*. I will not discuss the two speeches *Against Aristogeiton*, which are forgeries composed after the classical period.[6] At the end I will briefly discuss the role of written documents at the *euthynai* of officials and the nature of accounts and inventories

1 Harris 1989, 72. In support of his view he cites an essay of Pasquali about illiterate traders, which has now been refuted. See Harris 2013c, who shows that several lead letters reveal that traders were far from illiterate.

2 Gagarin 2008, 196, 197.

3 Gagarin 2008, 206. Cf. Gagarin 2008, 207: "limiting the role of writing in judicial procedure (...)", and Gagarin 2008, 209: "the restricted role given to written texts in Athenian trials (...)".

4 Cohen 2003, 96.

5 Thomas 1989, 70: Aeschines "seems to show a realization about their (i.e. documents) possible use that is new".

6 See Harris 2018, 193–236.

kept by public officials. The topic of written documents used in private actions must await a separate study.[7]

Before starting, however, it is important to bear in mind the variety of documents kept in the public archive and by public officials.[8] When one thinks of the Metroon, one tends to think of laws and decrees of the Assembly, but these represent only two types of documents kept there and in other public offices such as the Council building.[9] First, there were records of trials. When an accuser brought a charge before an official, he wrote on an indictment (*engklēma*) his name with patronymic and demotic, the name of the defendant with patronymic and demotic, the name of the procedure and the nature of the charge, that is, how the defendant had violated the substantive part of the law under which he brought his charges. If the charge was a public action against an illegal decree, the accuser would list the laws violated by the decree. After the trial, the indictment would be kept on file in the Metroon and could be cited in subsequent litigation (Dem. 32.37; 38.6).[10] Second, there were letters from Athenian officials, especially generals. When requesting reinforcements for the Athenian troops in Sicily, Nicias sent a letter to the Assembly (Th. 7.10–15). When Timotheus praised the assistance he received from Menelaus, a Pelagonian, in his campaign against Amphipolis and the Chalcidians, he probably wrote this in a letter to the Assembly (*IG* ii^2 110 [363/2]). Aeschines (2.90) reports that Chares sent to the Assembly a letter about the defeat of Cersebleptes in Elaphebolion 346. Third, there were letters from foreign kings. In the speech *Against Aristocrates*, there are letters from Cersobleptes and other Thracian kings read to the court (Dem. 23.174, 178). Demosthenes has several letters of Philip II of Macedon entered as evidence (Dem. 18.39, 221; 19.39–40, 51, 187).[11] Fourth, there were catalogues of trierarchs and

7 On documents kept by private individuals: Pébarthe 2007, 79–110, 325–6. There were extensive records about property ownership in Athens and other Greek *poleis*. See Faraguna 1997 and Faraguna 2000. One can find no reference to these essays in Gagarin 2008. Maffi 1989 is brief and superficial on the use of documents in private actions.

8 On public records and the Metroon in general: Sickinger 1999. On documents kept in the Metroon: Pébarthe 2007, 147–159. On archives kept by officials: Pébarthe 2007, 185–243. Bonner 1905: 58–66 devotes very little space to the nature of written records produced in court and examines primarily private cases.

9 Osborne 2012 has claimed that all decrees enacted had to be inscribed on *stēlai*, but see Lambert 2016.

10 Lanni 2004 and Gagarin 2008, 195 believe that records were not kept of trials, but see the evidence collected in Harris 2013a. Cf. Faraguna 2017, 28: "indictments were as a rule stored in the archive of the magistrate who was responsible for the charge and in the case of an *eisangelia* in the archive of the council and of the Assembly".

11 On these letters and their role: Ceccarelli 2012.

public debtors. For instance, Demosthenes at the trial of Ctesiphon has the clerk read a list of trierarchs compiled before his reform and a list of those compiled after his reform (Dem. 18.106). Fifth, there were records of import duties paid on grain kept by the *sitophylakes* (Dem. 20.32). Sixth, there were accounts and inventories kept by other officials. For example, the tribal commanders (*phylarchoi*) of the cavalry kept records of the sums advanced (*katastaseis*) to members of the cavalry to buy horses (Lys. 16.6–7). We will return to these later. Seventh, in the *antidosis* procedure, each litigant made a detailed inventory of his estate (Dem. 42.11–16). Eighth, the *pōlētai* kept records of leases of mines and sales of confiscated property.[12] Ninth, there were records of citizens kept in the demes.[13] Finally, honorary decrees about Athenian citizens passed by other states might also be kept in the Metroon. Aeschines (3.44–48) reports how these might be announced in the theatre of Dionysus. At the trial of Ctesiphon Demosthenes (18.89–90, 92) has the clerk read out decrees from Byzantium, Perinthus and the Chersonnese.

Let us start with Andocides' speech *On the Mysteries* delivered at his trial on a charge of impiety in 400/399 BC. Cephisios' charge was that Andocides had committed impiety by violating the terms of the decree of Isotimides by attending the Mysteries after being convicted of impiety in 415 BC. The first part of the speech discusses the parody of the Mysteries (11–33) and the mutilation of the Herms (34–70). To prove that he did not participate in the parody, Andocides provides the lists of those denounced by Andromachus (13) and Teucer (14). To confirm the list of Andromachus, however, he calls on Diognetus who was one of the investigators (14). For the Mysteries he provides another list of Teucer (35) and one of Diocleides (47). But Andocides also calls witnesses. At 18 he calls Callias, Stephanus, Philippus and Alexippus, who were denounced by Lydus (18–19). At 27 he has several witnesses testify about the rewards given to Andromachus and Teucer, which was the subject of a decree of the Assembly (28). To prove that the Council decided to arrest Andocides and others on the basis of Diocleides' statement, he has the *prytaneis* of that year, Philocrates and others, testify, though it is hard to believe that all surviving *prytaneis* of the fifty who served that year would have spoken (46). There was apparently no decree of the Council recorded or kept about the arrest. Next to show that several were released because of Andocides, more testimony of witnesses is read out (69). But the main weight of his defence rests mainly on the written documents even though he says that the information in Diocleides' list was false.

---

12 On the *pōlētai*: [Arist.] *Ath. Pol.* 47.2–3 with Langdon in Lalonde, Langdon and Walbank 1991, 53–143.

13 See [Arist.] *Ath. Pol.* 42.1 with Pébarthe 2006, 193–206.

To prove that the decree of Isotimides was no longer valid, Andocides has the decrees of Patrocleides (73–76, 80), a decree about the examination of the laws (82, 85) and several laws enacted in 403/2 BC. To show that Epichares should have been put to death for serving in office during the Thirty, Andocides has the clerk read a law of Solon about killing tyrants (95).[14] It should come as no surprise that the legal part of his defence relies on texts of laws and decrees. In the final part of his speech, Andocides discusses the charge that he placed a suppliant bough on the altar made by Callias and calls Eucles the herald to testify about the incident (112). He also has witnesses testify about the daughter of Epilycus (115–123) and about the oath sworn by Callias about the legitimacy of his son by Chrysilla (124–127). These were events for which there were no written documents. These allegations are not pertinent to the main charges but are attempts to damage the credibility of one of his opponents. Andocides provides both written documents and witnesses to make his case, but his most important evidence for refuting the charges are the lists of men condemned and the laws and decrees relevant to the amnesties.

The accuser in the speech of Lysias, *Against Agoratus* also uses many documents to support his accusation. The defendant Agoratus is accused of having "clearly" (*ep' autophōrō*) caused the death of Dionysodorus and therefore being subject to arrest.[15] There is some uncertainty about the nature of the procedure used by the unnamed accuser: it was not the private action for homicide (*dikē phonou*) but another procedure, possibly the "arrest for murder" (*apagōgē phonou*), in which the accused was taken to prison until the trial (Dem. 23.80–81).[16] The main charge is that Agoratus denounced Dionysodorus to the Thirty and that Agoratus caused the death of Dionysodorus (*aitios phonou*), who was executed as a result of his denunciation. Agoratus was apparently a metic because the accuser

14 The documents at Andoc. 1.77–79, 83–84, 85, 87, and 96–98 are forgeries and do not contain reliable evidence. See Canevaro/Harris 2012. The attempt of Sommerstein 2014 to defend the authenticity of the decree of Demophantus and the attempts of Hansen 2016a and Hansen 2016b to defend the authenticity of the decrees of Patrocleides and Tisamenus are not convincing. See Harris 2013/4 and Canevaro/Harris 2016 with detailed refutation of these essays and additional evidence against authenticity and the endorsement of Dilts/Murphy 2018, who rightly place brackets around all these documents.

15 On the meaning of *ep' autophōrō*: Harris 2006, 373–390. The term is mistranslated by Todd 2000, 145 with note 19, and by Wohl 2010, 220, whose mistake completely undermines her analysis of the speech. For the semantics of the verb *kteinein* and their implications for Athenian homicide law: Harris 2016, 391–404.

16 For discussion of Dem. 23.80–81 with references to earlier analyses: Harris 2018, 58–59.

states that Athens was not his native land and that he could have been tortured (27).[17]

The accuser bases the most important parts of his case on written documents. He begins by recalling the events leading up to the surrender of Athens in 404 BC (5–17). He then states that certain oligarchs persuaded Agoratus to denounce generals and taxiarchs (18). These men sent Theocritus to the Council, and Theocritus denounced Agoratus to the Council shortly before the Thirty entered power. The accuser then reads out a decree of the Council instructing certain members to go to the Peiraeus and find Agoratus (22–23). Agoratus was allowed to provide sureties, who were Athenian citizens, for his appearance before the Council. Agoratus and his sureties then sat as suppliants at the altar in Munichia (24). According to the accuser, Agoratus discussed with his sureties the possibility of fleeing Athens to avoid giving testimony, but decided to remain in Athens (25–28). To prove that Agoratus remained willingly, the accuser has another decree of the Council read out and the testimony of a witness, but does not specify the contents of the decree. As a result of this decree, the accuser charges that Agoratus willingly rose from the altar even though Agoratus claims that he was removed by force. The evidence provided would appear to support the accuser's version, but one wonders why Agoratus willingly left the altar. Normally, one supplicated to make a request and did not rise from an altar willingly until the request was granted.[18] The request of Agoratus was probably to be granted immunity from torture.[19] The accuser suppresses this grant of immunity because it would undermine his argument in the previous section that Agoratus risked torture (27). The accuser then produces decrees of the Assembly to prove that Agoratus denounced several Athenians (33) and another decree of the Assembly to prove that these men were to be tried before a court of two thousand (35). Instead of being tried in this court, the accused were tried in the Council under the Thirty and sentenced to death. The accuser then has a document containing the names of these men read to the court (38). What is interesting about this document is that it was created under the Thirty and obviously kept in the archives after their regime was overthrown. Next he has several witnesses testify that Dionysodorus declared before friends that Agoratus was responsible for his death and ordered

17 For the torture of non-citizens: for instance Dem. 18.133 with Harris 2013b, 10–11. Naiden 2006, 192 mistakenly calls Agoratus a public slave.

18 See Naiden 2006, 105–171 for acceptance and rejection of requests by suppliants. For suppliants rising and leaving an altar after a request is granted: Soph. *OT* 1–77.

19 See Gernet who rightly compares Lys. 13.55–56. For supplicating in order not to be tortured: Andoc. 1.44. On this supplication: Naiden 2006, 192–193 who does not analyze the two different versions in detail.

Dionysius, the accuser and his friends to punish Agoratus. He also ordered his wife to tell the child whom she was about to bear that Agoratus had killed him, and to order him to punish Agoratus (41–42). In response to Agoratus' denial of the charges, the accuser brings forward decrees of the Council and Assembly, stating that Agoratus denounced certain people, which may be the same decrees as those at 33 and 35. But the accuser also has the clerk read out a decision that Agoratus be acquitted or released because he had given true testimony (50), which must have been made under the Thirty. This was the usual procedure for cases of denunciation (Andoc. 1.20. Cf. Lys. 13.56): if the information given was true, the informer was given immunity, but if they were shown to be false, the informer was put to death. Here again we find another document from the reign of the Thirty kept in the archives.

After concluding his case against Agoratus, he turns to the argument that Menestratus was the one who denounced Dionysodorus. The accuser states that Menestratus was denounced by Agoratus and then given immunity in return for denouncing others. To prove this, the accuser has the decree of the Assembly read out (55). It is striking that the accuser does not have other documents about Menestratus read to the court, which may have been a weak point in his case. In fact, the speaker admits that Dionysodorus may have been executed as a result of information given by Menestratus, but argues that because Agoratus denounced Menestratus, he was still responsible for the death of the men he denounced because he in effect forced Menestratus to give their names (57). The accuser then contrasts the conduct of Agoratus with that of Aristophanes of Cholleis, who was accused of falsely claiming citizenship and ran the risk of being tortured, but still did not denounce others though it would have been to his advantage. The accuser has a decree of the Assembly read to prove his statement but does not summarise the contents of the decree aside from implying that it concerned Aristophanes (58–61).

In the following section the accuser discusses the family background of Agoratus and alleges that his father was a slave and that his three brothers were put to death for various crimes, one in Sicily, another in Corinth (62–66). For all these executions he provides witnesses and not documents though for the brother put to death in Athens there might have been a written record. He also claims that Agoratus was convicted for being a sycophant and for seducing women, and produces witnesses and not documents though records were kept of trials (68). We should not make the mistake of calling this evidence "non-legal" or "extra-legal". This evidence is designed to show that Agoratus was the kind of person who had a propensity to commit the kinds of crimes with which he is charged and was thus indirectly relevant to the accusations in the plaint. After slandering his family, the accuser anticipates the claim of Agoratus that he helped to kill Phrynichus and was made an Athenian citizen (70). He disproves this by producing the decree granting citizenship to Thrasybulus of Calydon and Apollodorus of Megara for killing Phrynichus and another decree, whose contents he does not summarise.[20] He also claims that after Agoratus joined the rebels at Phyle, the men in the camp wished to put him to death but were stopped by the general Anytus. Because he was polluted for causing the death of several people, the men would not share his table or tent.[21] To prove these statements, he calls on the *taxiarch* to testify (79). For these events there would have been no written documents. In general, the most important charges in the speech are supported by written documents; witnesses are called mainly to testify about the character of Agoratus.

The limits of documentation under the Thirty are illustrated by another speech delivered in this period, the speech of Lysias, *Against Eratosthenes*. Lysias brought the charges at a special procedure for those who held office during the Thirty ([Arist.] *Ath. Pol.* 39.6).[22] The case against Eratosthenes is similar to that against Agoratus insofar as neither defendant is accused of causing death by direct physical violence. Lysias charges that Eratosthenes arrested his brother Polemarchus, who was later put to death by the Thirty (4–22). Lysias relies first on questions posed to the defendant, who admits he arrested his brother Polemarchus (25), and witnesses to his conduct under the Four Hundred when as trierarch he deserted his ship and fled from the Hellespont (42), and that he was an *ephoros* under the Thirty (47), and about other events under the Thirty (61). One of the main arguments of Eratosthenes' defence was that he was ally of Theramenes who was put to death by the Thirty and opposed their execution of innocent men. Lysias anticipates this argument by alleging that Theramenes was no different from the rest of the Thirty (62–78). Here there were unlikely to have been any documents or living witnesses, and Lysias has to rely on the knowledge of the judges (61: "you yourselves know these facts"). The reliance on witnesses and the judges' knowledge was, therefore, not caused by any reluctance to use written documents but by the absence of such documents for this period.

There are fewer documents found in other public speeches from the Lysianic corpus, but this is because they often concern matters for which no public records

20 Fragments of a decree dated to 410/9 about rewards for Thrasybulus have been preserved. See *IG* i^3 102 with Osborne 1982, 16–21.

21 On pollution for homicide: Harris 2015.

22 There is no reason to believe that the Amnesty of 403 allowed for prosecution only in cases where the defendant had killed with his own hand. See my analysis of [Arist.] *Ath. Pol.* 39.5 in Harris in Joyce 2015, 45–49 with criticism of Rhodes 1981, 468 and Carawan 2013, 139–170, who implausibly claims that the speech *Against Agoratus* could not have been delivered.

existed. For instance, in the speech *On the Property of Aristophanes* (Lys. 19), the defendant is accused of holding some property from a confiscated estate. Because we do not have the speech of his accusers, we do not know what evidence they used. The defendant bases his case on the argument that Aristophanes did not have that much property and that he was generous in his public services. He relies mostly on the testimony of witnesses for his statements about private transactions and his will (23, 27, 41, 58, 59), but he has two documents read to the court, the *apographē*, which was probably the record of his confiscated properties (27), and a document about his liturgies (57).[23] The latter may have included entries from the records about trierarchs and those for dramatic and choral performances.

In the speeches delivered in cases about the inspections of qualifications for magistracies (*dokimasia*) most of the arguments concern the personal conduct of the candidates and rely on the testimony of witnesses because there were no public records about these events (Lys. 16, 25, 26, 31). For instance, in *Against Philon* the accuser charges that the candidate lived in Oropos as a metic and summons witnesses because there were no records about Oropos at Athens (Lys. 31.14). In one speech, however, the defendant Mantitheus relies on records kept by the tribal leaders to ensure the recovery of payments made to buy horses (*katastaseis*) to show that he was not a member of the cavalry during the Thirty (Lys. 16.6–7).[24] On the other hand, Mantitheus indicates that his accusers rely on a list of the cavalry kept under the Thirty but argues that this document was not reliable because it contains the names of several men who were abroad and omits the names of several who did serve (Lys. 16.6). This is one of the few passages I have found in the Attic orators in which the reliability of the information in a public document is questioned.

There are no speeches in public cases preserved from around 390 BC until the late 350s BC. During the late 350s Demosthenes wrote and delivered the speech *Against Leptines* in 355/4 BC,[25] and wrote *Against Androtion* for Diodorus

---

23 At Lys. 19.27, some manuscripts read ἀπογραφὴ χρημάτων. Reiske emended this to ἀπογραφὴ χαλκωμάτων and Carey to ἀπογραφὴ ἐπίπλων on the basis of the previous sentences. But there is no reason to emend the text. The previous sentence states the inventory included "what he left behind" and the following sentence states that there was little in his estate, which would indicate that the inventory covered the entire estate, not just part of it. For the term *apographē* and the procedure: Harrison 1971, 211–217.

24 On these records: the inscriptions published by Kroll 1977.

25 For the date: Harris 2008, 17; Canevaro 2016, 8–11.

to deliver in 355/4,[26] *Against Aristocrates* for Euthycles to deliver in 352/1,[27] and *Against Timocrates* for Diodorus to deliver in 353/2 BC.[28] Leptines had enacted a law abolishing exemptions for public service (2, 55, 160). Apsephion brought a public action against the law because it was "inappropriate", that is, because it clashed with several other Athenian laws (*graphē nomon mē epitēdeion theinai*). Phormio and Demosthenes addressed the court as supporting speakers (*synēgoroi*). Because of the nature of the charge, the main evidence against the law are other laws, but Demosthenes draws on other evidence to support his charges. The main argument against the law is that it takes away the power of the people to award honours, which are an important incentive to encourage public service at home and support from foreign allies (2–6, 102–103). To remind the court about the benefits gained from foreign benefactors, Demosthenes has the clerk read decrees for Leucon (29–40), an honorary decree for Epicerdes (41–45), a decree for Corinthian exiles (52–55), decrees for men of Byzantium and Thasos (61–64), honorary decrees for Conon (67–74), a list of Chabrias' achievements (75–84) and honorary decrees for Chabrias (86). When calculating the amount of grain shipped from Leucon's kingdom, Demosthenes cites the records of the Grain Supervisors (*sitophylakes*) even though he does not have these extensive figures read out for obvious reasons (32). We cannot tell precisely how many decrees were read out to support Demosthenes' arguments in this section, but there must have been at least ten and probably more.

The next section of the speech deals with the law about legislation (*nomothesia*) and procedural issues. To enact a law, the Assembly had first to pass a decree permitting proposals to be made.[29] These proposals were read out at meetings of the Assembly until the third meeting when a decree appointing *nomothetai* was passed. If there were any laws contrary to the proposed law, the proposer had to bring a public action against these laws on the grounds that they were inappropriate (*graphē nomon mē epitēdeion theinai*) and have them repealed

26 For the date: Harris 2008, 168. The proposal of Lewis 1954, 43–44 to date the speech to 359/8 is refuted by Cawkwell 1962, 40–45.

27 For the date: Harris 2018, 20 with n. 13.

28 For the date: Harris 2018, 109 with n. 9.

29 On the procedure of *nomothesia*: Canevaro 2013b, who shows that the document inserted into the text at Dem. 24.20–23 is a forgery. Hansen 2016 attempts to defend the document's authenticity, but his arguments ignore key evidence and are not convincing. For detailed refutation: Canevaro 2018.

before the new proposal could be enacted (Dem. 20.93; Dem. 24.32, 34–35).[30] Demosthenes' argument is that Leptines failed to repeal the law requiring that all awards made by the people are to remain valid before enacting his law abolishing awards of exemption from certain liturgies (88–101). The only written documents relevant in this section are, therefore, the laws about legislation, which are cited several times (92, 95, 96–98). The rest of the speech contains various arguments. To refute the claim that the Athenians did not grant honours in the past, Demosthenes has a decree passed by Alcibiades for Lysimachus read out (115–116).[31] To show that the families of Harmodius and Aristogeiton did not have exemptions from religious duties, he has the decree about their privileges read out (127–128). To prove that one cannot serve as a public advocate more than once, Demosthenes has the relevant law read out (151–153). What is striking is that the speech relies exclusively on written documents, mostly laws and decrees of the Assembly. Not a single witness is called to corroborate any statement.

In the same year Demosthenes also wrote the speech *Against Androtion* for Diodorus to deliver. This speech was delivered in an accusation against an illegal decree (*graphē paranomōn*) to grant a crown to the Council of 355/4 BC. The indictment was brought by Euctemon, who charged that Androtion has violated three laws: first, he proposed his decree without a preliminary motion from the Council (5–8); second, the Council did not deserve honours because it had not had triremes constructed as required by law (9–20); and third, Androtion was barred from moving proposals because he had been a homosexual prostitute (25–32). The speaker Diodorus addresses the court as a supporting speaker and devotes his speech mainly to anticipating objections by Androtion and to undermining his credibility by recalling his abusive conduct in collecting public debts and melting down dedications (42–78). Diodorus does not have any laws or decrees read to the court and calls no witnesses. The explanation for this absence of written documents and oral testimony should be clear: Diodorus spoke after Euctemon, who brought the actual charge and presented the main evidence. This left Diodorus free to spend his time refuting possible arguments he and Euctemon expected Androtion to make in his response. One should, therefore, not draw the wrong conclusion from the absence of written documents in this speech.

---

30 Kremmydas 2012 uncritically relies on the view of Hansen 1979–1980 about the legal procedure followed by Apsephion in bringing the case against Leptines' law, but Hansen's analysis contains many errors and is refuted in detail by Canevaro 2016b.

31 Davies 1971, 50–52 argues convincingly that this document from the fifth century was a forgery. Cf. Canevaro 2016, 376–377.

During the next year, 353/2, Demosthenes composed another speech for Diodorus to deliver against a politician named Timocrates.[32] Like the speech *Against Leptines* delivered two years before, this speech was written for a public action against an inappropriate law (*graphē nomon mē epitēdeion theinai*). Timocrates had enacted a law allowing a public debtor to avoid going to prison by providing sureties (39–40).[33] The first charge is that Timocrates did not follow the correct procedures for enacting a law (17–32), which he supports by citing the law about *nomothesia* and its provisions (17, 24–26) and the decree passed to enact the law (27–32). To introduce the rest of the charges, he has the law allowing a public charge against inappropriate laws (32–38) and the law of Timocrates (39–41) read out. In each case, the evidence to prove the main charges are laws: the statute that laws go into effect when they are enacted (41–44), the law not permitting any proposal about cancelling debts unless immunity is granted (45–49), the law forbidding anyone to supplicate the Assembly with a request to overturn a court's verdict (50–53), the law about *res iudicata* (54–55), the law making the decisions of private arbitrators binding and the law about judgments under the Thirty (56–57), the law forbidding *ad hominem* legislation (59–62), a law of Timocrates about placing debtors in prison (63–65) and a law about theft (102–105). To refute Timocrates' argument that the Oath of the Council allows men to avoid going to prison if they provide sureties, Diodorus has the clerk read the Judicial Oath, which does not contain such a restriction (144–148, 150–154). The final part of the speech repeats many of the attacks on Androtion made by Diodorus in his case against him. As in the *Against Androtion*, Diodorus does not produce documents or witnesses to prove these charges (170–186). As in the speech *Against Leptines*, there are no witnesses brought forward. All the charges are supported by written documents.

During the next year, 352/1 BC, Demosthenes wrote the speech *Against Aristocrates* for Euthycles. Euthycles had accused Aristocrates of proposing an illegal decree granting protection for the general Charidemus. The speech falls into two major parts: first, the argument that the decree violates several laws about homicide (22–94), and second, the argument that Charidemus has often betrayed Athenian interests and does not merit the protection granted by the decree (95–186). For the first part Euthycles has eleven laws read out and two or more

32 For the date of the speech: D.H. *Amm.* 1.4 with Harris 2018, 109, note 9. Rhodes in Lewis 1997, 230, note 1 claims that an unpublished inscription confirms the proposal of Lewis 1954, 32 to date the speech to 354/353. M. Richardson has allowed me to see her text of the inscription, which *pace* Rhodes in no way confirms the proposal of Lewis.

33 For discussion of the document at Dem. 24.40: Canevaro 2013a, 113–120.

decrees, but this is what we would expect in a case against an illegal decree where the accuser had to prove that the decree violated specific laws. What is interesting for the topic of written documents is the second part of the speech. In ninety-two sections of this part of the speech, there are only two witness statements read out, one at 151 about Charidemus' conduct during the Athenian campaign against Amphipolis and another made by trierarchs at 168 about campaigns in the Chersonese. By contrast, the speaker relies far more on written documents: there are fourteen letters from Thracian kings, from Charidemus and from Athenian commanders. These include two letters of Cotys to the Athenians (115), a letter of Iphicrates, a letter of Timotheus (151), a letter of Charidemus (159, 160), four letters from commanders stationed in the Chersonese (161–162), a letter from a commander and a letter of Berisades (174), letter from Cersobleptes to Athenians (178), a letter from other Thracians kings (178), and a letter of Chares (183). There are two Athenian decrees read out, one about hostages and another about the demands of Charidemus (151, 177). There are also two treaties read out (175, 176). That makes eighteen documents as opposed to just two witness statements. Euthycles argues that one of Charidemus' letters contained false statements, but to show that the statements in these letters are false, he produces letters from Athenian commanders and a decree, not oral testimony. But he assumes that the letters themselves are genuine. This impressive array of documents reveals once more the wealth of written information available in the archives. Despite the fact that the events covered in the narrative were relatively recent (the speech was delivered in 352/1, and the events in the narrative start in the early 360s BC and end about in 356 BC),[34] Euthycles does not rely on the judges' knowledge of public events. Just as Aeschines (3.73) says that written documents are the best way to examine the conduct of public officials and to keep them accountable, Euthycles uses letters, decrees and treaties to show that Charidemus is not to be trusted.

One might argue that the reason for the prominence of written documents in three of these speeches is that they concern legal issues rather than issues of fact.[35] On the other hand, the speech of Demosthenes and the speech of Aeschines delivered at the latter's trial in 343 concern a charge of treason and focus on the defendant's action during three embassies to Philip II of Macedon.[36] In 346 Demosthenes brought several charges against Aeschines at his *euthynai*: 1) Aeschines did not make truthful reports and prevented Demosthenes from reporting the

34 For a summary of the events recounted in this part of the speech: Harris 2018, 18–20.

35 On the nature of issues in Athenian legal speeches: Harris 2013a, 381–386. Most speeches concern issues of fact.

36 On these embassies: Harris 1995, 41–106.

truth, 2) none of Aeschines' proposals were advantageous for the city, 3) Aeschines carried out none of the orders given by the Assembly, 4) Aeschines caused delays that caused the Athenians to lose opportunities, and 5) Aeschines accepted bribes to commit all these actions (Dem. 19.8).

He has thirteen witness statements read out and in several cases the statements contained testimony from more than one witness.[37] Yet Demosthenes places more weight on public documents: he has at least twenty texts read to the court: a *probouleuma* (32), a letter of Philip (39–40), a decree (47), letters of Philip (51), an alliance of Phocians and Athenians (61), an agreement of Phocians and Philip (62), a resolution of Amphictyons (63), a decree of Diophantus (86), a decree of Callisthenes (86), a decree of Assembly in Skirophorion 346 (130), a decree of Council (154), a decree of the Assembly about taking oaths from Philip (161), a letter of Philip (161), a decree of Philocrates (161), letters of Philip (187), a decree of the Assembly about those who betrayed Olynthus (267), a stele about Arthmius of Zeleia (270), a decree of the Assembly about trial of Epicrates (276 – quoted at 277–279). As in the speech *Against Aristocrates*, there are several letters from a foreign king, in this case, Philip. There are also treaties and a document from the Amphictyons at Delphi. Not only does Demosthenes cite these documents; in several cases he quotes or summarises them extensively. For instance, he quotes many passages from the decree of Philocrates (47–50), some phrases from the agreement of Philip and the Phocians (62–63) and from the decree for Philip (87) and summarises his own decree of the Council passed in Munichion of 346 (154–155). Demosthenes, therefore, considers written documents far more important for his case than the testimony of witnesses, which he almost never summarises or discusses.

At this trial Aeschines also places much weight on the evidence of written documents: he cites at least thirteen decrees and three letters. Like Demosthenes, he also quotes extensively from some documents: two decrees of Philocrates, two of Demosthenes two (19), a decree of Demosthenes about the First Embassy (46), several decrees (54), a decree (55), a decree of Allies (60), a decree (61), a decree (65), a decree (73), a letter (90), a decree (91), a letter (128), a letter of general

37 Dem. 19.32, 130 (several witnesses), 146 (Olynthian witnesses), 162 (witnesses about Philip in Chersonnese, and response to Philip), 165 (testimony about Philip's rely to Eucleides), 168 (testimony of Apollophanes and others), 170 (several witnesses), 200 (several witnesses about Aeschines' character), 213 (several witnesses testifying that Aeschines tried to prevent Demosthenes from presenting his accounts), 214 (single witness, content of testimony unclear), 233 (witnesses testifying that Phrynon sent his son to Philip), 236 (testimony about Demosthenes hosting Macedonian ambassadors). At 176 Demosthenes challenges witnesses to testify, but it is not clear whether they did or not.

Proxenus (134) and a decree (170). This makes at least fourteen decrees and three letters. On the other hand, Aeschines has ten witness statements read out, but this figure is a little deceptive because in several cases there are more than one witness.[38] At 46 he calls his fellow ambassadors on the first embassy to corroborate his story of events in Macedonia and he calls them again at 107 and 127 about key events. Since there were eleven ambassadors who went to Pella but we can deduct Aeschines, Demosthenes and Philocrates who was in exile, this makes eight ambassadors testifying three times.[39] One must bear in mind that none of Demosthenes' fellow ambassadors testified on his behalf. But the largest number of witnesses is called to prove that not he, but Demosthenes tried to prevent Critobulus of Lampsacus, the representative of Cersobleptes, from swearing the oaths to the peace with Philip. At 85 to 86 Aeschines calls *proedroi* at the meeting, who would have numbered nine in 346 BC and the ten generals and the representatives of the allies.[40] We do not know precisely how many of the third group there were (although the highest number was around seventy, there were fewer after the Social War), but there must have been at least two or three dozen.[41] That would make anywhere between fifty and sixty witnesses testifying. This was quite a crowd, and we must not underestimate the visual impact of this large number on the judges and bystanders. And the group of *synēgoroi* from the Phocians and the Boeotian exiles who spoke at 143 must have also been large. Finally, we should add the three *synēgoroi* Phocion, Eubulus and Nausicles at the very end of the speech. One gets the impression that the two orators were competing to see who could bring to his side the largest number of witnesses. Demosthenes calls at least two dozen witnesses, but Aeschines outdoes him by calling at least double that number. Yet even if we take these numbers into account, Aeschines still spends more time discussing the written documents he cites. He does not give preference either to the testimony of witnesses or documents; he was on trial for his life in a hostile atmosphere and was using every weapon at his disposal. Aeschines judged oral testimony and written documents equally effective in proving his innocence. Yet is also clear that Aeschines is not unusual in his use of written documents: he relies on them in much the same way Andocides does

---

38 Statement made in absence by Aristodemus and those who witnessed it (19), testimony of ambassadors (eight – eleven minus Philocrates, Demosthenes and Aeschines) 46, 55, 68, 85, 86, 107, 127, 134, 156, 170 (eleven - but some are more than one witness).

39 For the number of members of the First and Second Embassy: Harris 1995, 53.

40 For the nine *proedroi* who presided over meetings of the Assembly: [Arist.] *Ath. Pol.* 44.2.

41 On the number of members of the Second Athenian League: Cargill 1981.

in his speech *On the Mysteries*, Lysias in the speech *Against Agoratus* or Demosthenes in his *Against Leptines* and *Against Aristocrates*.

The balance between the testimony of witnesses and written documents is much different in the speeches of Aeschines and Demosthenes written for the trial of Ctesiphon for proposing an illegal decree in 330. Aeschines made three charges in his indictment: 1) Ctesiphon violated the law about awarding crowns because he made his proposal before Demosthenes passed his *euthynai*, 2) Ctesiphon proposed that Demosthenes' honours be announced in the theatre when the law forbid this, and 3) Ctesiphon violated the law by placing in his decree false statements about Demosthenes speaking and acting for the benefit of the Athens. Sections 9–48 deal with the first two charges and at least five laws are read out and probably more (15, 22, 30, 32, 39), two decrees (27, 33) and one curious document that proves Demosthenes was elected manager of the Theoric Fund on a specific day, in a specific month and in specific year (24). I am not sure what kind of document this was; it may have been a document recording the results of elections or a decree recording Demosthenes' election. But this is what we would expect in arguments aimed at proving Ctesiphon's decree was illegal. What is striking is that when Aeschines reviews Demosthenes' political career, he uses only written documents and no testimony of witnesses. There are two decrees of Philocrates about sending ambassadors to Philip, two decrees of Demosthenes about meetings of the Assembly on 18 and 19 Elaphebolion (68), a resolution of Athenian allies (70), a decree of Demosthenes about swearing oaths to Philip (75), a decree of Demosthenes awarding seats at Dionysia to Macedonian ambassadors (76), a decree about a treaty with the Euboeans (93), which is discussed and quoted at length, a decree of Demosthenes for the people of Oreus (101), a decree of Oreus about revenues and a loan of Demosthenes (104) and a decree of the Amphictyons about punishing Amphissans (124).

In his defence of Ctesiphon Demosthenes relies overwhelmingly on written documents.[42] There are a decree of Demosthenes (29), a decree of Callisthenes (37–38), a letter of Philip (39), an indictment (54), a decree of Eubulus (73–75), two decrees of Aristophon, a decree of Hegesippus, a decree of Philocrates, a decree of Cephisophon (75), a letter of Philip (76–79), a decree of Aristonicus (83–84), crowns voted by Byzantines and Perinthians (89–90), decrees of the people in the Chersonnese (92), a decree of Demosthenes (105), a catalogue of trierarchs before Demosthenes' law, a catalogue of trierarchs after Demosthenes' law (106), a decree for Diotimus, a decree for Charidemus, a decree for Neoptolemus (114–

42 The documents inserted into the text of Dem. 18 are all forgeries. See Canevaro 2013a, 237–318 with full discussion and references to earlier analyses.

115), a decree of Ctesiphon (118), a law about awarding crowns (120), two resolutions of the Amphictyons (154), a letter of Philip (156–157), decrees of the Assembly (at least two – 163–165), a reply of Philip, a reply of the Thebans (166–168), a decree of Demosthenes (180–188), a letter (212), another reply of the Thebans (214), Athenian decrees about sacrifices (217), letters of Philip (221), decrees of praise for Demosthenes, one indicted by Diondas (222) and a list of allies brought by Demosthenes (305). This makes over twenty decrees for the Assembly as well as other types of documents, some from Athens and others from foreign communities and letters from Philip. By contrast, there are only three witness statements (135, 137, 267). For recent events neither relies on knowledge from oral tradition or on word of mouth.

But Demosthenes does not use written documents just about his political career. Demosthenes argues that Aeschines first two charges rest on mistaken interpretations of the law (111–125). Aeschines claims the ban on crowns for officials who have not based their *euthynai* applied to all decrees of praise. Demosthenes argues that it only applied to decrees of praise for an official's conduct during his entire term of office (113). Now some scholars have claimed that the interpretation of the laws was purely a matter of rhetoric and that there was no way of establishing which was the standard interpretation. One scholar has gone so far as to make the extreme and tendentious statement that the attempt to determine the correct interpretation is "futile".[43] Actually it is "futile" only if one does not bother to look at the evidence, which this scholar did not take the effort to do. Aeschines presents no evidence to prove his interpretation is correct; he simply asserts it. But Demosthenes cites several decrees of praise for individual acts of valour awarded to officials who had not yet passed their *euthynai* and shows that the law applied only to decrees of praise for overall performance in office (115–116). The evidence of inscriptions proves that Demosthenes was correct: in a study of almost thirty inscriptions I have shown that it was Demosthenes' interpretation that was always followed.[44] This has major implications for our view of open texture in Athenian law and for the concern with consistency in the application of the law. There were written documents that provided guidance about the normal way statutes were interpreted and applied.[45] Officials and proposers of decrees obviously followed these normal practices, and litigants used them in court. It would be a serious mistake to believe that the Athenians took an *ad hoc* approach to legal decisions. They were concerned with consistency in the enforcement of the law and

43 Extreme view: Gagarin 2012.
44 Harris 2017.
45 On this topic: Harris 2013a, 246–273 with detailed refutation of Lanni 2004.

used written documents. Any interpretation was not just rhetorical but constrained by the evidence of laws and decrees, which provided a yard-stick to judge which interpretation was the standard one followed by officials and the courts. This was a key feature of the rule of law.

Aeschines and Demosthenes were not the only litigants to make ample use of the written records found in the Metroon and the offices of magistrates. In the speech *Against Demosthenes* written by Dinarchus for a speaker at his trial in 323 BC, there are several documents read out about events in recent Athenian history. There is a decree about Timotheus (16), a decree of the Thebans and several letters (27), a decree of Demosthenes about citizens fighting and assigned to public works (79), a decree of Demosthenes about the Areopagus (82), and another decree of Demosthenes (83) and two witness statements (27, 52). The speech is unusual because the main charges against Demosthenes had been proven by the report of the Areopagus, and the court was deciding only about the penalty (3, 18, 84, 105).[46] As a result, the speakers reviewed Demosthenes' entire career and could rely on the knowledge of the judges for the main events. Yet even in this case there is more weight placed on written documents than on the testimony of witnesses.

Before ending, it is necessary to say a few words about the importance of the accounts of officials. At the end of their term of office, all officials were required to present their accounts to a board of accountants (*logistai*) and their assessors (*paredroi*) ([Arist.] *Ath. Pol.* 54.2; Aeschin. 3.9–31). These officials checked the accounts, and if the official who presented them was guilty of embezzlement, bribery or another offense, the accountants presented the charge to a court for trial. Some of these records were inscribed on steles and could be quite detailed. For instance, the inventories of the Treasurers of Athena contain detailed descriptions of items held in the Parthenon, the Erechtheion, the Opisthodomos and the Chalkotheke.[47] These were financial documents, but they were also legal documents because they had to be presented to officials presiding over the legal procedure of *euthynai* and could lead to legal proceedings in court. The supervisors of the fleet kept extensive records about triremes and naval equipment and listed those who served as trierarchs and returned naval equipment or did not.[48] The

46 For the unusual nature of the case: Harris 2013b, 135.

47 On the inventories of treasures in the Parthenon and Erechtheion: D. Harris 1995. For the lists from 434/3 to 405/4 BC: *IG* i^3 292–362 and *IG* ii^2 1382 and 1383. One can find no discussion of these written documents in Gagarin 2008.

48 On these records: Gabrielsen 1994. One can find no discussion of these written records in Gagarin 2008.

failure to return naval equipment would lead to legal proceedings, and these records contain several accounts of trials (e.g. *IG* ii^2 1629, ll. 746–749, 771–780, 796–799; 1631, ll. 115–120, 140–143, 148–152). The supervisors of the shrine of Asclepius kept extensive records as part of their public duties,[49] and so did the officials of the sanctuary of Demeter and Kore at Eleusis.[50] There were dozens of public officials in Athens, who must have produced thousands of documents. These written records played a central role in keeping magistrates accountable, one of the key features of the rule of law. The evidence of inscriptions shows, therefore, that the written records cited by litigants in court are just the tip of the iceberg. The Athenian legal system relied heavily on written documents, provided places to store these documents and made it easy for litigants to consult them.[51] It would be a serious mistake to claim that the Athenians attempted to exclude writing from the administration of justice or that the role of writing in Athenian trials was circumscribed. Written records were very important in keeping officials and public speakers accountable, one of the key features of the rule of law.

Bibliography

Aleshire, S.B. (1989), *The Athenian Asklepieion: The People, Their Dedications, and the Inventories*, Amsterdam.

Bonner, R.J. (1905), *Evidence in Athenian Courts*, Chicago.

Canevaro, M. (2016a), *Demostene 'Contro Leptine': Introduzione, traduzione, e commento storico*, Berlin/Boston.

Canevaro, M. (2016b), 'The Procedure of Demosthenes' *Against Leptines*: How to Repeal (and Replace) an Existing Law', in: *JHS* 136, 39–58.

Canevaro, M. (2018), 'The Authenticity of the Document at Dem. 24.20–23, the Procedures of *Nomothesia* and the So-Called ἐπιχειροτονία τῶν νόμων', in: *Klio* 100, 70–124.

Canevaro, M. (2019), 'Honorary Decrees and νόμοι ἐπ' ἀνδρί: on *IG* II^3 1 327; 355; 452', in: L. Pepe/L. Gagliardi (eds.), *Dike: Essays on Greek Law in Honour of Alberto Maffi*, Milano, 71–86.

Canevaro, M./Harris, E.M. (2012), 'The Documents in Andocides' *On the Mysteries*', in: *CQ* 62, 98–129.

Canevaro, M./Harris, E.M. (2016), 'The Authenticity of the Documents at Andocides' *On the Mysteries* 77–79 and 83–84', in: *Dike* 19, 7–48.

Caravan, E. (2013), *The Athenian Amnesty and Reconstructing the Law*, Oxford.

49 On the inventories of Asclepius: Aleshire 1989.

50 On the financial records of Eleusinian officials: Clinton 2005–2008.

51 On this topic: Sickinger 2004.

Ceccarelli, P. (2013), 'The Use (and Abuse) of Letters in the Speeches of the Attic Orators', in: U. Yiftach (ed.), *The Letter: Law, State, Society and the Epistolary Format in the Ancient World. Proceedings of a Colloquium Held at the American Academy in Rome*, Wiesbaden, 83–104.
Clinton, K. (2005–2008), *Eleusis: The Inscriptions on Stone: Documents of the Sanctuary of the Two Goddesses and Public Documents of the Deme*, Athens.
Cohen, D. (2003), 'Writing, Law and Legal Practice in the Athenian Courts', in: H. Yunis (ed.), *Written Texts and the Rise of Literate Culture in Ancient Greece*, Cambridge, 78–96.
Davies, J.K. (1971), *Athenian Propertied Families*, Oxford.
Detienne, M. (ed.) (1988), *Les savoirs de l'écriture. En Grèce ancienne*, Lille.
Dilts, M.R./Murphy, D.J. (2018), *Antiphontis et Andociodes orationes*, Oxford.
Faraguna, M. (1997), 'Registrazioni catastali nel mondo greco: il caso di Atene', in: *Athenaeum* N.S. 85, 1–33.
Faraguna, M. (2000), 'A proposito degli archivi nel mondo greco: terra e registrazioni fondiarie', in: *Chiron* 30, 65–115.
Faraguna, M. (2006), 'Alcibiade, Cratero e gli archivi giudiziari ad Atene', in: M. Faraguna/ V. Vedaldi Iasbez (eds.), *Dynasthai didaskein: studi in onore di F. Cassola per il suo ottantessimo compleanno*, Trieste, 197–207.
Faraguna, M. (2017), 'Documents, Public Information and the Historian: Perspectives on Fifth Century Athens', in: *Historika* 7, 23–52.
Fröhlich, P. (2005), *Le contrôle des magistrats dans les cités grecques*, Paris.
Gabrielsen, V. (1994), *Financing the Athenian Fleet: Public Taxation and Social Relations*, Baltimore.
Gagarin, M. (2008), *Writing Greek Law*, Cambridge.
Gagarin, M. (2012), 'Law, Politics, and the Question of Relevance in the Case *On the Crown*', in: *ClAnt* 31.2, 293–314.
Game, J. (2009), *Les actes de vente dans le monde grec: témoignages épigraphiques*, Lyon.
Hansen, M.H. (1979–1980), 'Athenian *Nomothesia* in the Fourth Century BC and Demosthenes' Speech *Against Leptines*', in: *C&M* 32, 87–104.
Hansen, M.H. (2016a), 'The Authenticity of the Law about *Nomothesia* Inserted in Demosthenes *Against Timokrates* 20–23', in: *GRBS* 56, 438–474.
Hansen, M.H. (2016b), 'Is Teisamenos' Decree (Andoc. 1.83–84) a Genuine Document?', in: *GRBS* 56, 34–48.
Harris, D. (1995), *The Treasures of the Parthenon and the Erechtheion*, Oxford.
Harris, E.M. (1995), *Aeschines and Athenian Politics*, New York/Oxford.
Harris, E.M. (2008), *Demosthenes, Speeches 20–22*, Austin.
Harris, E.M. (2013a), 'The Plaint in Athenian Law and Legal Procedure', in: M. Faraguna (ed.), *Archives and Archival Documents in Ancient Societies*, Trieste, 143–162.
Harris, E.M. (2013b), *The Rule of Law in Action in Democratic Athens*, Oxford.
Harris, E.M. (2013c), 'Were there Business Agents in Classical Greece? The Evidence of Some Lead Letters', in: U. Yiftach-Firanko (ed.), *Legal Documents in Ancient Societies (LDAS) I. The Letter: Law, State, Society and the Epistolary Format in the Ancient World*, Harrassowitz/Wiesbaden, 105–124.
Harris, E.M. (2013–2104), 'The Document at Andocides 1.96–98', in: *Tekmeria* 12, 1–32.
Harris, E.M. (2015), 'The Meaning of the Legal Term *Symbolaion*, the Law about *Dikai Emporikai* and the Role of the *Paragraphe* Procedure', in: *Dike* 18, 7–36.

Harris, E.M. (2016), 'The Legal Foundations of Economic Growth in Ancient Greece: The Role of Property Records', in: E.M. Harris/D.M. Lewis/M. Woolmer (eds.), *The Ancient Greek Economy. Markets, Households and city-states*, Cambridge, 116–148.
Harris, E.M. (2017), 'Applying the Law about the Award of Crowns to Magistrates (Aeschin. 3.9–31): Epigraphic Evidence for the Legal Arguments at the Trial of Ctesiphon', in: *ZPE* 202, 105–117.
Harris, E.M. (2018), *Demosthenes, Speeches 23–26*, Austin.
Harris, W.V. (1989), *Ancient Literacy*, Cambridge, MA.
Harvey, F.D. (1966), 'Literacy in the Athenian Democracy', in: *REG* 79, 585–635.
Joyce, C. (2015), 'The Athenian Reconciliation Agreement of 403 BC', in: *Antichthon* 49, 24–49.
Kremmydas, C. (2012), *Commentary on Demosthenes'* Against Leptines, Oxford.
Kroll, J. (1977), 'An Archive of the Athenian Cavalry', in: *Hesperia* 46, 83–140.
Lalonde, G.V./Langdon, M.K./Walbank, M.B. (1991), *Inscriptions: Horoi. Poletai Records. Leases of Public Lands*, *Agora* XIX, Princeton.
Lambert, S.D. (2016), 'The Selective Inscribing of Laws and Decrees in Late Classical Athens', in: *Hyperboreus* 22, 217–239.
Lanni, A. (2004), 'Arguing from "Precedent": Modern Perspectives on Athenian Practice, in: E.M. Harris/L. Rubinstein (eds.), *The Law and the Courts in Ancient Greece*, London, 159–171.
Lewis, D.M. (1997), *Selected Papers in Greek and Near Eastern History*. Edited by P.J. Rhodes, Cambridge.
Maffi, A. (1989), 'Écriture et pratique juridique dans la Grèce ancienne', in: M. Detienne (ed.), *Les savoirs de l'écriture. En Grèce ancienne*, Lille, 188–210.
Osborne, M.J. (2012), 'Secretaries, *psephismata* and *stelai* in Athens', in: *An So* 42, 33–59.
Pébarthe, C. (2006), *Cité, démocratie, et écriture: Histoire de l'alphabétisation d'Athènes à l'époque classique*, Paris.
Sickinger, J. (1999), *Public Records and Archives in Classical Athens*, Chapel Hill.
Sickinger, J. (2004), 'The Laws of Athens: Publication, Preservation, Consultation', in: E.M. Harris/L. Rubinstein (eds.), *The Law and the Courts in Ancient Greece*, London, 93–111.
Thomas, R. (1989), *Oral Tradition and Written Record in Classical Athens*, Cambridge.
Todd, S.C. (2000), *Lysias*, Austin.

Asako Kurihara

Rumour and Hearsay Evidence in the Athenian Law-courts

Abstract: Legal historians concur in the view that hearsay evidence was generally rejected in the Athenian legal system, apart from a few exceptions. However, the reliance on hearsay evidence (*akoē*) as the second best information (*opsis*), according to Herodotus and his contemporaries, invites us to re-examine the rationale behind the acceptance and rejection of hearsay in the Athenian law-courts. First, it will be argued that Athenian courts were willing to accept hearsay witnesses insofar as they made absolutely clear that their testimony simply constituted hearsay. If they failed to do so, they could be accused of bearing false witness. Second, the use of rumours as common knowledge in the Athenian law-courts can be explained as a variation of the use of hearsay evidence, which was to be substantiated by "the citizen jurors as witnesses".

1 Direct evidence and hearsay in Herodotus

It is well known that Herodotus favoured direct observation (*opsis*) over a theory-based approach.[1] At the same time, the historian also made use of hearsay (*akoē*) information.[2] In his famous declaration on the methodology of his investigation, he states (Hdt. 2.99.1):

> μέχρι μὲν τούτου ὄψις τε ἐμὴ καὶ γνώμη καὶ ἱστορίη ταῦτα λέγουσα ἐστί, τὸ δὲ ἀπὸ τοῦδε Αἰγυπτίους ἔρχομαι λόγους ἐρέων κατὰ τὰ ἤκουον: προσέσται δὲ αὐτοῖσί τι καὶ τῆς ἐμῆς ὄψιος.

1 Lateiner 1986; Thomas 2000, esp. 190–212 on the influence of contemporary medical writers on Herodotus. Fowler 1996 on *opsis* as the premium resource. Dewald 1987 and Marincola 1997, 68–86, on the reliance and nuanced treatment of *opsis* by Herodotus and Thucydides. Schepens 1980 on the monuments as visible proofs to his narrative.

2 Gray 2001 on Herodotus' heavy reliance on *opsis*, still escorted by *akoē* evidence in Arion's story. His preference of "seeing" to "hearing" is reflected in Gyges' remark that the eyes are more reliable than ears (Hdt. 2.8.2). Hartog 1988 on the importance of hearsay for Herodotus and the various distances of 'hearsay' evidence from the original source.

https://doi.org/10.1515/9783110751970-003

> So far, all I have said is the record of my own autopsy and judgment and inquiry. Henceforth I will record Egyptian chronicles, according to what I have heard, adding something of what I myself have seen. (Loeb translation)[3]

First he saw for himself (*opsis*), next he asked local people who knew (*akoē*). He traced the Nile river up to Elephantine to witness himself, and only after that point did he collect hearsay information from the locals. He writes (Hdt. 2.29.1):

> ἄλλου δὲ οὐδενὸς οὐδὲν ἐδυνάμην πυθέσθαι. ἀλλὰ τοσόνδε μὲν ἄλλο ἐπὶ μακρότατον ἐπυθόμην, μέχρι μὲν Ἐλεφαντίνης πόλιος <u>αὐτόπτης</u> ἐλθών, τὸ δὲ ἀπὸ τούτου <u>ἀκοῇ</u> ἤδη ἱστορέων.

> I was unable to learn anything from anyone else, but this much further I did learn by the most extensive investigation that I could make, going as far as the city of Elephantine to look myself, and beyond that by question and hearsay.

These passages show the historian's reliance on *opsis* in preference to *akoē*. All the same, it is noticeable that he relies on *akoē* when it is necessary, and that he tries to clarify the sources. His awareness of the need to clarify the sources appears most distinctly in his description of the labyrinth. He makes a sharp distinction between what he has seen and what he has heard (Hdt. 2.148.5–6).

> τὰ μέν νυν μετέωρα τῶν οἰκημάτων αὐτοί τε ὡρῶμεν διεξιόντες καὶ αὐτοὶ θεησάμενοι λέγομεν, τὰ δὲ αὐτῶν ὑπόγαια λόγοισι ἐπυνθανόμεθα: οὕτω τῶν μὲν κάτω πέρι οἰκημάτων ἀκοῇ παραλαβόντες λέγομεν, τὰ δὲ ἄνω μέζονα ἀνθρωπηίων ἔργων αὐτοὶ ὡρῶμεν.

> We ourselves viewed those that are above ground, and speak of what we have seen, but we learned through conversation about the underground chambers. Thus we can only speak from hearsay of the lower chambers; the upper we saw for ourselves.

Herodotus never dismissed hearsay evidence, but was aware of the need to clarify the difference between the sources, and to examine the reliability of each, and if he had no direct eyewitnesses, to make use of indirect hearsay (*akoē*) information (i.e. information given by someone else who had heard from others), as did he in his investigation on the farthest land in Scythai (Hdt. 4.14.1–2) and the source of the Nile (Hdt. 2.32–33). On occasion, he collected the local traditions of the remote past, transmitted either in oral or written forms (Hdt. 2.118.1, 121–123).

In his investigation (*historiae*), Herodotus seems to have used direct observation (*opsis*) as the primary source, but, at the same time, he relied on hearsay evidence as well. He was keen to clarify what were his resources and to

3 In this chapter, translations are based on the *Loeb Classical Library* unless otherwise stated.

differentiate between direct (*opsis*) and the indirect based on what he had heard (*akoē*). This reliance on hearsay evidence alongside the preference over direct information can also be attested in the practice of the Athenian law-courts.

It has been commonplace among legal historians that hearsay evidence was not generally taken in the Athenian legal system apart from a few cases such as death-bed messages, family pedigrees, disease and absence, which are also accepted in a modern context due to high credibility or necessity.[4] More recently, S.C. Todd has argued that the restrictive and negative attitude towards hearsay evidence was a direct result of the Athenian expectation for witnesses to appear in court as supporters of the litigants,[5] which seems to have become a standard view since S.C. Humphreys.[6] According to Todd, the role of the witness in the Athenian context was not to offer evidence to find the facts but to show up in person. Here he found the reason why the Athenian law-courts ruled out hearsay evidence. However, the reliance on hearsay evidence by Herodotus and his contemporaries suggests that it is worthwhile investigating the rationale lying behind the rejection (or acceptance) of it in the Athenian law-courts. In this chapter, through the re-examination of the relevant cases already collected in previous studies, I will try to show hearsay evidence based on what witnesses had heard from someone else was supposed to be an eligible source of information, even though it ranked second to testimony provided by eye witnesses.

2 Law of hearsay evidence

I will start by examining the law of hearsay, and will clarify how hearsay witnesses were incorporated into the Athenian legal system. Dem. 46, *Against Stephanos* 2, has a law on hearsay witness inserted; §8 is as follows:

Νόμος: ἀκοὴν εἶναι μαρτυρεῖν τεθνεῶτος, ἐκμαρτυρίαν δὲ ὑπερορίου καὶ ἀδυνάτου.

4 Leisi 1908; Lipsius 1905–1912, 886; MacDowell 1978, 243; Harrison 1968–1971, vol. 1, 145–147. Bonner 1905 refers to the death-bed messages and declarations by the deceased concerning pedigree and matters relating to family history as the exceptions to the hearsay rule commonly attested both in the Athenian and English practice.

5 Todd 2003.

6 Humphreys 1985. The view is slightly modified by Rubinstein 2005, who has shown that there is a difference between public and private suits, and that fact-finding was still an essential purpose of witnessing.

Law: One is to testify to hearsay evidence from the dead person, and *ekmartyria* from those who are absent and incapable.[7]

The first half of the law tells that one can testify as a hearsay witness of what one has heard from the deceased. The second half of the law is an instruction that those who are absent or do not have abilities to appear in court should testify in writing (*ekmartyria*). As a whole, the law instructs how to find witnesses when direct witnesses are unavailable.

In Isae. 6.54, *Against Philoctemon*, the speaker approves hearsay witnesses of what has happened in a previous generation.

Οἷς μὲν γάρ τις παρεγένετο, δίκαιον, ὦ ἄνδρες, μαρτυρεῖν, οἷς δὲ μὴ παρεγένετο, ἀλλ' ἤκουσέ τινος, ἀκοὴν μαρτυρεῖν.

It is justified to testify on what one was present at. On what one was not present at but has heard from someone else, it is justified to testify on hearsay.[8]

In Isae. 8, *On the Property of Chiron*, the speaker distinguishes what belongs to the remote past from what one has experienced during his lifetime. For the former, one can testify to what one has heard from the person who was present, and for the latter, the direct witness testifies (Isae. 8.29, see also 6). The preference for direct witnesses over indirect hearsay information is the rule. However, when the law of hearsay witness is described in the law-courts, the reference is more than often negative. In Dem. 44 (*Against Leokhares*), the speaker explains how the opponent should have provided witness in a *diamartyria*, a legal procedure to bar the action by providing a sworn witness in inheritance cases, refers to the law and criticises the opponent who provided hearsay evidence when a direct witness from his father was available.

Dem. 44.55:

ὁ δέ γε νόμος ἀκοὴν τῶν τετελευτηκότων κελεύει διαμαρτυρεῖν, οὐ ζῶντος τοῦ πατρὸς τὰ ὑπ' ἐκείνου πραχθέντα.

Well, the law does allow us to testify to the hearsay evidence of the dead but not to that of a living father concerning that father's own deeds! (Translated by Scafuro)[9]

7 Translation here is mine.

8 Translation here is mine.

9 Scafuro 2011.

The first half is an instruction of how to make a bar of action (*diamartyria*) when the direct witness has already died. This citation corresponds to the law of hearsay inserted in Dem. 46.8. The second half is, however, a negative repetition of the same provision. Again, in Dem. 46.7 (a), Apollodoros introduces the law in a restrictive way as following:

> ἀκοὴν δ' οὐκ ἐῶσι ζῶντος μαρτυρεῖν, ἀλλὰ τεθνεῶτος...
>
> And the laws do not permit a witness to testify to the hearsay statements of a living man but only to those of a dead man....
>
> (Translated by Scafuro)

The law on hearsay which is inserted in the next paragraph (Dem. 46.8) is a positive provision instructing hearsay witnesses how to act when the direct witness is dead. However, the speaker interprets the provision to prohibit a hearsay witness when the direct witness is alive.

3 *Ekmartyria* and divided responsibility

Ekmartyria, a document by an absentee witness may explain the reason for the negative attitude. The speaker Apollodoros continues; Dem. 46.7 (b):

> .... τῶν δὲ ἀδυνάτων καὶ ὑπερορίων ἐκμαρτυρίαν γεγραμμένην ἐν τῷ γραμματείῳ.
>
> ... and also (the law permits to testify) to the absentee testimony (*ekmartyria*) of those who are incapacitated or abroad, provided that it has been written on the tablet.
>
> (Translated by Scafuro, slightly modified)

In Isae. 3, *On the Property of Pyrrhos* 20, it is more precisely explained that those who lack the ability are the sick (τῶν ἀσθενούντων) and the absent (τῶν ἀποδημεῖν). The modern interpretation of *ekmartyria* usually takes this explanation. In the case of those who are sick or absent, they are allowed to provide written evidence.

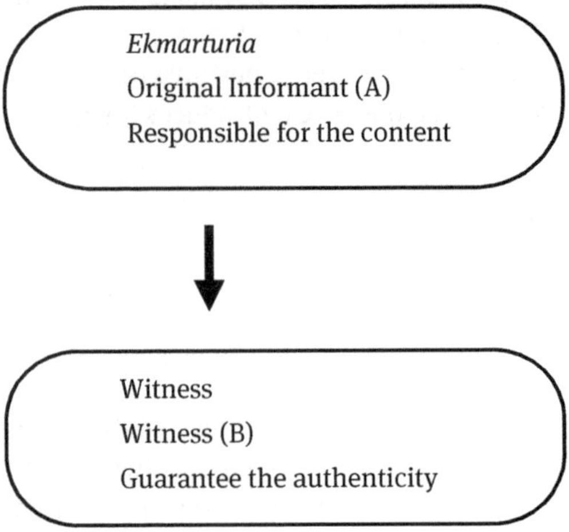

Fig. 1: *Ekmartyria* and the responsibility of the witness.

Once the original informant (A) has written the document, the witness who was present at the deposition (B) will testify to the authenticity of the documents in front of citizen-juries. The documents will be firmly attested as genuine if one has provided the documents with trustworthy witnesses (Isae. 3.20–21). The *ekmartyria* shows how keen the Athenian legal system was to establish the authenticity of the evidence indirectly transmitted to the law-court scene. Apollodorus, then, explains the limits of responsibility of the witness (B).

Dem. 46.7 (c):

> καὶ ἀπὸ τῆς αὐτῆς ἐπισκήψεως τήν τε μαρτυρίαν καὶ ἐκμαρτυρίαν ἀγωνίζεσθαι ἅμα, ἵν' ἐὰν μὲν ἀναδέχηται ὁ ἐκμαρτυρήσας, ἐκεῖνος ὑπόδικος ᾖ τῶν ψευδομαρτυρίων, ἐὰν δὲ μὴ ἀναδέχηται, οἱ μαρτυρήσαντες τὴν ἐκμαρτυρίαν.
>
> And the testimony of both the witness who appears in court and of the one who is absent can be subjected to litigation through the same procedure of objection (episkepsis), so that if the absentee witness acknowledges the testimony he is liable to a suit for giving false testimony, and if he doesn't acknowledge it, then the witnesses to the abentee testimony who appear in court are liable.
>
> (Translated by Scafuro)

If the original informant admits that the written document is genuine, he is the one to be responsible (*hypodikos*) for the content. If not, the hearsay witnesses own the whole responsibility. This is perhaps because, in the latter instance, the written document was regarded as a fabrication of the witness (B). In the case of *ekmartyria*, the Athenian legal system made it clear who owns the responsibility for the given information. So far as the authenticity of the document is unquestionable, the witness (B) was immune to the content of the testimony. Up to here, it is clear who is responsible for the given hearsay information. So far as the original informants admit the documents, the witnesses at law-courts were responsible only for the fact that the document was authentic. They were immune to the content of the testimony.

4 Hearsay witness and the limit of responsibility

Suppose who was to own responsibility if the original informant provided no written document. This was what happened with the hearsay witness. The speaker in Dem. 57, *Against Eubulides, an Appeal*, perceived the hearsay witness to be problematic and refers to the limit of responsibility of the hearsay witness; see Dem. 57.4–5:

> οὕτω γὰρ τοῦτ’ ἄδικον καὶ σφόδρα πάλαι κέκριται, ὥστ’ οὐδὲ μαρτυρεῖν ἀκοὴν ἐῶσιν οἱ νόμοι, οὐδ’ ἐπὶ τοῖς πάνυ φαύλοις ἐγκλήμασιν, εἰκότως· (a) ὅπου γὰρ εἰδέναι τινὲς ἤδη φήσαντες ψευδεῖς ἐφάνησαν, (b) πῶς ἅ γε μηδ’ αὐτὸς οἶδεν ὁ λέγων, προσήκει πιστεύεσθαι; ἀλλὰ μὴν (c) ὅπου γε μηδ’ ὑπεύθυνον καθιστάνθ’ ἑαυτὸν ἔξεστιν, δι’ ὧν ἂν ἀκοῦσαι τις φῇ, βλάπτειν μηδένα, (d) πῶς ἀνυπευθύνῳ γε λέγοντι προσήκε βλάπτειν μηδένα, πῶς ἀνυπευθύνῳ γε λέγοντι προσήκει πιστεύειν ὑμᾶς;
>
> Such a procedure [i.e. to deprive of citizenship based on hearsay evidence] has from time immemorial been recognised as so clearly unjust that the laws do not admit the production of hearsay testimony even in the case of the most trifling charges; and with good reason; for when persons who claim to have sure knowledge have now been convicted of falsehood, how can it be right to give credence in matters regarding which even the speaker himself has no knowledge? And when it is not permitted for a man to harm another by evidence which he declares he has heard with responsibility, how can it be right for you to give credence to one who speaks without responsibility?
>
> (Loeb translation, modified)

First, the speaker tells that the laws do not permit testimony on hearsay information even for trivial matters. This might be an exaggeration judging from what we have seen in the law of hearsay. What is interesting is the speaker's comparison between the different categories of witness. The comparison is between those who testify on what they know and those who testify on what they have heard from a direct witness. While even the witnesses who have direct knowledge are accused of false testimony (line a), those who testify on hearsay evidence are less reliable (line b). The speaker points out that one cannot hold responsibility (*hypeuthynos*) for the information by hearsay (line c). In other words, those who testify based on hearsay evidence are immune to the charge of false witness (*dikē pseudomartyriōn*) about the facts testified on hearsay. The speaker of Dem. 57 distinguishes between those who testify with responsibility and those who do not bear responsibilities.

The connection between hearsay evidence and the lack of responsibility also appears in Dem. 44, *Against Leochares*, in which Leostratos has made a sworn testimony to bar an action (*diamartyria*), alleging that he is the legitimate heir of the estate. An issue is whether his father was capable of adopting Leostratos into the family, after his father had been adopted into another family. In response to the allegation, the speaker accuses Leostratos of false witness on the grounds that (1) the adoption was invalid, and (2) the son Leostratos had testified on what happened before he was born. It is reproached that the father who is responsible (*hypeuthynos*) skipped the responsibility, and that the son testified on what he could not really hold responsibility.[10]

The speaker, meanwhile, putting aside the question of whether the contents written in the *diamartyria* are true or false, concentrates on the responsibility of the witnesses. If Leostratos' father Leocrates made the *diamartyria* himself, the testimony concerned what happened during Leocrates' own lifetime and he himself had experienced these things as a witness. Nevertheless, as a matter of fact, his son Leostratos testified on what occurred before he was born. It is unthinkable that he could testify as a direct witness on what happened before he was born. It must have been hearsay from his father.

The content of the testimony is not the matter here, but it is supposed, first, that the father of Leostratos, still alive, evaded the responsibility and, second, that Leostratos acted as witness on the matter for which he could not hold responsibility. His responsibility is restricted to the fact that he had heard his father talking on some issues. These two cases suggest that the hostility towards hearsay evidence was connected to the requirement that witnesses had to be responsible

10 Dem. 43.30 may provide another example of the requirement that the witness has to take his responsibility. The speaker criticises Theopompus of "his being short of any witness who would have been responsible to us (i.e. the speakers), having only his associates to corroborate what he said" (μάρτυρα μὲν οὐδένα παρασχόμενος, ὅστις ἔμελλεν ὑπεύθυνος ἡμῖν ἔσεσθαι, συνομολογοῦντας δ' ἑαυτῷ ἔχων τοὺς κοινωνούς...).

for the facts they testified, and that the one who could bear the best responsibility should testify. Hearsay witness was put under question in this regard. Witnesses have to be responsible for the facts they testify. In both cases, it was not the information given by the hearsay witnesses, but the lack of responsibility on their part that was criticised.

5 Examples of hearsay evidence from those other than the dead

Now that our observation suggests that it was the lack of responsibility of the hearsay witnesses that the Athenian law-court speeches criticised, it is time to re-examine the known cases of hearsay witnesses. Along with the information given by the deceased, especially in family troubles which related to past generations, we have some hints that the use of hearsay evidence was accepted more widely than the knowledge of the deceased in family history.

Tab. 1: Cases of hearsay witnesses.

	oasis	***akoē***	**the contents**
Lys. 12. 43ff.	*hetaireiai*	investigator?	conspiracy
Dem. 41.24	Spudias' wife	those who were present	the authenticity of the document
Lys. 32.18	orphans' mother	male relatives	maltreatment
Lys. 13.39	Dionysodoros	wife → male relatives	inheritance/vengeance/ dying message
Dem. 34.11, 20, 46	Lampis	those who were present	maritime loan

First, Lys. 12, *Against Eratosthenes* (43ff.) reports that the members of the *hetaireia* refrained from presenting testimony on the anti-democratic conspiracy because the oath of trust bound them. The speaker reproaches their reluctance to appear, but as a matter of fact, he had to rely on hearsay witnesses. The courts admitted a hearsay witness to substitute. The speaker, in this case Lysias himself, reproaches the members of the *hetaireia* that they should have given testimony in order to help the *polis* in punishing the culprits rather than being bound by the oath. It is evident that the speaker, Lysias, considers the direct witness far more reliable than the hearsay witness. But when he knew that it was difficult to persuade the member to act as an informant, he relied on the hearsay witness.

Next, three cases in which the direct informants were women are to be considered. In Dem. 41, *Against Spudias* 24, it is witnessed by "those who were present" that Spudias' wife recognised the seal of the will of her father as authentic. Those who were present had given testimony of the fact that Spudias' wife agreed to the authenticity. This is hearsay. In Lys. 32, *Against Diogeiton*, the mother of orphans accused her father at the table of private arbitration, telling what had happened up to the moment. The speaker introduces her report word by word, together with the compassionate response of the audience, and calls witnesses who heard her words to testify. The mother did not appear in person in the courtroom. In this case, the mother proposed that she was willing to swear an oath, but the proposal was not accepted. In Lysias 13, *Against Agoratos* 41, 42, Dionysodoros in prison told his wife that the defendant Agoratos caused his execution, and asked her to convey his wish to retaliate. The words of Dionysodoros (the original informant) were transmitted from him to his wife (the first hearsay witness) and then to other male relatives, friends and to Dionysodoros' son who was about to be born (the hearsay witnesses once removed).

Our last case concerns the exemption from the maritime loan in the case of shipwreck. This case offers an occasion in which the information obtained by a possible slave was introduced into the court as hearsay evidence by both parties. In the maritime loan, there was a provision that the borrower was to be exempted from the payment in the case of shipwreck. Accordingly, it was crucial for the litigants to clarify whether or not Phormion, the borrower, had entrusted the payment to Lampis, the captain of the ship, when it was shipwrecked. The speaker, Chrysippos, Phormion's investor, demands the money back, insisting that Lampis was not with Phormion's money when shipwrecked and that the money was safe, and he tries to prove the statement by providing three sets of witnesses.

1) Those who were present and heard Lampis' explanation that Phormion, the defendant, had not left his money in the hands of Lampis at the Bosporus, and that Lampis had not held the money when he had been shipwrecked. This happened soon after Lampis sailed back to Athens. The same witnesses later testified at the private arbitration (46) and the present trial (11, 46).
2) Those who witnessed the summons of Phormion at the perfumer's shop (15).
3) Those who were present at the table of private arbitration with Phormion, where Lampis also participated. Lampis admitted that he had not received the money from Phormion, but he later changed the statement, explaining that he was out of mind on the previous occasions (20).

Against this, the opponent Phormion seems to maintain that he had deposited the money with Lampis, which was lost in the sea. Lampis' status as a slave and the legal competence of a slave to testify are under question.[11] Still, it is clear at least that Lampis was present at the three out-of-court occasions, and that he did not testify before the citizen-jurors. I will come back to this private arbitration in the next section. These examples of the use of hearsay witnesses show that, in spite of the laws on hearsay witness, the Athenian courts admitted hearsay evidence in some instances. This happened when, for one reason or another, it was not possible for direct witnesses to come forward.

6 Two levels of responsibility

If the Athenian law-courts admitted hearsay witness, how far were hearsay witnesses expected to bear responsibility for the information transmitted by someone else? Lampis' case shows that theoretically there were two levels of responsibility for the witness. Chrysippos explains; Dem. 34.46:

> Τοῦ μὲν οὖν δανεῖσαι ἡμᾶς τὰ χρήματα αἵ τε συνθῆκαι καὶ αὐτὸς οὗτός ἐστι μάρτυς· τοῦ δ' ἀποδεδωκέναι οὐδείς ἐστι μάρτυς ἔξω τοῦ Λάμπιδος τοῦ συναδικοῦντος. καὶ οὗτος μὲν είς ἐκεῖνον μόνον ἀναφέρει τὴν ἀπόδοσιν, ἐγὼ δ' εἴς τε τὸν Λάμπιν αὐτὸν καὶ (a) τοὺς ἀκούσαντας αὐτοῦ ὅτε οὐκ ἔφη ἀπειληφέναι τὸ χρυσίον. τούτῳ μὲν οὖν τοὺς ἐμοὺς μάρτυρας ἔξεστι κρίνειν, εἰ μή φησι τἀληθῆ μαρτυρεῖν αὐτούς· (b) ἐγὼ δ' οὐκ ἔχω τί χρήσωμαι τοῖς τούτου μάρτυσιν, οἵ φασιν εἰδέναι τὸν Λάμπιν μαρτυροῦντα ἀπειληφέναι τὸ χρυσίον.

> That we lent the money is attested both by the terms of the agreement and by Phormion himself; that he has repaid it is attested by nobody except Lampis, his accomplice. Phormion claims to have relied on Lampis alone. But I rely not only on Lampis himself but also on those who heard him say he had not received the gold. So Phormion can put my

11 In Isager/Hansen 1975, 156–169, there are possible scenarios of this complicated story. On the debates over Lampis' status, see Harrison 1968–1971, vol. 1, 167–168 n. 6. There remains a possibility that he was a freed metic, but Lampis was most likely a slave of Dion, possibly an independent slave (Dem. 34.5, 10). Reed 2003, 105; Isager/Hansen 1975; Whitehead 1977, 25 n. 87. Slaves were not permitted to testify in the ordinal courts, but Cohen 1992, 96–98, argues that "slaves appear to have had full court access, as parties and as witnesses, in cases involving commercial matters (p. 96)", especially in the case of *chōris oikountes* in *dikē emporikē*. The possibility that slaves had some legal competences in commercial matters has been noticed since Gernet 1955, 162–163. However, as Cohen 1973, 121 n. 48 notices, that Lampis did not actually give witness. This may be either because Lampis could participate in the private arbitration but lacked legal competence to formally testify before the citizen-juries, or that he was absent from Athens at the time of trial.

> witnesses on trial, if he says their testimony is untrue; but I have no way of dealing with his witnesses, who say they know that Lampis testified that he had received the gold.
> (Translated by MacDowell)[12]

Chrysippos continues that if Lampis had come forward as a witness in court, he could have accused Lampis of false witnessing, but he did not act as a witness. So Chrysippos had no one to prosecute the false witness. Lampis' case provides us with an excellent example to show that the Athenian law-courts distinguished between the two levels of hearsay witness. In line (b) the speaker tells the citizen-jurors that as far as the witnesses merely testify that they have heard Lampis testifying, and refrain from verifying that Lampis told the truth, they cannot be accused of false witnessing on the contents of Lampis' words. They are risk free and without legal responsibility. Nor should Lampis be prosecuted because neither did the opponent provide the document written by Lampis himself, the speaker complains. In (a), Chrysippos asserts that, if Phormion considers that the contents of the testimony is not correct, he may prosecute Chrysippos' witnesses in *dikē pseudomartyriōn*. The speaker considers that *dikē pseudomartyriōn* cannot be applied to the former, but it is applicable to the latter. This suggests that witnesses on the speakers' side did not stop at reporting that they heard Lampis' words, but they testified beyond their direct knowledge or they could have been charged of fabricating the story. Now it has become more apparent what the speaker of Dem. 57 wanted to argue. The reason why the speaker criticised the hearsay witnesses was that they could not give witness with responsibility (thus being irresponsible) because they were immune to the contents of the information they had heard so far as they stayed within their direct experience.

This distinction between the two levels of hearsay evidence becomes even more explicit in Dem. 45, *Against Stephanos I*. The legal opposition originated in a suit for damage, but in the trial Stephanos, a witness on Phormion's side, testified at the table of *proklēsis* (challenge) in the course of the *paragraphē* (bar of the action). A *proklēsis* is a legal procedure in which one of the litigants asks the other side for some legal act. In this case, Phormion demanded that Apollodoros should either admit that the document posted before the arbitrator was the authentic copy of the will of Pasion' or open the copy. Apollodoros insisted that the document called the "will of Pasion" was fake, but did not accept the *proklēsis*. According to Apollodoros, the speaker of Dem. 45, there was something wrong with the *proklēsis* from the beginning. A man with a legitimate son was not allowed to leave a will because it would lack legal ground. Moreover, the witness

---

12 MacDowell 2004.

testimony which Phormion provided was fragmentary. None of the witnesses dared to testify that the copy was Pasion's will.

Apollodoros, in 45.26, continues:

> ἔχ' αὐτοῦ. οὐδ' ἂν εἷς ἔτι δήπου τοῦτ' ἐμαρτύρησεν, εἰ μή τις καὶ παρῆν διατιθεμένῳ τῷ πατρὶ τῷ ἐμῷ: ἀλλ' εὐθὺς ἂν εἶπε 'τί δ' ἡμεῖς ἴσμεν εἴ τινές εἰσι διαθῆκαι Πασίωνος;' καὶ γράφειν ἂν αὐτὸν ἠξίωσεν, ὥσπερ ἐν ἀρχῇ τῆς προκλήσεως 'εἰ μή φημ' ἐγὼ ἀντίγραφα εἶναι τῶν διαθηκῶν', οὕτως 'ὧν φησι Φορμίων Πασίωνα καταλιπεῖν', οὐ 'τῶν Πασίωνος'. τοῦτο μὲν γὰρ ἦν εἶναι διαθήκας μαρτυρεῖν, ὅπερ ἦν τούτοις βούλημα, ἐκεῖνο δὲ φάσκειν Φορμίωνα: πλεῖστον δὲ δήπου κεχώρισται τό τ' εἶναι καὶ τὸ τοῦτον φάσκειν.
>
> Stop right there. I daresay no one would have confirmed this testimony unless he had been present when my father was drawing up his will. Instead, he would have immediately said, "But how do we know whether Pasion had any will" and he would have asked Phormion to write, just as at the beginning of the challenge, "if I deny the document is a copy..."—not "of Pasion's will" but "of the will which Phormion says Pasion left behind". For their expression was equivalent to saying that a will exists - which is the very thing they want you to believe, whereas the other expression was equivalent to saying that Phormion claimed there is a will. And doubtless there is a very great difference between a thing that exists and a thing that someone claims exist.
>
> (Translated by Scafuro)

It was not inconceivable that the copy presented at the *proklēsis* might have been the same document as the one preserved at Cephisophon's hand, but even if it had been, Stephanos would not have been in the position to tell whether the will was Pasion's or not. His testimony was not supported by his own experience but was based on the explanation made by Phormion. This was the reason why Apollodoros prosecuted Stephanos for false witness. He should not have included the word "the will of Pasion" in his testimony because it was only hearsay. He could not have known whether it was authentic or not, unless he was present when Pasion made the will. If he was about to testify based on the truth, he had to question on what basis he could regard the copy as Pasion's authentic will. Stephanos testified that it was Pasion's will, but actually he should have testified on "the document which Phormion calls Pasion's will". Apollodoros maintains that it was not illegal if he stopped short of testifying on what he had heard from someone else. In Dem. 46, which was composed for the same trial, Apollodoros argues that the witness in the *proklēsis* was to remain *hypodikos* (4). He had to inform only what he can be responsible for.

Dem. 46.6:

οἱ δέ γε νόμοι οὐ ταῦτα λέγουσιν, ἀλλ' ἃ ἂν εἰδῇ τις καὶ οἷς ἂν παραγένηται πραττομένοις, ταῦτα μαρτυρεῖν κελεύουσιν ἐν γραμματείῳ γεγραμμένα, ἵνα μήτ' ἀφελεῖν ἐξῇ μηδὲν μήτε προσθεῖναι τοῖς γεγραμμένοις.

Yet the laws do not so stipulate but enjoin that a man is to testify to what he knows and to events at which he was present and that these details are to be written on a tablet so that it's impossible to add or subtract anything to what has been recorded.

Stephanos is responsible (*hypodikos*) for the false witness because he stated what he heard from Phormion, as if it was what he himself listened to. Here the speaker demands not to mix up hearsay information with direct experience. Likewise, Leostratos, discussed above, should not have made a sworn testimony (*diamartyria*) on what happened before he was born. If I borrow the word of Demosthenes in Dem. 57 cited above, he cannot be *hypeuthynos*. Only the father, the source of information, could. It was necessary to clarify whether the information was based on direct experience (*opsis*) or on hearsay (*akoē*). So far as the witnesses carefully limited their responsibility to the fact that they have heard the story and refrained from testifying to the veracity of the words they have heard, hearsay witnesses could stay responsible (*hypodikos, hypeuthynos*) within the limit of their knowledge and the courts did not reject them.

In the three *pseudomartyriōn* cases – Dem. 44, 45, 46 – the speakers refer to the law on hearsay witness, though partly reproaching the hearsay witnessing. In all of them, they refer to the failure of witnesses to clarify the hearsay, or the avoidance of the direct witnesses to take their own responsibility. In the Athenian legal practice, primary sources were privileged over the secondary sources. Direct witnesses were to testify when available. When the direct witnesses were "incapable" or "absent", they should testify by *ekmartyria*. However, when *ekmartyria* was not applicable because of legal incapability or reluctance of the witnesses, it seems to have been allowed for someone else to act as a witness for hearsay evidence. Even if the testimony was based on *akoē*, the Athenian courts did not accuse witnesses who testified merely on the facts that they had heard. However, if one would go too far as to verify the contents of the information, or failed to elucidate that it was hearsay, then he was charged with *dikē pseudomartyriōn*.

7 Rumour as witness

The reliance on hearsay (*akoē*) can be further attested in the litigant's use of rumour, too. Law-court speeches rely heavily on hearsay and rumour as sources of information. One prominent example is the use of rumour by Aeschines, who succeeded in prosecuting Timarchos without presenting any direct witness for his sexual behaviour and prostitution. Instead, he reminded the citizen-jurors of how they had reacted to Timarchos' speech in the popular Assembly (at which they were supposed to have been eyewitnesses), and of the personal conversations and reputations prevailing in the town at the time. He alleged that:

Aeschin. 1.89:

> εἰ μὲν τοίνυν ἦν ὁ ἀγὼν οὑτοσὶ ἐν πόλει ἐκκλήτῳ, ὑμᾶς ἂν ἔγωγε ἠξίωσα μάρτυράς μοι γενέσθαι, τοὺς ἄριστα εἰδότας ὅτι ἀληθῆ λέγω: εἰ δ' ὁ μὲν ἀγών ἐστιν Ἀθήνησιν, οἱ δ' αὐτοὶ δικασταί μοι καὶ μάρτυρές ἐστε τῶν λόγων, ἐμοὶ μὲν ἀναμιμνῄσκειν προσήκει, ὑμᾶς δέ μοι μὴ ἀπιστεῖν.

> Now if this trial were taking place in another city, and that city should have demanded that city were the referee, I should have demanded that you should be my witnesses, you who best know that I am speaking the truth. But since this trial is in Athens, and you are at the same time judges and witnesses of the truth of what I say, it is my place to refresh your memory, and yours not to disbelieve me.

Aristotle does not count rumour as a way of proof in his *Rhetoric*, but Aeschines does. For Aeschines, rumour served as the hearsay evidence, which is based on common knowledge. He refers to the response of the popular Assembly to Timarchos' speech and to personal conversation in the *polis*, and equates the response as "witness" of the common knowledge the *dēmos* shared about the man. Then he continues, "if the trial is held in some other *polis*... I would have asked you to act as witnesses". However, because the trial is held in Athens, where the citizen-jurors were themselves the witnesses, he declares, it is enough to recall the memory of the citizen-jurors. He further justifies rumour as evidence citing a verse that is attributed to Hesiod. For Aeschines, rumours served as testimony confirming the common local knowledge in the Athenian community. Demosthenes, who had criticised Aeschines' use of rumour at that time, later in turn re-emphasised the force of rumour as a form of evidence (Dem. 19.243).[13]

This reliance on common knowledge and the use of citizen-jurors as witnesses was not limited to the experience in political meetings. Gossip on personal

13 On (the deification of) rumour in Aeschin. 1: Serafim 2020, 34–36.

characters was another common topic on which citizen-jurors might have heard (Dem. 21 *passim*; Dem. 36.41, 44–45). The Athenian courts could also explore the memory of the past as evidence. Routine expressions to recall the memory of older members of the citizen-jurors such as "the older among you all know" or the representation of the facts as something that everyone knows reflects how the Athenian law-courts relied on common knowledge of history and past trials, which the judges acquired not necessarily from personal experience but as news and rumour. On family matters, it was necessary to provide witness to share the family knowledge with the citizen-jurors, but when it comes to public matters, the speakers could rely more on shared knowledge among the citizen-jurors. This might be one reason why the public suits do not have as many witnesses as the private suits. Rumour, as a commonly held hearsay knowledge, did not have to be testified by individual witnesses, but it was witnessed by the citizen-jurors themselves.

8 Conclusion

Todd explained that the Athenians restricted the use of hearsay evidence for a different reason from modern jurisdiction. For Todd, the avoidance of hearsay witness in Athens was the consequence of the purpose of witnessing, to act as supporters of the litigants rather than to verify the fact. This chapter has slightly modified this view. The Athenian law-courts distinguished between direct evidence and hearsay evidence, privileged the former over the latter. The strategies of persuasion employed in the Athenian courts, however, did include hearsay information. As Herodotus did, the Athenian courts were open to hearsay evidence as the second best source of information. The Athenian law-courts evaluated the original witness (*opsis*), and required a direct witness who was present to testify in person. When the direct witness was incompetent or absent, however, there was *ekmartyria*, and when even *ekmartyria* was not available by death, by legal incapability or by reluctance of the witness, it seems to have been possible to ask for hearsay witnesses to substitute. These witnesses were required to stay responsible, but so far as they carefully limited their responsibility to the fact that they had heard the story and so refrained from carelessly testifying to the veracity of the original information, the hearsay witnesses could stay *hypeuthynoi* within the limit of their knowledge. Witnesses were asked to clarify the source of information and to remain responsible (*hypodikos, hypeuthynos*) to the information they had given. The Athenian law-courts were keen to establish the distinction between the different levels of information. In contrast, in the narrative, even rumour was considered reliable so far as being witnessed by the general public. It was not necessary to call witnesses because everyone, including the citizen-jurors should have already heard the rumour – here lies the democratic feature of the Athenian law-courts and the danger.

Bibliography

Bonner, R.J. (1905), *Evidence in Athenian Courts*, Chicago.
Cohen, E. (1973), *Ancient Athenian Maritime Courts*, Princeton.
Cohen, E. (1992), *Athenian Economy and Society: A Banking Perspective*, Princeton.
Dewald, C. (1987), 'Narrative Surface and Authorial Voice in Herodotus' *Histories*', in: *Arethusa* 20, 147–170.
Fowler, R.L. (1996), 'Herodotos and His Contemporaries', in: *JHS* 116, 62–87.
Gernet, L. (1955), *Droit et société dans la Grèce ancienne*, Paris.
Gray, V. (2001), 'Herodotus' Literary and Historical Method: Arion's Story (1.23–24)', in: *AJPh* 122.1, 11–28.
Harrison, A.R.W. (1968–1971), *The Law of Athens*, 2 vols., Oxford.
Hartog, F. (1988), *The Mirror of Herodotus: The Representation of the Other in the Writing of History*, Trans. by Janet Lloyd, Princeton.
Hesk, J. (2012), 'Common Knowledge and the Contestation of History in Some Fourth Century Athenian Trials', in: J. Marincola/L. Llewellyn-Jones/C.A. Maciver (eds.), *Greek Notions of the Past in the Archaic and Classical Eras: History without Historians*, Edinburgh, 207–226.
Humphreys, S.C. (1985), 'Social Relations on Stage: Witnesses in Classical Athens', in: *History and Anthropology* 1, 313–369.
Isager, S./Hansen, M.H. (1975), *Aspects of Athenian Society in the Fourth Century B.C.: A Historical Introduction to and Commentary on the Paragraphe-Speeches and the Speech Against Dionysodorus in the Corpus Demosthenicum (XXXII-XXXVIII and LVI)*, Odense.
Lateiner, D. (1986), 'The Empirical Element in the Methods of Early Greek Medical Writers and Herodotus: A Shared Epistemological Response', in: *Antichton* 20, 1–20.
Leisi, E. (1908), *Der Zeuge im Attischen Recht*, reprinted 1979, New York.
Lipsius, J.H. (1905–1912), *Das attische Recht und Rechtsverfahren: mit Benutzung des 'Attischen Processes' von M.H.E. Meier und G.F. Schömann dargestellt*, Leipzig.
MacDowell, D. (2004), *Demosthenes, Speeches 27–38*, Austin.
Marincola, J. (1997), *Authority and Tradition in Greek Histriography*, Cambridge.
Ober, J. (2008), *Democracy and Knowledge: Innovation and Learning in Classical Athens*, Princeton.
Reed, C.M. (2003), *Maritime Traders in the Ancient Greek World*, Cambridge.
Rubinstein, L. (2005), 'Main Litigants and Witnesses in the Athenian Courts', *Symposion* 2001, 99–120.
Scafuro, A. (1994), 'Witnessing and False Witnessing. Proving Citizenship and Kin Identity in Fourth-Century Athens', in: A. Scafuro/A.L. Boegehold (eds.), *Athenian Identity and Civic Ideology*, Baltimore/London, 156–198.
Scafuro, A. (2011), *Demosthenes, Speeches 39–49*, Austin.

Schepens, G. (1980), *L''Autopsie' dans la méthode des historiens grecs du Ve siècle avant J.-C.*, Brussels.
Schepens, G. (2007), 'History and Historia: Inquiry in the Greek Historians', in: C. Dewald/J. Marincola (eds.), *Companion to Greek Historiography*, vol. 1, Oxford, 39–55.
Serafim, A. (2020), *Religious Discourse in Attic Oratory and Politics*, New York/London.
Steinbock, B. (2013), *Social Memory in Athenian Public Discourse: Uses and Meanings of the Past*, Michigan.
Thomas, R. (2000), *Herodotus in Context Ethnography, Science and the Art of Persuasion*, Cambridge.
Todd, S. (2003), 'The Purpose of Evidence in Athenian Courts', in: P. Cartledge/P. Millett/S. Todd (eds.), *Nomos: Essays in Athenian Law, Politics and Society*, Cambridge, 19–40.
Whitehead, D. (1977), *The Ideology of Athenian Metics: Some Pendants and a Reappraisal*, Cambridge.

Part II: **The Rhetoric of Information-Gathering and Decision-Making**

Guy Westwood

Audience Memory as Evidence in the Trial on the Crown

Abstract: This chapter takes its cue from the curious near-absence of formal witness testimony in the extant speeches from the trial on the Crown in 330 BC (Aeschines, *Against Ctesiphon*; Demosthenes, *On the Crown*). It argues that both orators base their cases on the understanding that the trial audience – above all, the judges – could act as proxy witnesses because many of them had experienced events central to Aeschines' prosecution, namely Demosthenes' policy of resistance to Macedon and his public activities before, during, and after the war of 340–338 BC. But whereas Aeschines largely just assumes that the judges will accept his negative versions of these events and activities, Demosthenes overtly mobilises the judges' personal memories, and in a positive direction. The judges' status as "witnesses" therefore becomes a powerful way for him to assert both the appropriateness of the honours proposed for him by Ctesiphon and, consequently, Ctesiphon's innocence on Aeschines' main charge.

1 Introduction

In 330 BC, eight years after Philip's defeat of the Theban-Athenian alliance at Chaeronea, Aeschines conducted a prosecution of another politician, Ctesiphon, for proposing an honorific crown for Demosthenes (which would be his third since 340 BC). Aeschines' claim was that Ctesiphon's decree was illegal – the procedure used was the *graphē paranomōn* (indictment of an illegal proposal) – and he had launched it as long ago as 336 BC. He possibly revived it now in response to a renewed proposal of the decree itself, though this is a vexed issue.[1] He lost, and apparently failed to gain a fifth of the judges' votes.[2] Speeches survive which represent Aeschines' prosecution (3, *Against Ctesiphon*) and Demosthenes' defence of Ctesiphon, as (apparently sole) *synēgoros* (18, *On*

1 Carawan 2019; Harris 2019, 83–93 argues that there is no need to posit a renewed proposal (or a revived action). For earlier discussions, see e.g. Burke 1977, 334–340; Harris 1995, 140–142; Sawada 1996, 60–71; Worthington 2000, 96–97; Yunis 2001, 10–11; Martin 2009, 86–87; Todd 2009, 162–163.
2 Plut. *Dem.* 24.2–3.

https://doi.org/10.1515/9783110751970-004

the Crown).[3] Ctesiphon's own speech, which must have opened the defence case, does not survive in any form, and we have little sense of its length or coverage.[4] But *Against Ctesiphon* and *On the Crown* leave us in no doubt that it was the proposed honorand, Demosthenes, who really mattered in this trial, and that the main issue was his political career to date. One of the three elements of Ctesiphon's decree to which Aeschines objected was its very framing: it honoured Demosthenes explicitly "for his virtue and integrity" (ἀρετῆς ἕνεκα καὶ ἀνδραγαθίας) and "because he consistently speaks and acts in the best interests of the people" (ὅτι διατελεῖ λέγων καὶ πράττων τὰ ἄριστα τῷ δήμῳ).[5]

As Demosthenes and his political group had been instrumental in bringing Athens to a state of war with Philip, in building up a formidable alliance system to confront him, and in dealing with the fallout when Athens was defeated, the part of Demosthenes' career on which both he and Aeschines lay particular emphasis in the Crown speeches is the sixteen-year period since 346 BC and the negotiation of the Peace of Philocrates, which involved both of them. The relative importance of the two more technical charges in Aeschines' *graphē* (that Demosthenes was still subject to audit for his office as *teichopoios* – and so could not be crowned – and that his crown could not legally be proclaimed in the Theatre) has been much discussed, usually as part of assessments of the strengths and weaknesses of the prosecution and the defence,[6] but I focus here on Aeschines' "third" charge (treated by him as the most serious one: 3.49–50): that Ctesiphon's claims about Demosthenes' outstanding statesmanship were simply false.

While Demosthenes' and Aeschines' surviving speeches from their previous major court battle, the "Embassy trial" of 343 BC, make much use of witness testimonies (e.g. from fellow envoys), the Crown trial speeches make very little use of them even though they make ample use of other familiar types of documentary evidence. Demosthenes only calls witnesses twice (18.135, 137), and

3 Editions used in this chapter: Dilts 1997 for Aeschines 3; Dilts 2002 for Demosthenes 18. Translations: Carey 2000; Yunis 2005 unless otherwise noted. Although these speeches are the products of post-trial revision, the rhetoric I discuss is so pervasive in Demosthenes' case that even if some of the individual passages I examine do not reflect material that appeared in the live version, we can still be confident of its importance to his approach. On the revision issue, see e.g. Yunis 2001, 26–27; Hubbard 2008, 193–195; Westwood 2020, 284–286.

4 Aeschin. 3.201 – highly misleading – is the best we can do; see also e.g. Harris 2000, 60–61 n. 60, 61.

5 Aeschin. 3.49, 101, 237. On the honorific terms: Whitehead 1993, 47–62; Cook 2009; 2012, 228.

6 For which see e.g. Harris 1994, 141–148; 2000, 59–67; Cook 2012, 227–229; Gagarin 2012; Harris 2013, 225–233; 2017.

Aeschines never calls any. I argue in this chapter that Demosthenes' near-avoidance of witnesses is part of a concerted strategy to co-opt the judges (and the citizens in the informal trial audience)[7] as the most significant "witnesses" to his own career (and Aeschines'), and part of a wide-ranging effort to capitalize on Aeschines' failure (at least judging by *Against Ctesiphon* as we have it) to build explicit meaningful connection with the judges based on their past shared experiences and on their recollection of how the *dēmos* – many of the listeners included – had personally endorsed Demosthenes' policies, especially in the critical years 341–338 BC.[8]

It was open to Aeschines to support his tendentious versions of the recent past (where Demosthenes' bad policies led directly to Athenian defeat in 338 BC) with appropriately-curated appeals to the audience's recollections – for example their memory of moments where an alternative course of action had been possible (and popular).[9] So it is intriguing that he takes very few opportunities to do so directly. Aeschines' decision – and his active embrace of his own low profile in the period concerned (3.215–220) – gave Demosthenes the chance to spin negative versions of that profile and to activate positive recollections of the decisions he himself and the audience had taken together since 346 BC. In one notable case (18.229), which I discuss below, Demosthenes even uses the formal language of witnessing (μαρτυρέω and its cognates, in this case μάρτυσι) to appeal to their memories, and this is notable because both he and Aeschines concentrate most of their usage of μαρτυρέω-cognates in these speeches on the straightforward designation of witness testimony itself and how their opponent's behaviour "bears witness to/against" his own failures or wrongdoing.[10] Broader appeals to audience members' knowledge and experiences are more important to Demosthenes' strategy, and I will discuss some key examples from *On the Crown* later. The strategy aims, ultimately, to present the audience with a positive and inspiriting vision of Athens' present and future at a time when the failed uprising by Agis III of Sparta earlier in the year had shown that open resistance to Macedonian power was not presently an option.[11] Articulating this

7 Several of the points I make below apply equally to the judges and to the wider audience, so the term "audience" is used relatively loosely in what follows.

8 See in general on the "rhetoric of community" involved here Serafim 2017a, 47–54; 2017b.

9 Demosthenes occasionally indicates (e.g. 18.143–144, 236) that there were times when he was simply not listened to, even during his political ascendancy between 341 and 338 BC.

10 The other instances: Aeschin. 3.27, 31, 41, 96, 119, 249; Dem. 18.118, 136, 217, plus the two witness testimonies (135, 137), and 267–268, which I discuss below.

11 See Aeschin. 3.133. For a summary of the uprising and the evidence for it: Kralli 2017, 68–75.

vision involves constructing positive, affirming versions of both the recent and the more distant past, as Harvey Yunis has shown.[12] In particular, it encourages the judges to deploy their memories of Demosthenes' and Aeschines' own activities, especially over the past decade, not only to uphold the terms of Ctesiphon's decree and secure his acquittal and Demosthenes' award of the crown, but also to validate *dēmos* endorsement – i.e. up to a point, their *own* endorsement – of Demosthenes' policies in the crucial 341–338 BC period.

The basic technique of co-opting judges and other audience members as witnesses (whether with μαρτυρέω-cognates or not) – witnesses to the speaker's life and activities up to now, of his liturgies, and so on – can be found in many other speeches from public or private cases, notably Aeschines' *Against Timarchus*;[13] and the "rhetoric of seeing" (and thus "knowing"), explored recently by Peter O'Connell, is a fundamental part of this.[14] Demosthenes applies the technique in *On the Crown* on numerous occasions, and in a distinctive way: appeals to the knowledge and experiences of the judges and wider audience effectively *take the place of* actual witness testimony. This is not true of *Against Timarchus*, where the two techniques operate alongside, and complement, one another;[15] and so it is a surprise, given Aeschines' many appeals to the judges in that speech to use their own knowledge of the defendant, that he makes only a small number of such appeals in *Against Ctesiphon* – and all the more surprising given his ambitious deployment in it of *enargeia* and related imaginative visualization techniques (e.g. asking the audience to imagine a past event they could not have witnessed, or a hypothetical future one, or that they see something other than the real trial in front of them in the present).[16] I will discuss Aeschines' reticence first, and then how Demosthenes capitalises on it.

---

12 Yunis 2000; 2001, 13–17; 2005, 30; see also Westwood 2020, 275–327, especially 324–327.

13 For examples, see e.g. the list in Harrison 1971, 138 n. 2; also Mirhady 2002, 264–265, singling out *Against Timarchus*.

14 O'Connell 2016; 2017a, especially 86–112; 2017b.

15 See e.g. Aeschin. 1.50 (appeal to popular knowledge combined with a witness statement); 1.65–66 ("you all know" followed by a witness statement); 1.115–116 (witness statement followed by an acknowledgement that these were "things you knew").

16 See e.g. Aeschin. 3.153–157, 180, 244, 257–259. Discussions: Hobden 2007; Webb 2009; O'Connell 2017a 124–136, especially 128–131; 2017b, 241–242; Serafim 2017a, 101–102; Westwood 2017; 2020, 301–305.

2 Aeschines' prosecution

The policies and events most at issue in the Crown trial would have been well within the competence of most of the judges. Even those only just over the age-limit for dicastic service would have completed their *ephēbeia* shortly before war with Philip broke out. Though some judges, for various reasons (distance, military service, etc.), would not have engaged continuously with political developments in the critical 341–338 BC period, many present would have voted on the key decisions, or fought at Chaeronea (or lost relatives and/or friends there), or have taken part in the mass evacuation from the Attic countryside into the city after the defeat. Many of them would also have seen the leading anti-Macedonian politicians hounded by their opponents in the courts across the 330s[17] BC – something Demosthenes describes as especially familiar to the judges in *On the Crown* (18.249: "you certainly know and remember..."[18] [ἴστε γὰρ δήπου καὶ μέμνησθε]) – and so they would have heard several of the arguments made by Aeschines and Demosthenes in the Crown trial before (cf. 18.125), in trials like the prosecution of Hyperides by Diondas (probably in 334 BC) from which the fragmentary *Defence Against Diondas* derives.[19] This series of prosecutions had been overwhelmingly unsuccessful (18.10, 250), and Demosthenes' resilience in particular (as well as his two previous crowns) would have served to foster favourable popular versions of his activities in the 341–338 BC period at a time when he appears to have been less politically active.[20] But hostile alternative arguments were clearly available and well-used.[21] Demosthenes could be targeted for failing to support the Theban revolt in 335 BC, for example (and Aeschines claims he had Persian money for this purpose: 3.156, 239–240) – so Aeschines' failure to make plausible alternatives stick was not a foregone conclusion: but the fact that he does not invoke the audience's memory for Demos-

17 Dem. 18.222–223, 249–250, 322; Hyp. *Dion.* 3.145r9–144v22; Plut. *Dem.* 21.1.

18 Literal translation mine; Yunis 2005, 93 has "surely you recollect...".

19 This is probably the same as Diondas' legal attack on Hyperides and Demomeles for proposing the second of Demosthenes' earlier crowns: Dem. 18.222–223; cf. [Plut.] *Vit. Hyp.* 848f. Date: Horváth 2014, 10–23.

20 See e.g. Worthington 2000; 2013, 285–293.

21 See e.g. Martin 2009, 86–88, noting Demades' criticism in Arist. *Rh.* 1401b32–34.

thenes' (non-)role in supporting Thebes five years earlier is already a good sign of the limited room for manoeuvre he seems to have had.[22]

Like most Athenian litigants in surviving trial speeches, Aeschines appeals to the judges (and members of the wider audience) in *Against Ctesiphon* in a wide variety of ways that do not seek to build a particular experience-based relationship with them (pleading with them in §61, warning them in §215, focusing their attention in §64, and so on). But only in a few places (3.144, 166, 175–176, 235) does he appeal directly to their knowledge of relevant facts and events – and of those instances only §144 solicits audience awareness of a specific issue from the period when Demosthenes was a key policymaker, namely his alleged bribe-taking to arrange that the Thebans would have overall command of the allied forces in the campaign that led to Chaeronea (part of a cluster of popular attack routes on the anti-Macedonian politicians in and after 338 BC, according to Aeschines here and as Hyperides' *Diondas* speech shows).[23] §166, by contrast, recalls an incident from only the past year: a speech Demosthenes made in the Assembly during Agis' war. (Aeschines only spends three paragraphs on this recent period, perhaps because he and Demosthenes had been in basic agreement that Athens should not join Sparta.) Conversely, §235 solicits much more distant knowledge (of events of the late fifth century). Finally, §§175–176 raise an issue with wider application.[24] Aeschines alludes here to Demosthenes' alleged flight from the battlefield at Chaeronea, framing this as part of a *general* predisposition towards cowardice on his part; and although he is prepared to say that the judges are well-informed about this (ὑμεῖς σύνιστε), and that he would only need to discuss the matter further if they did not know the facts (εἰ...ὑμεῖς μὴ συνῄδετε), he does not appeal to their knowledge or memory *directly* or for any particular *instance* of Demosthenes' cowardice – and this is part of a pattern in *Against Ctesiphon* where audience memory or knowledge is alluded to or conveniently assumed rather than directly invoked. In a few places, for example,[25] Aeschines refers to the judges as possessing the

22 Especially so if Diodorus is right (17.8.5–6) that Demosthenes did try to persuade the Athenians to join the revolt (which pushes against Aeschines here, and also Din. 1.10, 18–21; Plut. *Dem.* 17).

23 Hyp. *Dion.* 4.145v8–12.

24 Cook 2012, 232–242 reads this theme as key to the speech, and in rationalising Aeschines' reticence in going into detail on any particular instance of cowardice (240–241) comes to conclusions similar to those arrived at here on audience memory.

25 See Aeschin. 3.53, 80, 130–131, as well as the instances in the main text. 3.8, 176, 203 – which entreat the judges to remember matters raised *during* the trial – might also be added to the list.

knowledge that can disprove his opponents' claims or buttress his own, but does not appeal directly to them to use it: in §§221 and 237, these comments are even couched in fictive addresses to Demosthenes and Ctesiphon respectively (in §237, for example, Ctesiphon is accused of insulting "people who know the facts and are alert" [τοὺς δ' εἰδότας καὶ αἰσθανομένους]) – a way of indicating that the audience's knowledge is taken for granted (and one which Demosthenes also uses), but hardly a way to build community with them.

In other places, Aeschines almost seems to *avoid* opportunities for forging such a connection, even when the context might invite it (e.g. in the long passage §§244–254). In §§125, 217 and 224, for example, he tells the audience about occasions when he and they were both present in the Assembly to hear speeches he made (standing up to Demosthenes in two of those cases: 125, 224) – but in none of these three (isolated) cases does Aeschines invite the judges to recall the occasions concerned directly.[26] §224 is a particularly good example: Aeschines claims here that when he made Demosthenes admit in the Assembly to having Anaxinus of Oreus, his former host, executed as a spy because he "valued the city's salt more than the shared table of hospitality", "the *dēmos* ('the whole Athenian citizenry [ἅπασιν Ἀθηναίοις]', Aeschines tells us) and all the foreign observers at the Assembly [cried] out". Given that Aeschines is as ready as usual elsewhere in the speech to appeal to the audience's cognitive faculties (whether via visualization techniques or by other means: see e.g. §255), the fact that there is no appeal here to his listeners' own memories of an event he claims so many of them actually witnessed (e.g. by saying "you remember…") does not suggest that he is delicately avoiding dwelling on an already well-known and unpleasant incident, but that he is misrepresenting the incident and/or the reaction. Many of the judges who were in that Assembly audience might have approved of Anaxinus' execution, or have thought there were good grounds at least for arresting him; in *On the Crown*, Demosthenes simply takes Anaxinus' spying activity as read (18.137) (though that need not prove anything either).

As Aeschines does not often ask audience members to tap into their memories directly, and does not lay much emphasis on his own public activities – indeed his personal role in the Anaxinus incident is only marked by ὑπ' ἐμοῦ (3.224), and the only extended section in the speech where he does highlight his own public role is the Delphi sequence (3.115–124), which none of the judges witnessed – his possibilities for the construction of community with his audience are restricted. It is possible that his aim in invoking audience memories as obliquely as he does was to build a suitably insidious pattern of *suggestion* –

26 Aeschin. 3.94 offers a looser example of the same phenomenon (βλεπόντων).

and that this was simply too subtle, in the end, to compete with the optimistic and overt team-building of *On the Crown*. But that seems at odds with the authoritative tone of much of Aeschines' speech, so it is better to posit that he was simply playing safe with the judges: doing his best to avoid provoking the negative response that asking them to remember overly distorted versions of Demosthenes' public activities might yield.

This fits with Aeschines' occasional signs of awareness that some of his claims will actively clash with audience members' recollections. In *Against Ctesiphon* 59, for example, when trying to show that Demosthenes and Philocrates took bribes from Philip, he admits that such a claim may "[strike] some of you as rather suspect on suddenly hearing it (εἰ δέ τισιν ὑμῶν ἐξαίφνης ἀκούσασιν ἀπιστότερος προσπέπτωκεν ὁ τοιοῦτος λόγος)"; predictably, Demosthenes easily demolishes it in *On the Crown* (18.228). Later, when highlighting his allegation that Demosthenes took Theban bribes (3.144), Aeschines observes that although others criticize Demosthenes for this too, "you (i.e. the audience) know it (σύνιστε) and feel no anger. This is what Demosthenes has done to you; you are already habituated to hearing of his crimes, and as a result you feel no surprise". This is an important moment: as well as indicating Aeschines' awareness of the scale of his task in reversing popular perceptions, it is one of a number of moments in the speech where Aeschines seems to make his nurturing of a close speaker-audience relationship even harder to achieve. The implication that the audience's wits have become dulled risks alienating them, an outcome he risks elsewhere by accusing them of insensitivity (ὦ σιδηροῖ: 3.166),[27] by criticising the behaviour of judges in general (see e.g. 3.192, 251), by laying emphasis on the practical inferiority of present-day Athenians compared with their distinguished forebears (3.178), and by issuing his listeners with distasteful veiled threats about how an acquittal of Demosthenes might be seen by Athens' Macedonian masters (3.254). Although Demosthenes also occasionally criticises his audience too (e.g. 18.138), Aeschines risks offending them on several occasions. So while we can assume that Aeschines' versions of matters relevant to the third charge might already struggle to compete with Demosthenes' (at least for most listeners), we can also see that he does not obviously succeed in finding a good alternative means of getting the judges and wider audience on his side.

His strategic engagement with his audience's experiences can therefore be seen as bipartite. One part of the strategy, the "factual" part, seeks a kind of objectivity in presenting a narrative of Demosthenes' activities which is supported

---

27 Following Todd 2007, 686.

not (for the most part) by directly harnessing audience knowledge/recollection of experiences they shared with Aeschines (who, as we saw, downplays his own public contributions), but instead by three other interrelated methods. First, as noted above, Aeschines sometimes performs the assumption that the judges *do* remember what he wants them to (the way he wants them to), and mentions that obliquely, without actually appealing to them personally. Second, he supports his narrative with numerous documents (especially laws and decrees) of varying relevance (this is the speech, after all, where he goes out of his way to praise the practice of preserving public documents: 3.75). Third, he sometimes attempts to forestall the connection Demosthenes will seek to make with the judges by divorcing his opponent's policy disasters from the *dēmos* who voted for them. But this frequently (though not always: 3.125–126) involves depicting those who so voted, and are now listening, as swallowing Demosthenes' deceptive rhetoric (e.g. 3.72, 93–94, 142, 166–167), which in turn risks alienating them in the way mentioned above, and also leaves ample room for a much more positive and gratifying spin on the audience's past decisions by (Ctesiphon and) Demosthenes. Meanwhile, the other part of Aeschines' overall strategy (the "fictive" part) relies on the production of vivid alternative scenarios (past, present, and future) mentioned above: examples include the passages where Aeschines asks the audience to imagine the public shame Athens (and the audience) will incur when Demosthenes is crowned (3.153–156); his dramatic evocation of the plight of the Thebans after Alexander's destruction of their city in 335 BC (3.157, supported by a familiar formal "witnessing" term, παρεγένεσθε[28]); his tour of the Agora monuments, not visible to the judges, though nearby (3.183–187); and his conjuring up of the figures of Solon, Aristides, and others as co-pleaders in the *epilogos* (3.257–259).[29]

The problem with this twin strategy is that Aeschines does not – and clearly cannot easily – combine the two parts (i.e. the professedly factual and the overtly fictive) in this speech as he had in *Against Timarchus*. This is strikingly reflected in the fact that although he often uses the most common verb of seeing, ὁράω, in *Against Ctesiphon*, he never uses it to get the judges to recall particular relevant sights they have witnessed in the past (e.g. "you all saw how Demos-

28 Thür 2005, 153; O'Connell 2017a, 87. Elsewhere in the speech Aeschines uses both παραγίγνομαι and another formal "witnessing" term, πάρειμι, to refer to those watching the trial now (3.8, 56; cf. 247), but only once in relation to the judges' previous experiences (3.71), though without encouraging them to recall them.

29 For discussions of these passages, see above n. 16.

thenes did X").[30] A middle-way option – actively and frequently inviting the audience to tap into their memories and recall the experiences they shared with the speaker, rather than just alluding to them – is left largely untried; and that is the strategic route Demosthenes is then free to take unhindered in *On the Crown*.

3 Demosthenes' defence

Like Aeschines (e.g. 3.221), Demosthenes shows himself conscious (at points when it suits him) of the possible effects of the lapse of time between 338 and 330 BC on the clarity of his audience's memory (e.g. 18.226), accepting that some listeners may be too young to recall the pre-338 BC events accurately (and using that as an excuse to produce authoritative versions of those events) (18.50). He also envisages limits on the audience's ability to recall Aeschines' misdemeanours in the run-up to war (18.138), a moment which comes directly after the two moments in the speech where he has offered regular witness testimony (18.135, 137) to events to which a majority of judges would not have been privy (an Areopagus meeting and an alleged private meeting between Aeschines and Anaxinus) – though this does fall within the same few minutes as three separate assertions that the audience *will* remember Aeschines' role in key events (18.132, 136, 142). There are also well-known events which Demosthenes insists on giving documentary proof for (on some occasions with variations on the formula ἵν' εἰδῆτε, "so that you may know": 18.173, 218, 305), even though a plurality of judges will have been present, and also plenty of moments where he appeals to the judges' memories only obliquely, like Aeschines (e.g. 18.215, 283). In general, though, *On the Crown* sees Demosthenes investing to a much greater degree than Aeschines in techniques of community-building: a prominent one is his use of the language of *eunoia* to posit a reciprocal relationship of goodwill between himself and the judges.[31] This is especially notable in §8, in phrases repeated from the proem (1): "I pray…that in this trial you have as much concern for my welfare as I have always had for yours" (εὔχομαι…ὅσην εὔνοιαν ἔχων

30 As for other familiar "seeing" verbs, Aeschines uses βλέπω (and ἀποβλέπω) several times in *Against Ctesiphon* but only once (and very obliquely) to recall a situation supposedly involving the judges (3.94); he does not use θεάομαι at all; and both he and Demosthenes only use θεωρέω to draw audience attention to what can be "seen" from the current speech itself.

31 Hernández Muñoz 1989; Whitehead 1993, 52–54; Cook 2009; 2012, 249–251; Sanders 2016, 168–175.

ἐγὼ διατελῶ τῇ τε πόλει καὶ πᾶσιν ὑμῖν, τοσαύτην ὑπάρξαι μοι παρ' ὑμῶν εἰς τουτονὶ τὸν ἀγῶνα) (echoing, in διατελῶ, the honorific language of Ctesiphon's proposal). He also solicits more reactions in general from the audience, the best-known of which is his open encouragement to them to join him in calling Aeschines a hireling (52: μισθωτὸς or indeed μισθωτός).[32] His appeals to the audience as witnesses to his (and Aeschines') activities intersect with, and complement, related techniques like this, in order to construct this audience not only as observers of Demosthenes' past actions, but also as his supporters (like regular lawcourt witnesses)[33] – as people who have not only shared difficult times with him but have also endorsed his political responses to the events concerned.

A key example is the section (18.227–231) where (as noted above) Demosthenes dismisses Aeschines' attempt (3.59–61) to refashion *him* as the one who took bribes from Philip – something Aeschines knows the audience will find doubtful (3.59). There, Aeschines had used the image of accounting at audit (λογισμός) to encourage the judges to listen to his version fairly – a significant choice given the charge in his current *graphē* that Demosthenes was still subject to audit (ὑπεύθυνος), and given that ideas of audit and the frame of the *euthyna(i)* procedure are consequently important to interpreting both speeches' rhetoric. In *On the Crown* 229 – after exposing Aeschines' refashioning attempt to the audience and reworking Aeschines' imagery for his own purposes (227–228)[34] – Demosthenes uses "accounting" as a foil to introduce an itemised list of his own successful policies (229–231), as follows:

> καὶ μὴν ὅτι γε οὐ δίκαια λέγει μεταθέσθαι ταύτην τὴν δόξαν ἀξιῶν, ἐγὼ διδάξω ῥᾳδίως, οὐ τιθεὶς ψήφους (οὐ γάρ ἐστιν ὁ τῶν πραγμάτων οὗτος λογισμός, ἀλλ' ἀναμιμνήσκων ἕκαστα ἐν βραχέσι, **λογισταῖς ἅμα καὶ μάρτυσι τοῖς ἀκούουσιν ὑμῖν χρώμενος**.
>
> Yet I will easily demonstrate that he is wrong to demand that you change your opinion. I will not add up figures, which is no way to examine policy. Instead, I'll briefly recount all the particulars and use you, the audience, as both accountants and witnesses.

Where Aeschines had encouraged the judges to "audit" his version of Demosthenes' activities objectively, Demosthenes makes it a *subjective* matter: he is encouraging the judges and the wider audience (τοῖς ἀκούουσιν) to "audit" *his*

32 On this passage see Wankel 1976, 354–356; Yunis 2001, 139–140; Serafim 2017a, 53–54; 2017b, 35–37.

33 See the works cited in n. 49; Mirhady 2002 pushes against the idea that witnesses were primarily supporters.

34 See Yunis 2001, 236–237 on the imagery in 18.227–229.

version of his activities not just on the basis of what they hear now but also on the basis of what they themselves know already. He extends the scope of μάρτυσι beyond its immediate reference (presumably) to the witnesses who might be present at an official audit, to include the audience's "witnessing" of his past policies more generally (i.e. as participants in Assembly debates on them, as participants in the campaign that ended at Chaeronea, etc.), and also the function they can now perform as proxies for regular witnesses in court. In addition, his rejection of Aeschines' auditing/accounting analogy as insufficient – because it sticks to figures and does not take into account the lived reality of audience members' experiences[35] – helps to mark Aeschines' whole prosecution as frivolous and false to how the wider community had chosen to recall the period in question; so does the passage's link with Demosthenes' earlier reference to his own appearances before the auditors (λογισταί) (18.117), one of the many (seventy-two?)[36] moments in the speech where he makes the argument that Aeschines had ample opportunities for accusing him personally before now (indeed was *present* [παρὼν], like a witness, on key occasions: 18.83, 117, 222, 239), but did not speak out – another sign of the bad faith of his prosecution.

Also important here, and closely related, is Demosthenes' use of ἀναμιμνήσκων. The notion of "reminding" the judges of what they are assumed to know already has a fundamentally collaborative quality, helping to break down the speaker-audience divide. Aeschines uses ἀναμιμνήσκω four times in *Against Ctesiphon*, but only to get the judges to recall (or to point to his own recall of) matters outside the scope of the accusation (3.31, 112, 154, 177). For Demosthenes in *On the Crown*, "reminding" enables him to impute knowledge to – and so work with – his hearers, as here at §229; it also introduces important narratives of Philip's rise and Demosthenes' resistance to him in the 340s earlier in the speech, at §17 (ἀναμνῆσαι) and §60 (ἀναμνήσω). Furthermore, it buttresses (136: ἀναμιμνήσκεσθε) – and indeed introduces (131: ἀναμνήσω) – his factually dubious discussion of the activities he alleges Aeschines undertook on behalf of the enemy (i.e. 131–138): his defence of the alleged Macedonian agent Antiphon, his support for Philip's envoy Python, and his fraternising with Anaxinus. This is the section where Demosthenes calls his two sets of regular witnesses, probably to attest more neutral versions of the sensational claims that frame them: at §135, for example, the witnesses probably attested merely that Aeschines had been replaced by Hyperides as Athens' advocate at Delos, not that the Areopa-

35 And also because it cannot take account of what those who voted for Demosthenes' policies *hoped* they would achieve: Donnelly 1941, 309.
36 Σ *ad* Dem. 18.14 (48 Dilts).

gus judged him a traitor, as Demosthenes claims.[37] The high concentration of the language and actuality of "recalling" and "witnessing" in this sequence probably points to its high level of exaggeration. But the factual basis of Demosthenes' claims only mattered up to a point. Crucial to being believed, or to having his exaggerations overlooked by the audience, was the establishment of community with them; and this is what his willing submission to the scrutiny of the judges at §229 helps to achieve. I now offer some more examples of this.

In §§87–89, Demosthenes recalls one of his key policy achievements in the run-up to war with Philip – cementing friendship between Athens and Byzantium in 340 (88–89):

> ἀλλὰ τίς ἦν ὁ βοηθήσας τοῖς Βυζαντίοις καὶ σώσας αὐτούς; τίς ὁ κωλύσας τὸν Ἑλλήσποντον ἀλλοτριωθῆναι κατ' ἐκείνους τοὺς χρόνους; ὑμεῖς, ἄνδρες Ἀθηναῖοι. τὸ δ' ὑμεῖς ὅταν λέγω, τὴν πόλιν λέγω. τίς δ' ὁ τῇ πόλει λέγων καὶ γράφων καὶ πράττων καὶ ἁπλῶς ἑαυτὸν εἰς τὰ πράγματα ἀφειδῶς δούς; ἐγώ. [89] ἀλλὰ μὴν ἡλίκα ταῦτ' ὠφέλησεν ἅπαντας, **οὐκέτ' ἐκ τοῦ λόγου δεῖ μαθεῖν, ἀλλ' ἔργῳ πεπείρασθε·**
>
> But who was it who helped the Byzantians and saved them? Who was it who prevented the Hellespont from falling into foreign hands at that time? It was you, Athenians, and when I say you, I mean the city. And who was it who addressed the city, moved decrees, took action, and in truth devoted himself unsparingly to the situation? It was I. [89] But you do not need a report to teach you how much everyone benefited; you lived through the actual events.

The passage neatly encapsulates what we might call the "synergy rhetoric" of *On the Crown* – that both the Athenians themselves and Demosthenes as their chief policymaker were working together to enact the only course consistent with Athens' reputation and core identity. Demosthenes will shortly develop this aspect by recalling (18.96–100) a series of circumstances where the Athenians took action in defence of other states since the 390s – thus involving the total age-range of his audience.[38] Λέγων καὶ γράφων καὶ πράττων in §88 keeps his reminder of his record relevant to the legal case by recalling the terms of Ctesiphon's proposal (λέγων καὶ πράττων); but synergy is the keynote, and all the more emphasised by the misleading nominative singulars here (τίς ἦν ὁ βοηθήσας...καὶ σώσας...; τίς ὁ κωλύσας...) which then culminate not in fact in (the singular) Demosthenes at all, but in the true achievers, the *audience*, the Athenians themselves (ὑμεῖς, ἄνδρες Ἀθηναῖοι) as a civic body. Demosthenes goes out of his way to specify this (τὸ δ' ὑμεῖς ὅταν λέγω, τὴν πόλιν λέγω) –

37 Yunis 2001, 189; cf. Wankel 1976, 748 on Anaxinus.
38 For a discussion of this passage's strategy, see Westwood 2020, 27–29.

ὑμεῖς on its own could usually denote the *dēmos* wherever gathered and at whatever time, and not just the present judges, so would have been sufficient for Demosthenes' purposes here, but laying emphasis on the πόλις helps to remind the judges that the city's physical and political essence as well as its communal life were in danger in the war with Philip, and that the interrelated actions of Demosthenes and his audience were aimed at preserving the *totality* of Athens itself and its people.[39] Crucial in the passage for our purposes, though, and for the sustaining of Demosthenes' "synergy rhetoric", is his open reminder of their lived – and shared – experience (ἔργῳ πεπείρασθε, "you lived through the actual events").

This passage is one of many in *On the Crown* where Demosthenes seeks to activate audience recollection by invoking it directly (here with πεπείρασθε), and, predictably enough, his clearest efforts to co-opt the audience as witnesses to his actions come with uses of forms of οἶδα,[40] especially ἴστε,[41] though he does use alternative verbs of perception and recall for this purpose too (including, as we saw above, ἀναμιμνῄσκω).[42] By contrast, ἴστε is notably avoided by Aeschines when addressing the judges in *Against Ctesiphon* (except – as with his uses of ἀναμιμνῄσκω – in a handful of cases, none of which ask his audience to recall Demosthenes' activities in the period at issue: 3.6, 119, 246, 247). An alternative, σύνοιδα/σύνιστε, is only deployed on three occasions to invoke audience knowledge of Demosthenes' activity and behaviour,[43] and only once in the case of a specific, relevant event: in *Against Ctesiphon* 144, as we saw above, referring to 339/8 BC and the Theban command of the allied forces. This is a case where Aeschines as good as admits he is not going to get the reaction from the judges that he wants (ὑμεῖς σύνιστε καὶ οὐκ ὀργίζεσθε), and is also one of only two occasions in the speech where the judges' *aural* memory is directly invoked (ἀκούειν).[44] Alternative lexical means of directly invoking audience

39 Not least the measures he took in 338 BC to improve the city's defences: Aeschin. 3.236 (cf. Lycurg. 1.44).

40 For this verb's centrality in witnessing, see e.g. Thür 2005, 153–155; O'Connell 2017a, 12, 87, 100–104 (esp. 101).

41 The relevant instances are Dem. 18.10, 168, 249, 268; relevant variations can be found at 18.129, 130, 282 (ἴσασι); 18.50, 95 (εἰδότες/ας); cf. also 18.85, 132, 205, 315 for the τίς...οὐκ οἶδε; formulation type.

42 Beyond compounds, μιμνῄσκω/μέμνημαι and cognates are rarely used of the judges' memory here, but see 18.226, 249, 269, 283; cf. 18.138 (μνήμην) and 142 (μνημονεύοντας).

43 Aeschin. 3.175 (two forms) and 232, as well as 144.

44 The other is at Aeschin. 3.166 (ἀκροώμενοι).

memories are rare in the speech,[45] as we saw above with appeals to visual memory (e.g. via ὁράω). But while, like Aeschines, Demosthenes also seems to miss what look like some ideal opportunities for appealing to audience memory directly (with relatively few direct cues to the judges to recall things they saw and heard), the moments where he *does* draw on it directly are carefully placed: for example, although he does not solicit direct support from the audience for the speech he made in the Assembly the morning after the news arrived of Philip's taking of Elatea (18.169–180) – at which at least some of them must have been present – he prefaces the whole passage with a claim that *all* of his audience know (ἴστε μὲν ἅπαντες) about the alarm it caused at Athens and that he will only tell "just a few of the most important points" (μικρὰ δ' ἀκούσατε ὅμως αὐτὰ τἀναγκαιότατα). His claim about their knowledge, as framed, is entirely plausible: and although not all audience members will have witnessed the panic at first hand, the claim also embraces those who heard of it at second hand and in doing so assimilates their experience to the more vivid and relevant experience of those who were there. Nobody is left out.

On the Crown 268 is another example of a moment where Demosthenes includes a general appeal to audience memory – one which applies to his whole record, not just a time-specific part of it – and places it at a point where it can have special synoptic impact for a whole passage. Here he has just had a list of his liturgies read out to illustrate his public record. This piece of documentary evidence supplements earlier expressions of confidence like §110, where (after discussing his successful reform of the trierarchy in response to war in 340 BC) Demosthenes had claimed that even if he were to say nothing about the rest of his domestic policy achievements, audience knowledge could supply them anyway (ὁμοίως παρ' ὑμῶν ἑκάστῳ τὸ συνειδὸς ὑπάρχειν μοι). A similar moment is reached here in §268, where Demosthenes turns towards his record as a private citizen:

> ἐν μὲν τοίνυν τοῖς πρὸς τὴν πόλιν τοιοῦτος· ἐν δὲ τοῖς ἰδίοις **εἰ μὴ πάντες ἴστε** ὅτι κοινὸς καὶ φιλάνθρωπος καὶ τοῖς δεομένοις ἐπαρκῶν, σιωπῶ καὶ οὐδὲν ἂν εἴποιμι οὐδὲ παρασχοίμην περὶ τούτων οὐδεμίαν μαρτυρίαν, οὔτ' εἴ τινας ἐκ τῶν πολεμίων ἐλυσάμην, οὔτ' εἴ τισιν θυγατέρας συνεξέδωκα, οὔτε τῶν τοιούτων οὐδέν.
>
> That is my record in public life. If any of you are unaware that in my private life I am generous, compassionate, and helpful to the needy, I'll say nothing. I would rather not utter a word or provide any testimony about those matters, for instance, about any prisoners of

45 Aeschin. 3.152 ("are we to suppose your ability to remember [ἡ ὑμετέρα μνήμη] will die along with the dead men?") is one – and rather oblique.

war whom I ransomed from the enemy, or about the daughters of any citizens whose dowry I provided, or about any similar matters.

We know Demosthenes had ransomed prisoners in the past,[46] and so can probably assume that he was known to have provided at least some dowries; the *paraleipsis* here clearly supports an appeal to the knowledge of the *entire* audience – as in §168 – to corroborate his positive reputation (and to counteract Aeschines' various attacks on it). The most striking point for us here, though, is his effective rejection of the primacy of documentary evidence (μαρτυρία, to which the μαρτυρίαν here must at least partly refer given its proximity to the reading-out of the μαρτυρίαι about his liturgies) in favour of the personal knowledge he claims all judges have and can deploy to support him. This may partly respond to Aeschines' smug highlighting of the capacity of preserved written documents to convict people like Demosthenes (3.75 and 103–105) – Demosthenes certainly targets Aeschines' former career as secretary to the Boule in *On the Crown* (18.127, 209), as he had done in *On the False Embassy* – but the principal effect is to elevate the judges to the status of witnesses who can testify in Demosthenes' favour from what they know, just as in §89 the judges had needed no λόγος to remind them of their support for Byzantium but could rely on the ἔργον of their shared experience.

The way that Demosthenes frames their knowledge here in §268 – as part of a negatively-pitched conditional – also responds to a similar framing in a similar passage just after the proem (10) where Demosthenes – again, placing it at the very start of an extended discussion (10–52) that he figures as simply a necessary response to the extraneous attacks Aeschines had launched – had made a striking request of the judges:

περὶ μὲν δὴ τῶν ἰδίων ὅσα λοιδορούμενος βεβλασφήμηκεν περὶ ἐμοῦ, θεάσασθ' ὡς ἁπλᾶ καὶ δίκαια λέγω. **εἰ μὲν ἴστε** με τοιοῦτον οἷον οὗτος ᾐτιᾶτο (οὐ γὰρ ἄλλοθί που βεβίωκ' ἢ παρ' ὑμῖν), μηδὲ φωνὴν ἀνάσχησθε, μηδ' εἰ πάντα τὰ κοινὰ ὑπέρευ πεπολίτευμαι, ἀλλ' ἀναστάντες καταψηφίσασθ' ἤδη.

Consider how simply and fairly I can answer all the outrageous slanders he devised about my personal life. If you know me to be the kind of person he has alleged – and I have not lived anywhere else except among you – do not allow me to go on, not even if my entire public career has been exemplary, but stand up and convict me now.

These direct appeals in §10 and §268 (both with εἰ...ἴστε) engage audience memory much more compellingly than Aeschines does when covering the same

46 Dem. 19.166–171; see also: Wankel 1976, 1170–1171; Usher 1993, 263.

topic: in *Against Ctesiphon* 53, for example, Aeschines had asserted that the "details" of Demosthenes' early life were "so certain and familiar to the hearers" (οὕτως...πιστὰ καὶ γνώριμα τοῖς ἀκούουσιν) that they did not need more exploration by him – without any accompanying appeal to the judges to recall any of them themselves, even the three specific anecdotes he had actually just mentioned at 3.52. By contrast, Demosthenes shapes *On the Crown* 10 and 268 in such a way as to emphasise the complete sufficiency of the judges' knowledge to settle – on its own – the whole issue of his own life-long good character (and his personal/private character, not his public performance): in both cases he undertakes to stop speaking (either under their instruction, in §10, or voluntarily, in §268) if they refuse to validate his claim. It is fair to point out that Demosthenes cannot have expected to be stopped at §10, and that his daringly succinct (cf. ἁπλᾶ) request is to some extent purely rhetorical; but by offering the judges the *opportunity* to shut him down, he affirms his trust in "them" – both as representatives of the democratic civic community he has always been part of, and as an audience of individuals some of whom *have* observed his entire career – and does so in a way which gratifies them (in reminding them of the extent of their power) and complements the reciprocal *eunoia* with them that he had prayed for moments earlier (8). Shortly after §268, Demosthenes will deploy their knowledge in a similar way against Aeschines, challenging the abusive terms the latter has used against him ("sophist", "conjurer", etc.) (276):

> ἐγὼ δ' οἶδ' ὅτι **γιγνώσκετε τοῦτον ἅπαντες**, καὶ πολὺ τούτῳ μᾶλλον ἢ ἐμοὶ νομίζετε ταῦτα προσεῖναι.
>
> But I am confident that all of you know him and realize that those terms apply far more to him than they do to me.

Although the referential field of γιγνώσκετε *could* be restricted to the judges' awareness as gleaned during Aeschines' behaviour in the trial so far (i.e. γιγνώσκετε here as a proxy for "see", or indeed "see through"), knowledge of his political activity since 346 BC is very likely to be implicated; even if not, this sentence still qualifies – just as much as the previous examples do – as a move to encourage the audience to play the role of witnesses: this time as witnesses to what *all* participants in the trial have seen together.[47]

47 Assertive poetic rhythms – two dactylic hexameter half-lines, assuming the presence of Attic correption – underline the views he wants the judges to take (γιγνώσκετε τοῦτον ἅπαντες – νομίζετε ταῦτα προσεῖναι).

4 Conclusion

As these examples demonstrate, Demosthenes' chosen strategy for combating Aeschines' own as effectively as possible involves calculated – and often striking – direct appeals (as well as many less direct appeals) to the judges' and wider audience's recollection of their experiences in the period at issue in the trial. The strategy's effectiveness consists partly in its reliance on repeated reference to events and circumstances which Demosthenes could easily represent as reflecting well on the Athenians in spite of their ultimate failure to beat Philip, and as the right thing to do both at the time and with Athens' future in mind. There are certainly sections where he invokes the language (and actuality) of witnessing to buttress weak points (e.g. in 18.131–137, as we saw above), but – lethally for Aeschines' case – Demosthenes' discussion is sustained by its emphasis on what he actually did do and say (thus sticking close to the terms of Ctesiphon's proposal and Aeschines' *graphē*: λέγων καὶ πράττων) and on how many of those present among the judges and wider audience approved his proposals.

This becomes especially clear if we consider that some of the passages where we might expect reference to audience memory of specific major events do not in fact have any direct signposting to the listeners, because Demosthenes could take it as read that they would draw on their memories of them anyway.[48] His account of his election to deliver the funeral oration for the dead of the Chaeronea campaign (18.285–288) is a good example: even if they could quarrel with his *presentation* of the facts, no audience member could deny that Demosthenes *had* been elected to deliver the oration (287) or that the funeral meal *had* been held at his house (288). This part of the speech is supported by clear reminders that (many of) the judges have witnessed his career (272: ἐμὲ τὸν παρὰ τουτοισὶ πεπολιτευμένον) and voted for his policies (note the deft claim that he was only doing what the *dēmos* wanted: ταὐτὰ γὰρ συμφέρονθ' εἱλόμην τουτοισί: 281). Judges' memories of the lengthy period covered by the dispute might well be hazy, and some judges might doubt aspects of Demosthenes' versions (or, as just noted, object to his presentation of them) – but what Demosthenes apparently succeeds in doing is constructing a narrative which, for a

48 This is why he does not bother connecting two formally separate claims in *On the Crown* 248: (1) that all his listeners (οἱ πάντες ὑμεῖς), i.e. the citizen body, elected him as grain-commissioner after Chaeronea; and (2) that the *dēmos*, who "knew and had seen" everything he had done (ὁ δῆμος, εἰδὼς καὶ ἑορακὼς πάντα ὅσα ἔπραττον ἐγώ), and who could reasonably have chosen *not* to elect him, did so anyway.

large plurality of judges, underpinned a more convincing and dynamic reading of Athens' actions and priorities over the last decade than Aeschines' did – and one that looked powerfully forward in highlighting the immortality of Athens' core values. Ultimately, the question becomes not why Demosthenes succeeded, but why Aeschines failed to present a cogent enough alternative or communicate it to the judges, and although there are several possible answers (including an over-reliance on suggestion rather than overt enunciation, as mentioned above), the most obvious is that the facts left him a limited range of possibilities, and so he could not risk drawing sustained attention to the alternative facts about 346 BC onwards that he does present (as, e.g., in 3.59) by trying to use the judges' memories to buttress them. As part of a lively and engaging narrative, they might get through or be seen as relatively venial; inviting judges to confirm them was a different matter.

As modern work on Athenian witnesses has shown, the surviving speeches indicate that orators selected witnesses whose brief oral endorsement of the text prepared for them was not their only, or even perhaps their most important, contribution to the trial: their very appearance and known attributes (including those mentioned by the orator himself) were important too.[49] In the Embassy trial in 343 BC, for example, Aeschines' claim to distinguished military service in Euboea will have been very seriously bolstered by the appearance for him of the eminent commanding general Phocion (later called as a *synēgoros*: 2.184), of his own *taxiarchos*, and of some of his fellow soldiers (2.169–170). In *On the Crown*, Demosthenes rhetorically empowers the judges – many of whom had fought with him at Chaeronea as fellow-soldiers, or had voted for war with Philip on his proposal, or had come to his house for the funeral meal for the fallen – to do something similar for Ctesiphon: to attest, with their vote (and, like contemporary witnesses, without independent speech) that the versions of events offered by Demosthenes, whatever their flaws, were truer to their lived experiences than Aeschines' unheroic alternatives.

Bibliography

Burke, E.M. (1977), '*Contra Leocratem* and *De Corona*: Political Collaboration?', in: *Phoenix* 31, 330–340.
Carawan, E. (2019), 'How the "Crown Case" Came to Trial and Why', in: *GRBS* 59, 109–133.
Carey, C. (2000), *Aeschines*, Austin.

49 See Humphreys 1985, especially 350–351; Todd 1990; Rubinstein 2005; Thür 2005, 164–166.

Cook, B.L. (2009), 'Athenian Terms of Civic Praise in the 330s: Aeschines vs. Demosthenes', in: *GRBS* 49, 31–52.
Cook, B.L. (2012), 'Swift-Boating in Antiquity: Rhetorical Framing of the Good Citizen in Fourth-Century Athens', in: *Rhetorica* 30, 219–251.
Dilts, M.R. (ed.) (1997), *Aeschinis Orationes*, Stuttgart/Leipzig.
Dilts, M.R. (ed.) (2002), *Demosthenis Orationes: Tomus I*, Oxford.
Donnelly, F.P. (1941), *The Oration of Demosthenes On the Crown: a Rhetorical Commentary*, New York.
Gagarin, M. (2012), 'Law, Politics, and the Question of Relevance in the Case on the Crown', in: *CA* 31, 293–314.
Harris, E.M. (1994), 'Law and Oratory', in: I. Worthington (ed.), *Persuasion: Greek Rhetoric in Action*, London, 130–150.
Harris, E.M. (1995), *Aeschines and Athenian Politics*, Oxford.
Harris, E.M. (2000), 'Open Texture in Athenian Law', in: *Dike* 3, 27–79.
Harris, E.M. (2013), *The Rule of Law in Action in Democratic Athens*, Oxford.
Harris, E.M. (2017), 'Applying the Law about Crowns to Magistrates (Aeschin. 3.9–31; Dem. 18.113–117: Epigraphic Evidence for the Legal Arguments at the Trial of Ctesiphon', in: *ZPE* 202, 105–117.
Harris, E.M. (2019), 'The Crown Trial and Athenian Legal Procedure in Public Cases against Illegal Decrees', in: *Dike* 22, 81–111.
Harrison, A.R.W. (1971), *The Law of Athens: Procedure*, Oxford.
Hernández Muñoz, F.G. (1989), '*EYNOIA* como elemento estructural del discurso *Sobre la Corona*', in: *Minerva* 3, 173–188.
Hobden, F. (2007), 'Imagining Past and Present: a Rhetorical Strategy in Aeschines 3, *Against Ctesiphon*', in: *CQ* 57, 490–501.
Horváth, L. (2014), *Der 'Neue Hypereides': Textedition, Studien und Erläuterungen*, Berlin.
Hubbard, T. (2008), 'Getting the Last Word: Publication of Political Oratory as an Instrument of Historical Revisionism', in: E.A. Mackay (ed.), *Orality, Literacy and Memory*, Leiden, 185–202.
Humphreys, S. (1985), 'Social Relations on Stage: Witnesses in Classical Athens', in: *History and Anthropology* 1.2, 313–369.
Kralli, I. (2017), *The Hellenistic Peloponnese: Interstate Relations*, Swansea.
Martin, G. (2009), *Divine Talk: Religious Argumentation in Demosthenes*, Oxford.
Mirhady, D.C. (2002), 'Athens' Democratic Witnesses', in: *Phoenix* 56, 255–274.
O'Connell, P.A. (2016), 'The Rhetoric of Visibility and Invisibility in Antiphon 5, *On the Murder of Herodes*', in: *CQ* 66, 46–58.
O'Connell, P.A. (2017a), *The Rhetoric of Seeing in Attic Forensic Oratory*, Austin.
O'Connell, P.A. (2017b), '*Enargeia*, Persuasion, and the Vividness Effect in Athenian Forensic Oratory', in: *Advances in the History of Rhetoric* 20, 225–251.
Rubinstein, L. (2005), 'Main Litigants and Witnesses in the Athenian Courts: Procedural Variations', in: R.W. Wallace/M. Gagarin (eds.), *Symposion 2001: Vorträge zur griechischen und hellenistischen Rechtsgeschichte*, Vienna, 99–120.
Sanders, E. (2016), 'Generating Goodwill and Friendliness in Attic Forensic Oratory', in: R. Caston/R. Kaster (eds.), *Hope, Joy, and Affection in the Classical World*, Oxford, 163–181.
Sawada, N. (1996), 'Athenian Politics in the Age of Alexander the Great: A Reconsideration of the Trial of Ctesiphon', in: *Chiron* 26, 57–82.
Serafim, A. (2017a), *Attic Oratory and Performance*, London.

Serafim, A. (2017b), 'Conventions in/as Performance: Addressing the Audience in Selected Public Speeches of Demosthenes', in: S. Papaioannou/A. Serafim/B. da Vela (eds.), *The Theatre of Justice*, Leiden, 26–41.

Thür, G. (2005), 'The Role of the Witness in Athenian Law', in: M. Gagarin/D.J. Cohen (eds.), *The Cambridge Companion to Greek Law*, Cambridge, 146–169.

Todd, S. (1990), 'The Purpose of Evidence in Athenian Courts', in: P. Cartledge/P. Millett/S. Todd (eds.), *Nomos: Essays in Athenian Law, Politics and Society*, Cambridge, 19–39.

Todd, S. (2007), *A Commentary on Lysias: Speeches 1–11*, Oxford.

Todd, S. (2009), 'Hypereides *Against Diondas*, Demosthenes *On the Crown*, and the Rhetoric of Political Failure', in: *BICS* 52, 161–174.

Usher, S. (1993), *Demosthenes: On the Crown*, Warminster.

Wankel, H. (1976), *Demosthenes: Rede für Ktesiphon über den Kranz*, Heidelberg.

Webb, R. (2009), 'Eschine et le passé athénien: narration, imagination et construction de la mémoire', in: *CEA* 46, 129–147.

Westwood, G. (2017), 'The Orator and the Ghosts: Performing the Past in Fourth-Century Athens', in: S. Papaioannou/A. Serafim/B. da Vela (eds.), *The Theatre of Justice*, Leiden, 57–74.

Westwood, G. (2020), *The Rhetoric of the Past in Demosthenes and Aeschines*, Oxford.

Whitehead, D. (1993), 'Cardinal Virtues: The Language of Public Approbation in Democratic Athens', in: *C&M* 44, 37–75.

Worthington, I. (2000), 'Demosthenes' (In)activity during the Reign of Alexander the Great', in: I. Worthington (ed.), *Demosthenes: Statesman and Orator*, London, 90–113.

Worthington, I. (2013), *Demosthenes of Athens and the Fall of Classical Greece*, Oxford.

Yunis, H. (2000), 'Politics as Literature: Demosthenes and the Burden of the Athenian Past', in: *Arion* 8, 97–118.

Yunis, H. (2001), *Demosthenes: On the Crown*, Cambridge.

Yunis, H. (2005), *Demosthenes, Speeches 18 and 19*, Austin.

Noboru Sato

Additional Information in Witness Testimonies in Classical Athens

Abstract: The purpose of this chapter is to investigate the rhetorical functions of the witness testimonies that include additional information that the main speeches do not provide. Some litigants disclosed the identities of their witnesses or their source of information only in the documents of witness testimonies. By providing such information only through the documents, a litigant in a private case could save his allotted time and avoid the risk of losing the audience's interest, especially when he produced many witnesses at once. Others provided detailed information regarding his own or his opponents' character only through the witness testimonies to avoid praising himself or abusing opponents from his own mouth, by which the judges could be offended. Although the opportunities to use the witness testimonies with additional information were limited, they were beneficial for law-court speakers as far as they could use them.

1 Introduction

In 346 BC, the Athenian ambassadors to Philip II delivered their respective speeches upon returning from Macedonia. Demosthenes ascended the platform as the last speaker and, instead of delivering an elaborate oration, ordered a clerk to read the decree that had authorised their embassy. Subsequently, the Athenian statesman simply remarked that the decree was what they had been sent for and what they had done. He then asked the clerk to read Philip's letter, instead of explaining the negotiation with this king in his own words. Following the letter, the statesman said concisely that this was Philip's answer and that it remained for the people in the Assembly to deliberate.[1] It is apparent that these written documents, the decree and the letter, were not only used to explain the diplomatic negotiation between the Athenian embassy and the Macedonian king, but they were also skilfully used as a substitute for the orator's detailed

I am grateful to P.J. Rhodes for helpful suggestions.

1 Aeschin. 2.50–51.

https://doi.org/10.1515/9783110751970-005

accounts. Even Aeschines, Demosthenes' rival, admitted that, while there had been an uproar at the Assembly, at least some of the participants had praised Demosthenes' ability and his succinct speech. This episode suggests that the strategy of using written documents as a substitute for a part of a public speech seemed to have been employed in Athens during the fourth century BC. If a speaker at the Assembly could substitute a decree or a letter for his own detailed account, it is interesting to know whether Athenian litigants could also use the witness testimonies in the same manner.

Athenian witness testimonies have not been analysed from such a point of view. Some scholars have focused on a witness' social status and personal connection with the litigant whom he was supporting, while others have advocated that the main function of the Athenian witness was to prove the truth.[2] However, the substance of the witness testimonies, or the information contained in the witnesses' statements, have been largely neglected.[3] It is true that the content of the witness testimony is mostly omitted from the texts of the extant forensic speeches. Moreover, witness testimony is used, presumably in most cases, for mere confirmation of the information that a litigant provides in his own speech. However, not a few witness testimonies are likely to include additional information that is not mentioned in the main speeches.

The main purpose of this chapter is to investigate the rhetorical functions of such kinds of witness testimonies in the Athenian law-courts. First, this chapter investigates the contexts in which the witness testimonies which contain additional information are used, and classifies them into four categories: (a) a witness' identity and his source of information, (b) "character" evidence for the speaker's own side, (c) such evidence against the opponent's side, and (d) parallel cases.[4] Second, this chapter argues that, although the opportunities to use

---

2 E.g. Humphreys 1985; Todd 1990; Scafuro 1994; Carey 1995; Cohen 1995, 107–112; Mirhady 1996; Rubinstein 2005. On the procedure concerning witness testimonies, see Harrison 1971, 136–147; Thür 1977; MacDowell 1978; Todd 1993; Thür 2005; Martin 2008.

3 E.g. "the part played by the witness in the fourth century was restricted to a mere confirmation of a statement [...] the identity of the witness was more important than the actual information that he was called to corroborate"; Rubinstein 2005, 99. Rhetorical manipulation of witness testimony, including slaves' testimony through torture, have been discussed. For example, Carey 1994 analyses a number of choices that a litigant or a speech writer can make when using witness testimonies. Mirhady 1996 discusses the rhetorical strategies of references to torture; see also Thür 1996. Rubinstein 2015 suggests the emotional effects of the presence of the third-party victim in the court of law.

4 For a more recent discussion concerning character evidence, see, e.g., Lanni 2006, esp. 59–64, 167–168; Adamidis 2017.

witness testimonies with additional information are limited, such testimonies were beneficial for law-court speakers in some aspects as far as they could use them.

Before investigating the roles of witness testimonies with additional information in the Athenian law-courts, it is necessary to discuss how we know whether a particular witness testimony contained additional information. On the one hand, the majority of the witness testimonies are not preserved in the surviving forensic speeches. Moreover, the authenticity of the documents that are preserved under the heading of *martyria(i)* or *martys* (or *martyres*) in the extant texts is mostly doubted as spurious, or needs to be carefully examined case by case.[5] It seems possible, however, to obtain a general idea of their contents based on the context in which the witness testimonies are supposed to be read aloud. Witness testimonies are basically used to confirm a part of the main speech, usually to confirm the speaker's statements just before the testimonies are read. They are usually introduced by phrases such as "to confirm the truth of my statement, please take the depositions". Following the depositions, moreover, a speaker sometimes paraphrases their content, whether distorting it or not. Hence, the context of the main body before and/or after a witness testimony often suggests what information the document is likely to provide.

Judging from imagined or recited witness statements mentioned in the main body of the speeches,[6] any such statement usually contains simple and specific facts: the witness' identity (e.g. his name and deme) and the specific event which he attended, or the specific incident which he saw or which he himself experienced, as far as they are not negative testimonies.[7] In some cases, it can contain some more detailed information such as the amount of damages or the date when an incident happened. But it should not be supposed that a witness testimony is richly informative, describing an event in much greater detail than

5 Cf. Canevaro 2013.

6 Some orations contain imagined or recited witness testimonies in the main body of the speech. E.g Aeschin. 2.67; Dem. 29.31, 46.5, 54.31. Although it is not certain to what extent their words and phrases precisely reflect the reality, their style and the types of information they contained are presumably similar to the actual witness testimonies. On the authenticity of Dem. 29, see MacDowell 1989; 2009, 45–53.

7 E.g. "now what was the declaration of the witnesses? That they were present before the arbitrator, Notharchus, when Aphobus admitted that Milyas was a freeman, having been emancipated by Demosthenes' father" (Dem. 29.31). On witness formulas, see Thür 1977, 128–129; 2005, 152–153. A witness could testify that he did not see a specific incident. In this case, he did not reveal any more detailed information than the speaker whom he supported.

the account provided by the main body of the speech in which the testimony is cited.

2 Identity and source of information

First, the information regarding a witness' identity is frequently provided only in the witness statement. It is true that litigants sometimes disclose in their own words their witnesses' identity, e.g. their personal names, demes, social status, positions in office and relationships to the litigants themselves.[8] For example, Andocides, in his oration *On the Mysteries*, calls some of his witnesses by their names and clarifies their backgrounds. After providing detailed accounts of Lydus' *mēnysis* on the mysteries performed at a private house, Andocides presents some witnesses to prove that he has told the truth.[9] The orator calls his witnesses by name, Callias, Stephanus, Philippus and Alexippus, from his own mouth, and explains that they are relatives of Acumenus and Autocratus, who have gone into exile because of the information Lydus had provided, and that the witnesses certainly know best who caused their relatives' exile.[10] However, quite a few witnesses in the extant Attic forensic speeches are simply called to the platform without any information or with just a general remark on their identity in the litigant's or his *synēgoros*' main speeches. For example, when Aristodemus, the speaker of the Demosthenic oration 44, calls witnesses in order to prove his own statements about his kin filiations at the beginning of the speech, any information about the witnesses' identity is not provided in the main speech.[11] In another example, Ariston, the plaintiff of the assault case against Conon, also calls witnesses without identifying them in any way. At the beginning of his speech, he provides detailed accounts of his conflict with Conon's son and his fellows at Panacton three years ago.[12] In order to prove his statement so far, he introduces some witnesses without providing any information about their identities. Subsequently, he presents a vivid narrative of the assault which was caused by Conon, his son and his fellows against him, and introduces witnesses of the event, without adding any information about their

8 Rubinstein 2005, esp. 103, discusses the significance of identifying the witness in the main text of a speech.

9 Andoc. 1.17.

10 Andoc. 1.18.

11 Dem. 44.14.

12 Dem. 54.3–6.

identity in his own speech.[13] Since a witness' testimony in Attic forensic speeches usually begins with the witness' personal name and his deme, as we have seen above, the information about witnesses' identity is provided only in the depositions in these cases.[14]

Regardless of whether the witnesses' identities are provided in the actual speeches or in the depositions, such information is presumably of importance, at least to make their depositions more credible for the Athenian judges. As mentioned earlier, Andocides clearly explains the reasons he summoned those particular witnesses, which suggests that detailed information about witnesses' identity frequently functioned as a means to make their testimonies more trustworthy. As Mirhady clearly shows, the main motivation for providing the information regarding witnesses' identities was to show that they are in a good position to know the fact that they are going to testify.[15] For example, Euphiletus, who is seeking to prove his citizenship at the court hearing his appeal, introduces the witnesses of his birth, identifying them as his relatives, members of his phratry and fellow demesmen, who are most likely to have knowledge concerning his birth.[16] Although he does not refer to them by name, their identification as the relatives, *phrateres* or fellow demesmen of the litigant, seems to let the audience believe that the depositions were confirmed by those with better knowledge of his birth.

It is true that there was not always the necessity to add more detailed information about witness' identity than the main speaker provided. For example, if a litigant identifies his witnesses as his fellow phratry members from his own mouth, the judges may focus less on more detailed information provided in the deposition, such as their personal names or their demes. Thus, although witnesses are often summoned without being identified in detail in an actual speech, it is uncertain whether the information about the identity of the witnesses that is provided only in their depositions is crucial for enhancing the credibility of their testimonies.

Yet, in some cases, the detailed information about the witnesses' identities which are contained only in their depositions seeks to enhance their credibility. For instance, in the case concerning Hagnias' estate, Sosias, the birth father of Eubulides III, one of the claimants of the estate, summons a series of witnesses

13 Dem. 54.6–9.

14 For examples of the witnesses who were not identified in the main speech, see Mirhady 2002, 262 n. 29 and Rubinstein 2005, 115–116, 117–118.

15 Mirhady 2002.

16 Dem. 57.38–40.

in order to prove his statement regarding the parentage of Phylomache I, Eubulides III's step-grandmother.[17] When introducing the witnesses, Sosias asks the clerk to read the depositions proving that Phylomache I is sister by the same parents of Polemon, the father of Hagnias, and the depositions about kin filiation (*genos*), but he does not call the witnesses by name nor disclose their background information. Since they are not to attest their presence at an event or an accident, but to give detailed information about the parentage of Phylomache I, the witnesses' identity as her close relatives is certainly of key importance to enhance the credibility of their depositions. Moreover, there seems another feature which is likely to make the witnesses' identity more important: the witnesses in this case were presumably summoned to confirm the *hearsay* information. Since Phylomache I died a few decades before the trial at which Sosias delivered his speech, there was apparently no one who could attest her parentage through first-hand account.[18] While hearsay testimonies were legitimately used in Classical Athens to prove a statement about the person who was previously deceased,[19] the source of the information must have affected the credibility of such testimonies. If we are to believe the wording in the preserved depositions at Dem. 43.36,[20] the great-grand-children of a cousin of Hagnias' father, Polemon, heard from their father what they testify. Another witness, a son of Archimachus, a relative of Hagnias' father, also asserts that they have heard Phylomache I's parentage from his grandfather and other relatives (37). Although it is impossible to prove that the wording in the depositions preserved in the text is the same as what the witnesses really confirmed in the court of law, it is less likely that the source of those hearsay information was never clarified in the depositions. If this is the case, the important information which makes the witness testimonies more trustworthy is not provided by the speaker himself, but in the depositions of the witnesses.

17 Dem. 43.35–41.
18 Scafuro 2011, 132.
19 Dem. 46.7.
20 MacDowell 2009, 84–85 claims that the speech preserves "what apparently the genuine texts of all the documents, both laws and witness testimonies, which are read out to the jury". Scafuro 2011, 153 n. 70, following Thompson 1976, 88–89, argues that "a forger would not have been clever enough to have forged" details that only appear in the witness-testimonies.

3 Character evidence and parallel cases

Another context is providing "character" evidence for the speaker's side, which includes the contributions to the city or his fellow citizens either by the speaker himself or by his friends and family.[21] For example, when Demosthenes, in his oration *On the Crown*, asks the clerk to read the witness testimonies regarding the liturgies he had performed, they clearly provide much more information than the oration itself.[22] For, Demosthenes does not provide any specific information regarding his liturgies prior to the testimonies but, subsequently, he simply states that "I am such a person towards the city (ἐν μὲν τοίνυν τοῖς πρὸς τὴν πόλιν τοιοῦτος)". He adds that he has been generous and helpful to his fellow citizens in private life, too, but he does not offer specific information or detailed accounts about his private generous activities. Instead, he simply explains that "I believe that the recipient of a favour should remember it for all time if he is to act honourably, and the one who conferred the favour should forget it immediately if he is to avoid mean-spiritedness (18.269: μικροψύχου)".[23] Hence, it is apparent that the witnesses testify that they themselves know or attended the specific public contributions that Demosthenes performed, which are never mentioned in the orator's own speech.

Similarly, such witness testimonies are also used in Demosthenes' *For Phormio* (*Or.* 36). Almost at the end of the speech, the *synēgoros* of the defendant, Phormio, claims that any piece of evidence of the defendant's character, of his uprightness and his generosity, is relevant to the present trial. The speaker then suggests that it is unlikely that a man who has never wronged anybody, but who has voluntarily done good to many people, has wronged only Apollodorus, the plaintiff (Dem. 36.55). Subsequently, he introduces the witnesses' depositions by telling the clerk to "read [the witness testimonies on] how much publicly beneficial this man (i.e. Phormio) has been" (ἀνάγνωθι ... ὅσα δημοσίᾳ χρήσιμος τῇ πόλει γέγονεν οὑτοσί), without specifying even the types of services the defendant has performed. Thus, it is most likely that the witnesses' statements include specific information regarding Phormio's activities beneficial to the city and the Athenian citizens.

In another case, Nicobulus, an Athenian money-lender, possibly uses this type of witness testimonies, too. When charged by Pantaenetus for damage

21 E.g. Dem. 18.267; 36.55, 56; Lys. 19.58, 59; 20.29.

22 Dem. 18.267.

23 Dem. 18.269 (Trans. Yunis 2005).

(*blabē*), Nicobulus attempted to prevent the case from going to trial by bringing a special plea (*paragraphē*). In his speech at the *paragraphē* trial, Nicolaus anticipates that Pantaenetus will exploit the Athenians' general antipathy against the money-lenders in order to win over the judges. Although Nicobulus admits that there are, in fact, bad money-lenders, he also asserts that not all the people who are engaged in that business should be disliked. The speaker subsequently asks the clerk to read the depositions to show how he has behaved towards other money-lenders and those who needed his help, possibly those who borrowed money from him (τίς ἐγὼ πρὸς τοὺς συμβάλλοντας ἄνθρωπος καὶ πρὸς τοὺς δεομένους εἰμί).[24] It is possible that these witnesses' statements contain individual witnesses' specific experience which would suggest the speaker's agreeable personality, while the speaker himself does not give any specific information about what he has done to these people.

Conversely, witness testimonies with additional information are also used to provide character evidence *against* the opponent's side.[25] The witness testifies to prove that the speaker's opponent, his family or his supporters are harmful to the city and their fellow citizens sometimes contain more detailed information than, or somewhat different accounts from, the main speech itself. For example, Phormio's *synēgoros* produces this type of witness testimonies in the context of criticising their opponent, Apollodorus. The speaker predicts that in order to gain sympathy from the audience rather than prove the main legal issues, Apollodorus will argue that he spent a huge amount of money in performing liturgies for the city. The speaker seeks to deny Apollodorus' claim by showing that he has spent only a small part of the huge amount of his assets. To show Apollodorus' asset and the liturgies he has performed, the speaker asks the clerk to read a document, a challenge and some testimonies.[26] Unfortunately, the contents of these testimonies are not certain, since the speaker only vaguely refers to Apollodorus' liturgies both before and after the depositions. It is possible, however, that the witness testimonies describe the specific liturgies that Apollodorus had performed, including the amount of money spent on them, which gives the

24 Dem. 37.54.

25 E.g. Dem. 36.21, 40, 56; 47.82; 49.61; 54.36; 58.35; Lys. 12.42; 13.66; 31.19; Isoc. 9.20.

26 Dem. 36.40: ἵνα δ' εἰδῆτ', ὦ ἄνδρες Ἀθηναῖοι, τό τε πλῆθος τῶν χρημάτων ὧν εἴληφε, καὶ τὰς λῃτουργίας ἃς λελῃτούργηκεν, ἀναγνώσεται ὑμῖν καθ' ἓν ἕκαστον. λαβέ μοι τὸ βιβλίον τουτὶ καὶ τὴν πρόκλησιν ταυτηνὶ καὶ τὰς μαρτυρίας ταυτασί "So that you may know, men of Athens, the amount of property he has received, and the public services he has performed, the clerk shall read them to you one by one. Please take this document and this challenge and these dispositions".

audience the impression that he has not fairly contributed to the city.[27] Later, he also introduces a document which most likely contain more specific information regarding Apollodorus' evil character. When presenting the witness testimonies to prove Phormio's honesty and kindness, as mentioned earlier, he also asks the clerk to read the testimonies to prove Apollodorus' baseness (ἴθι δὴ καὶ τὰς κατ' Ἀπολλοδώρου τῆς πονηρίας).[28] The *synēgoros* does not provide any specific information about their opponents' behaviour from his own mouth, but simply suggests that Phormio's character is exactly the opposite of Apollodorus. Specific information regarding Apollodorus' dishonest character is presumably provided only in the witness testimonies.

In the false witness trial (*dikē pseudomartyrias*) against Euergus and Mnesibulus, the witness testimonies regarding defendants' wrongdoings are furnished by the victims themselves.[29] Through these testimonies, the plaintiff aims to prove that his opponents were not guileless nor fond of quiet (ἀκάκους καὶ ἀπράγμονας) at the time of the previous trial, for which the present defendants gave false testimonies. These offences are obviously not the main legal issues at the trial, but there are other offensive activities conducted by the speaker's opponent group. The speaker does not provide details about those wrongdoings from his own mouth. Instead, he plainly admits that his allotted time does not allow him to recount the whole story in his own main speech. In this case, those witness statements clearly attest specific facts regarding wrongdoings of the speaker's opponent group.

In the trial concerning Timotheus' debts to Pasion, Apollodorus, Pasion's son, also produces witness testimonies which possibly contain additional information. Having explained Timotheus' debts to his father in detail, Apollodorus anticipates the defendant's argument that he has already repaid those moneys to the creditor. Against this claim, the plaintiff argues that the defendant was not well provided with funds at the time, and he calls for a single witness to prove that he had borrowed money from some Athenians without security.[30] The speaker does not provide any detailed information about these debts, either the amount of debts or the names of creditors, but such specific pieces of information may have been provided by the witness testimony. In this case, although this witness statement supports the speaker's counter-argument against Timotheus, the debts to various people other than Pasion have no direct relevance to

27 One of the testimonies may be a testimony by the witness who attended the challenge.
28 Dem. 36.56.
29 Dem. 47.82.
30 Dem. 49.61.

the main issue. Hence, this part of Apollodorus' argument aims simply at highlighting Timotheus' defrauding habits.

Finally, witness testimonies which include additional information are likely to be produced in order to present a series of parallel cases to the main issues in the present trial, too.[31] A good example is provided by the plaintiff of the false witness case against Euergus and Mnesibulus, the speaker of the Demosthenic oration 47. This case originally derived from a series of conflicts between the plaintiff and Theophemus, for whom the defendants testified in a previous law suit for battery (*dikē aikeias*). The speaker of Demosthenes 47 was selected as a trierarch and had to retrieve equipment of the trireme he was appointed from his predecessor, Theophemus. When the speaker went to Theophemus' house, their dispute turned violent. Theophemus subsequently prosecuted the speaker for battery and won the case with the help from Euergus and Mnesibulus. In the false testimony case against the two witnesses, the plaintiff aims to justify his behaviour as a trierarch against Theophemus by explaining that he was required to recover the equipment in accordance with a law and a decree. In the course of his justification, he claims that he was one of many trierarchs that took similar measures in accordance with the decree. The speaker then asks the clerk to read their depositions regarding his fellow trierarchs.[32] Although the speaker does not give any detailed accounts about them, the depositions presumably include the specific information regarding at least their identities and the names of those who owed to the state the equipment that these trierarchs were ordered to recover. Thus, the witness testimonies may sometimes provide specific information regarding some parallel cases to one of the main issues which the litigant himself sought to prove.

4 Benefits of providing information through witness testimonies

One of the greatest benefits of using the witness testimonies which contain additional information is obviously saving time. The water clock at a private

31 E.g. Dem. 47.48; Lys. 23.4.
32 Dem. 47.48.

case was stopped as the clerk read a deposition aloud.[33] By using witness testimonies to provide detailed information regarding the fact that the speaker did not clearly recount in his own speech, a speaker could save his allotted time, while presenting additional information to the judges.

This strategy must have been remarkably beneficial for a litigant presenting a large number of witnesses at once, as Euphiletus or Sosias did in their cases.[34] It is true that, when summoning a large number of witnesses to prove a particular point, a litigant could, in theory, either provide all the information of every witness from his own mouth before their depositions were be read aloud by the clerk, or else call each of them to the platform, indicating his identity one by one. In either case, however, the litigant's explanation could take such a long time that he would waste a large amount of his allowance. Moreover, he would also run the risk of losing the judges' attention or patience by making too long an interruption in his main argument. By providing detailed information about the witnesses' identity and their source of information, if necessary, only through witness testimonies, a litigant could save time and minimise the risk of losing the judges' interest.

This strategy seems to have been effective also when a litigant or his *synēgoroi* spoke about a matter which was not directly related to the main legal issues. In the Athenian law-courts, the speaker was required to explain the main legal issues and to recount the important incidents directly related to their conflict in detail in their own speeches. But they knew the usefulness of the topics which, by our modern standards, were not directly related to the main issues. However, when witness testimonies with additional information were used to prove certain facts which were not directly related to the main issues, they must have been beneficial for a speaker, since he could save time and provide the judges with specific pieces of information. In fact, as we have seen, witness testimonies with additional information are often produced to prove facts which are not directly related to the main issue, i.e. as a part of character evidence or parallel cases. Those facts only indirectly reinforced the speaker's main narratives and legal arguments, but they were still important as a means of persuading the audience.

Second, witness testimonies with additional information helped a speaker to avoid presenting his own opinion in an egocentric manner. Aristotle, in his

---

33 Arist. *Ath. Pol.* 67.3. On the other hand, since the allowance for a public case was calculated according to daylight of the shortest day in December, the water clock was not stopped throughout the speech.

34 See above n. 16–17.

Rhetoric, explains that a speaker should use another individual in his place to describe moral character (*ēthos*): when describing his own good character, a speaker sometimes makes the audience envious, speaks for too long or creates a contradiction; when speaking of another man, he may be accused of abusive language or coarseness.[35] It is true that Aristotle does not recommend here that a speaker uses his witness testimonies for this purpose: the philosopher refers to Isocrates as an example, who sometimes puts some sort of character portrayal in the mouth of his friends or an imagined character in the main body of his speech, rather than calling a witness to provide detailed information.[36] Even so, it is obvious that Aristotle thought that self-praise and verbal abuse against opponents from the speaker's own mouth could have a detrimental effect, at least in some cases, on his persuasion of the audience.

Presumably contemporary law-court speakers also recognised this risk and sometimes sought to avoid it by resorting to witness testimonies. In fact, some litigants ostensibly present themselves as refraining from using abusive language, especially related to violence, sexual behaviour and domestic conflicts, since it could annoy their audiences.[37] For example, the plaintiff of the perjury case against Nicodemus cites the witness-testimonies which had been produced in the previous trial, in order to highlight the promiscuous sexual behaviour of the defendant's sister and to create the impression that his testimony that she had been legally married to Pyrrus was perjurious.[38] Prior to asking the clerk to read the document, the speaker claims that:

> If we had to list these people [*i.e.* those who had dealings with Nicodemus' sister] one by one, it would certainly be no small task. So if you command it, I'll mention some of them; but if it's as distasteful to some of you to hear about this as it is for me to say anything about it, I'll produce for you the documents from the previous trial, none of which my opponents saw fit to contest.[39]

According to this statement, the speaker is obviously ready to produce these documents in order to avoid abusive language which might sound unpleasant to the judges,[40] though it is uncertain how much information these particular

35 Arist. *Rh.* 1418b25ff.

36 E.g. Isoc. 5.4–7, 15.132–139, 141–149. Besides Isocrates, Aristotle refers to, as examples, Archilochus (fr. 15, 74) and Haemon in Sophocles' *Antigone* (688–700).

37 E.g. Isae. 1.9; 5.39; 6.17; Dem. 18.103; 21.79; 23.202; 24.7; 40.9; 45.3; 48.52; 54.9.

38 Isae. 3.11–12.

39 Trans. Edwards 2007.

40 In this case, the speaker simply refers to some scandalous behaviour in general terms, but not in detail, from his own mouth.

documents actually add to his own statement. As in this case, the Athenian lawcourt speakers who briefly refer to their opponents' wicked character, providing more concrete information only through the witness testimonies, presumably aim to avoid annoying the audience with uttering abusive language from his own mouth.[41]

Presumably, a speaker who wants to present his own good character could also seek to avoid the risks that Aristotle suggests by employing witness testimonies to provide somewhat detailed information. Certainly, it was advantageous for defendants to present their harmlessness and benefit to the Athenian society as a part of character evidence in order to win over the judges. However, if a speaker himself eloquently narrates his own liturgies and/or private contributions, he is likely to be regarded as garrulous, and incite the judges' envy against himself.[42] He could avoid creating such an impression by providing detailed accounts of his own contributions through witness testimonies, while restricting himself to a brief general remark on them. In fact, as mentioned earlier, when referring to his liturgies and private contributions while providing more detailed information only through his witness testimonies, Demosthenes claims that those who provided such benefits should remember it through his life, while those who have given a benefit should immediately forget them.[43] Presumably, the orator is seeking to avoid arousing the audience's envy against him, since he had presumably made a substantial contribution to the city and

41 It is not clear what kind of emotion witness testimonies themselves actually aroused. Rubinstein 2014, 162 argues that "the visual impact of the witness may very likely have contributed further emotional amplification through a silent appeal to the judges' pity", in the case where "the speakers' voices are replaced by the voice of the court attendant, accompanied by the spectacle of the opponents' victims on the witness stand". Although she may be correct, it is also likely that a speaker sought to avoid arousing bad emotion against himself among the audience, as Aristotle suggests.

42 There is no need to think that an Athenian litigant always sought to avoid describing his own or his family member's liturgies in detail and arousing the judges' envy against himself. Each litigant had certainly different priorities in accordance with the situation he was located in. The speaker of Lys. 21 recounts the liturgies he had performed in great detail in his own words. The speaker of Lys. 19 also recounts his father's liturgies but not in so great detail. Perhaps the documents and the witness testimonies he produces in this contexts provide more detailed information about the liturgies his father, Polystratus, performed than speaker's own explanation. Moreover, prior to referring to his father's liturgies, the speaker asks the judges to forgive him for reporting what his father had spent on the city and makes an excuse that he is doing so "not from the desire for glory (οὐ ... φιλοτιμίας ἕνεκα) but as evidence that the same man does not both spend a great deal voluntarily and want to steal part of the public property despite very great danger"; Lys. 19.56 (trans. Todd 2000).

43 See above, n. 23.

his fellow citizens. It is important to note that this long speech was composed for delivery in a judicial public case. Since the water clock was not stopped in such a case, avoidance of causing a bad impression on the audience may have been more important than saving time, at least in this case.

5 Conclusion

Although the majority of the witness testimonies do not seem to have added any substantial information to the main speeches they were supporting, some witness statements included specific information which the main speech does not provide. For example, witnesses' identities or their source of information were presumably often disclosed only in the document of the witness testimonies. By providing such information only through the documents, a litigant in a private case could save his allotted time and avoid the risk of losing the audience's interest, especially when he produced a number of witnesses at one time. In other cases, litigants provided detailed information regarding the speakers' own or his opponents' characters only through their witness testimonies: some included specific examples of public and/or private contributions on the speaker's side. Others provided more information than the main speech about the opponents' specific wrongdoings. Presumably, litigants did not use witness testimonies in such ways only to save their allotted time. They may also have sought to avoid praising themselves or abusing opponents from the speaker's own mouth, by which the judges could be offended. Although the number of examples is limited, it is clear that, if the conditions were right, an Athenian litigant in the fourth century BC could have strategically provided various specific pieces of information through witness statements.

Bibliography

Adamidis, V. (2017), *Character Evidence in the Courts of Classical Athens*, Abingdon/New York.
Canevaro, M. (2013), *The Documents in the Attic Orators: Laws and Decrees in the Public Speeches of the Demosthenic Corpus*, Oxford.
Carey, C. (1994), 'Artless' Proofs in Aristotle and the Orators', in: *BICS* 39, 95–106.
Carey, C. (1995), 'The Witness's *Exomosia* in the Athenian Courts', in: *CQ* 45, 114–119.
Cohen, D. (1995), *Law, Violence, and Community in Classical Athens*, Cambridge.
Edwards, M. (2007), *Isaeus (The Oratory of Classical Greece, 11)*, Austin.
Harrison, A.R.W. (1971), *The Law of Athens*, vol. II, *Procedure*, Oxford.

Humphreys, S.C. (1985), 'Social Relations on Stage: Witnesses in Classical Athens', in: *History and Anthropology* 1.2, 313–369.
Lanni, A. (2006), *Law and Justice in the Courts of Classical Athens*, Cambridge.
MacDowell, D.M. (1978), *The Law in Classical Athens*, London.
MacDowell, D.M. (1989), 'The Authenticity of Demosthenes 29 (Against Aphobos III) as a Source of Information about Athenian Law', in: G. Thür (ed.), *Symposion 1985. Vorträge zur griechischen und hellenistischen Rechtsgeschichte*, Köln, 253–263.
MacDowell, D.M. (2009), *Demosthenes. The Orator*, Oxford.
Martin, G. (2008), 'The Witness's *Exomosia* in Athens', in: *CQ* 58.1, 56–68.
Mirhady, D. (1991), 'Non-Technical Pisteis in Aristotle and Anaximenes', in: *AJPh* 112, 5–28.
Mirhady, D. (1996), 'Torture and Rhetoric in Athens', in: *JHS* 116, 119–131.
Mirhady, D. (2002), 'Athens' Democratic Witnesses', in: *Phoenix* 56, 255–274.
Rubinstein, L. (2005), 'Main Litigants and Witnesses in the Athenian Courts: Procedural Variations', in: R.W. Wallace/M. Gagarin (eds.), *Symposion 2001: Vorträge zur griechischen und hellenistischen Rechtsgeschichte*, Vienna, 99–120.
Rubinstein, L. (2014), 'Evoking Anger through Pity: Portraits of the Vulnerable and Defenceless in Attic Oratory', in: A. Chaniotis/P. Ducrey (eds.), *Unveiling Emotions II: Emotions in Greece and Rome: Texts, Images, Material Culture*, Stuttgart, 135–165.
Scafuro, A.C. (1994), 'Witnessing and False Witnessing: Proving Citizenship and Kin Identity in Fourth-Century Athens', in: A.L. Boegehold/A.C. Scafuro (eds.), *Athenian Identity and Civic Ideology*, Baltimore, 156–198.
Scafuro, A.C. (2011), *Demosthenes, Speeches 39–49. (The Oratory of Classical Greece 13)*, Austin.
Thompson, W.E. (1976), *De Hagniae hereditate: An Athenian Inheritance Case*, Leiden.
Thür, G. (1977), *Beweisführung vor den Schwurgerichtshöfen Athens*, Wien.
Thür, G. (1996), 'Reply to D.C. Mirhady: Torture and Rhetoric in Athens', in: *JHS* 116, 132–134.
Thür, G. (2005), 'The Role of the Witness in Athenian Law', in: M. Gagarin/D. Cohen (eds.), *The Cambridge Companion to Ancient Greek Law*, Cambridge, 146–169.
Todd, S.C. (1990), 'The Purpose of Evidence in Athenian Courts', in: P. Cartledge/P. Millett/S. Todd (eds.), *Nomos: Essays in Athenian Law, Politics, and Society*, Cambridge, 19–40.
Todd, S.C. (1993), *The Shape of Athenian Law*, Oxford.
Todd, S.C. (2000), *Lysias (The Oratory of Classical Greece 2)*, Austin.
Yunis, H. (2005), *Demosthenes, Speeches 18 and 19, The Oratory of Classical Greece*, Austin.

Pasquale Massimo Pinto

Self-Quotations as Witnesses and Evidence: The Case of Isocrates' *Antidosis*

Abstract: This chapter aims to explore the role of the self-quotations in Isocrates' *Antidosis* in connection to the fictitious judicial framework of the speech. Pretending to defend himself in a trial for a charge of corrupting youth through his own teaching, Isocrates produces written evidence that consists of large extracts from his previous works. A clerk was also asked to read out these passages, thus turning the imaginary court into a place for a public reading. By introducing and commenting on this "auto-anthology", Isocrates offered an authorised interpretation of his writings; at the same time, however, these pieces of evidence – together with the silent witnesses produced by his pupils – proved functional both to the rehabilitation of the author's reputation in the *polis* and to the transformation of traditional rhetorical forms into new literary products.

1 Isocrates' *Antidosis*

Isocrates' *Περὶ τῆς ἀντιδόσεως*, usually referred to as *Antidosis*, is a huge and complex speech and, for several reasons, one of central importance within the works of Isocrates. As is well known, the *antidosis* procedure was prescribed by Athenian law when a citizen refused to take up a *liturgy* for which he thought he had been unjustly appointed, in which case, he had the option of indicating another citizen as wealthier and better qualified to provide the public service in question. The citizen thus challenged might agree to take up the liturgy or decide to exchange his own property – this would be a proper *antidosis* – with the challenger. Although some aspects of this procedure are still disputed, it seems clear that in the event of no agreement between the two parties, the *liturgy* might be assigned by a court in a *diadikasia*.[1]

This is apparently what happened to Isocrates during the years of the Social War, in a case concerning a *trierarchy*: ἀντιδόσεως γενομένης περὶ τριηραρχίας

1 On the *antidosis* procedure and its controversial aspects: Harrison 1971, 236–238; MacDowell 1978, 162–164; Gabrielsen 1987; Christ 1990; Todd 1993, 120–121; Gabrielsen 1994, 91–95; Della Libera 1997; McCannon 2017.

https://doi.org/10.1515/9783110751970-006

καὶ περὶ ταύτης ἀγῶνος "having been challenged to an exchange of property on the question of a trierarchy and subjected to a trial on that issue" (*Ant.* 4).[2] We know from a well-informed source – the first-century BC critic Dionysius of Halicarnassus, who in turn relied on records of Alexandrian origin – that Isocrates was involved in a trial connected to *antidosis* in the summer of 356 BC. Dionysius dated it to the time when the general Timotheus held his *stratēgia* with Chares, Iphicrates and Menestheus, the one that ended in the defeat of Embata in August 356 BC and the subsequent indictment, sentence and exile of Timotheus. We also learn that the citizen who challenged Isocrates for the *antidosis* was called Megacleides and that Isocrates' stepson, Aphareus, acted for his elderly father before the court.[3] At the end of the procedure the judges decided against Isocrates, as he himself recalls (*Ant.* 5): ἔγνωσαν ἐμὴν εἶναι τὴν λειτουργίαν ("they imposed the trierarchy upon me").

For Isocrates, who was already in his eighties at the time, the *antidosis* trial and its unfavourable outcome were a real eye-opener[4] as far as his standing among his fellow citizens was concerned, since he realised that public opinion was hostile to him. In particular, during the trial the prosecutor had highlighted the number of Isocrates' pupils and the wealth he had obtained through school

2 Transl. by Norlin 1929, as in the rest of the paper. Isocrates himself states in *Ant.* 145 that he and his son had been previously appointed for trierarchy: εἰς δὲ τοὺς διακοσίους καὶ χιλίους τοὺς εἰσφέροντας καὶ λειτουργοῦντας οὐ μόνον αὑτὸν παρέχεις, ἀλλὰ καὶ τὸν υἱόν, καὶ τρὶς μὲν ἤδη τετριεραρχήκατε, τὰς δ' ἄλλας λειτουργίας πολυτελέστερον λειτουργήκατε καὶ κάλλιον ὧν οἱ νόμοι προστάττουσιν ("you have enrolled not only yourself but your son among the twelve hundred who pay the war-taxes and bear the liturgies, and you and he have three times discharged the trierarchy, besides having performed the other services more generously and handsomely than the laws require").

3 The information can be read in the treatise that Dionysius devoted to Dinarchus, in a list of speeches falsely attributed to that orator, cf. D.H., *Din.* 13.8: εἴρηται γὰρ ἐπὶ τοῦ στρατηγοῦ Τιμοθέου ζῶντος κατὰ τὸν χρόνον τὸν τῆς Μενεσθέως στρατηγίας, ἐφ' ᾗ τὰς εὐθύνας ὑποσχὼν ἑάλω, "for it was delivered while the general Timotheus was still alive, about the time of his command with Menestheus, when he was convicted during his audit". Dionysius also knew the name of the eponymous archon of that year: ἐπὶ Διοτίμου τοῦ μετὰ Καλλίστρατον (the manuscripts of the treatise break off after this point). Apart from Isocrates' own statements, this is the only reliable evidence we have on the "prehistory" of the *Antidosis*. Dionysius was also able to quote the title (ὑπὲρ ἀντιδόσεως <πρὸς> Μεγακλείδην) and the incipit of the speech delivered by Aphareus for his father and knew some of its content, see D.H., *Isoc.* 18.2 (Aphareus stated that no judicial speech was written by his father). The garbled evidence contained in the *Lives of the ten orators* (Plu. *Mor.* 837a, 838a, 839c) and repeated by Photius (*Bibl.* 260, 486b 20–22, 487b 19–25) should not be taken into serious account.

4 The expression was used by Misch 1949[3], 170: "in diesem Prozess wurden ihm 'die Augen geöffnet'".

fees (*Ant.* 5): τοῦ γὰρ ἀντιδίκου, περὶ μὲν ὧν ἡ κρίσις ἦν οὐδὲν λέγοντος δίκαιον, διαβάλλοντος δὲ τὴν τῶν λόγων τῶν ἐμῶν δύναμιν καὶ καταλαζονευομένου περί τε τοῦ πλούτου καὶ τοῦ πλήθους τῶν μαθητῶν ("my opponent made no argument whatever on the merits of the case, and did nothing but decry my "cleverness" of speech and indulge in extravagant nonsense about my wealth and the number of my pupils"). For this reason, two years later, in 354 BC, the innuendos and accusations uttered on that occasion induced him to write an apology for himself in order to counter the "bad press". This decision turned into a profitable yet demanding creative opportunity for the skilled prose writer, notwithstanding his old age and physical weakness. To achieve his purpose, he devised a court speech which had nothing to do with an *antidosis* procedure;[5] on the contrary, the author explicitly pretended to defend himself, like a new Socrates, against a charge of corrupting youths through his teaching.[6] This charge was brought by a fictitious prosecutor, a sycophant, whom Isocrates named Lysimachus and whom he imagined repeating the slanders uttered in the real trial of two years before. The resulting text, the *Antidosis*, actually turns out to be an elaborate defence of the life, works and educational approach of the eighty-two year old author included in the framework of a fictional judicial speech. Its title, however, was chosen by the author in order to recall the trial of 356 BC, which marked a decisive moment in his life and was therefore at the origin of the speech.[7]

As a literary work, the *Antidosis* can be considered – and was considered, to a certain extent, by Isocrates himself – an experimental text, an attempt to try out new ways of writing prose works: accordingly, a carefully worked-out preface explains the structural features of the speech and, besides giving recommendations for a proper public performance, warns the readers about the contents of the work (*Ant.* 10).[8] In fact, the fictional legal framework embraces different components: extensive self-quotations from previous speeches; an

---

5 Cf. *Ant.* 8: εἰ δ' ὑποθείμην ἀγῶνα ("if I were to *adopt the fiction* of a trial"); *Ant.* 13: τὴν ἀπολογίαν τὴν προσποιουμένην περὶ κρίσεως γεγράφθαι ("my defence, which *purports* to have been written for a trial").

6 It is worth stressing this point, since confusion has often arisen about the fictional nature of the case devised by Isocrates. As Bonner 1920, 194 clearly pointed out: "the speech does not purport to have been written for a διαδικασία in connection with a trierarchy or any other liturgy". The imitation of Plato's *Apology of Socrates* was recognised by Hieronymus Wolf as early as the 16th century (Wolf 1570, I, 455) and was investigated by 19th-century German philologists: Vollnhals 1897; Vasold 1898. See, more recently, Ober 1998, 260–263.

7 On the title of the speech: Pinto 2012.

8 Pinto 2018.

encomium of the general Timotheus, Isocrates' former pupil, including an address by the author himself (§§101–139); a supportive speech by a friend (§§142–149); large sections discussing cultural and educational issues (§§167–292); and, in the closing pages, a celebration of Athenian culture (§§293–309). As a whole, the *Antidosis* is the longest of Isocrates' works, stretching far beyond the average length of an Athenian judicial speech.

2 Fictional legal setting and self-quotations

In spite of the attempt made by Isocrates to change the form of the judicial speech into a new literary "container", something that he calls a μικτὸς λόγος,[9] the legal structure of the *Antidosis* maintains a certain consistency.[10] First of all, several common elements of forensic oratory are included in the proem of the speech (*Ant.* 13–28): the appeal to the judges for a fair hearing together with the warning against forming hasty judgements clouded by anger; the mentioning of the harmful activities of sycophants against innocent men; the speaker's claim to lack experience in litigation. Following the proem, the reading of the indictment by a clerk likewise presents us with a scene typical of an Attic trial.[11] Isocrates also refers more than once to the prospective punishment, suggesting that a capital sentence, a μεγίστη τιμωρία, should be the penalty for the losing party (*Ant.* 28, 272, 322). Other judicial elements are scattered throughout the speech – though more sporadically in the extensive section of the second part (*Ant.* 167–292) that is devoted to the discussion of the value of education and culture.[12] The legal background is mentioned again at the end of the speech, where Isocrates makes an oblique reference to the clepsydra, the tool that measured the time allowed for each speaker in court, apologises for his long speech,[13] and, after affirming that he will not call on relatives and friends to plead for him, finally invites the judges to cast their votes.

---

9 Papillon 1997; Nicolai 2004b, 54–58.

10 In general, on the legal setting of the speech: Bonner 1920.

11 The exact wording of the indictment is not given in the speech; the manuscripts only show at this point the lemma ΓΡΑΦΗ. As Bonner 1920, 195 points out, at no point is the indictment classified: a technical classification was probably avoided by Isocrates on purpose.

12 At §272, for instance, Isocrates alludes to the lack of patience of the judges.

13 *Ant.* 320: τὸ μὲν ὕδωρ ἡμᾶς ἐπιλεῖπον, αὐτὸς δ' ἐμπεπτωκὼς εἰς λόγους ἡμερησίους καὶ κατηγορίας ("the water in the clock is giving out, while I myself have fallen into thoughts and recriminations which would exhaust the day").

As far as proof is concerned, namely evidence and witnesses, this is not – as may first appear – lacking in the speech either. Rather, one might say that this is actually the aspect of the judicial speech which the author exploited in order to write the most innovative part of the *Antidosis* and try to achieve his apologetic purpose. In fact, Isocrates decided to present his speeches and pupils as his special means of proof.[14] These two elements are dealt with in different ways and their inclusion in the body of the speech has different effects.

Early in the speech, in commenting on the imaginary indictment read by the clerk, Isocrates mentions the accusation concerning his pupils: "my accuser endeavours to vilify me, charging that I corrupt young men by teaching them to speak and gain their own advantage in the courts contrary to justice".[15] He also pretends that the fictitious prosecutor claimed in his speech "that I have had as my pupils not only private persons but orators, generals, kings and despots; and that I have received from them and am now receiving enormous sums of money" (*Ant.* 30).[16] However, Isocrates' primary concern was his literary output. His λόγοι were the concrete expression of his long career as a refined writer and as a political and moral adviser;[17] but they were also the clear sign of his commitment to Athens and were tightly connected to his school and his teaching.[18] For this reason they are given a significant place in the *Antidosis*.

Isocrates' speeches are introduced in the fictional judicial framework through a subtle line of reasoning. After dramatically asking for the ultimate punishment for himself if he fails to show that his speeches are superior to any others (*Ant.* 51), the author announces that he will show the judges what his eloquence exactly is. This strategy is based on the idea that, unlike other defendants, Isocrates is in a position to exhibit the crime itself for which he is being prosecuted:

> Ἔχει γὰρ οὕτως· ἐγὼ καλλίστην ἡγοῦμαι καὶ δικαιοτάτην εἶναι τὴν τοιαύτην ἀπολογίαν, ἥτις εἰδέναι ποιεῖ τοὺς δικάζοντας ὡς δυνατὸν μάλιστα, περὶ ὧν τὴν ψῆφον οἴσουσι, καὶ μὴ πλανᾶσθαι τῇ διανοίᾳ μηδ' ἀμφιγνοεῖν τοὺς τἀληθῆ λέγοντας. Εἰ μὲν τοίνυν ἠγωνιζόμην ὡς περὶ πράξεις τινὰς ἡμαρτηκώς, οὐκ ἂν οἷός τ' ἦν ἰδεῖν ὑμῖν αὐτὰς παρασχεῖν, ἀλλ' ἀνα-

14 They could be labelled, according to Aristotle, as *pisteis atechnoi*, which included laws, documents and witnesses. On their rhetorical use cf. Calboli Montefusco 1998; for their role in the orators cf. Carey 1994.

15 *Ant.* 30: ὡς διαφθείρω τοὺς νεωτέρους λέγειν διδάσκων καὶ παρὰ τὸ δίκαιον ἐν τοῖς ἀγῶσι πλεονεκτεῖν "that I corrupt young men by teaching them to speak and gain their own advantage in the courts contrary to justice".

16 On Isocrates' pupils see at least Sanneg 1867, Johnson 1957, Engels 2003.

17 On the "genre" of Isocrates' λόγοι see Nicolai 2004b, 37–127.

18 Cf. Johnson 1959; Pinto 2015, 326–327.

> γκαίως ἂν εἶχεν εἰκάζοντας ὑμᾶς ἐκ τῶν εἰρημένων διαγιγνώσκειν ὅπως ἐτύχετε περὶ τῶν πεπραγμένων· ἐπειδὴ δὲ περὶ τοὺς λόγους ἔχω τὴν αἰτίαν, οἶμαι μᾶλλον ὑμῖν ἐμφανιεῖν τὴν ἀλήθειαν. αὐτοὺς γὰρ ὑμῖν δείξω τοὺς εἰρημένους ὑπ' ἐμοῦ καὶ γεγραμμένους, ὥστ' οὐ δοξάσαντες, ἀλλὰ σαφῶς εἰδότες ὁποῖοί τινές εἰσι, τὴν ψῆφον οἴσετε περὶ αὐτῶν.
>
> The best and fairest defence, in my opinion, is that which enables the judges to know the facts, so far as this is possible, in regard to the issues on which they are to vote, and which leaves no room for them to go astray in their judgement or to be in doubt as to which party speaks the truth. If, however, I were being tried for some criminal act, I should not have been able to produce the act itself before your eyes but you would have to conjecture the facts from what I said and pass judgement as best you might. But since I am charged with offending by my speeches, I think that I shall be in a better position to make you see the truth; for I shall present in evidence the actual words which I have spoken and written, so that you will vote upon my discourses, not from conjecture, but with clear knowledge of their nature.[19]

Isocrates then goes a little further (*Ant.* 56):

> Καὶ γὰρ ἂν πάντων εἴην καταγελαστότατος, εἰ τοῦ κατηγόρου διαβάλλοντος ὅτι τοιούτους γράφω λόγους οἳ καὶ τὴν πόλιν βλάπτουσι καὶ τοὺς νεωτέρους διαφθείρουσι, δι' ἑτέρων ποιοίμην τὴν ἀπολογίαν, ἐξὸν αὐτοὺς δείξαντι τούτους ἀπολύσασθαι τὴν διαβολὴν τὴν λεγομένην περὶ ἡμῶν.
>
> It would be the height of absurdity if in a case where my accuser denounces me for writing the kind of speeches which both hurt our city and corrupt our youth I used other speeches in my defence, when I can clear my name of the calumnies which are been heaped upon it by producing before you the very discourses of which he complains.

It is no coincidence that he goes back to this argument at the very end of the speech: αἰσχυνθείην ἂν εἰ δι' ἄλλο τι σῳζοίμην ἢ διὰ τοὺς λόγους τοὺς προειρημένους ὑπ' ἐμοῦ καὶ γεγραμμένους "I should be ashamed to owe my life to any other plea than to the words which you have just heard" (*Ant.* 321).

Through this rhetorical strategy, Isocrates' speeches, despite being the object of accusation, become a weapon in the hands of the defendant. What is more, they are transformed into the equivalent of written documents presented in support of one of the litigants, in a manner consistent with the legal procedure in force probably since the 370s,[20] which required that litigants should lay before the judges any law or decree relevant to their case. The documents thus submitted were to be written down and read out at the trial by a clerk of the court. Consequently, in the fictional space of the *Antidosis*, Isocrates asks the

---

19 *Ant.* 52–54, transl. by Norlin 1929 with slight changes.
20 Cf. Bonner 1905, 46–53; Calhoun 1919; Pringsheim 1955.

γραμματεύς, through the usual formula ἀνάγνωθι (*Ant.* 30, 59, 65, 72), to read out "documents" from three of his previous works, the *Panegyricus*, the speech *On the peace* and the parainetic address *To Nicocles*. Of course, they cannot be produced (ἐξενεγκεῖν) in their entirety because of the fictional duration of the trial and the restrictions inherent in the structure of the text; yet large parts of these speeches will be presented to the pretended and real audiences (for this purpose Isocrates uses the image of a selection of fruits).[21] Each of these extracts, amounting to several pages of a modern edition, is introduced by a presentation by the author and is followed by his comments, while the clerk (a second voice in the actual performance of the *Antidosis*?) is given a clear indication as to the point of the book from which he has to make the reading.[22]

These three speeches are selected by Isocrates as representative of different periods and different expressions of his rhetorical art, but they also perform different roles in his apologetic strategy.[23] The first one, the *Panegyricus*, written around 380 BC, was the most renowned and celebrated of his works: it was entirely devoted to celebrating the glory of the Athenian past and, on the basis of that glorious history, claimed political hegemony for the city. Isocrates singled out from this speech the pages (*Paneg.* 51–59) concerning how the other Greeks were militarily indebted to Athens (the story of the Athenian exploits goes from the time of the Heraclids to the Persian Wars). This extract was intended by Isocrates as a proof of his patriotism and of the civic and – at the same time – artistic value of his oratory (*Ant.* 60–61):

> Ἐνθυμήθητε δὲ πρὸς ὑμᾶς αὐτούς, εἰ δοκῶ τοῖς λόγοις διαφθείρειν τοὺς νεωτέρους, ἀλλὰ μὴ προτρέπειν ἐπ' ἀρετὴν καὶ τοὺς ὑπὲρ τῆς πόλεως κινδύνους, ἢ δικαίως ἂν δοῦναι δίκην

21 *Ant.* 54: ἅπαντας μὲν οὖν διὰ τέλους εἰπεῖν οὐκ ἂν δυναίμην· ὁ γὰρ χρόνος ὁ δεδομένος ἡμῖν ὀλίγος ἐστίν· ὥσπερ δὲ τῶν καρπῶν, ἐξενεγκεῖν ἑκάστου δεῖγμα πειράσομαι. μικρὸν γὰρ μέρος ἀκούσαντες ῥᾳδίως τό τ' ἐμὸν ἦθος γνωριεῖτε καὶ τῶν λόγων τὴν δύναμιν ἁπάντων μαθήσεσθε ("I cannot, however, present them all in complete form; for the time which has been allowed me is too short. But just as is done with fruits, I shall try to produce a sample of each kind. For when you have heard a small portion of them you will easily recognize my true character and appreciate the force of all my speeches").

22 See in particular *Ant.* 59, where Isocrates invites the clerk to read the passage from the *Panegyricus* beginning from the line marked in the margin of the book with a παραγραφή, namely a dash.

23 Two more self-quotations are included in the speech, though in a looser way: one from the speech *Against the sophists* 14–18 (*Ant.* 194) and one from *Nicocles* 5–9 (*Ant.* 253–257); there is no introduction to the latter except for the words ἅπερ ἤδη καὶ πρότερον εἶπον ("as I have already said on a former occasion"). On the meaning and role of self-quotations in the speech: Pinto 2003.

ὑπὲρ τῶν εἰρημένων, ἀλλ' οὐκ ἂν χάριν κομίσασθαι παρ' ὑμῶν τὴν μεγίστην, ὃς οὕτως ἐγκεκωμίακα τὴν πόλιν καὶ τοὺς προγόνους καὶ τοὺς κινδύνους τοὺς ἐν ἐκείνοις τοῖς χρόνοις γεγενημένους ὥστε τούς τε πρότερον γράψαντας περὶ τὴν ὑπόθεσιν ταύτην ἅπαντας ἠφανικέναι τοὺς λόγους, αἰσχυνομένους ὑπὲρ τῶν εἰρημένων αὐτοῖς, τούς τε νῦν δοκοῦντας εἶναι δεινοὺς μὴ τολμᾶν ἔτι λέγειν περὶ τούτων, ἀλλὰ καταμέμφεσθαι τὴν δύναμιν τὴν σφετέραν αὐτῶν.

But, I beg of you, consider well whether I appear to you to corrupt the young by my words, or, on the contrary, to inspire them to a life of valour and of dangers endured for their country; whether I should justly be punished for the words which have been read, or whether, on the contrary, I deserve to have your deepest gratitude for having so glorified Athens and our ancestors and the wars which were fought in those days that the orators who had composed discourses on this theme have destroyed them all, being ashamed of their own efforts, while they who to-day are reputed to be clever dare no longer to speak upon this subject, but confess the feebleness of their own powers.

The second quotation comes from a work that Isocrates circulated a short time before the *Antidosis*, namely the oration *On the peace*, written in the years of the Social War in the form of a speech held before the Assembly. Isocrates presents two sections from this speech, the first one (*Pac.* 25–56) concerning the political and moral situation in Athens during the war compared with that of the ancient Athenians; and the second one, which contains the actual conclusion of the speech (*Pac.* 132–145), advising a peace settlement and appealing especially to the young. Through this second instance of his new oratory, which despite its fictitious form pursued concrete goals,[24] Isocrates offers an example of his commitment also to current issues of political significance (*Ant.* 63: ἐν ᾧ φανήσομαι περὶ τούτων ἁπάντων πολλὴν ἐπιμέλειαν πεποιημένος "in which [selection] it will be seen that I have given much attention to all these questions").

The third extract requires a chronological step back: it is culled from the speech *To Nicocles* (§§14–39, with cuts),[25] a series of pieces of political and moral advice sent by Isocrates to his former pupil Nicocles, the king of Salamis of Cyprus, soon after his accession to the throne after the death of his father Evagoras in 374 BC. Nicocles was already dead by the time of the *Antidosis*;

24 On this aspect, see Moysey 1982, 123: "there is no reason to doubt the validity of the testimony given in this oration concerning the purpose of *On the Peace*. Indeed, the fact that *On the Peace* is one of only three of his orations from which Isocrates chose to quote verbatim in his defence makes his testimony all the more noteworthy".

25 This quotation was actually a "new edition", since, due to the parainetic structure of the speech, Isocrates was able to delete some of the short sections of the original passage without altering the meaning of the sequence. Cf. Pinto 2003, 172–176.

however, his discipleship was a delicate issue, since the Cypriot king had allegedly rewarded Isocrates with huge and valuable gifts, as we learn in a previous passage of the *Antidosis* (*Ant.* 40):

> Ἠκούσατε δὲ καὶ τοῦ κατηγόρου λέγοντος ὅτι παρὰ Νικοκλέους τοῦ Σαλαμινίων βασιλέως πολλὰς ἔλαβον καὶ μεγάλας δωρεάς. Καίτοι τίνι πιστὸν ὑμῶν ἐστιν ὡς Νικοκλῆς ἔδωκέ μοι ταύτας ἵνα δίκας μανθάνῃ λέγειν, ὃς καὶ τοῖς ἄλλοις περὶ τῶν ἀμφισβητουμένων ὥσπερ δεσπότης ἐδίκαζεν.
>
> But you have heard also from my accuser that I have received many great presents from Nicocles, the king of the Salaminians. And yet, could any one of you be persuaded that Nicocles made me these presents in order that he might learn how to plead cases in court – he who dispensed justice, like a master, to others in their disputes?[26]

This third quotation is appended by Isocrates in order to show that all his speeches tend toward virtue and justice and that he has always behaved correctly towards monarchs too. In addition, he intends that the speech should be seen as evidence of his *democratic* sentiment. The point of his specious argument is that, since when addressing a king he spoke in favour of the king's subjects, he would be even more categorical in exhorting those who live in a democracy to defend the interests of the (*Ant.* 69–70):

> Διὰ τὴν αὐτὴν δὲ ταύτην πρόφασιν καὶ νῦν αὐτὸν ὑμῖν δεῖξαι προειλόμην, οὐχ ὡς ἄριστα τῶν λοιπῶν γεγραμμένον, ἀλλ' ὡς ἐκ τούτου μάλιστα φανερὸς γενησόμενος ὃν τρόπον εἴθισμαι καὶ τοῖς ἰδιώταις καὶ τοῖς δυνάσταις πλησιάζειν· φανήσομαι γὰρ πρὸς αὐτὸν ἐλευθέρως καὶ τῆς πόλεως ἀξίως διειλεγμένος, καὶ οὐ τὸν ἐκείνου πλοῦτον οὐδὲ τὴν δύναμιν θεραπεύων, ἀλλὰ τοῖς ἀρχομένοις ἐπαμύνων καὶ παρασκευάζων καθ' ὅσον ἠδυνάμην τὴν πολιτείαν αὐτοῖς ὡς οἷόν τε πρᾳοτάτην. Ὅπου δὲ βασιλεῖ διαλεγόμενος ὑπὲρ τοῦ δήμου τοὺς λόγους ἐποιούμην, ἦπου τοῖς ἐν δημοκρατίᾳ πολιτευομένοις σφόδρ' ἂν παρακελευσαίμην τὸ πλῆθος θεραπεύειν.
>
> It was with the same motive that I decided to present this discourse to you on the present occasion, not that it is the best written of my works, but that through it you will best see in what spirit I am wont to deal with princes as well as with private men; for you will see that I have expressed myself to Nicocles as a free man and an Athenian should, not paying court to his wealth nor to his power, but pleading the cause of his subjects, and striving with all my powers to secure for them the mildest government possible. And since in addressing a king I have spoken for his subjects, surely I would urge upon men who live under a democracy to pay court to the people.

---

26 According to an ancient tradition, stemming from the Alexandrian biographer Hermippus, Isocrates was paid twenty talents or more by the prince for the speech *To Nicocles*. Cf. Phld., *Rh.* 2.178 Sudhaus; Plin. *Nat.* 7.110; the anonymous life and the hypotheses to the speeches *To Nicocles* and *Evagoras* (in Mathieu-Brémond 1928, xxxvi; Mathieu-Brémond 1938, 97, 145).

At the end of the presentation of the three extracts, Isocrates goes back to the value of the works that have just been read out and, while stressing in particular the character and contents of the *Panegyricus*, reminds the judges of the usefulness of all three speeches (*Ant.* 76–78). The inclusion of these passages as evidence in his defence strategy allows Isocrates to insert a real anthology of his literary output into the new work, the *Antidosis*, while, at the same time, giving recommendations on how to approach it correctly.[27]

The analogy with written documents, brilliantly exploited by Isocrates, is not only highly remarkable for the study of ancient literary composition and for the history of ancient criticism, but also has some decisive implications for a correct assessment of the manuscript tradition of the speech. The most ancient manuscript of Isocrates, the Urbinas gr. 111 from the end of the 9th century, which is the origin of one of two families of Isocratean manuscripts,[28] transmitted the self-quotations in a shortened form that preserves just the beginning and the end of the quoted passages connected by the phrase μέχρι τοῦ ("as far as"). However, several features show that this form of the text was the result of editorial work carried out in Late Antiquity and cannot be considered the author's text.[29] This idea is confirmed precisely by the analogy with the judicial situation, in which the documents were read out by a secretary in their entirety. The laws and documents exhibited in a trial were considered to be valuable evidence, and integrity was required of a secretary, who would have been responsible for any alteration of them:[30] this is a clear sign of the central role of the quotations, in their complete form, within the literary design of the *Antidosis*.

3 Pupils as witnesses

Immediately after the section containing his "anthological" evidence, Isocrates moves on to the second piece of proof, namely his pupils. In his defence strategy speeches and pupils are closely linked, since he intends to make clear that he obtained his pupils thanks precisely to speeches like those read out in the imag-

---

27 This auto-anthology is the most impressive instance of excerpting in the fourth century. In particular, the introductions to and comments on the long passages included in the *Antidosis* are a good example of the control that Isocrates exerted over his writings and clear evidence of his mature self-consciousness as an author. Cf. also Nicolai 2004a.

28 On the manuscript tradition of Isocrates, cf. Martinelli Tempesta 2014.

29 Cf. Pinto 2003, 91–101.

30 On Athenian secretaries, see in general Ferguson 1898; Brillant 1911.

inary court: "for the writing and publication of them has won me distinction in many parts of the world and brought many disciples, no one of whom would have remained with me had they not found in me the very kind of man they expected to find".[31] Isocrates proceeds in his defence first by dwelling on the weakness of the position of the fictitious prosecutor, who has emphasised the gravity of Isocrates' alleged offence, the corruption of youth, yet has produced no proof, no ἀπόδειξις, to show how Isocrates teaches his pupils to prevail in the courts against justice (*Ant.* 89). He goes on to state that he will defend himself on pertinent and just grounds (*Ant.* 92: ἐξ ὧνπερ προσήκει καὶ δίκαιόν ἐστι). Therefore, after producing evidence in the form of written documents, he turns to witnesses. Starting from *Ant.* 93, one of the most important pieces of information on his own school, Isocrates introduces eight of his Athenian pupils as witnesses. They are presented as those who have remained by their teacher's side even after the years of the school, real friends, some being the same age as Isocrates:

> Καὶ τοὺς μὲν λόγους ὀλίγῳ πρότερον ἀνέγνωμεν ὑμῖν, τοὺς δὲ κεχρημένους ἐκ μειρακίων μοι μέχρι γήρως δηλώσω, καὶ μάρτυρας ὑμῶν αὐτῶν παρέξομαι περὶ ὧν ἂν λέγω, τοὺς κατὰ τὴν ἡλικίαν τὴν ἐμὴν γεγενημένους. ἤρξαντο μὲν οὖν ἐν πρώτοις Εὔνομός μοι καὶ Λυσιθείδης καὶ Κάλλιππος πλησιάζειν, μετὰ δὲ τούτους Ὀνήτωρ, Ἀντικλῆς, Φιλωνίδης, Φιλόμηλος, Χαρμαντίδης.
>
> I had my speeches read to you a moment ago; I shall now bring before you the men who have been associated with me from the time of my youth to the days of my old age, and from your own number I shall present men of my own years to bear witness to the truth of what I say. Among the first to begin studying with me were Eunomous, Lysitheides and Callippus; and following them were Onetor, Anticles, Philonides, Philomelus and Charmantides.

Isocrates does not push the judicial fiction too far in this case, since the pupils he mentions do not give evidence in the fictional court of the *Antidosis*, but are simply imagined as being present there, as living but silent examples of the successful teaching of Isocrates, who in turn gives evidence on himself through

---

31 *Ant.* 87: Τούτων γὰρ γραφέντων καὶ διαδοθέντων καὶ δόξαν ἔσχον παρὰ πολλοῖς καὶ μαθητὰς πολλοὺς ἔλαβον, ὧν οὐδεὶς ἂν παρέμεινεν, εἰ μὴ τοιοῦτον ὄντα με κατέλαβον οἷόν περ προσεδόκησαν. On the meaning of verb διαδιδόναι cf. Hudson-Williams 1949, 66: "Isocrates uses three verbs in connexion with the publication of his works, διαδίδωμι, ἐκδίδωμι, and ἐκφέρω. These are all used in a wide sense, and would include publication either in book form or by readings".

their lives.[32] As he states (*Ant.* 94), they were all awarded golden crowns for their services to Athens (and in fact we find evidence that some of them featured in 4th-century Athenian public and political life).[33] For this reason, Isocrates is ready to envisage an extreme case (*Ant.* 99):

> Ἀξιῶ γάρ, εἰ μέν τινες τῶν ἐμοὶ συγγεγενημένων ἄνδρες ἀγαθοὶ γεγόνασι περὶ τὴν πόλιν καὶ τοὺς φίλους καὶ τὸν ἴδιον οἶκον, ἐκείνους ὑμᾶς ἐπαινεῖν, ἐμοὶ δὲ μηδεμίαν ὑπὲρ τούτων χάριν ἔχειν, εἰ δὲ πονηροὶ καὶ τοιοῦτοι τὰς φύσεις οἷοι φαίνειν καὶ γράφεσθαι καὶ τῶν ἀλλοτρίων ἐπιθυμεῖν, παρ' ἐμοῦ δίκην λαμβάνειν.
>
> For I ask this of you: if any of those who have been associated with me have turned out to be good men in their relations to the state, to their friends, and to their own households - I ask you to give them the praise and not to be grateful to me; but if, on the other hand, any of them have turned out to be bad - the kind of men who lay information, hale people into court, and covet the property of others - then to let the penalty be visited on me.

And he even declares himself ready – a typical forensic strategy – to yield the floor to the accuser or to anyone who is able to name one of his pupils who does not enjoy good reputation (*Ant.* 100).

However, the most important witness that Isocrates brings into play cannot be imagined as present at the trial. In fact, the section devoted to his pupils (*Ant.* 93–100) gradually culminates in the remembrance of one of them, the *stratēgos* Timotheus, the son of Conon, a former pupil to whom Isocrates was linked by a strong friendship[34]. Timotheus is mentioned as dead in *Ant.* 101 (ἀνδρὸς τετελευτηκότος): he probably died during the very period in which Isocrates was writing the *Antidosis*. The friendship with Timotheus, the scion of an internationally well-connected family and one of the unsuccessful generals in the battle of Embata in 356 BC, afterwards condemned by the Athenians, had been most likely included among the arguments of the real prosecutor in the *diadikasia* connected to the *antidosis* procedure of 356 BC, as the information provided by Dionysius of Halicarnassus seems to imply.[35] For this reason, the argument is also put into the mouth of Lysimachus, the fictitious accuser of the speech: "my accuser has mentioned also the friendship which existed between

32 On the nature and role of witnesses, see Harrison 1971, 136–147; Thür 2005; for witnesses as supporters, cf. Humphreys 1985, 328–333.

33 Cf. Trail 1994–2011, nos. 133220 (Anticles); 440305, 440310, 440315 (Eunomous); 559370 (Callippus); 614405 (Lysitheides); 748105, 748110 (Onetor); 939780 (Philomelus); 957490 (Philonides); 987670 (Charmantides). For their involvement in the political life of the time, cf. e.g. Rowe 2000.

34 On Timotheus, see Bianco 2007.

35 See also above pp. 97–98.

me and Timotheus, and has attempted to calumniate us both", Isocrates states; and then he adds: "he has laid greater stress upon his arraignment of Timotheus than upon the charges which he has preferred in his indictment".[36] In this case again, through his overturning strategy, Isocrates makes clear that he considers Timotheus the most important witness on his side (*Ant.* 102):

> Ἐγὼ δ' ᾤμην μέν, εἰ καὶ φανερῶς ἐξηλεγχόμην ἀδικῶν, διὰ τὴν πρὸς ἐκεῖνον φιλίαν σῴζεσθαί μοι προσήκειν· ἐπειδὴ δὲ Λυσίμαχος καὶ τοῖς τοιούτοις ἐπιχειρεῖ με βλάπτειν ἐξ ὧν δικαίως ἂν ὠφελοίμην, ἀναγκαίως ἔχει διαλεχθῆναι περὶ αὐτῶν. Διὰ τοῦτο δ' οὐχ ἅμα περὶ τούτου καὶ τῶν ἄλλων ἐπιτηδείων ἐποιησάμην τὴν μνείαν, ὅτι πολὺ τὰ πράγματα διέφερεν αὐτῶν.

> But I, for my part, should have thought that even if I were proved guilty beyond a doubt, yet because of my friendship with him I should be entitled to go free. But since Lysimachus is attempting to hurt me by the very means which ought to help my case, I am compelled to go into this question. I must explain that I did not mention Timotheus when I named my other associates because he was a very different case from them.

As in the case with the quotations from his previous speeches, here too the analogy with pieces of proof gives Isocrates the opportunity to include an additional *logos* in the expandable structure of the *Antidosis*. The explanation of the difference between Timotheus and the rest of his pupils takes the form of a self-contained text, an encomium of Timotheus covering nearly forty sections of a modern edition. Of course, Isocrates justifies this inclusion in judicial terms: he asks the judges not to treat the *logos* about Timotheus as irrelevant to the case, nor to think that he is straying beyond the limits of the indictment.[37] The subsequent encomium then gives first-hand, detailed information about the achievements of Timotheus and describes, with psychological insight, the qualities of the man and the politician. Though not explicitly signalled, the analogy with documents added to the record recurs. At the same time, through an example of his refined art of eulogy Isocrates seeks again to defend and rehabilitate himself in the eyes of his fellow citizens through rhetoric and, one might say, literature.

---

36 *Ant.* 101: Ἐμνήσθη δὲ καὶ τῆς πρὸς Τιμόθεόν μοι φιλίας γεγενημένης καὶ διαβάλλειν ἡμᾶς ἀμφοτέρους ἐπεχείρησεν; *Ant.* 103: περὶ δὲ τὴν Τιμοθέου κατηγορίαν μᾶλλον ἐσπούδασεν ἢ περὶ ὧν ἀπήνεγκε τὴν γραφήν.

37 *Antid.* 104: Χρὴ δὲ τὸν ὑπὲρ ἐκείνου λόγον οὐκ ἀλλότριον εἶναι νομίζειν τοῖς ἐνεστῶσι πράγμασιν οὐδ' ἐμὲ λέγειν ἔξω τῆς γραφῆς.

4 Conclusion

It can be said conclusively that the treatment of evidence and witnesses in the fictional framework of the *Antidosis* is functional to the achievement of the general purpose of the work, that is to say the transformation of a situation highly typical of the life of a democratic *polis*, namely the trial, and of a well-known rhetorical form, the judicial speech, into something new. Ironically but all the more significantly, this project was carried out by a renowned teacher of rhetoric and an influential intellectual who apparently tried all his life to have his past as a logographer forgotten. The result was a highly elaborated literary text that interweaves different levels of authorial discourse: the autobiographical, the apologetic and the political.

Bibliography

Bianco, E. (2007), *Lo stratego Timoteo torre di Atene*, Alessandria.
Bonner, R.J. (1905), *Evidence in Athenian Courts*, Chicago.
Bonner, R.J. (1920), 'The Legal Setting of Isocrates' *Antidosis*', in: *CPh* 15, 193–197.
Brillant, M. (1911), *Les secretaries athéniens*, Paris.
Calboli Montefusco, L. (1998), 'La force probatoire des *pisteis atechnoi*: d'Aristote aux rhéteurs Latins de la République et de l'Empire', in: G. Dahan/I. Rosier-Catach (eds.), *La Rhétorique d'Aristote. Traditions et commentaires de l'antiquité au XVIIe siècle*, Paris, 13–35.
Calhoun, G.M. (1919), 'Oral and Written Pleading in Athenian Courts', in: *TAPhA* 50, 177–193.
Carey, C. (1994), '"Artless" Proofs in Aristotle and the Orators', in: *BICS* 39, 95–106, repr. in: E. Carawan (ed.), *Oxford Readings in* The Attic Orators, Oxford 2007, 229–246.
Christ, M.R. (1990), 'Liturgy Avoidance and Antidosis in Classical Athens', in: *TAPhA* 120, 147–169.
Della Libera, M. (1997), 'ΑΝΤΙΔΟΣΙΣ', in: *Patavium* 5, 17–47.
Engels, J. (2003), 'Antike Überlieferungen über die Schüler des Isokrates', in: W. Orth (ed.), *Isokrates. Neue Ansätze zur Bewertung eines politischen Schriftstellers*, Trier, 175–194.
Ferguson, W.S. (1898), *The Athenian Secretaries*, New York.
Gabrielsen, V. (1987), 'The Antidosis Procedure in Classical Athens', in: *C&M* 38, 7–38.
Gabrielsen, V. (1994), *Financing the Athenian Fleet*, Baltimore/London.
Harrison, A.R.W. (1971), *The Law of Athens*, II, Oxford.
Hudson-Williams, H.L. (1949), 'Isocrates and Recitations', in: *CQ* 43, 65–69.
Humphreys, S.C. (1985), 'Social Relations on Stage: Witnesses in Classical Athens', in: S.C. Humphreys (ed.), *The Discourse of Law*, London, 313–369, repr. in: E. Carawan (ed.), *Oxford Readings in The Attic Orators*, Oxford 2007, 140–213.
Johnson, R. (1957), 'A Note on the Number of Isocrates' Pupils', in: *AJPh* 78, 297–300.
Johnson, R. (1959), 'Isocrates' Methods of Teaching', in: *AJPh* 80, 25–36.
Martinelli Tempesta, S. (2014), 'Missing "Archetype": The Transmission of the Isocratean Corpus and the Problems of the *constitutio textus*', in: Ch. Brockmann/D. Deckers/

L. Koch/S. Valente (eds.), *Handschriften- und Textforschung heute. Zur Überlieferung der griechischen Literatur*, Festschrift für Dieter Harlfinger aus Anlass seines 70, Geburtstages, Wiesbaden, 43–54.
Mathieu, G./Brémond, É. (1928), *Isocrate. Discours*, texte établi et traduit par G.M. et É.B., I, Paris.
Mathieu, G./Brémond, É. (1938), *Isocrate. Discours*, texte établi et traduit par G.M. et É.B., II, Paris.
McCannon, B.C. (2017), 'Who Pays Taxes? Liturgies and the Antidosis Procedure in Ancient Athens', in: *Constitutional Political Economy* 28, 407–421.
MacDowell, D.M. (1978), *The Law in Classical Athens*, London.
Misch, G. (1949[3]), *Geschichte der Autobiographie*, I.1, Bern.
Moysey, R.A. (1982), 'Isokrates' *On the Peace*: Rhetorical Exercise or Political Advice?', in: *American Journal of Ancient History* 7, 118–127.
Nicolai, R. (2004a), 'Isocrate e le nuove strategie della comunicazione letteraria: l'*Antidosi* come "antologia d'autore"', in: R. Pretagostini/E. Dettori (eds.), *La cultura ellenistica. L'opera letteraria e l'esegesi antica*, Roma.
Nicolai, R. (2004b), *Studi su Isocrate. La comunicazione letteraria nel IV sec. a.C. e i nuovi generi della prosa*, Roma, 187–197.
Norlin, G. (1929), *Isocrates*, with an English translation by G.N., II, London/Cambridge, MA.
Ober, J. (1998), *Political Dissent in Democratic Athens. Intellectual Critics of Popular Rule*, Princeton.
Papillon, T.L. (1997), 'Mixed Unities in the *Antidosis* of Isocrates', in: *Rhetoric Society Quarterly* 27, 47–62.
Pinto, P.M. (2003), *Per la storia del testo di Isocrate. La testimonianza d'autore*, Bari.
Pinto, P.M. (2012), 'The Title of Isocrates' *Antidosis*', in: *Hermes* 140, 362–368.
Pinto, P.M. (2015), 'L'École d'Isocrate: un bilan', in: C. Bouchet/P. Giovannelli Jouanna (eds.), *Isocrate: entre jeu rhétorique et enjeux politiques*, Lyon, 319–329.
Pinto, P.M. (2018), 'Sulla prefazione dell'*Antidosis* di Isocrate', in: P. Davoli/N. Pellè (eds.), *Polymatheia. Studi offerti a Mario Capasso*, Brescia/Lecce, 589–596.
Pringsheim, F. (1955), 'The Transition from Witnessed to Written Transactions in Athens', in: Aequitas und bona fides*: Festgabe zum 70. Geburtstag von August Simonius*, Basel, 287–297.
Rowe, G.O. (2000), 'Anti-Isocratean Sentiment in Demosthenes' *Against Androtion*', in: *Historia* 49, 278–302.
Sanneg, P. (1867), *De schola Isocratea*, I, Halle.
Thür, G. (2005), 'The Role of the Witness in Athenian Law', in: M. Gagarin/D. Cohen (eds.), *The Cambridge Companion to Ancient Greek Law*, Cambridge, 146–169.
Traill, J.S. (1994–2011), *Persons of Ancient Athens*, 1–20, Toronto.
Vasold, J. (1898), *Über das Verhältnis der isokratischen Rede περὶ ἀντιδόσεως zu Platons Apologia Socratis*, Munich.
Vollnhals, W. (1897), *Über das Verhältnis der Rede des Isokrates περὶ ἀντιδόσεως zu Platos Apologie des Sokrates*, Bamberg.
Wolf, H. (1570), *Ἰσοκράτους ἅπαντα. Isocratis scripta*, quae quidem nunc extant, omnia, Graecolatina, postremo recognita. Annotationibus novis et eruditis illustrata, castigationibuśque necessariis expolita, Hieronymo Wolfio Oetingensi interprete et auctore, Basel.

Robert Sullivan

Antiphon's Witnesses: Extending the Earliest Greek Theories of Argumentation

Abstract: The surviving *corpus* of the Attic orator Antiphon consists of three complete instances of his logography, each directed to a homicide case, and his *Tetralogies*, sets of abstracted cases that are most likely to have been used to teach litigation strategy. Almost all of these texts prominently feature attempts to qualify or disqualify the testimony of witnesses, often drawing the audience's attention to criteria by which these attempts can be characterised. This chapter extends our understanding of the earliest sophistic theories of argumentation by attending to Antiphon's argumentative practices in relation to forensic witnesses, and more particularly to the paratextual statements made by him regarding the criteria by which such arguments could be judged. The chapter's findings point to a nascent, quasi-technical vocabulary and conceptual structure, and support for a position that sophistic argumentation in the 5th century BC was more sophisticated than the standard account would lead one to expect.

This chapter seeks to advance our understanding of how argumentation was conceived in the earliest Greek rhetorical theory. It does so by examining a body of arguments, and the paratextual statements made about those arguments, as they are found in the works of the Attic orator Antiphon (480–411 BC) in situations where he attempts to either qualify or disqualify witnesses and their testimony. Antiphonic statements about testimony and witnesses are an excellent candidate for an entry point into sophistic argumentation. A robust body of scholarship addressed to the most general notions of Antiphonic argumentation already exists, particularly the warranting of arguments by recourse to *eikos*, the notion of "probability" or "plausibility".[1] We have learned a good deal from these studies about the structure of sophistic reasoning, but their findings are focused almost entirely on the single, but very important, concept of *eikos*. In addition, a number of scholars have provided very helpful accounts of the pragmatics of Antiphonic argument, describing his tactical manoeuvring by the

1 Gagarin 1990; Goebel 1989; Schmitz 2000. Due 1980 and Tindale 2010 have established the complexity of *eikos* argumentation in early sophistic, and particularly in Antiphon's use of the concept where it is used to encompass a variety of ideas well beyond simple "probability" or "likelihood," in many cases describing an argument's "rationality" or "reasonableness".

https://doi.org/10.1515/9783110751970-007

use of "commonplaces", allowing us to see the theory *in situ*, as it were.[2] This chapter extends both classes of studies by describing what seem to be other, generally unaddressed premises of sophistic argumentation and nascent ideas about the criteria by which arguments might be judged.

These premises are not expressed by Antiphon in a complete or systematic form as his arguments are found in situationally based hypotheticals and "genuine" forensic speeches. We can, however, abstract his theories by reference to the author's paratextual statements about matters of argument at stake. Such paratextual statements could include any number of author's references that explain what is meant by some feature of the text. These could be as simple as a parenthetical clause within a sentence or as complex as an extended theoretical digression. Taken together, Antiphon's paratextual statements give us the fullest sense of how argument theory was understood by him and how the criteria used in the judgement of argumentation might be imagined. For the purposes of this study, we will accept as a theoretical statement any statement made within a discourse that seeks to give an account of how a witness or piece of testimony is to be judged. Antiphon's paratextual statements about witnesses and their testimony are then analysed inductively, in order to see if there are patterns or consistencies to be observed.

Antiphon's corpus is valuable for our purposes for a number of reasons. First, Antiphon's texts are among the very earliest surviving remains of Greek rhetoric, his materials having been composed between the 440's and his death in 411 BC.[3] Written when they were, well before both the Platonic critiques of sophistic argumentation[4] and the Aristotelian codification of the standards of reasoning (and their application to the rhetorical proofs in his *Technē Rhetorikē*),[5] these materials can be taken as instances of more or less "pure" sophistic argumentation. Second, Antiphon's texts also constitute the largest set of remains we have of rhetoric from this earliest period. There are works from this period by Andocides, Gorgias, Lysias and possibly Isocrates, but either they are less extensive (Andocides), removed from normative public practice (Gorgias),

2 The best structural accounts of the pragmatics of argumentation in Antiphon are Edwards/Usher 1985; Carawan 1993; Gagarin 2003.

3 Disputes over the authorship and date of composition of the *Tetralogies* continue; Sealey 1984, 71–85. This essay accepts Antiphon as author of the *Tetralogies* following Gagarin 1998, 4; Gagarin 1997; Edwards 1994 as it does the early dates of composition for these materials. Gagarin argues out that the *Tetralogies* were probably Antiphon's earliest writings, suggesting that they may have been written as early as the 440's.

4 As, for instance in Plato, *Phaedr.* 273a–274a.

5 Aristotle's critique of sophistic argument by *eikos* in *Rh.* 1401a.10–11.

or their dates of composition are not as completely contained within the period under discussion (Lysias, Isocrates). Third and most importantly, Antiphon's literary remains include both speeches that were written for presentation in the Athenian courts, as well as a variety of theoretical or technical writings. Though we do not have all of the works which in antiquity were ascribed to Antiphon,[6] we do have three complete courtroom speeches, significant remains of Antiphon's unsuccessful *apologia* at his trial for treason, a number of fragments, as well as the *Tetralogies*, highly abstracted hypothetical cases that lay out for students a variety of strategies for litigators.

Witnesses and testimony play a vital role in almost all of Antiphon's discourses.[7] Antiphon uses variants of μαρτυρία, roughly "testimony", μάρτυρος, "witness", or μαρτυρέω, the verbal form "to testify", no fewer than 170 times in his surviving corpus. Witnesses or testimony appear in all but the *Second Tetralogy*[8] and in his fragmentary "On the Revolution".[9] The author occasionally uses a participial construction of the verb παραγιγνώσκω, "to be present", such as παραγενομένων, roughly "bystanders", as a term to describe eyewitnesses eighteen times.[10] The word ὀπτήρ makes a single appearance in Antiphon 5. In any case, there seems to be no important distinction between the meanings of the words.

The chapter now turns to the statements of witnesses and their testimony in the Antiphonic corpus. The *Tetralogies* will be treated first, followed by the "genuine" forensic cases, in the standard order (1, 5, 6) in which they appear in modern texts. Our best surmise is that the *Tetralogies* are instructional materials meant to supply students with a variety of commonplace lines of argument, presented in the form of hypothetical cases deploying abstracted lines of argument available to opposed advocates. Sophistic rhetorical instruction focused teaching techniques of strategic maneuvering within the parts of a speech, and this was effected by bringing students to emulate models of argumentation coordinated with those speech parts.[11] In this way, students were introduced to

---

6 Maidment 1941, 298 describes how approximately sixty works were in circulation under Antiphon's name in antiquity, many of which were believed at that time to be spurious.

7 The literature on role of witnesses in Athenian trials is quite extensive. Rubinstein 2000 provides the best general account, supplemented by excellent studies by Bonner 1912; Gagarin 1996, 1997; Martin 2008; Mirhady 1991b, 1996, 2002.

8 All subsequent citations are to Antiphon's works using the modern number and section identifiers.

9 Fr. B.1.

10 Nine times in 2, eight time in 6, once in 1.

11 See particularly Kennedy 1959; 1963, 30–32, 130–131.

lines of argument, both *pro* and *contra* that were (more or less) commonly encountered in litigation. Based on these hypotheticals, an apt student would be expected to be able to compose plausible arguments and counter-arguments within the purview of the commonplace.

The *First Tetralogy* (Antiphon 2) consists of a highly abstracted legal dispute regarding a murder. The body of a man has been discovered in a secluded area. The victim's companion, a slave, has been found with him, suffering from what would later prove to be fatal wounds. Before he dies, the slave identifies the defendant as the assailant. Accordingly, almost the entirety of the prosecution case relies on the testimony of an eyewitness, though one whose status as a slave will provide argumentative resources for both sides and, not surprisingly, a significant portion of the defendant's argument aims at the disqualification of the slave's testimony.

The prosecution's first challenge is that the foundation of their case is the testimony of a single witness. They anticipate the counter-argument by pointing out that, "had there been witnesses in large numbers we should have produced them in large numbers" (2.1.9: μάρτυρες δ' εἰ μὲν πολλοὶ παρεγένοντο, πολλοὺς ἂν παρεσχόμεθα).[12] But, as the witness was alone at the time of the crime, and dying, they will be forced to rely entirely upon his testimony. The actual witnesses imagined as testifying in the hypothetical trial would be the men who had come upon the scene. To these men the slave had spoken as he died, stating that the only assailant he could identify was the defendant. Based on this the prosecutor argues that the defendant's guilt "can be inferred both from probabilities and eyewitnesses" (2.1.9: ἐξελεγχόμενος δ' ὑπό τε τῶν εἰκότων ὑπό τε τῶν παραγενομένων).

Based on the foregoing the prosecutor brings forward a subsidiary line of argument which attempts to bolster this testimony, tainted as it is by the fact that they have but one eyewitness and that a dying slave. The prosecutor argues that it would be a violation of justice if the defendant were not to be convicted because, in spite of the eyewitness' deficiencies, the slave was, in fact, present during the crime and capable of making an identification of the perpetrator. It would be, the prosecution argues, an affront both to justice and expediency to acquit, as it would be impossible to convict any defendants at all if they could

12 Interestingly, this line of argument is signaled by a parallel stylistic construction, perhaps a mnemonic prompt. The text and translations are taken from the Loeb editions, with modifications to the translations where required.

not be convicted on the word of eyewitness that corroborate situationally based likelihoods.[13]

The defendant's reply to this testimony necessarily focusses on a series of arguments meant to discredit the credibility of the witness. The defence does this by attacking the credibility of slaves as a class, shifting the status of the witness from "eyewitness" to "slave". Why, he asks, should the testimony of this slave be given any credence?[14] First, the defence argues that any witness, in terror at the time of the attack, would be most unlikely to recognize his killer. Secondly, he argues that it is likely that the slave would, at the time of his interrogation, confirm the suggestions made to him by the victim's family to have committed the crime.[15] Immediately after this the defendant lays out a new line of argument aimed against use of the testimony of slaves as a general matter. "We are not persuaded by the testimony of slaves generally, why else would we torture them?" (2.2.7: ἀπιστουμένων δὲ καὶ τῶν ἄλλων δούλων ἐν ταῖς μαρτυρίαις, οὐ γὰρ ἂν ἐβασανίζομεν αὐτούς). How then could it be just to be put to death solely on the word of this one? The witness, a slave, has, of course, not been tortured, as he was *in extremis* at the scene of the crime and would die soon thereafter. Finally, even if the words of the slave are given any weight, the defendant deploys a new line of argument that it would be most unlikely for the defendant to plot his crime so poorly that there could be witnesses to his acts. Interestingly, each of these four counter arguments are deployed without reference to each other, unadorned by any evidence, in a single paragraph, seeming more like a list of argumentative *topoi* than consistently composed arguments.

The prosecution answers the defendant forcefully and directly. In the first instance, the defendant has argued that the murdered man may have been the victim of cloak thieves who hurried away before they could steal their clothes, perhaps because of the sudden appearance of others. The prosecutor points out that this has no bearing whatsoever on the case, given that regardless of the motive of the perpetrators, the dying slave testified that the defendant was the assailant. Furthermore, "it is not correct", the prosecutor says, "that the testi-

13 2.1.10: Note the striking similarity of the phrase οἵ τε γὰρ ἐπιβουλεύοντες ἀνεξέλεγκτοι ἂν εἶεν, εἰ μήτε ὑπὸ τῶν παραγενομένων μήτε ὑπὸ τῶν εἰκότων ἐξελέγχονται ("not only would it be impossible to convict deliberate criminals if they are not to be convicted by eyewitnesses and by such inferences") to the passage from 2.1.9 οἵ τε γὰρ ἐπιβουλεύοντες ἀνεξέλεγκτοι ἂν εἶεν, εἰ μήτε ὑπὸ τῶν παραγενομένων μήτε ὑπὸ τῶν εἰκότων ἐξελέγχονται.

14 2.2.7: Τοῦ δὲ ἀκολούθου ἡ μαρτυρία πῶς ἀξία πιστεύεσθαί ἐστιν "Why, moreover, should the evidence of the attendant be allowed any weight?".

15 The text suggests that the witnesses who testified that they had interrogated the slave were part of the family of the slave's owner. Nowhere else in 2 is this position refuted or developed.

mony of slaves is considered to be without credibility" (2.3.4: Ὀυκ ὀρθῶς δὲ τὴν τοῦ ἀκολούθου μαρτυρίαν ἄπιστον λέγουσιν εἶναι). For having given such evidence as this, he contends, slaves are not tortured, but in fact often given their freedom. It is only when slaves do such things as deny a theft or conspire with their masters to conceal a crime, presumably either by lying or remaining silent, that it is thought that torture will compel them to speak the truth. The prosecution returns at the conclusion of his second speech to the argument by which he concluded that if the judges refuse to convict when presented with arguments bolstered by both probabilities and the testimony of witnesses, then there is no possible way for justice to be obtained. The language the prosecutor uses here is very similar to that with which he uses in 2.1.9.[16]

In his second speech, the defendant once again returns to the credibility of the dying slave (2.4.6–7). How, he asks, can the evidence given by a slave be considered more trustworthy than that of a free man? (2.4.6–7: Τοῦ δὲ θεράποντος πῶς χρὴ πιστοτέραν τὴν μαρτυρίαν ἢ τῶν ἐλευθέρων ἡγεῖσθαι). The defendant points out that a citizen, if caught out in perjury can be fined and deprived of their citizenship, whereas this particular slave could have no such penalty held against his false testimony. Accordingly, there is no legal compulsion held against him that could guarantee his truthfulness.[17] Lastly the defendant argues, because the slave has died, he cannot be cross-examined and to condemn a man to death without the right of cross-examination would be an injustice. Following on this, the defendant then deploys a challenge, offering to turn over all his household slaves for examination under torture, holding that they will all support his contention that he was at home on the night of the murder.[18] This, he says, will prove his innocence not by mere likelihoods or conjectures, but Antiphon's word for "facts" is *erga*, which are in corroboration of the man's slaves as to his alibi. The defendant completes his counterargument by reiterating that the slave's testimony is not credible, all the more so because he cannot be cross-examined.

In the *Third Tetralogy* (Antiphon 4) an accusation of homicide, occasioned by a street brawl, is levelled against a defendant who offers a mitigating answer of self-defence to the charge. The prosecution's first speech is notably short and offers very little by way of argumentation, but focusses, in the main, on the pollution of the city caused by the death of the victim. The defendant offers a variety of plausible responses; that the deceased struck him first, that the vic-

16 See n. 13.
17 Cf. 2.2.7 where a free man's testimony is compared to that of a slave.
18 Cf. 1.6–13; 5.38, 74, 84; 6.27–28 for other similar challenges.

tim's death was unintentional, the likelihood of the younger, stronger victim being the aggressor in the assault, that intention is a central matter that must be proven in a homicide case, and that the fight was not the cause of the victim's death, that having been caused by the malpractice of the attending physician. As we should expect, refutation of these commonplaces is the focus of the prosecutor's second speech (4.3).

The defendant attacks those counter-arguments in the *prooimion* of 4.4. The prosecutions "inferences" (*tekmēria*) he says "are not plausible", as they could as easily be applied to the defence as the prosecution. He argues that the prosecutor's claim, for instance, that the defendant would be more likely to be the aggressor in the brawl than the victim because of his relative youth is absurd. If this were true then all youths would be automatically judged to be guilty and the jury would be forced to ignore their knowledge that many young men are prudent and that many older men are querulous. As these commonplaces could be bent to either position, they are argumentatively useless. All things being equal, that is to say the probabilistic arguments of the commonplaces working equally well for either side, the defendant argues that his case is stronger because he can produce witnesses that the victim struck the first blow,[19] and on account of this, the defendant must be acquitted. Finally, as he concludes his speech the defendant summarises his arguments and introduces an unimpeachable set of witness testimony. Returning to his claim that the physician's malpractice was the cause of the victim's death he cavalierly points out that this has been corroborated by the testimony of eyewitnesses.

If we look, then at these appearances of commonplaces regarding witnesses in the *Tetralogies*, several matters of note arise. What we find in the *Tetralogies* are not fully deployed arguments but a set of abstracts associated with highly generalised hypothetical cases. Within these "cases" what we see is much more like a list of possible lines of argument that could be deployed at greater length in actual forensic discourse. For instance, the entirety of the first four commonplace lines of argument in the defendant's first speech in *Tetralogy* 1 is expressed in four consecutive sentences:

> τοῦ δὲ ἀκολούθου ἡ μαρτυρία πῶς ἀξία πιστεύεσθαί ἐστιν; ὑπό τε γὰρ τοῦ κινδύνου ἐκπεπληγμένον αὐτὸν οὐκ εἰκὸς ἦν τοὺς ἀποκτείναντας γνῶναι, ὑπό τε τῶν κυρίων ἀναγιγνωσκόμενον ἐπινεῦσαι ἦν εἰκός. ἀπιστουμένων δὲ καὶ τῶν ἄλλων δούλων ἐν ταῖς

19 4.4.3: κοινοῦ δὲ τοῦ τεκμηρίου ἡμῖν ὄντος <καὶ> τούτῳ, τῷ παντὶ προέχομεν· οἱ γὰρ μάρτυρες τοῦτόν φασιν ἄρξαι τῆς πληγῆς "as the presumption supports us as much as it does the dead man, the balance is in our favour; for according to the witnesses, it was he who was the aggressor".

> μαρτυρίαις – οὐ γὰρ ἂν ἐβασανίζομεν αὐτούς – πῶς δίκαιον τούτῳ μαρτυροῦντι πιστεύσαντας διαφθεῖραί με;
>
> As for the attendant's testimony, how can you believe it? Terrified by the danger, is it not likely that he recognised the killers, but it is likely he was persuaded to agree with his masters. Since the testimony of slaves in general is untrustworthy – otherwise we wouldn't torture them – how can it be right for you to believe this witness' testimony and destroy me?

We can compare this to Antiphon's prolix (1.6–13) treatment by the speaker in *Against the Stepmother for Poisoning* of his spurned challenge to his step brother that they hand over their slaves for torture. There the argument is amplified for a full seven sections, two pages of the Greek text.

There are, however, a number of theoretical statements in the *Tetralogies* that place testimony in relationship with other modes of argumentation, particularly probabilistic inferences. So, clearly, theorists at this point were working out, even if at a very simplistic level, the problems of argumentative validity and critical primacy. The author has his defendant point out, for instance, that commonplace lines of argument provide probabilities of equal weight to either side. So, for instance, the defendant in *Tetralogy* 3 points out that the *tekmēria* associated with the commonplace generated by the relative age of the combatants, could easily be reversed and applied to either side. That being so, the *tekmēria*, the "indicator", cannot be used to judge the case. As that defendant has witnesses, he argues that the jury should ignore those probabilistic inferences. Many of these principles appear more fully developed, both with concrete details and parenthetical discussions, in Antiphon's "genuine" forensic speeches.

Against the Stepmother for Poisoning (Antiphon 1) is, by any account, an unusual speech. The speech is a *katēgoria*, levelled against a woman, accusing her of having murdered her husband several years previously. The case is brought by the woman's stepson, perhaps her husband's illegitimate son. The speaker claims to have been told by his father, while that man was on his death bed, that the defendant, the man's wife, had poisoned him. The speech's vivid narrative conveys the prosecution's story, describing how the speaker's father and his friend, a certain Philoneos, had been poisoned by Philoneos' "mistress", or *pallakē*,[20] under strange circumstances. It is alleged that Philoneos

20 The unfortunate παλλακή would have been a slave, owned by Philoneos, who would act as Philoneos' "mistress", though see Bushala 1969 for a contrary position on her status as a slave.

had determined to sell his companion to a brothel and that the desperate woman had confided her anxieties to the speaker's stepmother. She, in turn, is alleged to have suggested that the *pallakē* administer a "love potion", presumably an aphrodisiac, both to Philoneos and to the stepmother's husband in order to stimulate the ardor of both men towards their respective mates. The prosecution claims, however, that this was a ruse devised by the stepmother, who provided the *pallakē* with a deadly poison instead of a love potion. Philoneos would die immediately. The father would linger on for some weeks and, supposedly, during that period told the speaker of the "real cause" of his death, pledging the boy by oath to get vengeance. Immediately subsequent to these events the *pallakē* was tortured and executed for the murders. Now, years later, the speaker, having come into his majority, has come forward, claiming to be the agent of his father's revenge.

Virtually the entirety of the speaker's case relies on his vivid rehearsal of this alleged conspiracy and fulsome vituperation heaped upon the stepmother and her sons who have spoken in her defence. The prosecution also presents a sustained argument (1.6–13) that the greatest proof sustaining his accusation is that the family has refused to turn over their household slaves to the prosecution for interrogation under torture.[21] The prosecution begins by laying out in detail the terms of the challenge. First, he chides his brother. How can he say that he is certain his mother did not commit the crime when he refuses to engage the only means of determining the truth, interrogating the slaves under torture? The "reverse hypothetical" is then put forward. Surely, the speaker says, if the torture of the slaves had not implicated their mother, the defence would have taken this as incontrovertible evidence of the woman's innocence. Declining the challenge, on the other hand, must mean that the defence fears what the slaves will say. Accordingly, the prosecution can put into the slave's mouths what they would have said had he been allowed to interrogate them, particularly, that they had knowledge of the stepmother's attempt to poison her husband on a previous occasion, when having been caught she had claimed that she was giving him an aphrodisiac, and that more generally they would corroborate the prosecution's allegations as to the events that led to the man's death. The speaker says that if the slaves had not corroborated his account under torture would have forced the speaker to shape his accusations to those

---

In the narrative she is described as accompanying Philoneos in a variety of settings. Her sale to a brothel would have, among many other things, represented a drastic decline in her status.

21 Much has been made of the "challenge" to turn slaves over for torture. See Johnstone 1999, 70–93 for a review of the issue.

facts (1.10: ἡ βάσανος ἀναγκάζοι τὰ γεγονότα κατηγορεῖν), as testimony creates facts which require one to make properly formed accusations. Following upon this the prosecution lays out another "reverse hypothetical" argument that if the roles had been reversed, and the prosecution had refused to hand over their slaves for interrogation, the opposition would surely have taken this as the strongest indication, *tekmēria* that he was lying. The reverse being the case, it is only fair that the same presumption be applied to his argument.[22]

On the Murder of Herodes (Antiphon 5) is the longest and, in some ways, the most complex Antiphonic discourse. The speech is an *apologia* made by a Mytilenean by the name of Euxitheus, who had been accused of a murder alleged to have taken place during a trading expedition to Thrace. The prosecution has alleged that Euxitheus murdered his traveling companion, Herodes, after a drinking party, and disposed of the body with the assistance of a slave. The slave admitted under torture to his part in the killing and, following this admission, had been executed. As physical evidence at the scene was found to be ambiguous at best, and the body of Herodes was never found, the greater part of the prosecution's case is either highly circumstantial or rests on the testimony of a tortured slave who, having been killed, cannot be cross-examined by the defendant.

The defence strategy is highly complex, having three separate tactical foci.[23] First, the defence argues vociferously that they are being tried in an inappropriate court. Typically, homicides (*dikē phonou*) were presented before the Areopagus where specialised oaths and different procedural rules were in place.[24] The prosecution, however, has brought the case as one against a common criminal (*kakourgia*) to be argued before the *dikastēria*, where Euxitheus feels greatly at a disadvantage. The first part, then, of Euxitheus' speech (5.8–19), as well as a good deal of the *epilogos*, is a vehement argument about this issue of jurisdiction. Secondly, and allied to this jurisdictional issue, is the fact that Euxitheus' father seems to have been associated with the revolt by the Mytilenaeans from the Athenian hegemony during the Peloponnesian War. As this may well have exercised a powerful prejudice on popular jury, Euxitheus attempts to portray his father as having been pro-Athenian during the revolt (5.74–78). The substantial refutation of the charges then, (5.20–73) are then framed by attention to

22 1.12: similar "reverse hypothetical" arguments will also be found at 5.38, 74, 84; 6.27–28.

23 Discussed at length in Farenza 2006, 320–329 in which the defendant is described as "performing innocence". Gagarin 1989 47–78 more helpfully examines the relationship between Euxitheus' testimony and *eikos*.

24 The *locus classicus* remains MacDowell 1963.

these matters. As we might expect, within the refutation proper Euxitheus focusses a great deal on the credibility of the slave, whose testimony supports the prosecution's case.

To counteract this testimony Euxitheus himself presents a number of witnesses to establish aspects of his case that he sees as being crucial; that he and Herodes were traveling to Thrace on legitimate business (5.21), that the travellers had been forced to put shore on account of a storm (5.22), that while ashore the merchants had engaged in a bout of drinking, following which Herodes had gone missing, and the next day Euxitheus sent a slave back to Mytilene to inform Herodes' family that he was missing before Euxitheus re-embarked for Thrace (5.24). Each of these "facts" (*erga*) established by Euxitheus' witnesses contradict features of the prosecution's narrative which the jury would have just heard. The prosecution had claimed, for instance, that Euxitheus had followed Herodes off of the boat during the drinking party and had struck him with a rock on the head. Euxitheus' witnesses, however, corroborate under oath that Euxitheus had never left the boat on the night of Herodes' disappearance. Similarly, Euxitheus' witnesses swear though that Herodes' family at first had claimed that blood was found in the boat where the men had been drinking but had withdrawn that claim when witnesses had testified that the blood had come from a sheep.

The most powerful prosecution evidence seems to have been the testimony of a slave, seized by Herodes' family at the scene.[25] That slave, upon initial verbal interrogation denied any knowledge concerning the disappearance of Herodes. When tortured, however, he testified that he had led Euxitheus and Herodes from the boat and that, after Euxitheus had killed Herodes, he had assisted Euxitheus in disposing of the body by putting the corpse in a boat and throwing it into the sea. Once the torture ended, however, and Herodes' family told the slave that he was to be executed for his part in the slaying, the slave recanted his testimony and said that both he and Euxitheus were victims of an injustice. Building on these dramatic events Euxitheus' task is to argue that the slave's original and final testimonies were true while the testimony made while being tortured should be dismissed. Euxitheus submits two subsidiary arguments to bolster this position. The first is that the prosecution has killed the slave in order to prevent him from testifying as to the truth under interrogation by Euxitheus. A second argument is derived from a Mytilenaean citizen, who

25 For a full discussion of the possible status of the two tortured witnesses see Gagarin 1989, 58–63; Gagarin 1998, 58 n. 23; Edwards/Usher 1985, 68–124.

had also been interrogated under torture who had steadfastly refused to implicate Euxitheus before, during, or after his *basanos*.[26]

The torture of these two witnesses gives Euxitheus the opportunity to advance arguments against the credibility of testimony given under torture. For instance, at 32 Euxitheus appeals directly to conventional wisdom, "you know that those who are interrogated normally testify in favour of those who have most control over the interrogation and say whatever will be pleasing to them". Oddly, Euxitheus extends his critique by pointing out that, "If I had ordered him to be put on the rack for not telling the truth, this alone would likely make him recant his false accusations" (5.32). Obvious logical inconsistency does not detain Euxitheus from complaining that the torture of the prosecution had led almost inevitably to falsehoods, but that if he had been given access to the slave his tortures would have resulted in the slave telling the truth.

Because Euxitheus' case is so greatly concerned with the relative credibility of witnesses, enslaved and free, corroborating and contradictory, qualified by torture and oath, we should not be surprised that we find embedded in the speech a number of statements that, taken together, point towards a theory of interpretation. Some of these are mere re-statements of the conditions of commonplaces, adjusted in force to advance the speaker's strategic manoeuvres. For instance, we see an extended attack on testimony gained through torture (5.31–42), which is generally consistent with other arguments in several Antiphonic discourses. Similarly, we find the "reverse hypothetical" manoeuvre, expressed at 5.38 in a number of other places.[27]

This case, though, offers Antiphon the opportunity to air more abstract considerations. For instance, at 5.39–42 Euxitheus compares the testimony of the slave and the free Mytilenaean, both of whom had been interrogated under torture. The slave had testified that Euxitheus was innocent before the torture, had implicated Euxitheus during the torture, but had recanted once the *basanos* was completed. The free man had corroborated Euxitheus' positions though, before, during, and after his torture. Antiphon argues that "the truth compelled" (5.41: ἀναγκαζόμενος ὑπὸ τοῦ ἀληθοῦς) both the slave and the free man to corroborate Euxitheus' story, while only the "necessity" of the wheel compelled the slave to lie. The difference is alluded to at Antiphon 5.31 where it is alleged that the interrogators had "probably" (ἴσως) offered the slave his freedom in exchange for testimony against Euxitheus, only to withdraw the offer as soon as they had testimony that favoured their position. By 5.50 this has be-

26 See, in particular, Gagarin 1998, 62 n. 28 on the status of the Mytilenaean citizen.
27 Cf. 2.4.8; 5.74, 84; 6.27–28.

come a "reality" that explains why the free man has never wavered in his statements. Simply put, the prosecution could not shake the compulsion of the truth by means of appeal to a stronger "necessity". Who then is to be believed? The witness whose testimony does not change. Consistency, then, emerges as a criterion for determining the probative value of testimony.

One unique set of witnesses that Euxitheus invokes, though he cannot call them to the bar, are the gods (81). If, he argues, he had committed the crime as the prosecution has alleged, the gods would have surely punished him. However, as his voyage concluded safely and profitably, the gods themselves must be pointing towards his innocence. "Indications from humans and witnesses (τῶν ἀνθρωπίνων τεκμηρίων καὶ μαρτυριῶν)", having been presented, signs from the gods (ἀπὸ τῶν θεῶν σημείοις) should also be considered. Euxitheus concludes his arguments by an extended reiteration of the grounds by which his divine witnesses should be believed and the prosecution's not given any credence (5.84). He begins with yet another "reverse hypothetical" tactic, arguing that if his voyage had ended in disaster, surely the prosecution would have said that this was a divine sign of Euxitheus' guilt. However, these signs (σημείων) contradict the prosecution's hypothesised assertions as do the greatest number of witnesses. Euxitheus would have it that the prosecution calls upon the jury to disbelieve all of Euxitheus' witnesses and "signs", relying only on their words (λόγοι) to establish their case. In doing so, he says, "where all other men test arguments with facts, these would use arguments to discredit facts" (5.84: καὶ οἱ μὲν ἄλλοι ἄνθρωποι τοῖς ἔργοις τοὺς λόγους ἐλέγχουσιν, οὗτοι δὲ τοῖς λόγοις τὰ ἔργα ζητοῦσιν ἄπιστα καθιστάναι). This formula, appearing elsewhere,[28] helps establish an interpretive hierarchy where facts are superior to words alone, facts are indicated by *sēmeia* and *tekmēria*, and verdicts need to be determined by facts.

The argumentative economy of *On the Choreutes* (Antiphon 6) has a broad resemblance to that of the *Second Tetralogy*. The *Second Tetralogy* is an abstracted case of an accusation of homicide following the death of a student on a training field. In *On the Choreutes* the wealthy patron of a choir has been accused of murder when a chorister dies as the result of having been administered a (poisonous) medicinal draught by the patron's lieutenant. The defendant in this case employs a number of lines of argument that are rehearsed in the *Second Tetralogy*. The first argument (6.2) praises the law upon which the defendant rests his case, as does in the *Second Tetralogy*.[29] Much is also made of the

28 Cf. 6.47, 87; 6.3–6 and note in Loeb p. 22.
29 Cf. 3.2, 9–10; 3.4.10; 5.14.

spiritual proofs and consequences of civic miasma as we see in several of Antiphon's texts.[30]

The defendant first produces witnesses (6.16) to the effect that he neither told the boy to drink the potion, compelled him to do so, nor was even present at the event. Furthermore, he argues that he had taken an oath during the preliminary depositions that he neither instigated nor took any part in the killing. As the prosecution has sworn a similar oath, claiming that the defendant is responsible for the boy's death, the case must turn on which of these two opposing testimonies should be given credence. Again, arguments based on probabilities alone are seen as being of equal probative value for either side. Consistent testimony is superior to probabilities alone as testimony can point to the corroborating indicators of the truth of the matter.

At 18–19 the defendant points out that many murders take place in private spaces without witnesses, and in such cases as these the jury must rely on the accounts of the litigants alone, making their decisions based on conjectures rather than on certain knowledge.[31] This death, however, took place before a number of witnesses. Hence, a rule of argument might be that positions supported by witnesses, especially multiple witnesses, are superior to conjectures drawn from the statements of interested parties that are not corroborated by such testimony.[32]

The defendant then (23) lays out the strategic maneuver that he had made when first accused, challenging the prosecution to interrogate the witnesses, slave and free, who were present at the boy's death. The free citizens would have been interrogated under oath, as was appropriate to their status. The defendant says that he offered to make his slaves available for interrogation with or without *basanos*, and to convince the owners of any other slaves who had been present, presumably by buying or indemnifying them, to turn the slaves over for similar questioning. As the prosecution had rejected the challenge, the defendant claims that they did so because of their fear of the exonerating testimony that would have resulted.

The defendant expands on the entailments of this challenge (25–29) in a number of ways. First he argues that justice is most clearly obtained when a litigant's position is confirmed by witnesses and the more witnesses, slave or free, that can corroborate a proof the more secure we can be in the truth of the

30 Cf. 2.1.3, 9; 3.1.2; 4.3.6; 5.88, 96.

31 Cf. 6.18.

32 Cf. 2.4.

claims.[33] He reiterates that a free man's honesty is guaranteed by the making of an oath, while slaves are compelled to the truth by other "necessities", that is to say, torture.[34] He then goes on to praise the efficiency of these 'other means' as causing slaves to testify truthfully, even when the slaves know that it will lead to their own destruction, as their desire to relieve they immediate agony will outweigh their fears of what they will suffer in the future. Accordingly, the prosecution should not be believed.

Following upon this the defendant lays out a complex hypothetical argument, that if the prosecution had offered similar witnesses and the defendant had refused to interrogate them, the prosecution would have surely presented that as being the strongest evidence (μέγιστα τεκμήρια) that the defence was not speaking the truth.[35] This reverse hypothetical then should provide the jury with a powerful indication (τεκμήριον) that the prosecution is lying. Furthermore, the defendant invites the jury to consider how the prosecution would have argued if they had had the number of witnesses that the defence has produced. If they had had many witnesses they would have argued that this was a formidable proof of the truth of their claim. The opposite being the case, the defendant argues that it is only fair that they be given the same advantage. This is even surer, he argues because his many witnesses have testified consistently from the first that the defendant had nothing to do with the chorister's death.

Immediately following this (30–31) the defendant shifts to make an extremely important statement about the relative probative value of corroborated and uncorroborated arguments. If a position is advanced by words (λόγῳ) or arguments alone, but not supported by witnesses, one would say that the argument needed corroboration, just as if the testimony that was provided did not agree with the indications (or presumptions), the τεκμήρια drawn from the witnesses. More simply put, inconsistent testimony would be as suspect as a litigant's statement that could not be corroborated. However, he says, he has made a reasonable account and produced witnesses that agree with his account,[36] preceding with an interesting series. His facts, he says, are in accordance with the testimony (τοῖς μάρτυσι τὰ ἔργα), and with the indications drawn from those facts (τεκμήρια ἐξ αὐτῶν τῶν ἔργων), and that the strongest and greatest of

33 Cf. 1.11; 5.84.

34 On the use of oaths in Athesian trials see Mirhady 1991b, 2000; Gagarin 1997.

35 Cf. 1.4; 5.84.

36 Cf. 6.31: ἐγὼ τοίνυν τούς τε λόγους ὑμῖν εἰκότας ἀποφαίνω τοῖς λόγοις τοὺς μάρτυρας ὁμολογοῦντας "now in my own case, you are being presented with an account which is reasonable, with evidence which is consistent with that account".

these facts is that the prosecution has failed to accept the challenge offered by the defendant to produce his witnesses for interrogation. The series indicates that arguments need witnesses and witnesses need arguments, linking in a hierarchy reasonable accounts, witnesses that agree with those accounts, facts that can be established by that testimony, and presumptions drawn from those facts. Tellingly, in the conclusion, the defendant says that honest men attempt to establish arguments by means of facts but that the prosecution, in this instance, seeks to establish absurd facts by means of arguments alone.[37] So, at least in this case the speaker would take "facts" (ἔργα) as probative and arguments (λόγοι) as merely indicative.

We can now give shape to some general conclusions about Antiphon's conceptions of two related matters; the practical need to either qualify or disqualify the testimony of witness at trial, and the contribution of such testimony to a more general theory of argumentation. In doing so, it is important to note that no claim is made to Antiphon being an original theorist of argumentation. However, it would be just as mistaken to say that he operated under no theory of argumentation at all. These nascent theories can be gathered together from his paratextual statements and from them can be abstracted some preliminary, quasi-technical notions.

The first set of principles of argumentation are focused on the value of testimony drawn from different classes of witnesses. Premises such as these are hardly statements of theory at all, but merely mark opportunities for making tactical maneuvers within the operations of familiar commonplaces. Such premises would include statements such as: slaves are generally unreliable witnesses, are less credible then freemen, and can be expected to seek the approval of their interrogators. Allied to these are notions associated with the use of torture to qualify the testimony of slaves: that who have not been tortured can be assumed to be liars, and that the use of torture can force slaves to speak truthfully, and that on account of this, being unwilling to turn over slaves upon challenge is a strong sign of furtiveness. Adoption of these premises makes plausible the use of "reverse hypotheticals" that can be used to expose the probative value of an opponent's positions. Contrary positions in this game of tactical argumentation would be that slaves sometimes do testify truthfully and are rewarded for it, or that slaves are only tortured when accused of committing or

37 Cf. 6.47: ἄλλοι ἄνθρωποι τοῖς ἔργοις τοὺς λόγους ἐξελέγχουσιν οὗτοι δὲ τοῖς λόγοις ζητοῦσι τὰ ἔργα ἄπιστα καταστῆναι "whereas other people use the facts to prove the worth of mere assertion, they use mere assertion for the purpose of discrediting the facts". Cf. 5.84.

concealing a crime, and that torture causes witnesses to seek to gratify their interrogators with false testimony.

We also see a number of more general concepts related to witnesses that extend our understanding of the general functioning of sophistic argumentation. Several of these premises nuance the centrality of *eikos* as a criterion for the judgement of arguments. For instance, reliable witnesses corroborate and establish facts (*erga*) that would otherwise be weak arguments based on mere probabilities, and truth is better established by probabilities and witnesses than by probabilities alone. The quantity of evidence to be adduced is also raised, as the accuracy of an account is better established by many witnesses than fewer, less by one, and least of all by none. Indeed, multiple witnesses offer a higher level of corroboration of facts. Importantly, not only must there be a sufficiency of evidence to establish facts, testimony must be consistent across times and circumstances. Consistent witnessing is more credible than testimony that changes and is an important criterion for judgement of its truthfulness, while inconsistent testimony is as problematic as uncorroborated argument. In addition, the mere presence of testimony is not enough, testimony that cannot be cross-examined is not credible. Consistent, sufficient, examined testimony, then, is of powerful, probative value, to the extent that justice would be impossible if probabilities corroborated by witnesses could not persuade a finder of fact.

Finally, at the highest level of generality we find a number of criteria for the judgement of arguments. These can be described as unequivocally pointing towards an increasingly self-awareness of argumentative criteria and hierarchies within the probative values of arguments. The first matter to note is Antiphon's recognition of the weakness of the commonplace lines of argument themselves. He notes, for instance, that transposable arguments are neither credible nor reliable, as the "plausibilities" of uncorroborated *eikos* arguments are equally weighted for both interlocutors. Such probabilities, however, can be made reliable by witnesses. Indeed, witnesses can establish or corroborate statements (*logoi*) to such a degree that they become "facts" (*erga*). These facts (*erga*) are of a higher probative value than mere words (*logoi*); facts must establish arguments and words cannot disestablish facts. This points to a hierarchy of probative claims. Facts are established by witnesses and these allow arguers to base their contentions more securely than might conjectures (*eikazontas*). Arguments without facts or witnesses are either absurd (if opposed by facts) or mere conjectures or probabilities. These "facts", in turn, can be used to propose *tekmēria*. *Tekmēria* are the "indicators" that anchor arguments in reality. Antiphon's hierarchy seems to be that conjecture (*eikazontas*) can point towards probabilities (*eikos*), which, when corroborated by witnesses, can yield facts (*erga*), and these facts, in turn, can act as indications (*tekmēria*) of the truth of a statement. By this somewhat attenuated process testimony establishes facts that force parties to properly shape and advance arguments.

These notions are more abstract, and go to the criteria by which arguments can be assessed. Within these criteria Antiphon recognises interpretive hierarchies that govern the probative value of arguments. These concepts are probably not constructed systematically, indeed they are most likely conventional sophistic notions. That, in a way, makes them more important. The position of the chapter is that Antiphon is not original in his thinking but reflective of general sophistic positions and practices. These findings then point to a nascent, quasi-technical vocabulary and conceptual structure, and support for a position that sophistic argumentation in the 5th century was becoming more sophisticated than the standard account would lead one to expect.

Bibliography

Bonner, R.J. (1912), 'Evidence in the Areopagus', in: *CPh* 7, 450–456.
Carawan, E. (1993), 'The Tetralogies and Athenian Homicide Trials', in: *AJPh* 114, 235–270.
Dover, K.J. (1950), 'The Chronology of Antiphon's Speeches', in: *CQ* 44, 44–60.
Due, B. (1980), *Antiphon: A Study in Argumentation*, Copenhagen.
Edwards, M./Usher, S. (1985), *Greek Orators I: Antiphon and Lysias*, Warminster.
Farenga, V. (2006), *Citizen and Self in Ancient Athens: Individuals Performing Justice and the Law*, Cambridge.
Gagarin, M. (1989), *The Murder of Herodes: A Study of Antiphon 5*, Frankfurt am Main.
Gagarin, M. (1990), 'The Nature of Proofs in Antiphon', in: *CPh* 85, 22–32.
Gagarin, M. (1996), 'The Torture of Slaves in Athenian Law', in: *CPh* 91, 1–18.
Gagarin, M. (1997), *Antiphon: The Speeches*, Cambridge.
Gagarin, M. (2002), *Antiphon the Athenian: Oratory, Law, and Justice in the Age of the Sophists*, Austin, TX.
Gagarin, M. (2003), 'Telling Stories in Athenian Law', in: *TAPhA* 133, 197–207.
Gagarin, M./MacDowell, D.M (1998), *Antiphon and Andocides*, Austin, TX.
Gernet, L. (ed.) (1920), *Antiphon: Discours*, Paris.
Goebel, G.H. (1989), 'Probability in the Earliest Rhetorical Theory', in: *Mnemosyne* 42, Fasc. 1/2, 41–53.
Johnstone, S. (1999), *Disputes and Democracy: The Consequences of Litigation in Ancient Athens*, Austin, TX.
Kennedy, G.A. (1959), 'The Earliest Rhetorical Handbooks', in: *AJPh* 80, 169–178.
Kennedy, G.A. (1963), *The Art of Persuasion in Greece*, Princeton, NJ.
MacDowell, D.M. (1963), *Athenian Homicide Law in the Age of the Orators*, Manchester.
Maidment, K.J (1941), *Minor Attic Orators in Two Volumes: I Antiphon Andocides*, Cambridge, MA.
Martin, G. (2008), 'The Witness's "Exomosia" in Athens', in: *CQ* 58, 56–68.

Mirhady, D.C. (1991a), 'Non-Technical *pisteis* in Aristotle and Anaximenes', in: *AJPh* 112, 5–28.
Mirhady, D.C. (1991b), 'The Oath-Challenge in Athens', in: *CQ* 41, 78–83.
Mirhady, D.C. (1996), 'Torture and Rhetoric in Athens', in: *JHS* 116, 119–131.
Mirhady, D.C. (2002), 'Athens' Democratic Witnesses', in: *Phoenix* 56, 255–274.
Radermacher, L. (1951), *Artium Scriptores: Reste der voraristotelischen Rhetorik*, in: *Sitzungsberichte der Osterreichische Akademie der Wissenschafter, philosophisch-historische Klasse*, 227, no. 3.
Rubinstein, L. (2000), *Litigation and Cooperation: Supporting Speakers in the Courts of Classical Athens*, Stuttgart.
Schmitz, T.A. (2000), 'Plausibility in the Greek Orators', in: *AJPh* 121, 47–77.
Sealey, R. (1984), 'The *Tetralogies* Ascribed to Antiphon', in: *TAPhA* 114, 71–85.
Tindale, C. (2010), *Reason's Dark Champions: Constructive Strategies of Sophistic Argument*, Columbia, SC.

Part III: **Scripting Witnesses and Evidence: Prose and Verse Texts**

Andreas Serafim

The Questions in (Answering the Question about the Historicity of) Plato's *Apology of Socrates*

Abstract: This chapter aims to investigate the frequency of questions, their content and their placement in the transmitted script of Plato's *Apology of Socrates.* It will be argued that questions are used because they serve Socrates' interests in three specific ways: first, to help him get into the gist of the case and, using Meletus' answers and reactions to the interrogatories, to present rhetorical and, in some cases, non-verbal evidence for the defendant's innocence and for his accuser's lies; second, to describe the *ēthos* of litigants; and third, to convey a message to the audience about the verdict Socrates thinks the judges should cast about him. This chapter also aims to use questions as evidence of the factuality and veracity of the speech that Plato attributes to his teacher.

1 Introduction

The idea of preparing this chapter was given to me by Professor Gerhard Thür, who insisted that the rhetorical value of the questions in Plato's *Apology of Socrates* should at last be thoroughly examined, not least because they relate to, and shed useful light on, the features and functions of the Aristotelian "artful"/ "artistic" proofs (i.e. *ēthos*, *pathos* and *logos*), while also providing rhetorical evidence for Socrates' innocence and helping us think about the veracity of the speech that Plato puts into the mouth of his teacher.[1] Professor Thür and I agree that questions are thoughtlessly and mistakenly considered today as a hackneyed part of law-court etiquette, which makes it compulsory for speakers to include them in their speeches.[2] The truth is that there is no pattern of rhetorical persuasion mandatory for speakers to use because of the institutional etiquette

1 This paper is dedicated to Professor Gerhard Thür: his world-known erudition and intellectual scholarship has ignited the interest of researchers in, and further help the establishment of, the study of ancient Greek law and rhetoric in modern academia. I would also like to thank Millie Gall for reading and commenting on a draft of this paper.

2 On the features and value of interrogation, the article of Carawan 1983, 209–226 is still useful.

https://doi.org/10.1515/9783110751970-008

of a particular forum; they had at their disposal a pool of techniques they could use for persuasion, but it was their choice how and when to use them. That is why, for example, we can only find a few references to religious discourse even in speeches which are formally about religious matters.[3] Questions in Plato's *Apology of Socrates* are used because they are a means of serving the defendant's strategic interests and purposes in a legal case that he knew it would cost his life.

It is true, of course, that questions were customarily used in the legal process of *anakrisis*,[4] and the process of *elenchus*, cross-examination, in which, as Dem. 46.10 and Isae. 6.12 indicate, it was compulsory for the parties involved in the interrogation to answer to each other's questions. The transmitted script of the *Apology* "shows Socrates adapting his own characteristic method of argument to the conventions of the courts where the law required an answer, and for the most part the questioning is based on the wording of the indictment recorded at the *anakrisis*. This kind of cross-examination based on the arguments put forward at the *anakrisis* seems to be typical of *erōtēsis* in the extant speeches [cf. Lys. 12.24–26, 22.5; Isae. 11.4–6]".[5] But even in this case the defendant was not obliged to use questions as cleverly and strategically as Socrates did in his oration, and certainly not in the high frequency with which questions are used in the *Apology*: in 39 sections of the speech, a ratio of 31.2%.[6]

---

3 "There is a remarkable absence, in the speeches of Lysias, of references to the gods, the divine and other matters of religious importance from several speeches of all oratorical kinds – public forensic orations. It is surprising that two of the three speeches that relate to impiety (what is known in ancient Greek law as γραφὴ ἀσεβείας) do not include any examples of religious discourse, as one might reasonably expect. This is in sharp contrast with Demosthenes' *Against Androtion*, a public indictment for impiety, in which I counted ten instances of religious discourse. [...] This may point to Lysias' personal distaste for religious arguments, since there is no, or at least no explicit, manifest and artful rhetorical reason behind the general omission of religious references from public forensic speeches"; Serafim 2020c, 52, 74.

4 During *anakrisis*, the preliminary hearing of a case before an *archōn* of the city-state, who had the right to ask questions to the litigants, they themselves were also entitled to question each other, as they were obliged to disclose their arguments, witnesses and other evidence that would support the presentation of the case. The purpose of this legal process was to find out if the case should be presented before the court, and "how exactly the question was to be framed", as Harrison 1971, 96–97 points out. Further on *anakrisis*: Carawan 1983, 211–212; Kremmydas 2018, 110–131.

5 Carawan 1983, 216.

6 The percentage given in the brackets is the quotient of the number of sections with questions (39) and the total number of sections in the *Apology of Socrates* (125).

Much has been written in discussing the content of the *Apology*, its reflections upon the life of Socrates, his arguments, points of philosophy and rhetorical techniques of persuading the judges.[7] More can be said, however, about the content, style, place and importance of questions as "artful"/"artistic" proofs that aim for rhetorical persuasion, beyond what is said about questions being a customary part of *anakrisis* and *elenchus*, or aiming to serve Plato's choice to "recreate a specimen of the question-and-answer style that dominates the dialogues".[8] This chapter aims to investigate and discuss the content, place and rhetorical use of questions, as they are incorporated in the transmitted script of the *Apology*. It will be argued that these questions are used because they serve the defendant's interests in three specific ways: first, to help him get into the gist of the case and, using Meletus' answers to the interrogatories, to present rhetorical evidence for his innocence and for his accuser's lies; second, to describe the *ēthos* of litigants; and third, to convey a message to the audience about the verdict Socrates thinks the judges should cast about him. This chapter also aims, by referring to the use of questions in the *Apology*, to offer a solution to the conundrum of the historicity and factuality of the speech that Plato attributes to Socrates, i.e. whether or not it presents the *ipsissima verba* of what was said in court. A comparison between the two main accounts of Socrates' apology by Plato and Xenophon with regard to the use of questions in particular may reveal, as will be argued below, that the same pattern of questioning is adopted by both authors and attributed unanimously to their teacher.

Questions always serve an important rhetorical purpose; their use in oratorical texts is not without meaning or potential to affect the cognitive/emotional perception of the audience. In two recently published papers, "Language and persuasion in Attic oratory: Imperatives and questions", and "ΕΡΩΤΗΣΟΝ ΑΥΤΟΥΣ: Questions, rhetorical purpose and *hypocrisis* in Attic forensic oratory", I argue that questions, when used skilfully, become a powerful weapon in the rhetorical arsenal of the speaker, who is enabled to recount events or actions of the historical past and attack opponents; to cover up weaknesses of speeches;

---

7 On the rhetorical structure of the *Apology*, which consists of a preface, *tractatio* and epilogue: Burnet 1924, 64–67; Strycker and Slings 1974, 21–25; McCoy 2008, 26.

8 Miller and Platter 2010, 65. Memorable is the volume edited by Gower and Stokes 1992 on Socratic questions, with Kidd in that volume (pp. 82–92) examining them with the aim of reconstructing the philosophical portrait of Socrates, but not of exploring the oratorical character and purposes of questioning specifically in the *Apology*. McCoy 2008, 23–31 offers useful information about how rhetorical techniques are used, in the *Apology*, for persuasion and for making "philosophical claims about the nature of wisdom, courage, piety and justice" (p. 24); little attention is paid, however, on rhetorical questioning *per se*.

to defend and absolve himself; and to address the audience directly in order to instruct its members in what and how they should think about the case.[9]

Ancient rhetorical treatises also refer to the potential of questions to influence the audience: [Longinus], in *On the Sublime* 18.1–2, for example, argues that questions add to the vehemence of a speech, rendering it a means of attacking the opponents. This purpose of using questions is also underlined by Demetrius, who, in his treatise *On Style* 279, points out that "in speaking it is sometimes forcible to address questions to the audience without disclosing one's own view. For instance: 'nay, he was appropriating Euboea and establishing a fortress to command Attica; and in so doing was he wronging us and violating the peace, or was he not?' The orator forces his hearer into a sort of corner, so that he seems to be brought to task and to have no answer. If the positive statement 'he was wronging us and violating the peace' were substituted, the effect would be that of precise information rather than of cross-examination". For Hermogenes, in his treatise *On Types of Style* 239, the orators employ questions followed by answers in their speeches to make them distinct and to engage the audience. In his own words: "a speech also becomes distinct whenever the speaker asks himself a question and then replies after a brief pause. Demosthenes often does this by saying something like 'Why do I say this?' or 'How then is this true?' or 'Why is this so?' He uses many such devices in the speech *Against Aristocrates*, since he is examining an illegal procedure, a topic that demands a great deal of clarity".[10] In a similar vein, Tiberius recognises four functions of questions: to engage the audience and grasp the attention of its members, to clarify matters, to create vividness or to convey excitement, and to refute an opponent's arguments (*Figures* 13).

Modern scholars tend to focus on, and write about, the questions that are put to Meletus in the well-known interrogative *elenchus* from 24b3 to 28a5. Stokes, for example, argues that "Socrates' interrogation falls into two sections. The first section argues that Meletus has paid no attention to the subject concerning which he accuses Socrates, namely the education of the young. The second, though not announcing at 26b2 any change of tack, emerges at 27a1–7 with the conclusion that Meletus is a frivolous litigant; further debate down to 27e3 substantiates the frivolity by demonstrating self-contradiction, and is followed by the suggestion that the charge is trumped up in default of a true

9 Serafim 2020b, 1–19; Serafim 2020d.
10 Translation: Wooten 1987, 16–17.

one".[11] This succinct description of the content of the interrogation of Meletus by Socrates accurately describes the strategy of the speaker. It should be noted, however, that questions are not only included in the part of the speech that contains the interrogative *elenchus*, but also in other parts. I counted four such parts: 19b–23d, 24c–34d and 36b–41c; questions, as one can see, are evenly distributed throughout the speech, from exordium to peroration. Questions aim to serve a variety of rhetorical purposes: they can be *introductory* or *explanatory* (19b–23d), as they help the speaker get into the gist of the case, explain his arguments and present rhetorical evidence for his innocence and for Meletus' lies; *ēthos-depicting* (24c–34d), since these are used to describe the *ēthos* of litigants, i.e. to undermine the prosecutor, Meletus, and to present the defendant, Socrates, positively; and *investigatory* (36b–41c), in the sense that these questions are used as a means of determining what is the fair and measured punishment that Socrates should receive at the end of the trial.

It might be interesting to make the point here that questions in Plato's *Apology of Socrates* have some affinities with the patterns of using questions in Attic forensic speeches that I identified in my recently published papers about questions, which are cited above. Questions are used, *nach athenischem Muster* ("according to the Athenian way"), to paraphrase Thür,[12] as a means of attacking the opponents and referring to the speaker himself for the purpose of self-praise, defence and absolution (cf. Lysias 24–26 for a notable parallel to the line of interrogation in the *Apology*).[13]

2 Questions in the texts and contexts of the *Apology*

In what follows, I discuss some of the most salient passages in which questions are used as evidence to corroborate Socrates' key-arguments (as, for example, that he is not guilty of impiety or atheism), depict his *ēthos* positively, arouse emotions and persuade the audience. I do not side with those who think that

---

11 Stokes 1997, 128. A similar pattern of analysis can be found in Reeve 1989, 87, where we read: "The professed aim of Socrates' examination of Meletus is to show three things: (a) that Meletus has dealt frivolously with serious matters (24c9–25c4); (b) that he irresponsibly brought Socrates into court (25c5–26b2); and (c) that he professed to be seriously concerned with things about none of which he has ever cared (26b2–28a1)".

12 Thür 2014, 749.

13 On questions in Lysias 12: Edwards 1999, 96–97; Kapellos 2018, 51–64.

Socrates did not care about persuasion, or that his defence speech was inadequate or displayed rhetorical incompetence.[14] Socrates, in my view, did what any other orator would have done in his position, when delivering a defence speech: to defend himself, accuse his rivals and try to win over the audience, using all possible cognitive/emotional means of influencing the judges.

Let me start with the questions used in the first part of the *Apology* – the *introductory* or *explanatory* questions in 19b–23d. A notable passage is in 20c–d, where two questions are presented by an imaginary interlocutor:

> ὑπολάβοι ἂν οὖν τις ὑμῶν ἴσως: 'ἀλλ', ὦ Σώκρατες, τὸ σὸν τί ἐστι πρᾶγμα; πόθεν αἱ διαβολαί σοι αὗται γεγόνασιν; οὐ γὰρ δήπου σοῦ γε οὐδὲν τῶν ἄλλων περιττότερον πραγματευομένου ἔπειτα τοσαύτη φήμη τε καὶ λόγος γέγονεν, εἰ μή τι ἔπραττες ἀλλοῖον ἢ οἱ πολλοί. λέγε οὖν ἡμῖν τί ἐστιν, ἵνα μὴ ἡμεῖς περὶ σοῦ αὐτοσχεδιάζωμεν'.
>
> Now perhaps someone might rejoin: "But, Socrates, what is the trouble about you? Whence have these prejudices against you arisen? For certainly this great report and talk has not arisen while you were doing nothing more out of the way than the rest, unless you were doing something other than most people. So tell us what it is, that we may not act unadvisedly in your case".

Socrates has an imaginary interlocutor ask him two questions that would allow him to proceed with his speech and explain to the audience why the accusations against him are trotted out by his rivals. He could equally well have made an affirmative statement himself; the fact that he avoids making such a statement indicates that questions are not used randomly, thoughtlessly or without a specific purpose. Questions add to the dramatic solemnity of the moment, aiming to engage the audience and underline the importance of the defence that is about to begin (cf. Demetrius, *On Style* 279). That this is the purpose of Socrates, to increase dramatic tension and stir up emotions, is evident from the way in which he chooses to insert questions in the context of 20c–d: they are not to be taken as rhetorical questions, nor does the speaker direct them to himself (as, for example, the questions in other parts of the defence, e.g. in 20d and 21b); they are instead asked by an abstract interlocutor. This is *prosōpopoeia*, i.e. the act of having an abstract, imagined or absent entity speaking, which is a means of heightening the emotional character of a moment and maximising the influence of the speech on the audience.[15]

In this emotionally heightened context, Socrates attempts implicitly to present himself positively as a hero, who carries out noble actions. This technique

14 See, for example, Danzig 2003, 287.
15 On *prosōpopoeia* in Attic oratory: Westwood 2017, 57–74.

of positive self-description is more clearly articulated in the second section of the speech, especially in 28b–d, where Socrates refers to Achilles' unyielding adherence to principles, despite detrimental consequences for himself.[16] It is interesting that in 28b–d there is also an imaginary questioner who gets involved in conversation with Socrates:

> But perhaps someone might say: "Are you then not ashamed, Socrates, of having followed such a pursuit, that you are now in danger of being put to death as a result?" But I should make to him a just reply: "You do not speak well, Sir, if you think a man in whom there is even a little merit ought to consider danger of life or death, and not rather regard this only, when he does things, whether the things he does are right or wrong and the acts of a good or a bad man. For according to your argument all the demigods would be bad who died at Troy, including the son of Thetis, who so despised danger, in comparison with enduring any disgrace, that when his mother (and she was a goddess) said to him, as he was eager to slay Hector, something like this, I believe, "My son, if you avenge the death of your friend Patroclus and kill Hector, you yourself shall die; for straightway, after Hector, is death appointed unto you; "he, when he heard this, made light of death and danger, and feared much more to live as a coward and not to avenge his friends, and said, "Straightway may I die, after doing vengeance upon the wrongdoer, that I may not stay here, jeered at beside the curved ships, a burden of the earth". Do you think he considered death and danger?

So, despite the difference in the purpose of the questions (with those in 20c–d aiming to explain the case, and those in 28b–d aiming for the description of *ēthos* of the speaker), Socrates uses ring composition in his attempt to associate himself with the unyielding nobility of heroic figures. It seems to me that the decision to employ an imaginary interlocutor is more rhetorically astute than researchers have supposed: by having an interlocutor ask questions which invite the speaker to present himself positively, Socrates tries to strengthen the favourable portrayal of himself in a *seemingly objective way*. Demetrius, in his treatise *On Style* 288, underlines the rhetorical force of a similar technique, which he calls "covert allusion", whereby Plato, in the dialogue *Phaedo*, assigns to someone else what he wishes to point out.[17]

---

16 Stokes 1997, 142–143 also identifies the link that Plato (as he says) tries to make between Socrates' and Achilles' ideals of justice, but he does not identify and comment on the strategy of Socrates (as I say) to liken himself to a heroic character.

17 Demetrius, *On Style* 288: "Good taste is shown in the *Phaedo*, where Plato desires to reproach Aristippus and Cleombrotus because they were feasting at Aegina when Socrates was lying for many days imprisoned at Athens, and did not cross to visit their friend and master, although they were less than thirty miles from Athens. He has not said all this in express terms (for that would have been an open reproach), but with fitting reserve as follows. Phaedo is

The questions in the two sections mentioned above, 20d and 21b, are also worthy of note because they are asked and answered by the defendant himself:

> 20d: The fact is, men of Athens, that I have acquired this reputation on account of nothing else than a sort of wisdom. What kind of wisdom is this? Just that which is perhaps human wisdom. For perhaps I really am wise in this wisdom.
> 21b: But see why I say these things; for I am going to tell you whence the prejudice against me has arisen. For when I heard this, I thought to myself: "What in the world does the god mean, and what riddle is he propounding? For I am conscious that I am not wise either much or little. What then does he mean by declaring that I am the wisest? He certainly cannot be lying, for that is not possible for him". And for a long time I was at a loss as to what he meant; then with great reluctance I proceeded to investigate him somewhat as follows.

To ask and answer questions yourself is known, in ancient rhetorical theory, as *hypophora*, a figure of speech which, as Tiberius in *Figures* 3 points out, adds beauty and verve (κάλλος καὶ ἐνέργειαν) to an oration. Quintilian also refers to the "pleasing effect" of this technique (*Institutio Oratoria* 9.2.14). *Hypophora* may also be taken as a form of climax where "the answers to the questions make use of the answer technique which gradually intensifies the argument in favour of the party concerned".[18] Climax in the suggested answers to the questions in the *Apology* 21b is achieved by the reference to the divine dictum, which implicitly points to Socrates as being liked and respected by the gods, an idea that is repeated implicitly in 33c.[19] Socrates, in a sense, changes the rhetorical style and content of a defence speech into that of an epideictic oration, where humans are praised because of their devotion to the gods (cf. Isocrates, *To Demonicus* 13; *Panathenaicus* 204).[20]

---

asked who were with Socrates. He enumerates the men one by one. Next he is asked whether Aristippus and Cleombrotus were present. 'No', he answers; 'they were in Aegina'. Everything that precedes owes its point to the words 'they were in Aegina'. The passage is all the more forcible because its point is conveyed by the fact itself and not by the speaker. So, although he might no doubt have reproached Aristippus and his companions without incurring any risk, Plato has done so under cover of a figure".

18 Lausberg 1998, 342–343.

19 *Apology of Socrates* 33c: "But, as I believe, I have been commanded to do this [i.e. to talk to people] by the God through oracles and dreams and in every way in which any man was ever commanded by divine power to do anything whatsoever".

20 On the appeal of references to the gods and the divine in Attic oratory: Martin 2009; Serafim 2020c. Religious discourse is used periodically throughout the defence, as, for example, in 26d with two questions from Socrates to be focused on issues of belief: "Do I not even believe that the sun or yet the moon are gods, as the rest of mankind do? "No, by Zeus, judges, since he says that the sun is a stone and the moon earth." Do you think you are accusing Anaxagoras,

The second part of the *Apology* (24c–34d) contains what I call *ēthos*-depicting questions, as the positive references to the defendant himself in 28b-d (which are discussed above) indicate. The depiction of the litigants' characters, *ēthopoiia* as it is called in rhetorical theory, is a powerful means of persuasion. As Aristotle points out, "the orator persuades by moral character when his speech is delivered in such a manner as to render him worthy of confidence" (1356a4–6); and "character has almost, so to speak, the greatest authority in winning belief" (1356a13; cf. 1377b20–24; 1378a6–15). In Attic forensic oratory, the speaker has often two interrelated goals: to create a persona for himself that is relatable and appealing to the audience, and to undermine the persona of his opponent so that he emphasises the gap that (seemingly) exists between his rival and the audience. An incessant game of unity and division lies behind references to *ēthos*; the impact of this game upon the audience is studied in a recently published volume.[21]

In the second part of Socrates' defence, 24c to 34d, one can find many notable passages, including those in the extended subsection 24c–25e, where 23 questions are included. It was usual for the parties involved in litigation to ask each other questions during *anakrisis*, but the fact that so many questions are used in a row in eight consecutive sections of the speech says a lot about Socrates' skilful rhetorical strategy. His aim is to bombard Meletus with questions he cannot answer, and then use the resulting bewilderment as evidence that his accuser is a slanderer – this is what I call *non-verbal evidence*, evidence collected through observation of the physical or, more generally, non-verbal reactions of the addressee. The passage in 24d points to that purpose:

> ἴθι δή νυν εἰπὲ τούτοις, τίς αὐτοὺς βελτίους ποιεῖ; δῆλον γὰρ ὅτι οἶσθα, μέλον γέ σοι. τὸν μὲν γὰρ διαφθείροντα ἐξευρών, ὡς φῄς, ἐμέ, εἰσάγεις τουτοισὶ καὶ κατηγορεῖς: **τὸν δὲ δὴ βελτίους ποιοῦντα ἴθι εἰπὲ καὶ μήνυσον αὐτοῖς τίς ἐστιν.** —ὁρᾷς, ὦ Μέλητε, **ὅτι σιγᾷς** καὶ οὐκ ἔχεις εἰπεῖν; καίτοι οὐκ αἰσχρόν σοι δοκεῖ εἶναι καὶ ἱκανὸν τεκμήριον οὗ δὴ ἐγὼ λέγω, ὅτι σοι οὐδὲν μεμέληκεν; ἀλλ' εἰπέ, ὠγαθέ, τίς αὐτοὺς ἀμείνους ποιεῖ; οἱ νόμοι.
>
> Come now, tell these gentlemen who makes them better? For it is evident that you know, since you care about it. For you have found the one who corrupts them, as you say, and you bring me before these gentlemen and accuse me; **and now, come, tell who makes**

---

my dear Meletus, and do you so despise these gentlemen and think they are as unversed in letters as not to know, that the books of Anaxagoras the Clazomenian are full of such utterances?". On the epideictic nature of the *Apology*, see Perysinakis in this volume.

21 On unity and division in ancient Greek literature, and its persuasive dynamics: Michalopoulos, Serafim, Vatri and Beneventano 2021. On the performativity and persuasiveness of *ēthopoiia* in Attic forensic oratory: Serafim 2017, 25–28.

> **them better and inform them who he is.** Do you see, Meletus, that **you are silent** and cannot tell? And yet does it not seem to you disgraceful and a sufficient proof of what I say, that you have never cared about it? But tell, my good man, who makes them better? "The laws".

The rhetorical construction of this passage is as skilful as the speeches of the greatest orators in classical Athens are, as it is designed to increase the force and vehemence of the words uttered against the accuser of Socrates. It is not simply that there are three questions in a row that leave Meletus literally speechless until the end of the passage; it is also that Socrates asks a question at the beginning of the passage, then proceeds with two affirmative clauses, the second of which contains an indirect question (in bold face in the passage above), and then, without allowing Meletus to say a word, he accuses him of being silent. Meletus, in other words, is bombarded with consecutive questions, and is left "in a sort of corner" (to use the words of Demetrius in his treatise *On Style* 279), unable to defend himself properly. This pattern of questioning is not used once, but quite regularly in the interrogation part of the speech, as, for example, in 25a–b, where three questions are directed at Meletus, who has no opportunity to reply to them, as he should during *anakrisis*; instead, Socrates replies to his own questions (*hypophora*).[22] That is why Meletus is often tricked into accepting the arguments of Socrates, as, for example, in 27c–d where he admits that Socrates is not an atheist – this admission can be called *verbal evidence* (in contrast to *non-verbal evidence* that I mentioned above).[23]

Questions are used not only with the purpose of undermining the adversaries of Socrates, but also of enabling him to profile himself in the most positive way, as in the passages in 28b and d, which are discussed above. With the

---

22 *Apology of Socrates* 25a–b: "But answer me; does it seem to you to be so in the case of horses, that those who make them better are all mankind, and he who injures them some one person? Or, quite the opposite of this, that he who is able to make them better is some one person, or very few, the horse-trainers, whereas most people, if they have to do with and use horses, injure them? Is it not so, Meletus, both in the case of horses and in that of all other animals? Certainly it is, whether you and Anytus deny it or agree; for it would be a great state of blessedness in the case of the youth if one alone corrupts them, and the others do them good".

23 *Apology of Socrates* 27c–d: "But do we not think the spirits are gods or children of gods? Yes, or no? "Certainly." Then if I believe in spirits, as you say, if spirits are a kind of gods, that would be the puzzle and joke which I say you are uttering in saying that I, while I do not believe in gods, do believe In gods again, since I believe in spirits; but if, on the other hand, spirits are a kind of bastard children of gods, by nymphs or by any others, whoever their mothers are said to be, what man would believe that there are children of gods, but no gods?".

question in 33b–c Socrates implies that he is adored by the people ("but why then do some people love to spend much of their time with me?") and with the question in 34b that he is sincere as a truth-lover ("but what reason could their relatives have, who are not corrupted and are already older men, unless it be the right and true reason, that they know that Meletus is lying and I am speaking the truth?"). One of the most salient passages, in which Socrates tries to present himself in a positive way, is in 34d:

> [...] I have relatives and, men of Athens, I have three sons, one nearly grown up, and two still children; but nevertheless I shall not bring any of them here and beg you to acquit me. **And why shall I not do so?** Not because I am stubborn, Athenians, or lack respect for you. Whether I fear death or not is another matter, but for the sake of my good name and yours and that of the whole state, I think it is not right for me to do any of these things in view of my age and my reputation, whether deserved or not.

Socrates implicitly presents himself in this passage as being sincere, honest and principled, since he declares he would avoid bringing his children in court to try to deceitfully win over the judges, as others in Athens did repeatedly. Ample evidence shows that to bring children into the law-court was indeed a common practice that aimed to influence the verdict of the judges by appealing to their *epieikeia*, a means of tempering the strictness of the written legal statutes about the litigant's transgressions (cf. Aristotle, *Rhetoric* 1374a27, 1374b1ff. and *Nicomachean Ethics* 1143a21ff.). Speakers are worried about this technique being abused to deceive the audience. In Lysias 20.34, for example, it is claimed that sometimes the judges are so much influenced by the whining of the speaker's children that "they overlook the father's transgressions on account of the children". Demosthenes, in 21.99, refers to the (alleged) tactic that Meidias was about to use in order to elicit the pity of the judges: "pity, forsooth! He will group his children round him and weep and beg you to pardon him for their sakes. That is his last move. But I need not remind you that pity is the due of those who unjustly suffer more than they can endure, not of those who are paying the penalty for the misdeeds they have committed" (cf. 19.310; 21.186, 188; 38.27). Socrates does not follow the masses in trying to trick the judges, even when knowing that the cost of this trial may be his life. The question asked before his important self-depicting statement is not, from a purely factual perspective, necessary. It is used, however, as a clever means of emphasising what Socrates says. In fact, he says the same thing twice: the two negations that are used in context ("I shall not" and "why I shall not") turn out to be a strong positive statement.

The last part of Socrates' defence, in 36b–41c, purports to determine the appropriate punishment – thus the similar focus of all 17 questions that are asked.

This investigation gets intense in two consecutive sections, 37b–c, where 8 questions are asked, 7 of which in a row.

> I am certainly not going to wrong myself, and to say of myself that I deserve anything bad, and to propose any penalty of that sort for myself. Why should I? Through fear of the penalty that Meletus proposes, about which I say that I do not know whether it is a good thing or an evil? Shall I choose instead of that something which I know to be an evil? What penalty shall I propose? Imprisonment? And why should I live in prison a slave to those who may be in authority? Or shall I propose a fine, with imprisonment until it is paid? But that is the same as what I said just now, for I have no money to pay with. Shall I then propose exile as my penalty? Perhaps you would accept that. I must indeed be possessed by a great love of life if I am so irrational as not to know that if you, who are my fellow citizens, could not endure my conversation and my words, but found them too irksome and disagreeable, so that you are now seeking to be rid of them, others will not be willing to endure them. No, men of Athens, they certainly will not.

This passage indicates the rhetorically astute way Socrates attempts to anticipate what the judges may think about his punishment, rejecting one possibility after another – thus trying to leave the judges with no further options to consider when the time for casting their votes arrives. To do so by asking questions, instead of making affirmative statements, is to put more verve in the speech, grasp the attention and engage the audience, especially the judges, inviting them to listen carefully to Socrates' arguments.

3 Questions as evidence of the historicity of the *Apology*

It is evident, so far, that questions, as skilfully used by Socrates, are important aspects of the rhetorical nature of the oration, with which the defendant seeks to win over the audience and influence its verdict at the end of the trial. This section of my chapter focuses on the value of questions as evidence in the persistent debate over whether or not the speech that is attributed to Socrates represents reliably what he said in court. There is an intense controversy among scholars on this issue, which dates back more than a century. Grote (1875), Taylor (1911), Burnet (1924), Field (1930), Guthrie (1975), Brickhouse and Smith (1989), and Thür (2008) and (2014) are in favour of the historicist approach to the Platonic *Apology*. In opposition, Oldfather (1938), Chroust (1945) and (1957), West (1979), Kato (1991), Rutherford (1995) and Kahn (1996) consider the speech of Socrates to be Plato's masterful forgery, with Danzig (2003) insistently propagating the view that "Plato does not expect the reader really to believe that this is the speech that Socrates spoke in court".[24] Some other scholars argue that the Platonic *Apology* is a masterful imitation of Gorgias' *Defence of Palamedes.*[25] This argument is not based on solid evidence, however; the fact, for example, that both Socrates and Gorgias start with the claim that they are at a loss about how to talk to the audience does not mean that one of the two works copies the other. In fact, both use the *topos of inexperience*, which is used regularly and in many occasions in the speeches of the Ten Attic Orators that have come down to us in a textual form (e.g. Lysias 1.3).[26] Similarly, the fact that both defences refer to the "unliveable life" does not indicate that the Platonic *Apology* duplicates Gorgias' speech, given that this expression is also attested in other works of Greek literature, both rhetorical (cf. Antiphon 2.2.10) and non-rhetorical (cf. Xenophon, *Memorabilia* 4.8.8; Aristophanes, *Wealth* 967–969).

Given these deeply polarising arguments about the historicity and factuality of the *Apology*, a fully satisfactory and unanimously acceptable answer to this question cannot be found. After all, we were not present in court when Socrates delivered his speech. In the absence of audio-visual records of the ancient law-court proceedings, some amount of speculation will always remain an inevitable weakness of any interpretative approach to the transmitted texts, and a complete reconstruction of the speaker's *ipsissima verba* will perpetually elude us. Scholars who argue for the reliability of the *Apology* offer many reasonable considerations in support of their arguments. One of them is that the Platonic work was composed close to the trial, and, given that its author was present at the trial of Socrates, he would have memorised a great part of the speech that his teacher delivered. We should not forget that the ancients had honed skills (more so than we have) in memorising passages to be delivered in oral performances.[27] Another argument is that common knowledge by a large segment of

24 Danzig 2003, 293.

25 On the links between the *Apology* and *Palamedes*: Christ and Schmid 1912; Gomperz 1912, 9–11; Morr 1929, 29–34; Schmid and Stählin 1940, 74; Chroust 1957, 216–218; Calogero 1957, 12–17; Coulter 1964, 269–303; McCoy 2008, 31–39; and relatively recently Wallace 2013, 100.

26 Lysias 12.3: "hence I have been often overcome with a great feeling of despondency, from a fear lest my inexperience might cause me to fail in making a worthy and able accusation on my brother's and on my own behalf. Nevertheless I will try to inform you of the matter from the beginning, as briefly as I can". On the themes and topics of the *topos of inexperience* in Attic oratory: Lateiner 1982, 5, 7–8; Ober 1989, 226–231; Carey 1992, 92; Gagarin 1997, 17, 106–107; Kapparis 1999, 194–195; Hesk 2007, 371–372; Serafim 2020a, 71–98.

27 Memory is considered one of the five parts of rhetoric (together with invention, disposition, elocution and delivery). Cf. [Cicero] *Rhetorica ad Herennium* 1.3; Quintilian, *Institutio Oratoria* 3.3.1–3, 11–15. On poetry, memory and performance: Thomas 1992, 113–128.

the Athenian population of what was said in court would have inhibited Plato from forging Socrates' speech. It has been argued, in fact, that only in the case of unknown figures did the orators have the freedom to present the case as they wanted before the historical audience, i.e. the people who may have had personal knowledge of what happened in a specific case and what individuals did. "[Orators] manipulate the depiction of themselves and their opponents by deliberately choosing, altering and/or highlighting events of the past to project their characters in a specific way, overemphasising some of their traits and deemphasising others, but never fully fabricating characters. A modern reader may argue that the degree of fabrication of characters in Aeschines 2, 3 and in Demosthenes 18, 19 is completely unacceptable and incredible. The two orators, however, were experienced and they knew to what extent they could distort and exaggerate characters and facts without losing the audience's trust and goodwill".[28] It is presumably for this reason that Xenophon in his *Apology* does not claim he was present at the trial, but rather admits he received information from Socrates' companion, Hermogenes.

Questions, a significant aspect of the oratorical nature of the speech, can also tell us a lot about this daunting "true-speech" inquiry. I would like here to make a few points that come out my study of the oratorically clever use of questions in the defence of Socrates. First, common sense would suggest that of all the things one might include in a written script after the event, questions are perhaps among the most unlikely additions. The nature of the questions makes it more likely than not that they were included in the original speech. Questions may have deliberately been retained from the oral version to give a sense of dramatic immediacy to the speech and to conjure up the setting of the speech in the minds of the listeners and readers of the revised version. Questions directed by the speaker to himself, his opponent or the audience bring the written script of the speech to life, and allow the readers to picture the original better.[29] Also, as Carawan argues, "it appears to be an authentic feature in Plato's account that Socrates' interrogation is directed to the wording of the charges, to refute the accusations of corruption of the youth (24d–26a) and impiety towards the gods of the state (26b–27a)".[30] If this is accepted, at least in principle, then it results that the 39 sections of the speech which contain questions are likely to be genu-

28 Serafim 2017, 19.

29 Cf. Carawan 1983, 214 where a similar point is made concerning Lysias 24–26: "although the extant speech may represent a version revised for publication, it is unlikely that Lysias would have misrepresented the actual proceedings".

30 Carawan 1983, 216.

ine. Given that these sections cannot be separated from the text that precedes and follows them (since the speech exhibits admirably robust coherence from section to section), the number of genuine sections may increase.

Second, there seems to be a pattern of using questions in both of the existing scripts of Socrates' defence, one by Plato and another by Xenophon in his description of Socrates' conduct before, during and after trial. Despite the differences between these two accounts (in terms of the content; the authorial purpose, which is indicated, for example, by the presence of a narrator in Xenophon's account; and structure), both include questions in high frequency. I counted 16 sections with questions out of a total of 34 sections in Xenophon's account (or 47%), and I recognised the same threefold way of using them: there are, in other words, three functions of questions, *introductory or explanatory* (as those six that are used in sections 3–5), *ēthos-depicting* (as the questions that are used in sections 16–18 to praise Socrates and the one used in section 19 to attack Meletus) and, finally, *investigatory* questions (as the one used in section 24). The similarity in the frequency and the use of questions in both accounts may indicate that what is attributed to Socrates is what he said in court. Scholars may think that Xenophon imitates the style and the content of the Platonic work.[31] It is doubtful, however, whether he would have been able to follow Plato's exact, masterful and intricate way of presenting interrogation during the trial, if he had not received information from Hermogenes, who was present at Socrates' speech. This doubt is maximised by the fact that we do not have steady historical evidence that points to Plato's *Apology* having been composed before that of Xenophon.

Third, the examination of the patterns, the placement and the frequency of questions undeniably point to the *Apology* being a masterpiece of rhetorical eloquence. That is why I do not agree with suggestions that the speech should be taken primarily as a philosophical, not as a rhetorical or historical, document.[32] The speech of Socrates has all the virtues the masterpieces of the Ten Attic orators have: through questions in the *Apology*, the speaker shows competence in appealing to the audience, arousing emotions, incriminating the opponents and presenting himself positively – in short, he adopts astute rhetorical

31 The dependence of Xenophon's works on those of Plato has been the subject of research for many years. Huss 1999, 13–18, for example, dated Xenophon's *Symposium* with reference to its dependence on Plato's homonymous work. Cf. Bury 1932, LXVIII; Wimmel 1957; Thesleff 1978. Waerdt 1994 argues that Plato was the model for Xenophon's Apology. It has also been argued that Xenophon draws on two other Platonic works, Crito and Phaedo, when writing his *Apology*; Hogenmüller 2015, 127–138.

32 Prior 2001, 41–57.

ways of persuading the audience. Diogenes Laertius corroborates this view when saying that (according to Idomeneus) Socrates was "formidable in the art of public speaking" (*Lives of Eminent Philosophers* 2.5: ἐν τοῖς ῥητορικοῖς δεινός).

There is an objection one should refute: that the transmitted speech is so highly refined in terms of the content and oratorical style that it is unlikely to have been delivered by Socrates. One may think that the ample use of questions in a limited space or consecutively may indicate post-delivery elaboration that would change or distort the liveliness of the defence that a speaker could deliver in court. To these reasonable objections one may reply that the same, if not a more elevated, level of stylistic rhetorical refinement can also be found in speeches of Attic oratory, with some of them having many questions being accumulated in a few sections or delivered one after another (as in the case of Aeschines 3.130–132 which contains 8 questions in rapid succession). Despite the reliability and veracity of these speeches still being a matter of controversy among researchers, it is argued, convincingly in my view, that the transmitted scripts are close to the delivered versions; changes may have been made, but the substantial rewriting of speeches in high profile trials would have been constrained by common knowledge.[33] To refine a speech post-delivery is one thing, but to prepare a completely fictional speech is quite different; refinement does not necessarily entail forgery, in other words. For, even in the case of Demosthenes being accused of refining his speeches (e.g. Dionysius of Halicarnassus, *Isaeus* 4.23–24: τῆς πολλῆς ἐπιτεχνήσεως), the accuser does not cast doubts on whether or not the speech belongs to the accused.

4 Conclusion

It has been argued that the examination of the frequency of questions, their content and their placement in Plato's *Apology of Socrates* can tell us a lot about the rhetorical nature of the speech, as well as about its historicity and veracity. Organised in three general groups (*introductory* or *explanatory* in 19b–23d; *ēthos-depicting* in 24c–34d; and *investigatory* in 36b–41c), these questions aim to maximise the forcefulness, vehemence, charm and verve of the *Apology*, and enable the speaker to appeal to the audience and to use the answers of Meletus to the interrogatories as evidence for the accusers' lies and his innocence – in a nutshell, to try to be as persuasive as possible. Rhetoric in Socrates' *Apology*

33 Harris 1995, 9–16. On a different view: Hubbard 2007, 185–202.

should be more thoroughly and meticulously explored, not simply in terms of arguments, however important these are for persuasion, but also in terms of the language (figures of speech, tenses and moods of verbs etc.). The examination of the use of questions gives us some further reasons to argue in favour of the veracity of the *Apology*. Other aspects of rhetoric can shed further light on the portrait of Socrates, while also enhancing our understanding of the techniques of persuasion and audience-control that are used in the ancient art of public speaking.

Bibliography

Brickhouse, T.C./Smith, N.D. (1989), *Socrates on Trial*, Princeton.

Burnet, J. (1924), *Plato's Euthyphro, Apology of Socrates, and Crito*, Oxford.

Bury, R.G. (1932), *The Symposium of Plato, Edited with Introduction, Critical Notes and Commentary*, Cambridge.

Calogero, G. (1957), 'Gorgias and the Socratic Principle Nemo Sua Sponte Peccat', in: *JHS* 77, 12–17.

Carawan, E. (1983), '"Erotesis": Interrogation in the Courts of Fourth-Century Athens', in: *GRBS* 24, 209–226.

Carey, C. (1992), *Apollodoros against Neaira: [Demosthenes] 59*, Warminster.

Christ, W. von/Schmid, W. (1912), *Geschichte der Griechischen Literatur*, Munich.

Chroust, A.-H. (1945), 'Socrates: A Source Problem', in: *American Catholic Philosophical Quarterly* 19, 48–72.

Chroust, A.-H. (1957), *Socrates, Man and Myth: The Two Socratic Apologies of Xenophon*, London.

Coulter, J. (1964), 'The Relation of the *Apology of Socrates* to Gorgias' *Defense of Palamedes* and Plato's Critique of Gorgianic Rhetoric', in: *HSCPh* 68, 269–303.

Danzig, G. (2003), 'Apologizing for Socrates: Plato and Xenophon on Socrates' Behavior in Court', in: *TAPhA* 133, 281–321.

Edwards, M. (1999), *Lysias: Five Speeches*, Bristol/London.

Field, G.C. (1930), *Plato and his Contemporaries*, London.

Gagarin, M. (1997), *Antiphon: The Speeches*, Cambridge.

Gomperz, H. (1912), *Sophistik und Rhetorik*, Leipzig/Berlin.

Gower, B.S./Stokes, M.C. (eds.) (1992), *Socratic Questions: New Essays on the Philosophy of Socrates and its Significance*, London/New York.

Grote, G. (1875), *Plato and the Other Companions of Socrates*, London.

Guthrie, W.K.C. (1975), *A History of Greek Philosophy*, Cambridge.

Harris, E.M. (1995), *Aeschines and Athenian Politics*, New York/Oxford.

Harrison, A.R.W. (1971), *The Law of Athens*. Volume II, Oxford.

Hesk, J. (2007), 'Despisers of the Commonplace: Meta-Topoi and Para-Topoi in Attic Oratory', in: *Journal of the History of Rhetoric* 25, 361–384.

Hogenmüller, B. (2015), 'The Influence of Plato's *Crito* and *Phaedo* on Xenophon's *Apology* of Socrates', in: *Kentron* 31, 127–138.

Hubbard, T.K. (2007), 'Attic Comedy and the Development of Theoretical Rhetoric', in: I. Worthington (ed.), *A Companion to Greek Rhetoric*, London, 490–508.
Huss, B. (1999), 'The Dancing Sokrates and the Laughing Xenophon, or the Other "Symposium"', in: *AJPh* 120, 381–409.
Kahn, C. (1996), *Plato and the Socratic Dialogue*, Cambridge.
Kapellos, A. (2018), 'Lysias Interrogating Eratosthenes on the Murder of Polemarchus (Lys. XII 25)', in: Erga-Logoi. *Rivista di storia, letteratura, diritto e cultura dell'antichità* 6, 51–64.
Kapparis, K. (1999), *Apollodoros against Neaira [D. 59]*, Berlin/New York.
Kato, S. (1991), 'The Apology: The Beginning of Plato's Own Philosophy', in: *CQ* 41, 356–364.
Kidd, I. (1992), 'Socratic Questions', in: B.S. Gower/M.C. Stokes (eds.), *Socratic Questions: New Essays on the Philosophy of Socrates and its Significance*, London/New York, 82–92.
Kremmydas, C. (2018), '*Anakrisis* and the Framing of Strategies of Argumentation in Athenian Public Trials', in: C. Carey/I. Giannadaki/B. Griffith-Williams (eds.), *The Use and Abuse of Law in the Athenian Courts*, Leiden/Boston, 110–131.
Lateiner, D. (1982), 'The Man Who Does not Meddle in Politics: A Topos in Lysias', in: *CW* 76, 1–12.
Lausberg, H. (1998), *Handbook of Literary Rhetoric*, Leiden/Boston/Köln.
Martin, G. (2009), *Divine Talk: Religious Argumentation in Demosthenes*, Oxford.
McCoy, M. (2008), *Plato on the Rhetoric of Philosophers and Sophists*, Cambridge.
Michalopoulos, A./Serafim, A./Vatri, A./Beneventano della Corte, F. (2021), *The Rhetoric of Unity and Division in Ancient Literature*, Berlin/Boston.
Miller, P.A./Platter, C. (2010), *Plato's Apology of Socrates: A Commentary*, Norman.
Morr, J. (1929), 'Die Entstehung der platonischen *Apologie*', in: *Schriften der Deutschen Wissenschaftlichen Gesellschaft in Reichenberg Heft* 5, 29–34.
Ober, J. (1989), *Mass and Elite in Democratic Athens: Rhetoric, Ideology and the Power of the People*, Princeton.
Oldfather, W. (1938), 'Socrates in Court', in: *CW* 31, 203–211.
Prior, W. (2001), 'The Historicity of Plato's *Apology*', in: *Polis* 18, 41–57
Reeve, C.D.C. (1989), *Socrates in the* Apology, Indianapolis.
Rosalind, T. (1992), *Literacy and Orality in Ancient Greece*, Cambridge.
Rutherford, R.B. (1995), *The Art of Plato*, London.
Schmid, W./Stiihlin, O. (1940), *Geschichte der griechischen Literatur*, Munich.
Serafim, A. (2017), *Attic Oratory and Performance*, London/New York.
Serafim, A. (2020a), '"I, He, We, You, They": Addresses to the Audience as a Means of Unity/Division in Attic Forensic Oratory', in: A. Michalopoulos/A. Serafim/A. Vatri/F. Beneventano della Corte (eds.), *The Rhetoric of Unity and Division in Ancient Literature*, Berlin/Boston, 71–98.
Serafim, A. (2020b), 'Language and Persuasion in Attic Oratory: Imperatives and Questions', in: *Argos. Journal of the Argentine Association of Classical Studies* 41, 1–19.
Serafim, A. (2020c), *Religious Discourse in Attic Oratory and Politics*, London/New York.
Serafim, A. (2020d), 'ΕΡΩΤΗΣΟΝ ΑΥΤΟΥΣ: Questions, Rhetorical purpose and Hypocrisis in Attic Forensic Oratory', in: G. Thür/S. Avramovic/A. Katanceviic (eds.), *Law, Magic and Oratory*, Belgrade, 229–248.
Stokes, M.C. (1992), 'Socrates' Mission', in: B.S. Gower/M.C. Stokes (eds.), *Socratic Questions*, London.
Stokes, M.C. (1997), *Plato: Apology of Socrates*, Warminster.
Strycker, E. de/Slings, S.R. (1994), *Plato's Apology of Socrates*, Leiden.

Taylor, A.E. (1911), *Varia Socratica*, Oxford.
Thesleff, H. (1978), 'The Interrelation and Date of the Symposia of Plato and Xenophon', in: *BICS* 25, 157–170.
Thür, G. (2004), 'Law of Procedure in Attic Inscriptions', in: D.L. Cairns/R.A. Knox (eds.), *Law, Rhetoric and Comedy in Classical Athens: Essays in Honour of Douglas M. MacDowell*, Swansea, 33–49.
Thür, G. (2008), 'The Principle of Fairness in Athenian Legal Procedure: Thoughts on the *Echinos* and *Enklema*', in: *Dike* 11, 51–73.
Thür, G. (2014), 'Antike Streitfälle im Rechtsunterricht', in: J. Hallebeek/M. Schermaier/R. Fiori/ E. Metzger/J.-P. Coriat (eds.), *Inter cives necnon perigrinos. Essays in honour of Boudewijn Sirks*, Göttingen, 741–750.
Vander Waerdt, P.A. (1994), *The Socratic Movement*, Ithaca.
Wallace, R.W. (2013), 'Plato Logographos: Defense of Socrates', in: *Philosophia* 43, 99–112.
West, T.G. (1979), *Plato's Apology of Socrates*, Ithaca/London.
Westwood, G. (2017), 'The Orator and the Ghosts: Performing the Past in Fourth-Century Athens', in: S. Papaioannou/A. Serafim/B. Da Vela (eds.), *The Theatre of Justice: Aspects of Performance in Greco-Roman Oratory and Rhetoric*, Leiden/Boston, 57–74.
Wimmel, W. (1957), 'Zum Verhältnis einiger Stellen des xenophontischen und des platonischen Symposions', in: *Gymnasium* 64, 230–250.
Wooten, C.W. (1987), *Hermogenes' on Types of Style*, Chapel Hill/London.
Wooten, C.W. (2013), 'Questions in Greek Rhetorical Theory and Demosthenes' *Philippics*', in: *Rhetorica* 31, 349–371.

Ioannis N. Perysinakis

Plato's *Apology of Socrates*: The Rhetoric of Socrates' Defence and the Foundation of the Ancient Quarrel between Philosophy and Poetry

Abstract: In Plato's *Apology of Socrates*, Socrates defends himself against both the accusers and the accusation proper. His re-evaluation of archaic moral values had motivated the allegations. Thus, all the above are vital components of the ancient quarrel between philosophy and poetry. By applying Socrates' teaching, Plato seeks to protect his adored teacher, thereby laying the foundations of his own philosophy. Anticipating Aristotle's *Rhetoric*, Socrates, as well as counteracting the prejudicial attack, deploys arguments aiming to disprove horrible suspicions; he contests the disputed points by both denying the alleged events and their supposed harmfulness and arguing for his beneficent influence on the Athenians. More than this, Plato portrays Socrates putting Meletus on trial for the same charge. It is therefore Socrates who brings his opponents to trial and eventually points the finger at the majority of the judges and their incompetence, while inveighing against the grave injustice inherent in the unfair trial brought against him.

1 Introduction

The standard division of the *Apology* conceals a broader tripartite structure, which underlines its relation with rhetoric. The first movement in Socrates' speech is the opening address and the defence against the ancient accusations (17a–24b2); the second is the defence against Meletus (24b3–28a1), which takes the form of an *elenchus*; *elenchus* is always defence of reason. In both these movements Socrates' characterization is largely negative. In the third movement, in the digression and the continuing through the counter-penalty to the end of the closing address (28b3–42a5), Socrates' characterization becomes more positive,

Professor M. Edwards read an early draft of the text, and the young scholar Georgios Alexakis the last one: thanks are due to them both for the improvement of the text.

https://doi.org/10.1515/9783110751970-009

and in fact pictures the true Socrates.[1] In the second movement Socrates argues: "I am not guilty". In the third movement, counteracting the prejudicial attack Socrates uses arguments that might refute an unpleasant suspicion; he contests the disputed points by denying the fact and its harmfulness, by offering a different reason that he did not intend harm, and substitutes one motive for another not only denying the charges against him but also arguing for the services he has provided to the Athenians.[2]

Plato made Socrates, his favourite character, his mouthpiece (cf. Diog. Laert. 3.52). And it is foremost the *Apology of Socrates* in which Plato uses Socrates as his mouthpiece. As for its historicity, the *Apology of Socrates* is Plato's literary work, a fictional literary composition of a historical case, an account of what Socrates could or should have said, in the way e.g. Thucydides composed his speeches: "fabricating speeches" (πλάττοντι λόγους) may be a reference to the *Apology* itself.[3] However, Xenophon's comment on Socrates' *megalēgoria* (defiance) may be instructive: all of those who have written about Socrates' defence "have captured his defiant way of speaking, which makes it clear that Socrates really did speak that way" (*Ap.* 1, Doyle). "Plato had his reasons for creating a main character named 'Socrates' to serve as the philosophical protagonist in his early dialogues. These reasons clearly include debt and tribute to the historical Socrates".[4] But the *Apology* is not a reliable source for the philosophy of the historical Socrates; it is Plato's literary composition. Glaucon's promise to Socrates in the *Republic* that "I won't desert you, I'll defend you where I can" (474a6–7) is the author's self-reference to the *Apology*, the *Republic* and other dialogues.

However, in composing the *Apology of Socrates*, Plato's purpose was twofold: first as forensic discourse as a defence of historical Socrates; and second as vehi-

1 Reeve 1989, 2–3; The division of the *Apology* follows Burnet 1924/2002; Hackforth 1933. Also, unless otherwise stated, the translation is R.E. Allen's.

2 The re-evaluation of virtues, the fundamental aspect of this "ancient quarrel", which is the main subject of the second digression, the epilogue, the counter-penalty, and the speeches after the sentence (though only at a few points), all of them consisting the more philosophical parts of the *Apology*, are not included in this paper. For this reason, Socrates' speeches after the sentence to the jurors, first to the condemners and then to the acquitters are striking departures from forensic *topoi*; they have no precedents in the surviving forensic genre.

3 A different discussion about the historicity and factuality of the *Apology* is offered by Serafim in this volume.

4 Wolfsdorf 2004, 37, 38. Rowe 2010: the *Apology* is Plato's manifesto. Burnet 1924/2002, 143, 146. Kahn 1998, 88–95: the historical Socrates. Morrison 2000; Prior 2001; Peterson 2011, 1–16; Dorion 2005; Tarrant 1955; Press 2000, 40. The historical or fictional character of Socrates is a major topic of Socratic studies.

cle to convey the philosophical programme of Plato and the defence of philosophy itself. And although it appears as a judicial discourse, it is in fact an *epideixis*, an epideictic speech and encomium of Socrates, and philosophy itself. In this sense, the *Apology* is both an encomium and an exhortation. "In including more than one genre here, Plato's dialogue goes well beyond conventional forensic speeches (whether constructed or historical) in serving as a defence, an encomium, and an exhortation to philosophize all at once".[5] Besides, this philosophical programme includes the re-evaluation of archaic moral values and the making of justice, which permeates many early, middle and transitional dialogues and the *Republic*: this constitutes the fundamental aspect of the "ancient quarrel".

In the second critique of poetry in Book X of the *Republic* Socrates and Glaucon agree that they were right to banish poetry from their city according to the demands of reason, and say to her "if she looks like accusing us of being harsh or uncultured, that there is an ancient quarrel between philosophy and poetry" (607b, Griffith with alter). I argue that the "ancient quarrel between philosophy and poetry" is a literary or rhetorical invention of Plato; and it is a second-round defence of Socrates, and constitutes a counter-defence against the accusations of poetry and politicians. The banishment is a condemnation of poetry based on the critique of poetry both in the second and third book and in the tenth book of the *Republic*; witnesses in the trial of poetry are therefore the passages drawn from poetry itself. It is helpful to remember that according to Aristotle's *Metaphysics* (995a7–8), there are people who will take seriously the arguments of a speaker (including those of a philosopher) only if a poet can be cited as a witness in support of them. I also argue that the fundamental chapter of the ancient quarrel between philosophy and poetry consists in fact of the re-evaluation of the archaic moral values and excellences (especially in Homer and the tragedians) in (some of) Plato's early and middle dialogues and in the *Republic*, of the banishment of literature in education, and of making *dikaiosynē* part or the whole of *aretē*.[6]

---

5 Cf. McCoy 2011, 53, 54. Cf. also de Strycker, *Plato's Apology*, 10–15, who points out that the ancient author of "On Figured Speeches" writes that Plato's *Apology* is (1) an *apologia* of Socrates; (2) an accusation of the Athenians for bringing such a man to court; (3) an encomium to Socrates; and (4) an exhortation, *paraggelma*, of what sort of person a philosopher ought to be.
6 Cf. Adkins 1960, 153, 171. I do not examine here the existing "ancient quarrels", but I cite the titles.

2 *Prooimion* (17a1–18a6)

In the *prooimion* Socrates addresses the jury (17a1–18a6), and distinguishes the kind of speech he plans to make from the speech made by the prosecution. Socrates begins his framing conversation (accounting of his past) in an abrupt manner: the accusers have warned the jurors that they should take care not to be deceived by a clever speaker like him; the defendant on the other hand, according to the rules of oratory, is required to declare that he will speak the truth. What is most shameless on their part is that they are not ashamed that they will immediately be refuted by what he is going to do, when he shows himself not to be a clever speaker – unless by a clever speaker they mean one who speaks the truth (17b). This is a clever rhetorical tactic. Socrates speaks about the accusers in terms of shame culture ("ashamed", αἰσχυνθῆναι). If it is cleverness for a person to speak the truth, Socrates will speak the truth: the virtue of the speaker is to speak the whole truth (17b8: τἀληθῆ, 18a6, 23d6, 33c8). It was always claimed by the poets that they would speak the truth (Hes. *Theog.* 27–28, Hom. *Il.* 2.485–486, Pi. *Ol.* 1.28b–29, Bach. 3.96), and all the philosophers after Plato also promised that they would speak the truth. Truth is repeated in the epilogue and second digression: Socrates exhorts the Athenians to care about having concern for wisdom and the greatest possible excellence of their soul (29d8–e2).

Other forensic introductions also attempt to arouse the jurors' suspicion of clever speech. In Antiphon's *On the Murder of Herodes* 5 the defendant states that many able speakers were believed although they told lies: "I request this of you, that if, on the one hand, I make some mistake in speaking, you will pardon me and attribute the error to inexperience (*apeiria*) and not to dishonesty (*adikia*); and if on the other hand, I express something well, you will attribute this to truthfulness (*alētheia*) and not to skill (*deinotēs*)" (Edwards and Usher).[7] Cf. also Gorgias' *Defence of Palamedes* 4.

This opening address to the jurors is part of the well-known Socratic irony.[8] The disclaimer of rhetorical ability is part of Socratic irony in the same sense that the disclaimer of knowledge of virtue or the definition of some part of virtue is Socratic irony and the beginning of the elenchus. What Socrates does not know is the new meaning in the re-evaluation of virtues. The truth (ἀληθῆ) the orator

---

7 McCoy 2011, 27, 34; Wallace 2013, 101; Danzing 2003, 297 n. 42.

8 Cf. Burnet 1924/2002, 147; Reeve 1989, 5–9; on Socrates' disclaimer of science and oratory cf. also 14–21. Brickhouse/Smith 1984a. Leibowitz 2010, 21–37 supports the irony. McCoy 2011 does not see Plato's main purpose here as parody or irony (40). On Socratic irony: cf. Vlastos 1991, 21–44; Lane 2011 and *ead.* 2006. Cf. below Seeskin n. 40.

has to speak in the case of Socrates is his teaching itself, his defence against the old accusers on the old prejudice, and especially his mission to Athens in his second digression. But the meaning of ἀληθῆ is ambiguous: on usual rhetorical standards and on the new meaning of the values. Socrates' speech may be a masterpiece of rhetoric and re-evaluation of traditional values, but it is not a masterpiece of the rhetoric he disclaims. In the epilogue Socrates argues that it does not seem just to him to beg a judge or to be acquitted by begging: "the judge does not sit to grant justice as a favour, but to render judgment; he has sworn no oath to gratify those whom he sees fit, but to judge according to law" (35c2–4). In this way in the final chapter of the *Apology* proper Socrates comes back in a sort of ring composition or cycle to what he maintained at the end of the *prooimium*: the virtue of the judge is to look strictly to this one thing, whether the defendant speaks justly or not, and the virtue of the orator is to speak the truth (18a4–6).

Socrates distinguishes between the deceptive, false plea of his prosecutors, which is intended to secure a conviction only to advance their own interests, and his own frank plea, which aims at the truth, justice, and the advancement of the interests of the Athenian audience (17a–18a). In the *prooimion* Socrates offers a sample of the argument in order that the jurors may know what the speech is about; he makes clear what is the ultimate objective of the speech. In the defendant's speech replies to attack come first, so the defendant must counteract the attack. He also tries to obtain their attention by seeming to be a reasonable person and by trying to induce laugher, when he says "unless they call a man a clever speaker if he speaks the truth", which over and above dissociates himself from the sophists and the rhetors-politicians.[9]

However, contrary to the established rules of rhetoric, Socrates does not attempt to make the jurors well-disposed to him in the *prooimion*, but instead prepares them to be questioned. "Socrates' aim is to improve the judges through subjecting them to his demand that they inquire into the state of their own souls". Throughout the defence, while Socrates uses rhetoric to affect the emotions of the jurors, he does so for the purpose of encouraging them to take care for virtue. Also, Socrates uses the conventions of probability argument and *ēthopoiia* in order to change the jury's opinion not only of himself but also of the virtues. Rhetoric is subjugated to the demands of virtue.[10]

---

9 In accordance with Aristotle's *Rhetoric* 1415a8–38, based on Kennedy 2007, 233–234; Yunis 2010, 79.

10 McCoy 2011, 40–42 the quotation from p. 42.

In the *prooimion*, Socrates says that his speech will not be in fine language embellished with choice phrases and words, and carefully arranged; on the contrary he will speak naturally in the words which happen to occur to him, but they will hear the whole truth (17b7–c2) – although in the *prooimion* Riddell and Burnet have recognised eight rhetorical *topoi* (Burnet 146–147). Ending his discussion on the uselessness and the corruption of philosophers in the *Republic*, Socrates says that most people have more often seen words purposely chosen to rhyme with one another instead of occurring spontaneously. "But a man whose meter is measured by virtue, and made like it so far as possible in word and deed, and who holds power in a city of the same sort – this they have never yet seen" (498e). This man is obviously the philosopher king – i.e. Socrates himself if he were to practice politics (496c4). And this is a splendid double self-reference: to Socrates about himself regarding his teaching and condemnation and about Plato as author regarding his diction.

3 The foundation of the ancient quarrel in the *Apology of Socrates*

3.1 The defence against the old accusers: διαβολή and ἀπέχθειαι (19a8–24b2)

In the *prothesis* (18a7–19a7) Socrates outlines his plan of defence. He distinguishes between two sets of accusations. The first accusation is always referred to as being in the past: πρῶτα, πρῶτοι, πάλαι (many times, 18a, 18e, 23e, 24b, πολὺν χρόνον 18c, ἐν πολλῷ χρόνῳ 19a, πρότερον 18e). This first accusation is referred to by the adjective παλαιά used in the famous expression of the *Republic* ("the ancient quarrel") and constitutes the subject of this paper. This παλαιά is fixed as being in the time of Socrates' life during which he tested the Athenians; it starts during the childhood of the jurors he is addressing. παλαιός is usually used to refer to one's lifetime; ἀρχαῖος, referring to the initial, is used in the case of generations: ἀρχαιοπλούτων δεσποτῶν (Aesch. *Ag.* 1043). Socrates is accused that he does not worship the old (ἀρχαίους) gods (*Euthphr.* 3b2–3). Plato speaks of the ἀρχαία φύσις of Glaucos or his body (*Resp.* 611d; *Symp.* 193c). Aristophanes' *Clouds*, to which Socrates himself referred (19c), was produced in 423 BC (the text of the *Clouds* we have is an adaptation made by Aristophanes himself). Parody or fiction, Plato was aware that the *Clouds* had seriously harmed Socrates and, in his role of rehabilitator of Socrates' reputation, endeavoured to divert the odium from him. The four poetic fragments Socrates quotes as evidence for poets attacking philosophy might come from the lost first version of Aristophanes' *Clouds*. As Brock suggests, the "ancient quarrel" is for Plato essentially a matter of comedy attacking philosophy.[11] For him, comedy in particular is responsible for Socrates' condemnation and death. The defence against the old accusers, the διαβολή and ἀπέχθειαι (19a8–24b2), which is repeated emphatically after Meletus' interrogation ("the enmity has risen against me among many people, and that is what will convict me", 28a5–8), establishes "the ancient quarrel". The ancient quarrel is a counter-defence of philosophy against poetry's accusations both in theatre (especially of Aristophanes), in traditional values and in its use in the education of the young. The symbolic birthday of the "ancient quarrel" is the production year of Aristophanes' *Clouds*. Chaerephon himself is parodied in the *Clouds*. Also, in Aristophanes' *Frogs* (405 BC) Aeschylus, almost in Socratic fashion, asks Euripides "why are poets admired", and Euripides replies "because we make the men in the cities better" (1009–1010). But if Euripides has in fact not done that, what should his reward for that be? Dionysus supplies the answer τεθνάναι (1010–1012). Aristophanes chooses Aeschylus. By his condemnation of Euripides, "that is, by the thesis that tragic poetry died with Euripides, died because Socrates' student Euripides made it intellectual and problematic and thereby secularised it, died therefore in the final analysis because of Socrates", Aristophanes condemns Socrates and his innovative moral values.[12] This "quarrel" is a condemnation of Socrates before the trial.

3.2 The Delphic oracle. "I do not think I know what I do not"

Part of the old prejudice is the widespread view that Socrates is σοφός, that he possesses human wisdom (23a3–4, 20d7–e1); the slander against him has arisen from the oracle. According to the Delphic oracle (after Chaerephon's question),

---

11 Dover 1971/1980; Brock 1990, 40; Havelock 1972; Burnet 1924/2002, 157, 158, 161; Leibowitz 2010, 41–45; Konstan 2011; Strauss 1966; Adkins 1970; Most 2011, 12; McPherran 1996, 90–98; Parker 2000, 42–43; Corradi 2018, 86–89; Capra 2018: Aristophanes' effectiveness at determining the visual aspect, and the iconic status, of Socrates and his main contribution to the history of Socratism. Bromberg 2018: by reading Aristophanes as a representative of Old Comedy he can picture Socrates against the background of the thinkers and innovators of the late-fifth century parodied in the yearly comic festivals. Moore (2015): Aristophanes links the precept 'know yourself' with Socrates in the *Clouds*. P. Cruickshank, *Socrates in the* Clouds: *Excess and Impiety* (MA, McMaster Univ. 2008).

12 Kanicht 1988, 26–27.

no one is wiser than Socrates (21a).[13] "Socrates considers it a terrible slander to be labelled 'wise' in its ordinary use because the label implies that he is reputed wise about the biggest things and thus is in a position to do the worst harm to others". And it is a lie and a slander to say that Socrates has this divine capacity to teach virtue.[14] Puzzled for a long time over what the oracle meant, Socrates decided to inquire into the matter and went to someone in political life with a reputation for wisdom. Upon examining him, Socrates realised that he was wiser than that man, in one small respect "that this man thinks that he knows but he does not, while Socrates does not know, and does not think he does"; Socrates "does not think he knows what he does not" (21d4–6). This is the first (historical) expression of the famous Socratic principle, which is repeated later (οἴεσθαι εἰδέναι ἃ οὐκ οἶδεν, 29b, cf. 33c, 23c, 41b). This ignorance is again part of the well-known Socratic irony.

After the politician, Socrates went to the poets, the traditional[15] teachers of ethical values. Finally, Socrates went to the craftsmen. In each case the same pattern emerges. On the one hand there is a kind of knowledge or wisdom that the politicians, poets and craftsmen falsely believe they possess and that Socrates is aware he lacks – knowledge that would make its possessor the wisest of men, being knowledge of the most important things. On the other hand, there is the human wisdom Socrates possesses, and the others lack, precisely because of that lack of awareness. The Delphic oracle contains what was always characteristic Delphian thought, which is, commended anti-hubristic awareness of the human

---

13 The introduction to the story of the oracle ("the words I am about to speak are not mine") is an adaptation from Euripides' *Melannipe the Wise* (fr. 484.1 N^2/Kan.): κοὐκ ἐμὸς ὁ μῦθος, ἀλλ' ἐμῆς μητρὸς πάρα. Melanippe is beginning a tale of cosmogony. The words are alluded to again at Pl. *Symp.* 177a. The verse from *Melannipe the Wise* is quoted by Dionysius of Halicarnassus (*Rhet.* 9.11). In the *Poetics* (1454a31) Aristotle censures the ῥῆσις of Melanippe, in which she expounds certain cosmological doctrines, as a παράδειγμα ... τοῦ ἀπρεποῦς καὶ μὴ ἁρμόττοντος. Cf. Burnet 1924/2002, 169; West 1979, 55 n. 38.

14 Peterson 2011, 57, 27.

15 On Socrates' disclaimer of knowledge Reeve 1989, 53–62. Cf. Irwin 1977, 39–40; Kraut 1984, 270–274; Vlastos 1994, 42–44, 61–66; Lesher 1987; Woodruff 1992, 88–90. Yonezava 1995: when Socrates claims to know, he knows through direct or indirect human experience. Such knowing is quite compatible with his prudence or human wisdom, i.e. his awarenes of lacking the sort of wisdom available only to the gods. In fact the knowledge he claims in the *Apology*, that he should not disobey the better, and his claim that he is good are closely connected with his human wisdom. On Socratic ignorance cf. Morrison 2000, 256–264; Mackenzie 1988, the *Apology* is about Socrates' knowledge of ignorance (334); Brickhouse and Smith 1994, 30–38; 1989, 37–47, 100–108; Matthews 2006, 103–118; R. Bett 2011, 215–236, esp. 218–25. Tarrant 2006, 263–264, examines what is there to be known in the *Apology*.

limitation in wisdom. Anything that helps one to avoid something as repugnant to Apollo and inimical to human prosperity as *hybris* is of enormous significance to ethics and religion.[16]

Rhetores, artisans and poets are the three main classes of the Athenian society and Socrates' everyday interlocutors in his conversations, and characters in Plato's dialogues, not only in the *Apology*. It is mainly through them that he is led inductively in many dialogues to re-evaluation of virtues and the banishment of poetry.

What the politician, the poet, the artisan (to whom Socrates goes) and those examined in everyday conversations thought they knew were the traditional virtues. What Socrates (appears that he) does not know are the new virtues, which he tries to define by means of the elenchus; his disclaimer of knowledge is the introduction of his interlocutors to the new virtues. What they do not know is the new meaning in the re-evaluation of virtues, the new moral values on which he wants to found the new *polis*; those values are the content of the *aporetic* dialogues. Plato, in successive stages, establishes justice and founds the new city.

As for the oracle, the emphasis on Chaerephon in the *Apology* and the noise in the court in both Plato ("please do not make a disturbance", 21a and 30c2) and Xenophon ("the jury made more disturbance, reasonably", *Ap.* 14), seem rather to have a literary function in crucial points of the plot than to represent reality. Plato's mistrust towards laughter influenced subsequent authors.[17] Among few exceptions, recently Dorion argued that not only is this story a fiction invented by Plato, but also that we should consider it as a Platonic myth of origin, as are myths of this kind in Plato's dialogues.[18] The oracle seems to have been coined

16 Reeve 1989, 12, cf. 27–28.

17 Various dates for Chaerephon's purported visit to Delphi have been proposed, but most scholars now date it ca. 430 BC, or some thirty years prior to Socrates' trial in 399 BC: cf. Brickhouse/Smith 1983, 662 n. 11; Guthrie 1971 III.2, 85–86; Reeve 1989, 21; Ferguson 1964, 70–73; Parke/Wormell 1956, 1.401–403, 2.59; Fontenrose 1978, 34–35, 245; Burnet 1924/2002, 170–172; de Strycker 1975; McPherran 1996, 210–232 *passim*, 2002, 114–144 on elenctic interpretation and the Delphic oracle. Reeve 1989, 28–32 investigates "Why Delphi praised Socrates' wisdom". Some completely reject the oracle story as a Platonic invention, on the grounds that none of the candidates proposed for its origin is unproblematic. Leibowitz 2010, 63–69. Among those who reject the oracle story is M. Montuory (*Socrates: Physiology of a Myth* (Amsterdam, J.C. Gieben, 1981), 140), cf. Reeve 1989, 30; de Strycker 1975, 40, the prominence given to the oracle in the narration is chiefly a literary device; Stokes 1997, 115–116, outlines the principal arguments against the truth of the oracle-story, cf. *id.* 1992. Morrison 2000 argues that Plato's *Apology* is not a reliable source for the philosophy of the historical Socrates; Dorion 2012, 421–424; Jazdzewska 2018, 2005. On Chaerephon cf. Mooe 2013.

18 Dorion 2012, 432. Cf. Wallace 2013, 110; Danzing 2003, 304.

(or exploited) by Plato as an "*ad hoc* invention", a literary device. In the first book of the *Iliad* Homer makes Athena catch Achilles by his fair hair at the very moment when he was ready to kill Agamemnon (1.197). This is the way for the archaic man to represent the way he thinks in his mind. The mythological example of Meleager in the ninth book of the *Iliad* is an "*ad hoc* invention" of the poet which reflects the plot of the poem: it is analogous to Achilles' position.[19] The whole scene with the oracle and the visit to the politician, the poets and the craftsmen are analogous inventions of Plato which not only serve the "plot" of the *Apology*, but also describe in advance and foreshadow the content of the following dialogues down to the *Republic*, as well as Socrates' role in these dialogues. Just as in the mythological example of Meleager in the *Iliad* every person serves a particular place in the plot, in the same way the individuals Socrates examines after the oracle represent groups of men in Athenian life and are part of Socrates' interlocutors, but they also correspond to the three accusers of Socrates. Meletus is angry on behalf of the poets, Anytus on behalf of the craftsmen and politicians (Anytus himself was a master-tanner and statesman), and Lycon on behalf of the orators (23e–24a).

It must be noted that when Socrates says that he tries to refute the oracle (ἐλέγξων, 21c2), he does not attempt to refute the oracle *per se*, but only his own initial interpretation of its most obvious meaning; Socrates was puzzled for a long time what the oracle meant. He never claims that the oracle ought to be ignored or disobeyed. Both the meaning of the oracle argument and Socrates' elenchus in judicial terms is the case of Sophocles (in Aristotle's *Rhetoric*): it is not Socrates' fault that either people or the oracle say that he is wise. Seeking the meaning of the oracle, Socrates already asserts what he will say later in the *Apology*: that he lives according to a divine rather than a human standard and that his philosophical activity is grounded upon this divinely instituted mission; his main concern to inspire the Athenians, and the jurors, to pursue virtue is legitimate; he makes the judges witnesses. By appealing to Apollo, who cannot speak falsely, Socrates insinuates that anyone who might challenge this hearsay testimony is himself impious. Socrates acknowledges that his autobiographical disclosure will not have its intended effect (24a4–7). But "he leaves a pedagodical trail for others who wish to follow this path of self-inquiry and communal obligation".[20]

"Socrates' appeal to the oracle serves a positive purpose in his use of *ēthopoiia*. By appealing to a divine rather than a human witness, Socrates already asserts what he will say later in the *Apology*: that he lives according to a divine

19 Willcock 1964; Willcock 1977.
20 Cf. McCoy 2011, 48–51; Schultz 2015, 134.

rather than a human standard and that his philosophical activity is grounded upon this divinely instituted mission (29d)".[21] Also, "Socrates' risky choice to appeal to the oracle story forces each juror to make a choice: he must decide whether Socrates' philosophical activity is a moral and even religious virtue. If the mention of Delphi successfully convinces the judges that philosophical questioning can be an exhibition of piety and humility, then Socrates has not only won his case but also contributed further to his mission to the city". What *is* clear is that Socrates does not use *ēthopoiia* to build up only his own virtue but also to build up a new idea of the virtues in relation to philosophy.[22]

3.3 Socrates' "pupils" and *elenchus*

Apart from the oracle, another reason for such enmity and zealous slander is Socrates' "pupils", mainly young men of wealthy families who have the leisure to follow him of their own initiative, *automatoi* (23c2–3). These young men, rejoicing to hear men tested, imitate Socrates and undertake to test others; and next, they find many people who know little or nothing but think they have some knowledge. "As a result, those whom they test become angry at me, not at themselves, and they say 'this fellow Socrates is utterly polluted, and corrupts the youth'" (23c4–d2), a reference to his association with Charmides and Alcibiades, both of whom had revealed themselves to be hostile to Athenian democracy. Near the end of the second digression Socrates repeats that he has never been teacher to anyone, that he never did promise instruction and none did he teach, and comes to the psychological explanation of this stance: "Why is it then, that some people enjoy spending so much time with me? ... It is because they enjoy hearing people tested who think they are wise and are not" (33a5–6; 33b8–c4); again a reference to Alcibiades and Critias.[23] In the education of the philosopher- ruler

21 McCoy 2011, 50.

22 McCoy 2011, 51.

23 On Socrates' relations with Alcibiades and Critias see Xen. *Mem.* I.ii.12–16, 24–25, 40–46. Cf. Reeve 1989, 97–100; Vickers 1994: In Plato's *Gorgias* Callicles is a mask for Alcibiades and Polus for Critias. Emphasis on Alcibiades' relation to the Peloponnesian War and Critias' relation to the civil war, and their relationship with Socrates was recently given by Waterfield 2009, 186–190, 51–55; on Alcibiades 85–102; on Critias 122–136. Danzig 2014 argues that in the *Memorabilia* (1.2.41–46) Xenophon illustrates the skills that could be acquired by students of Socrates and reminds readers that very gifted men such as Alcibiades gained much by their association with Socrates (25–26). Pownall 2018, 365 argues that "through this effective use of foils, Xenophon demonstrates that Socrates could instill virtue even in those who were not naturally good" and

the young people "imitate those who have refuted them by refuting others themselves, and, like puppies, enjoy dragging and tearing with argument anyone within reach" (*Resp.* 539b4–7; cf. also 563a4–b2).

Socrates' method is inquiry and examination (cf. 22e1 asked myself, 22e6 examination, 23b5 search and inquire, 28e5–6 examining myself and the others). The Delphic oracle commended elenctic examination. Socrates repeatedly claims that Apollo has ordered him to inquire and to philosophise (23a5–c1, 28e4–6, 30a5, 33c4–7, 37e5–6). Plato assigns a divine and mythical origin to the Socratic *elenchus*. And elenchus is the practice of virtue qua moderation. In the counter-penalty speech he repeats that the unexamined life is not worth living for man (38a5–6), one of the most famous utterances in the *Apology*,[24] and he warns the jurors who condemned him that they will not be released from submitting to examination of their lives (39c7).

When he was describing his being the soldier of Apollo, Socrates maintained that the Athenians had gained no greater service in the city than his service to the god (30a5–7). He regards it most important "that the young should be as good as possible". By appealing to the oracle Socrates already asserts that his philosophical activity is grounded upon this divinely instituted mission, and his re-evaluation programme is activated. The "know yourself" principle is a good starting point. Counteracting the prejudicial attack and substituting one motive for another in the *Apology* Plato opens his philosophical programme of re-evaluating and interiorising virtues and making justice by making Socrates his own mouthpiece.

Regarding the refutation of the old accusations, in particular those regarding Socrates' "pupils", in forensic terms, Socrates seems to say that the act that "I am accused is a mistake or bad luck or a side-effect". It is not Socrates' fault that those whom the young pupils test become angry at him, not at themselves. Socrates not only did not intend harm the Athenians, not only was his objective different, but he "believes that no greater good for the Athenians has ever come about in the city than his service to the god" (30a5–7, Reeve). "Wickedness and being unjust involve deliberate choice" (*Rh.* 1374a11–12). Therefore, even in the case that a wrong has been done through the elenchus, this service is honourable and advantageous to them.

---

that "both Critias and Alcibiades behaved with restraint for the duration of their association with Socrates (*Mem.* 1.2.18 and 24)".

24 Cf. Goldman 2004 and 2009.

These young men are such as Hippocrates, who asks for recommendation from Socrates in order to be accepted by Protagoras as his pupil in the homonymous dialogue of Plato: "Hippocrates here is an Athenian, the son of Apollodorus, of a great and wealthy family, and in natural ability he seems the equal of anyone of his age. I think that he wants to become eminent in public life, and he thinks that that would be most likely to happen if he were to become a pupil of yours" (316b9–c3). Pheidippides in Aristophanes' *Clouds* is the best example, since his case stands for the opposite of Hippocrates. *Clitophon* describes a similar condition. These young men who enjoy hearing people tested are the audience in Plato's theatre in which Socrates is the hero protagonist.

The charges of impiety and corrupting the youth of Athens were already enough for a death sentence, but the prosecutors accused him of more. They asserted that Socrates was also an elitist who surrounded himself with politically undesirable characters and mentored those responsible for the defeat of Athens in the Peloponnesian war. This was the surface; the situation went deeper. What is examined in these courses are the moral values and political behaviour of the traditional *agathoi*; their transformation is the new learning. The young men spending their time with Socrates "enjoy hearing people tested who think they are wise and are not". These people examined in the presence of young men do not know the new values Socrates is introducing. Such a course is the dialogue between Socrates and Anytus in the *Meno*, which clearly interprets not only the motives for the accusation against Socrates, but also, more importantly, the difference and development of the philosophy of Socrates and Plato in comparison to the traditional moral values and political behaviour. Pheidippides is scornful of the ancient poets and thinks that the ancient social traditions do not stand up to reasoning (cf. *Clouds* 1361–1378, 1421–1422). This elenchus is taking place under the prospect to newly define *aretē*. At the core of Socrates' moral inquiry is his attempt to get his interlocutors to think as he does. Plato is interested in advancing morality and in interiorisation of virtue (*aretē*). This is the subject of each dialogue before the *Republic*.

It is part of the old prejudice that those examined by the richest young men, who follow Socrates, and pretend knowledge while knowing nothing, speak vigorously with zealous slander against him, because they are concerned for their pride (23c–e, 33c).[25] The reaction of the people examined is repeated indirectly in an *analēpsis* in the *Republic* where people think philosophers useless in the cities and philosophy corrupted (487b–e, 489b–490b). The dialogue between Socrates

---

25 Reeve 1989, 97–107 considers the motives of Meletus, Anytus and Lycon. Leibowitz 2010, 114–115.

and Anytus in the *Meno* (89e–96d) clearly interprets not only the motives for his accusation against Socrates, but also the cause of his condemnation, and more importantly, the difference and development of the philosophy of Socrates and Plato in comparison to traditional moral values and political behaviour. Anytus supports the traditional archaic moral view that an elder *agathos* teaches an *agathos* boy virtue and such as he learned from noble men while still a child, as is prescribed in Theognis' advice (27–28).[26] Socrates, on the contrary, argues, using examples, that noble men in Athenian politics (*agathoi ta politica*) sent their children to those who were regarded as experts to teach them the desired virtue. Anytus is speaking about the traditional *aretē*, Socrates is speaking about the moral philosophical *aretē*. The difference is fundamental for Athenian moral political thought.

3.4 The defence of Socrates against Meletus (refutation of the proper accusation, 24b3–28a1)

Although in Attic law either party was entitled to interrogate the other ("for the law requires you to answer", 25d1),[27] in the next chapters, in which Socrates refutes one by one (ἓν ἕκαστον, 24c2–3) the particulars of the accusation against him, his defence is developed by the well-known method of examination of his interlocutors – though more formal, i.e. what was to become the Socratic method is already prescribed in the *Apology*. Socrates claims that his discourse in court is the same as that which he uses to converse privately with fellow citizens outside the political institutions (17d4–18a3). The prosecution (*graphē*) of Socrates is founded on the old accusations. The wording of the actual *graphē* is preserved in Diogenes Laertius (2.40): "Socrates does injustice by not believing in the gods in whom the polis believes and by introducing other *kaina daimonia*; he also does injustice by corrupting the youth". This does not differ in any significant way from the summary Socrates produces in the *Apology* (24b8–10). The accusations are also mentioned by Xenophon (*Mem.* 1.1.1; *Ap.* 10) and by Plato in *Ap.* 24b7–c1 and in the *Euthyphro* (3b1–4).[28]

---

26 Perysinakis 2012, 470–472.

27 Burnet 1924/2002, 186. He quotes Arist. *Rh.* 1418b40–19a12 and cites Dem. 46.10: τοῖν ἀντιδίκοιν ἐπάναγκες εἶναι ἀποκρίνασθαι ἀλλήλοις τὸ ἐρωτώμενον, μαρτυρεῖν δὲ μή.

28 Burnet 1924/2002, 182; Reeve 1989, 74–75; Leibowitz 2010, 117. On the trial of Socrates and how the system worked cf. Waterfield 2009, 3–31; on Anytus' prosecution speech 195–202; Socrates as scapegoat 202–204. Cartledge 2009, 76–90: the trial of Socrates. On the later accusers see McPherran 1996, 116–130. Scholars are puzzled over this seemingly pointless interview with

In the dialectic examination that follows Socrates refutes the first charge of corrupting the youth, which is related to the education of the young: "that the young should be as good as possible" (ὡς βέλτιστοι οἱ νεώτεροι ἔσονται, 24d), which is repeated twice in the second digression (29d8–e2 and 30a7–b2; cf. *Euthphr.* 2d1–2, *Grg.* 503a7–8, 513e), and to the "no one does wrong voluntarily" principle (25e–26a), which is found for the first time in the *Apology* (i.e. the first time in the development of Plato's writing programme).[29] The interest for the young to be as good as possible is related to both the accusations and Socrates' teaching. *Aretē* (virtue) has always been the goal of education, and is always related to poetry and *leges*. *Leges*, too, make citizens better in the city (24d), and this is a recurring theme (*Cri.* 50c4–51c5 (*Leges* personified), *Resp.* 599e1–2, *Leg.* 770c–d).[30] Poets always make the citizens better in the city (Ar. *Ran.* 1008–1009).

In the interrogation, Meletus insists that Socrates corrupts the youth intentionally (25d5). Socrates' reply is: "I do not believe you, Meletus, and I do not think anyone else does either. On the contrary: either I do not corrupt the youth, or if I do, I do so unintentionally. In either case, you lie. And if I corrupt them unintentionally, it is not the law to bring action here for that sort of mistake, but rather to instruct and admonish in private" (25e5–26a5). In Meletus' cross-examination, Plato uses the topos of demonstrative [enthymeme] from opposites (*ek tōn enantiōn*), according to which "one should look to see if the opposite [predicate] is true of the opposite [subject], [thus] refuting the argument if it is not, confirming it if it is" (*Rh.* 1397a7–10, Kennedy). Socrates' argumentation is close to Gorgias' *Palamedes* (26). The prosecution (κολάζειν) would only be justified after instructing and reproving (after διδάσκειν and νουθετεῖν). Socrates pleads that a

---

Meletus: cf. Danzing 2003, 299–300; 2010, 44–47. In all of Xenophon's works, and a significant number of Plato's, the authors were not only addressing the topics they seem to be addressing, but were also defending Socrates' memory and creating our Socrates, according to the main approach of Danzig's work 2010. Cf. also Pangle 1985; Sage (academia.edu) on the two *Apologies*. Pownall 2018 argues that "the early part of the *Hellenica* reveals that Xenophon does offer very pointed political commentary on the trial and execution of Socrates" and that "the *Hellenica* is intended to be read as a defence of Socrates and a condemnation of the Athenian democracy". On Xenophon's on Socrates' trial and death cf. Waterfield 2012.

29 Cf. *Cri.* 49a, *Ap.* 25e–26a, 37a, *Menex.* 77b–78b, *Prt.* 345d–e, 358c–d, *Resp.* 589c, *Leg.* 731c, 734b, 860d, *Ti.* 86d.

30 Arist. *Pol.* 1336b20–22; *Eth. Nic.* 10.9, 1179a–1181b15 (τοὺς νομοθετοῦντας δεῖν μὲν παρακαλεῖν ἐπὶ τὴν ἀρετὴν καὶ προτρέπεσθαι τοῦ καλοῦ χάριν, 1180a6–7). In the *Gorgias*, the sophistry which promises to make people better is false care of the soul which imitates the true art of lawgiving (464b–466a), and the orator secures that the souls of the citizens shall be as good as possible (503a). On Socrates' obedience to the law cf. Vlastos 1974; Woozley 1971/1980; Brickhouse/Smith 1994, 141–155; Young 1974; for a reply cf. McLaughlin 1971.

man would not corrupt his associates willingly, because by having corrupt associates he would cause injury to himself (25c), which strongly foreshadows Plato's later explanation of the doctrine that wrongdoing is involuntary. At the end of the second digression, Socrates claims that all of the relatives of those whom he is supposed to have corrupted are actually ready to help him: "what reason could they have for supporting me except that it is right and just, because they know Meletus is lying and I am telling the truth?" (34a7–b5).

In his defence, anticipating Aristotle's *Rhetoric*, Socrates uses arguments describing ways of meeting a prejudicial attack. "One source of counteracting a prejudicial attack (*diabolē*) is to use arguments to refute an unpleasant suspicion... 2. Another topic is to make denial in regard to what is at issue: either that it is not true or not harmful or not to this person or not so much as claimed or not unjust, or not very, or not disgraceful or that it is not important. The question at issue [*amphisbētēsis*] concerns things like this... Or one may balance one thing against another when a wrong has been done, [saying that] although it was harmful, it was honourable [or that] though it caused pain, it was advantageous, or something of this sort. 3. Another topic: that [the act in question] is a mistake or bad luck or a necessity, as Sophocles said he was not trembling for the reason his accuser said – in order to seem old – but out of necessity; for it was not of his own volition that he was eighty years old. And it is possible to offer a different reason: that one did not intend harm but some other objective and not what the accuser alleged, but the accidental result was harmful: 'it would be just for you to hate me if I acted in order to bring this about'" (1416a4–20, Kennedy; cf. also 3.17.1 and 1.13.9–10).

Thus, the accusation against Socrates is prejudice and hostility coming from Aristophanes' *Clouds* and the slander among the Athenians; it is not his fault. Part of the old prejudice is the widespread view that Socrates is σοφός and he possesses human wisdom, all this coming from the Delphic oracle; but this is not his fault either. It is also not his fault, as we demonstrated above, that young men of the wealthy families who have the leisure followed him of their own initiative or that those tested by these young men become angry at him and not at themselves, because they know little or nothing but they think they have some knowledge. Meletus chose to write the present indictment relying on the same prejudice; it is not Socrates' fault. On the contrary, Socrates describes himself as a gift from the gods to the city (30e1). The Athenians had gained no greater service in the city than his service to the god (30a5–7; also 30a7–b2 and 30b2–4). Besides, Plato portrays Socrates as putting Meletus on trial on the same charge and seems to have treated the legal proceedings as a moral and intellectual test of the jurors themselves and their judicial incapacity.

Socrates' cross-examination of Meletus serves as an opportunity for the implicit cross-examination of each juror in the audience. By questioning Meletus Socrates "promotes self-knowledge in his entire audience, potentially inspiring it to recognize how philosophy promotes greater self-understanding". Plato relies upon *ēthopoiia* in order to reconstruct for us a new Socrates. Plato willingly argues from probability to show that Socrates cannot reasonably be believed to have willingly corrupted the youth. "Instead of being a corruptor, interested in destroying the city's values and replacing them with his own, Plato suggests that Socrates is both pious (in his obedience to the oracle at Delphi) and devoted to the good of the city (in his acting as the gadfly of Athens)".[31]

The dialogue between Socrates and Meletus may be typical of the Platonic art in the sense of characterization of an encounter between two individuals. Smith considers "the logic that underlines the content of Meletus' answers, with the aim of showing both that these responses are not as dramatically unconvincing as is sometimes thought, and that Plato's portrayal of Meletus serves to connect the drama of the events portrayed in the *Apology* to Plato's attempt to understand the nature of the sophist and what the success of sophistry teaches about the moral and political life of Athens".[32]

Smith's arguments may be right, but it is not Plato's main aim to show the career of the practitioner of sophistry. In fact, Meletus repeats the accusations of the old accusers and, by putting Meletus on trial on the same charge, it is Socrates who brings on trial the old accusers and eventually the majority of the jurors, and shows that the trial against him is unjust. Socrates himself argues that, when Meletus wrote the present indictment against him, he relied on the same slander (19b2–3). Meletus is not able to answer who makes the young better (24d7–8). When Meletus insists that every Athenian makes the young excellent except Socrates (25a7–8, b7–9), he simply repeats what Anytus supports in the *Meno* (89e–96d), which is the traditional belief of the *agathoi*. By appearing to dispute the right of the 'elder noble men' and the majority to form morally the youth, Socrates serves his *megalēgoria* and in real judicial terms underlines his position. After this conversation Socrates concludes that Meletus never cared about the matters for which he brings action against Socrates (25c4, 26b2). Socrates also shows that Meletus is in confusion regarding Socrates' beliefs in relation to Anaxagoras, as is the case in the *Frogs* (26d). Socrates then reverses the accusation against him and furthermore shows that Meletus is contradicting himself in his indictment by means of the use of *daimonia* and *daimōn* and *daimōn* and god and gods' children

31 McCoy 2011, 52, 39.
32 Smith 1995, 372–373, 388. Cf. Allen 1980, 3–16.

(27c2, 27d2–e1). This is a sophistic examination, but given that Meletus is speaking on behalf of the poets, we may recall that the poets "know nothing of the things they speak" (22c3). Interrogating Meletus Socrates tries to uproot or extinguish the common opinion of the old accusers eventually shared by the majority of the judges.

There is no paradox between Socrates' ignorance of moral virtue and his insistence on the supreme moral value of his philosophical mission, and thus on his innocence of any wrongdoing as a result of its pursuit.[33] The point is that the judges were among the spectators of the *Clouds* or the *Frogs* and other comedies at the theatre, or met him at the agora and the wrestling schools, and the majority of them did not agree with his updating of moral values. Besides, this seems to be Plato's aim in writing the *Apology*. The readers of the *Apology* are transferred to the "real" court with Socrates in front of the juries and his new accusers. Plato is representing Socrates' defence in light of the jury's verdict and sentence. But Plato's *Apology*, of course, does not aim at influencing the court, but rather at an educational and political influence. Therefore, Socrates seems to have treated the legal proceedings as a moral and intellectual test, or trial, of the jurors themselves and their judicial incapacity. "In that case, Socrates is putting on trial, not just those individual citizens, but the very legal system of democratic Athens".[34] As in other dialogues, Plato delivers a moral, political and philosophical lesson, with Socrates as the hero of his drama.

Plato in the *Apology* is presented with a dilemma. On the one hand Plato should be (though he was not) in a position to completely deny his similarity with the Sophists and the substance of accusations, on the other hand he had to support Socrates' teaching, the re-evaluation of standard moral values, of which in fact he was accused. Plato's Socrates fits some of the qualities of Plato's Sophists. The Sophists teach/sell virtue; for Socrates the greatest good is to discuss virtue every day (38a1–3), though this is a different virtue. Therefore, it was easier in his defence to make Socrates claim for himself the position of Achilles in Greek poetry and education, since the virtue of bravery was the least changed in the history of Greek ethics, as the conditions of life in this field had not shifted.

Service to the city is common topic in pleas to the jurors in forensic speeches. It is surprising to discover the pleas actually offered in Athenian courts of law. In Lysias 25 (*Δήμου Καταλύσεως Ἀπολογία*) the defendant is rebutting a charge of having subverted the democracy: it is evidently plausible that he had oligarchic sympathies. "This speaker is also protesting his innocence; but openly to avow

33 Cf. Brickhouse/Smith 1984.
34 Blyth 2000, 1–2.

(§12) that one has spent money in order to be thought more *agathos* and have a better chance in court if put on trial must appear to us to fly in the face of the justice that the jury swore to observe. Yet Lysias was a skilled speech-writer: he must have known what would sway the jury".[35]

On the other hand, the Athenians had gained no greater service in the city than Socrates' service to the god and his philosophical mission (30a5–7). Socrates goes around Athens attempting to persuade the Athenians not to care primarily or passionately about their bodies and about wealth, but about how their soul can be the best possible (30a7–b2); that "virtue does not come from money, but it is virtue that makes wealth and everything else, both public and private, good for a man" (30b3–5) (where *aretē* is both traditional and re-evaluated); that "the unexamined life is not for man worth living"; and his obedience to the law and his not leaving his position in the phalanx both literally and metaphorically: "to live in the pursuit of wisdom, examining myself and others" (28e5–6). All these in fact constitute the background, from which the old accusations come. Socrates' service to the city is modelled on such pleas in court law. The speaker in the above speech claims: "I spent more money on these than I was required to do by the city, so that I might be thought more *agathos* by you, and if some misfortune should come upon me, I might *ameinon agōnizesthai* (fare better in court)" (Adkins).[36] This is equivalent to Socrates' position in the *Apology*, too. With one difference: the speaker seeks to be *agathos* according to traditional standards; Socrates is *agathos* in completely new moral internal standards – and this is one of the clearest cases of re-evaluation of moral values.

In his real historical life, Socrates never left his position in the military phalanx and once as a member of the Council he acted in a manner worthy of a good man, never disobeyed his superior and the laws. Thus, it was easy for Plato to exploit these behaviours metaphorically and to apply them both to his mission to the god and the Athenians' neglecting of knowledge, virtue and their souls. Therefore, Plato depicts Socrates on the one hand presenting his thought as a radical break with the standard virtues and values, and on the other hand diminishing the distance between his mission in the city, and the new values he was introducing, by employing customary moral terms.

The eventual condemnation of Socrates and his consequent death is equivalent to the warrior's alternative for death, who enjoys honour and glory and im-

35 Adkins 1972, 121; 1960, 201–205. On similar cases cf. Lys. 30.26, 3.46ff., 12.38.

36 And there are other speakers: Lys. 30.26, 3.46ff., 12.38, 21.12; Aeschin. 3.8. The liturgies are a similar case.

mortality in Tyrtaeus' elegies. By his reference to Achilles in the second digression (28b8–d4), Socrates puts himself in Achilles' position after Patroclus' death; he appropriates for himself Achilles' status as 'best of the Achaeans', Achilles' *aretē*. Socrates speaks ambiguously both absolutely in terms of traditional competitive values and excellences in a shame culture and in terms of co-operative values and excellences. Achilles' competitive virtue corresponds to Socrates' internal morality. This is absolutely compatible both with the traditional competitive and the new interior co-operative values. If we go a little further: Plato himself with respect to Socrates is in the place of Homer with respect to Achilles. Achilles' fulfilment of his share and alternative destiny with respect to the day of his death according to the Thetis' *theopropie* equals Socrates' fulfilment of the oracle. The *kleos*, which Homer promises through his poetry to Achilles in his first alternative, is equivalent to Socrates' immortality by means of Plato's *Apology* and his dialogues in general. Plato substitutes himself in the place of Homer.

In the epilogue (34b6–35d9) Socrates disposes the jurors favourably towards him: he calls them to judge in accordance to justice, as he has told them the whole truth (33c2). But Socrates moves the jurors into an anti-emotional reaction; he will not beg them for his release. The epilogue of the *Apology* is not just a simple speech; it could be part of Socrates' real life, i.e. a speech which he could deliver on such a subject during his life. His own honour, the honour of the judges and that of the whole city would suffer, if he were to behave in this way. If one behaves in this way, it brings shame upon the city, so that a stranger might think that those men among the Athenians who are superior in virtue, and whom the Athenians themselves judge worthy of office and other honours, are no better than women (35b3). This last sentence must echo Archilochus 13W.7: "thrusting aside womanly mourning" (Gerber; γυναικεῖον πένθος ἀπωσάμενοι), (a poem which uses the warrior's vocabulary), but also the Athenian law as proposed by Plato that the most appropriate punishment for anyone who threw away his shield in battle would be to become a woman from a man (*Leg.* 944e). Such behaviour is neither honourable nor just nor holy, and this is repeated in the counter-penalty speech (38d9–e5). "Bringing these mournful dramas on to the stage" (35b7) is an ironic reference to the *choron didonai* or *didonai*, which are very common in tragedy or theatre. "When someone says things of that sort about gods (Aesch. fr. 350R), we will be angry: we will not give him a chorus nor allow teachers to use him for the education of the young" (*Resp.* 383c1–3). At this point Plato says: "So we will praise Homer for many things, but not for this". "These mournful dramas", on the other hand, refer to the sorrows and the emotions of the soul which are refused later in the *Republic* (388a–b; 605d–e; cf. Gorg. B 11a.33 DK), so that Homer and the poets of tragedy are banished from the city. This potential stranger

(35a8) imitates the well-known Homeric device of the objective observer καί κε τις ὧδ' ἐρέει (*Il.* 6.460, 2.271), which lends objectivity on the event.[37] The same is valid in the case of the three imaginary questions or conditions (20c4, 28b3, 29c6), which strengthen Socrates' answer much more. Throughout this section, Socrates uses the terms of a shame culture (reputation, honour, shame, disgrace, what a stranger [i.e. people] will say) and of competitive values (superior). Socrates' stance in the epilogue is equivalent to a warrior's position in the phalanx.

Socrates is also shown in the *Apology* to be able to beat the rhetoricians at their own game in a count-reverse of the accusation. "In an extraordinary mixture of humility and arrogance perhaps best captured in the famous gadfly passage", as Rutherford put it, he is far from making a defence for his own sake but that he is pleading them on their behalf lest they mistake the gift the god has given them and cast their votes against him (30d5–8). The god had attached him to the city as a gadfly – one that awakens, persuades, and reproaches each and every one of the Athenians and never stops alighting everywhere on them the whole day, and they will not easily find another like him (30e5–31a3). We do not know whence Socrates derives his amazingly firm conviction of his divine mission, "but Plato has brilliantly succeeded in making us both admire and value the dedication of Socrates to his task, and at the same time see very clearly exactly why the Athenians wanted to be rid of him".[38] Socrates closes the passage thus: "If you obey Anytus, you might easily kill me. Then you might spend the rest of your lives asleep, unless the god, in his compassion for you, were to send you someone else" (31a5–7, Reeve). This is the way Plato makes a subtle self-reference announcing his authoritative philosophical presence. Also, one may suggest that Socrates' deciphering of the oracle and his 'categorical' duty to philosophize anticipate Plato's commitment to compose the *Republic.*

The wide spread of the old accusations, the Delphic oracle and the way Socrates refutes it, the insinuation that anyone who might challenge this hearsay testimony is himself impious, on the one hand, and on the other hand the divine mission and Socrates' assertion that the Athenians had gained no greater service in the city than his service to the god, the treatment of the legal proceedings as a moral and intellectual test of the jurors themselves and their judicial incapacity, that in the refutation of Meletus Socrates seems to dispute the right of the "elder

37 Cf. Wilson 1979.

38 Rutherford 1995, 34–35; Konstan 2006, 67–68. Cf. Ober 1998, 174, 176, 177; Samaras 2003, 147–149. Cf. also Dorion 2005 on *megalēgoria*; Danzig 2003, 286–287, 300–309 and 2010, 26–34, 47–56 on Socrates' arrogance (refusal to beg, the oracle, the counter-penalty); cf. 2010, 26–34, 47–56.

noble men" and the majority to form morally the youth, that he is far from making a defence for his own sake but that he is pleading them on their behalf lest they mistake the gift the god has given them and cast their votes against him, that the god had attached him to the city as a gadfly – one that awakens, persuades, and reproaches each and every one of the Athenians, that perhaps they are angry against Socrates as men roused from the sleep are angry, but if they kill him they will continue to sleep out their lives, that he did not beg the judges with tearful supplications, that he abstained from politics, all these are important in philosophical terms and make a rhetorical and literary masterpiece, but in judicial and real political terms, before the court, may express an arrogance and *megalēgoria*, and thus may be crucial for the trial's outcome and "hard bill for many judges to swallow".[39] Socrates promised to tell the truth. And his military service to the city and his service as a member of the Council are true, but the rest service to the Athenians, his divine mission, as described in the digression and the counter-penalty though of course true, too, is useless for the Athenians, like the service of the useless philosophers described in book VI of the *Republic*. Thus, they condemned him by a vote of 280 to 220.

The very word *apektonate*, repeated three times in Socrates' final speech after the verdict of the judges who condemned him, constitutes the decisive foundation of the quarrel, and the "care that you will be as good as possible", its demanded content (38c4, 39c4 and 6). In fact, it is Socrates himself who lays the foundation of the quarrel; he says to those who condemned him: "you are to be accused ... of having killed Socrates, a wise man" (38c2). Plato confirms later in his life: "By some misfortune, some of those in power brought my friend Socrates into court, fabricating a most scandalous charge, and the least appropriate for Socrates; some of them accused him of impiety, while others condemned and executed him" (*Seventh Letter* 325b–d).[40] Xenophon also makes Socrates console himself after his condemnation by referring to Palamedes, who died in a similar way to him (*Ap.* 26). There are numerous echoes of Gorgias' *Defence of Palamedes* in Plato's text. But the mythical Palamedes forms an important part of the text's mythological structure and formulates Socrates' predicament in court. "Palamedes constitutes an apt model for the wise, σοφός, who though unjustly condemned will live forever in the works of those who tell his story". Plato's *Apology* "heaps scorn upon those who defeated Socrates, as it claims for its hero a fame

---

39 Cf. Samaras 2003, 114, 116, 128, 130, 146.
40 Cf. Aristotle's answer: καὶ πρὸς τὸν ἐρόμενον διὰ τί ἀπέλιπε τὰς Ἀθήνας, ἀπεκρίνατο ὅτι οὐ βούλεται Ἀθηναίους δὶς ἐξαμαρτεῖν ἐς φιλοσοφίαν, τὸ περὶ Σωκράτην πάθος αἰνιττόμενος καὶ τὸν καθ' ἑαυτὸν κίνδυνον (Ael. *VH* 3.36).

as long lasting as that secured by Euripides' Palamedes".[41] Socrates appropriates Palamedes, condemned to death by a wrong judicial sentence. Euripides' words "*ekanet' ekanete*" (*Palamedes* 588Ka; cf. D. Laer. 2.44) is close to the *apektonate.* In the place of the dead, Socrates associated with those heroes and the poets like Hesiod and Homer, whom he would test and question, as he did during his lifetime, "who among them is wise; who thinks he is and is not" (41b5–7). In a clever development and ambiguity, since it is about his life after death, about which no one knows (a reference to Orphism and the Eleusinian mysteries), Socrates refers to the principle "I do not think I know what I do not". This is the final allusion to the supposed wisdom of the poets, and the earliest chapter of the quarrel.

4 Conclusion

Plato's *Apology of Socrates* is a literary work, a fictional literary composition. However, in composing the *Apology of Socrates*, Plato's purpose was twofold: starting from the trial and exploiting Socrates' philosophy to protect him in judicial terms and lay the foundations of his own philosophy, a component of which was the re-evaluation of traditional morality. Besides, this re-evaluation of traditional morality constitutes fundamental aspect of the ancient quarrel.

Socrates defends himself by taking up from the beginning the charges, which have given rise to the prejudices, acquired by the Athenians a long time ago. Part of the old prejudice is the widespread view that Socrates is σοφός, that he possesses human wisdom (23a3–4, 20d7–e1); the slander against him has arisen from the oracle. And apart from the oracle, another reason for such enmity and slander is Socrates' 'pupils', mainly young men of wealthy families who have the leisure to follow him of their own initiative, *automatoi* (23c2–3). Nothing of these is Socrates' fault.

Furthermore, the first accusation is referred to by the adjective παλαιά, used in the famous expression of the "ancient quarrel between philosophy and poetry" in book ten of the *Republic.* This παλαιά is fixed as being in the time of Socrates' life, during which he tested the Athenians. Aristophanes' *Clouds* had seriously

41 Barret 2001, 26 and *passim*. Cf. Rutherford 1995, 33–34; Coulter 1964; Guthrie iv 1975, 76–77; Feaver-Hare 1981; Calogero 1976, 413, 415. Seeskin 1982, 94: *Apology* is a parody of existing commonplaces and Gorgias' speech as its prime example. *Id.* 1987 55–56, 58–61. Nightingale 1999, 29: Isocrates imitates the *Apology*. Hunter 2012, 109–120 on metamorphoses of the *Apology*. Wallace 2013: In the contest between rhetoric and philosophy Plato shows in the *Apology* he can out-*logographein* the *logographoi* by producing a masterly defence of the logographic type (111).

harmed Socrates, and from this examination much enmity and many slanders have arisen against him.

What the politician, the poet, the artisan (to whom Socrates goes) and those examined in everyday conversations thought they knew were the traditional virtues. What Socrates (appears that he) does not know are the new virtues, which he tries to define by means of the elenchus; his disclaimer of knowledge is the introduction of his interlocutors to the new virtues. What they do not know is the new meaning in the re-evaluation of virtues, the new moral values upon which he wants to found the new *polis*; those values are the content of the aporetic dialogues. After the prejudices Socrates' condemnation constitutes the ancient quarrel between philosophy and poetry, which is "invented" in the *Republic* X.

Forensic commonplaces are both reshaped and dismissed later in the speech. Anticipating Aristotle's *Rhetoric*, Socrates, counteracting the prejudicial attack, uses arguments that might refute an unpleasant suspicion; he contests the disputed points by denying the fact and its harmfulness, and substitutes one motive for another not only denying the charges but arguing for the services done to the Athenians. By appealing to the oracle Socrates already asserts that his philosophical activity is grounded upon this divinely instituted mission, and his re-evaluation program is activated.

In his interrogation Meletus in fact repeats the accusations of the old accusers. Plato portrays Socrates as putting Meletus on trial on the same charge. Thus, it is Socrates who brings on trial the old accusers and eventually the majority of the jurors and their judicial incapacity, and shows that the trial against him is unjust. When Meletus insists that every Athenian makes the young excellent except Socrates (25a7–8, b7–9), he simply repeats what Anytus supports in the *Meno* (89e–96d), what the traditional *agathoi* believe. Interrogating Meletus, Socrates tries to uproot or extinguish the common opinion of the old accusers eventually shared by the majority of the jurors.

Bibliography

Editions, Commentaries, Translations

Allen, R.E. (1984), *The Dialogues of Plato* vol. I, New Haven/London.
Barrow, R. (1977), *Plato, The Apology of Socrates*, London.
Burnet, J. (1924/ 2002), *Plato: Euthyphro, Apology of Socrates, Crito*, Oxford.
Dyer, L. (rev. T.D. Seymour) (repr. 1984) *Plato Apology of Socrates and Crito*, New Rochelle, N.Y.
Miller, P.A./Platter, C. (2010), *Plato's Apology of Socrates: A Commentary*, Oklahoma Press.
Reeve, CDC (2002), *The Trials of Socrates Six Classic Texts*, Indianapolis/Cambridge.

Samaras, Th. (2003), *Πλάτωνος* Απολογία Σωκράτους- Κρίτων, Thessaloniki.
Stokes, M.C. (1997), *Plato: Apology, with an Introduction, Translation and Commentary*, Warminster.
Strycker, E. de/Slings, S.R. (1994), *Plato's Apology of Socrates; A Literary and Philosophical Study with a Running Commentary*, Leiden.
West, T. (1979), *Plato's Apology of Socrates: an Interpretation with a new Translation*, Ithaca, N.Y.

Other works

Adkins, A.W.H. (1960), *Merit and Responsibility*, Oxford.
Adkins, A.W.H. (1970), 'Clouds, Mysteries, Socrates and Plato', in: *Antichthon* 4, 13–24.
Adkins, A.W.H. (1972), *Moral Values and Political Behaviour in Ancient Greece*, London.
Ahbel-Rappe, S./Kamtekar, R. (eds.) (2006), *A Companion to Socrates*, Oxford.
Allen, R.E. (1980), *Socrates and Legal Obligation*, Minneapolis.
Balot, R.K. (2008), 'Socratic Courage and Athenian Democracy', in: *Ancient Philosophy* 28, 1–14.
Barfield, R. (2011), *The Ancient Quarrel Between Philosophy and Poetry*, Cambridge.
Barrett, J. (2001), 'Plato's *Apology*: Philosophy, Rhetoric, and the World of Myth', in: *CW* 95, 3–30.
Benson, H.H. (1990), 'The Priority of Definition and the Socratic Elenchus', in: *OSAP* 8, 10–65.
Benson, H.H. (ed.) (1992), *Essays on the Philosophy of Socrates*, Oxford.
Benson, H.H. (2002), 'Problems with Socratic Method', in: G.A. Scott (ed.), *Does Socrates Have a Method*, University Park, Penn, 101–113.
Benson, H.H. (2006), 'Plato's Method of Dialectic', in: H.H. Benson (ed.), *Essays on the Philosophy of Socrates*, Oxford, 85–99.
Benson, H.H. (ed.) (2006), *A Companion to Plato*, Oxford.
Bett, R. (2011), 'Socratic Ignorance', in: D.R. Morrison (ed.), *The Cambridge Companion to Socrates*, Cambridge, 215–236.
Blyth, D. (2000), 'Socrates' Trial and Conviction of the Jurors in Plato's *Apology*', in: *Philosophy and Rhetoric* 33, 1–22.
Brickhouse, T.C./Smith, N.D. (1982), 'Socrates' Proposed Penalty in Plato's *Apology*', in: *AfGPh* 64, 1–18.
Brickhouse, T.C./Smith, N.D. (1983), 'The Origin of Socrates' Mission', in: *JHI* 44, 657–666.
Brickhouse, T.C./Smith, N.D. (1984), 'The Paradox of Socratic Ignorance in Plato's *Apology*', in: *History of Philosophy Quartely* 1, 125–131.
Brickhouse, T.C./Smith, N.D. (1984), 'Irony, Arrogance, and Sincerity in Plato's Apology', in: E. Kelly (ed.), *New Essays on Socrates*, Lanham, (1984), 'Irony, Arrogance, and Sincerity in Plato's Apology', in: E. Kelly (ed.), *New Essays on Socrates*, Lanham, 29–46.
Brickhouse, T.C./Smith, N.D. (1989), *Socrates on Trial*, Oxford.
Brickhouse, T.C./Smith, N.D. (1994), *Plato's Socrates*, Oxford.
Brock, R. (1990), 'Plato and Comedy', in: E.M. Craik (ed.), *Owls to Athens. Essays on Classical Subjects Presented to Sir Kenneth Dover*, Oxford, 39–49.
Bromberg, J. (2018), 'A Sage on the Stage: Socrates and Athenian Old Comedy', in: A. Stavru/C. Moore (eds.), *Socrates and Socratic Dialogue*, Boston, 31–63.
Calogero, G. (1976), 'Gorgias and the Socratic Principle *Nemo sua sponte pecats*', in: C.J. Classen (ed.), *Sophistik*, Darmstadt, 408–421 (= *JHS* 87, 12–17).

Capra, A. (2018), 'Aristophanes' Iconic Socrates', in: A. Stavru/C. Moore (eds.), *Socrates an Socratic Dialogue*, Boston, 64–83.

Cartledge, P. (2009), *Ancient Greek Political Thought*, Cambridge.

Colaiaco, J.A. (2001), *Socrates against Athens Philosophy on Trial*, New York/London.

Collobert, C./Destrée, P./Gonzalez, F.J. (eds.) (2012), *Plato and Myth Studies on the Use and Status of Platonic Myths*, Leiden/Boston.

Corradi, M. (2018), 'Protagorean Socrates, Socratic Protagoras: A Narrative Strategy from Aristophanes to Plato', in: A. Stavru/C. Moore (eds.), *Socrates and Socratic Dialogue*, Boston, 84–104.

Coulter, J. (1964), 'The Relation of the *Apology of Socrates* to Gorgias' *Defence of Palamedes* and Plato's Critique of Gorgianic Rhetoric', in: *HSCP* 68, 269–303.

Danzing, G. (2003), 'Apologizing for Socrates: Plato and Xenophon on Socrates' Behavior in Court', in: *TAPA* 133, 281–321.

Danzing, G. (2010), *Apologizing for Socrates*, Lanham.

Danzing, G. (2014), 'Alcibiades versus Pericles: Apologetic Strategies in Xenophon's *Memorabilia*', in: *G&R* 61, 7–28.

Danzing, G./Johnson, D./Morrison, D. (eds.) (2018), *Plato and Xenophon Comparative Studies*, Leiden/Boston.

Destrée, P./Herrmann, F.-G. (eds.) (2011), *Plato and the Poets*, Leiden/Boston.

Destrée, P./Smith, N.D. (eds.) (2005), *Socrates' Divine Sign: Religion, Practice, and Value in Socratic Philosophy*, Kelowna.

Dorion, L.-A. (2005), 'The *Daimonion* and the *Megalêgoria* of Socrates in Xenophon's *Apology*', in: P. Destrée/N.D. Smith (eds.), *Socrates' Divine Sign: Religion, Practice, and Value in Socratic Philosophy*, Kelowna, 127–142.

Dorion, L.-A. (2012), 'The Delphic Oracle on Socrates' Wisdom: a Myth?', in: C. Collobert/P. Destrée/F.G. Gonzalez (eds.), *Plato and Myth Studies on the Use and Status of Platonic Myths*, Leiden/Boston, 419–434.

Dover, K.J. (1971/1980), 'Socrates in the *Clouds*', in: G. Vlastos (ed.), *The Philosophy of Socrates: A Collection of Critical Essays*, New York, 50–77.

Edmundson, M. (1995), *Literature against Philosophy, Plato to Derrida: A Defence of Poetry*, Cambridge.

Edwards, M./Usher, S. (eds.) (1985), *Classical Texts Series: Greek Orators*, vol. I, Warminster, PA.

Feaver, D.A./Hare, J.E. (1981), 'The *Apology* as an Inverted Parody of Rhetoric', in: *Arethusa* 14, 205–216.

Ferguson, J. (1964), 'On the Date of Socrates' Conversion', in: *Eranos* 62, 70–73.

Fontenrose, J. (1978), *The Delphic Oracle: Its Responses and Operations* (Berkeley/Los Angeles/London.

Goldman, H.S. (2004), 'Reexamining the 'Examined Life' in Plato's *Apology of Socrates*', in: *The Philosophical Forum* 35, 1–33.

Goldman, H.S. (2009), 'Traditional Forms of Wisdom and Politics in Plato's *Apology*', in: *CQ* 59, 444–467.

Gould, T. (1990), *The Ancient Quarrel between Poetry and Philosophy*, Princeton.

Gower, B.S./Stokes, M.C. (eds.) (1992), *Socratic Questions: New Essays on the Philosophy of Socrates and its Significance*, London/New York.

Griffin, D.E. (1995), 'Socrates' Poverty: Virtue and Money in Plato's *Apology of Socrates*', in: *AncPhil.* 15, 1–16.

Griffith, T. (2000), *Plato* The Republic translated by- edited by G.R.F. Ferrari, Cambridge.

Guthrie, W.K.C. (1969–1986), *A History of Greek Philosophy*: vols. III-IV, Cambridge.
Hackforth, R. (1933), *The Composition of Plato's Apology*, Cambridge.
Havelock, E.A. (1972), 'The Socratic Self as It Is Parodied in Aristophanes' *Clouds*', in: *YCS* 22, 1–18.
Hobden, F./Tuplin C. (eds.) (2012), *Xenophon: Ethical Principles and Historical Enquiry*, Leiden/Boston.
Hunter, R. (2012), *Plato and the Traditions of Ancient Literature*, Cambridge.
Irwin, T. (1977), *Plato's Moral Theory. The Early and Middle Dialogues*, Oxford.
Jazdzewska, K. (2018), 'Laughter in Plato's and Xenophon's *Symposia*', in: G. Danzing/D. Johnson/D. Morrison (eds.), *Plato and Xenophon Comparative Studies*, Leiden/Boston, 187–207.
Kahn, C.H. (1998), *Plato and the Socratic Dialogue. The Philosophical Use of a Literary Form*, Cambridge.
Kannicht, R. (1988), *The Ancient Quarrel Between Philosophy and Poetry: Aspects of the Greek Conception of Literature*, Canterbury.
Kelly, E. (ed.) (1984), *New Essays on Socrates*, Lanham.
Kennedy, G.A. (2007), *Aristotle on Rhetoric A Theory of Civic Discourse*, Oxford.
Konstan, D. (2006), *The Emotions of the Ancient Greeks Studies in Aristotle and Classical Literature*, Toronto.
Konstan, D. (2011), 'Socrates in Aristophanes' *Clouds*', in: D. Morrison (ed.), *The Cambridge Companion to Socrates*, Cambridge, 75–90.
Kraut, R. (1984), *Socrates and the State*, New Jersey.
Lane, M. (2011), 'Reconsidering Socratic Irony', in: D. Morrison (ed.), *The Cambridge Companion to Socrates*, Cambridge, 237–259.
Leibowitz, D. (2010), *The Ironic Defence of Socrates. Plato's* Apology, Cambridge.
Lesher, J. (1987), 'Socrates' Disavowal of Knowledge', in: *JHPh* 25, 275–288.
Levin, S.B. (2001), *The Ancient Quarrel Between Philosophy and Poetry Revisited: Plato and the Greek Literary Tradition*, Oxford.
McCoy, M. (2011), *Plato on the Rhetoric of Philosophers and Sophists*, Cambridge.
McLaughlin, R.J. (1971), 'Socrates on Political Disobedience: A Reply to Gary Young', in: *Phronesis* 21, 185–197.
McPherran, M.L. (1996), *The Religion of Socrates*, University Park, Penn.
McPherran, M.L. (2002), 'Elenctic Interpretation and the Delphic Oracle', in: E. Scott (ed.), *Does Socrates Have a Method*, University Park, Penn, 114–143.
Mackenzie, M.M. (1988), 'The Virtues of Socratic Ignorance', in: *CQ* 38, 331–350.
Moore, C. (2013), 'Chaerephon the Socratic', in: *Phoenix* 67, 284-300.
Moore, C. (2015), 'Socrates and Self-Knowledge in Aristophanes' *Clouds*', in: *CQ* 65, 1–18.
Morrison, D.R. (2000), 'On the Alleged Historical Reliability of Plato's *Apology*', in: *Arch. Gesch. Philosophie* 82, 235–265.
Morrison, D.R. (ed.) (2011), *The Cambridge Companion to Socrates*, Cambridge.
Most, G.W. (2011), 'What Ancient Quarrel between Philosophy and Poetry?', in: P. Destrée/F.-G. Herrmann (eds.), *Plato and the Poets*, Leiden/Boston, 1–20.
Naddaff, R.A. (2003), *Exiling the Poets. The Production of Censorship in Plato's Republic*, Chicago.
Nakhnikian, G. (1971/1980), 'Elenctic Definitions', in: G. Vlastos (ed.), *The Philosophy of Socrates: A Collection of Critical Essays*, New York, 125–157.
Nightingale, A.W. (1997), *Genres in Dialogue. Plato and the Construct of Philosophy*, Cambridge.

Ober, J. (1998), *Political Dissent in Democatic Athens. Intellectual Critics of Popular Rule*, Princeton.

Pangle, T.L. (1985), 'The Political Defence of Socratic Philosophy: A Study of Xenophon's 'Apology of Socrates to the jury'', in: *Polity* 18, 98-114.

Parke, H.W./Wormell, E.E.W. (1956), *The Delphic Oracle*, vol. I: The History, vol. II: The Oracular Responses, Oxford.

Parker, R. (2000), 'The Trial of Socrates: And a Religious Crisis?', in: N.D. Smith/P.B. Woodruff (eds.), *Reason and Religion in Socratic Philosophy*, Oxford, 40–54.

Perysinakis, I.N. (2012), *Ἀρχαϊκὴ Λυρικὴ Ποίηση*. Ἀνθολογία ἀρχαϊκῆς λυρικῆς ποίησης μὲ βάση τὴν *ἀρετὴ* καὶ τὸν *ἀγαθὸν*, Athens.

Peterson, S. (2011), *Socrates and Philosophy in the Dialogues of Plato*, Cambridge.

Pownall, F. (2018), 'Socrates' Trial and Execution in Xenophon's *Hellenica*', in: *Mouseion* 15, 347–368.

Press, G.A. (2000), 'The Logic of Attributing Characters' Views to Plato'', in: G.A. Press (ed.) (2000), *Who Speaks for Plato? Studies in Platonic Anonymity*, Lanham, 27–38.

Press, G.A. (ed.) (2000), *Who Speaks for Plato? Studies in Platonic Anonymity*, Lanham.

Prior, W. (2001), 'The Historicity of Plato's Apology', in: *Polis* 18, 41–57.

Ramfos, S. (1978), *Η εξορία των ποιητών. Ένα πλατωνικό παράδοξο*, Athens.

Reeve, C.D.C. (1989), *Socrates in the Apology*, Indianapolis.

Rosen, S. (1988), *The Quarrel Between Philosophy and Poetry. Studies in Ancient Greek Thought*, London.

Rowe, C. (2010), *Plato and the Art of Philosophical Writing*, Cambridge.

Rutherford, R.B. (1995), *The Art of Plato. Ten Essays in Platonic Interpretation*, Duckworth.

Sage, D.K., 'The Two Apologies: A Comparison of the Defence Speeches of Plato and Xenophon', in: academia.edu.

Schultz, Anne-Marie (2015), 'Socrates on Socrates: Looking Back to Bring Philosophy Forward', in: *BACAP* 30, 123–141.

Scott, G.A. (ed.) (2002), *Does Socrates Have a Method*, University Park, Penn.

Seeskin, K. (1982), 'Is the *Apology* of Socrates a Parody?', in: *Philosophy and Literature* 6, 94–105.

Seeskin, K. (1987), *Dialogue and Discovery: A Study in Socratic Method*, New York.

Smith, L.R. (1995), 'The Interrogation of Meletus: *Apology* 24c4–28a1', in: *CQ* 45, 372–388.

Smith, N.D./Woodruff, P.B. (eds.) (2000), *Reason and Religion in Socratic Philosophy*, Oxford.

Stavru, A./Moore, C. (eds.) (2017), *Socrates and Socratic Dialogue*, Boston.

Stokes, M.C. (1986), *Plato's Socratic Conversations*, London.

Stokes, M.C. (1992), 'Socrates' Mission', in: B.S. Gower/M.C. Stokes (eds.), *Socratic Questions*, London, 26–81.

Strauss, L. (1966), *Socrates and Aristophanes*, New York/London.

Strycker, E. de (1975), 'The Oracle Given to Chaerephon about Socrates (Plato, *Apology* 20e 21a)', in: J. Mansfeld/L.M. de Rijk (eds.), *Kephalaion: Studies in Greek Philosophy and Its Continuation Offered to Professor C.J. De Vogel*, Assen/Van Gorcum, 39–49.

Tarrant, D. (1955), 'Plato as Dramatist', in: *JHS* 75, 82–89.

Tarrant, H. (2006), 'Socratic Method and Socratic Truth', in: S. Ahbel-Rappe/R. Kamtekar (eds.), *A Companion to Socrates*, Oxford, 254–272.

Vickers, M. (1994), 'Alcibiades and Critias in the *Gorgias*: Plato's 'Fine Satire'', in: *Dialogues d'histoire ancienne* 20, 85–112.

Vlastos, G. (ed.) (1971/1980), *The Philosophy of Socrates: A Collection of Critical Essays*, New York.
Vlastos, G. (1974), 'Socrates on Political Obedience and Disobedience', in: *The Yale Review* 63, 517–534.
Vlastos, G. (1991), *Socrates: Ironist and Moral Philosopher*, Cambridge.
Vlastos, G. (1984), 'Happiness and Virtue in Socrates' Moral Theory', in: *PrCPhSoc* 30, 181–213.
Vlastos, G. (1994), *Socratic Studies*, Cambridge, 1–31, 1–37.
Wallace, R.W. (2013), 'Plato *Logographos*: Defense of Socrates', in: *Philosophia* 43, 99–112.
Waterfield, R. (2009), *Why Socrates Died: Dispelling the Myths*, New York/London.
Waugh, J. (2000), 'Socrates and the Character of Platonic Dialogue', in: G.A. Press (ed.) (2000), *Who Speaks for Plato? Studies in Platonic Anonymity*, Lanham, 39–52.
Willcock, M.M. (1964), 'Mythological Paradeigma in the *Iliad*', in: *CQ* 14, 141–154.
Willcock, M.M. (1977), 'Ad Hoc Invention in the *Iliad*', in: *HSPh* 81, 41–53.
Wilson, J.R. (1979), 'Καί κέ τις ὧδ'ἐρέει: An Homeric Device in Greek Literature;, in: *ICS* 4, 1–15.
Wolfsdorf, D. (2004), 'Interpreting Plato's Early Dialogues', in: *OSCP* 27, 15–40.
Woodruff, P.B. (1992), 'Plato's Early Theory of Knowledge', in: H.H. Benson (ed.), *Essays on the Philosophy of Socrates*, Oxford, 86–106.
Woozley, A.D. (1971/1980), 'Socrates on Disobeying the Law', in: G. Vlastos (ed.), *The Philosophy of Socrates: A Collection of Critical Essays*, New York, 299–318.
Worthington, I. (ed.) (2010), *A Companion in Greek Rhetoric*, Oxford.
Yonezawa, S. (1995), 'Socratic Knowledge and Socratic Virtue', in: *Ancient Philosophy* 15, 349–358.
Young, G. (1974), 'Socrates and Obedience', in: *Phronesis* 19, 1–29.
Yunis, H. (2010), 'Plato's Rhetoric', in: I. Worthington, *A Companion in Greek Rhetoric*, Oxford, 75–89.

Vasileios Liotsakis

Witnesses and Evidence in Thucydides: The Institutional and Rhetorical Context of the Digression on the Tyrannicides

Abstract: This chapter examines Thucydides' digression about the tyrannicides, with which the historian questions the Athenians' memory of Harmodius and Aristogeiton and explains the truth about the tyrannicides and the Peisistratids. The point that is put forward is that Thucydides, in interrupting with this digression his account about Alcibiades' involvement in the case of the Herms, does not only criticise the flaws of his compatriots' collective memory about the tyrannicides, but he also conveys the message that the story of Harmodius and Aristogeiton was intentionally distorted by politicians and demagogues in their speeches against Alcibiades in the Assembly and in court. Thucydides' emphasis on the institutional and rhetorical context within which the tyrannicides were evoked as democratic symbols at the expense of Alcibiades' alleged plan to overthrow democracy emerges from specific verbal choices. The surviving works of 4th-century oratory which refer to the tyrannicides prove that in the Assembly and court the Athenians referred to Harmodius and Aristogeiton in an idealising fashion, which leads to the conclusion that Thucydides, by offering an account which belied the established idealised image of Harmodius and Aristogeiton, thus wishes, *inter alia*, to highlight historiography's superiority over oratory in terms of the degree of validity with which each genre contributed to the preservation of historical truth.

In his account of the episode of the Herms in 415,[1] which led to Alcibiades' exile, Thucydides undertakes an extensive digression on the Peisistratids' tyranny, with a special emphasis on Hipparchus' assassination by Harmodius and Aristogeiton (6.54–59). In the chapters both before and after the excursus (ch. 6.27–29, ch. 53, and ch. 60–61), the historian narrates that the statues of Hermes in the streets of Athens were mutilated shortly before the Sicilian expedition. The Athenians took the event as a sinister omen for the fate of the enterprise, while they also suspected that the perpetrators sought to express through their action their intention to overthrow democracy. Alcibiades was accused of participating

1 All dates in this paper refer to BC.

https://doi.org/10.1515/9783110751970-010

in the mutilation. After all, he was believed to have been involved in similar sacrileges in the past, such as the profanation of the Mysteries. Subsequently, his stained record, alongside with his voluptuous lifestyle, gave the opportunity to his political rivals to accuse him of participating in the mutilation of the Herms too and of aspiring to impose a tyranny. The Athenian people, remembering the harsh government of the Peisistratids in the last years of their tyranny, feared the return of a similar totalitarian regime. As a result, in an atmosphere of terror and suspicion, they condemned Alcibiades and other citizens without any meticulous scrutiny of the accusations at their disposal.

On the occasion of these events, Thucydides interrupts his narrative in order to relate how the tyrannicides killed Hipparchus in 514 and how the Peisistratids were later on (in 510) overthrown by the Alcmeonids with the help of the Spartans. His aim in this digression is to prove that the Athenians had a false picture of the Peisistratids' tyranny. In particular, he argues the following: (a) the tyrannicides did not kill Hipparchus in order to overthrow the tyranny, but were motivated by their homosexual love. Hipparchus unsuccessfully tried to seduce Harmodius. The latter rejected him and Hipparchus decided to insult him by excluding his sister from religious institutions. Harmodius revealed the situation to his lover Aristogeiton and the two men decided to kill Hipparchus. (b) Contrary to what many Athenians believed, it was not Hipparchus but his older brother, Hippias, who was tyrant at that time. And (c) the Peisistratids were not overthrown by Harmodius and Aristogeiton in 514 but by the Alcmeonids and the Spartans four years later (in 510).

This digression constitutes one of the most discussed passages in the entire *History*. It is typically described by modern scholars with characterizations such as "puzzling",[2] "unusual",[3] "a long and surprising jump",[4] or "strange and sudden".[5] Some critics can hardly recognise any connection between the excursus and its context. In the *floruit* of the Separatist Era, the digression was taken to be one of the strongest indications of the incomplete state of the work. Edward Schwartz argued that the excursus belongs to Thucydides' unpolished notes, which the editor clumsily incorporated at the point where we find it.[6] For others,

2 Connor 1984, 176.
3 Meyer 2008, 13.
4 *COT* III, 433.
5 Wohl 1999, 349.
6 Schwartz 1919, 181–184, followed by Grundy 1948, 424–427; Dover 1973, 20; Proctor 1980, 16, 195. Müller-Strübing 1873, 543ff. and followed by Classen, 91 and Smith 1913, 102 assumed that Thucydides' choice to compose the excursus was motivated by his family's origins from the Peisistratids. See, *contra*, Fornara 1968, 401 n. 6.

it was not the editor but Thucydides himself who put the digression at that point, in the hope that he would omit it in a final revision of the work; however, he never did so due to his unexpected death. What is more, he wrote such a detailed account of the Peisistratids' tyranny merely out of an aspiration to prove his methodological superiority over his predecessors, such as Herodotus and Hellanicus.[7] Others have suspected that the digression betrays the existence of different stages of the *History*'s composition: given that Thucydides also refers to the Athenians' false memories of the Peisistratids, outside of Book VI, at ch. 1.20.2, the two parts of this doublet have occasionally been believed to have been written in different periods.[8]

More recent scholarship has gradually adopted a more favourable attitude towards the excursus. This shift in attitudes was reinforced, as is usual in such cases, by an effort to connect the digression with its context. This methodological shift proved highly fruitful, as it revealed that the excursus has a central role in the way the reader perceives the episode of the mutilation of the Herms. Most importantly, the pluralism of views on the matter suggests, if anything, that the digression is not only closely related with its context, but also that it is connected to it on many different interpretive levels. On the one hand, for some readers, Thucydides intended through this excursus to show that the Athenians' false impression about their past led them to inappropriate political choices, with the most crucial of these being Alcibiades' removal. By seeking to demonstrate that distorted memories of the tyrannicides obscured the Athenians' judgment in 415, Thucydides focused on the aforementioned points at which the Athenians had an inadequate picture of their past.[9]

---

7 Dover 1965, 58–61. On Thucydides' digression as an open dialogue with Herodotus, see below n. 42 and with Hellanicus, see Jacoby 1949, 158–161; *HCT* IV, 323–325; Dover 1965, 59–60; Fornara 1968, 402; Connor 1984, 177 n. 47; de Bakker 2013, 29 n. 22.

8 Jacoby 1949, 338 n. 47 argued that Thucydides wrote ch. 1.20 at an earlier stage, namely after Hellanicus' *Atthis* appeared, and that ch. 6.54–59 were composed at a later stage. By contrast, Cwiklinski 1877, 54–55 believed that ch. 1.20 was written later than the digression of Book VI. See, *contra*, Grundy's 1948, 426–427 arguments.

9 For this direction of thought, see Edmunds' 1975, 194–195, 206 view that Thucydides endeavoured to show how Hipparchus' assassination by the tyrannicides was "a chance event, the recollection of which led to a bad fortune event"; Connor 1984, 116 and 177 n. 47; Orwin 1994, 125–126; Rutherford 1994 *passim*; Ober 1998, 54 n. 4; Greenwood 2006, 51; Rood 2012, 138. See, also, Ludwig's 2002, 74ff. view (followed by Shanske 2006) that the tragic way in which the Athenians were led to the Sicilian disaster due to their inadequate knowledge of their history resembles Attic tragedy and especially Oedipus' doom due to his ignorance of his past. Marchant 1897, 192 believed that the political connotations of Thucydides' narrative addressed, *inter alia*, young students.

Last, scholars also recognise in the digression Thucydides' intention to draw certain parallels between the events of 514 and those of 415. The tyrannicides' individualism and passions (expressed by their fear, rage, and hate) match with the self-interest of Alcibiades' rivals and the fears of the Athenian *dēmos*. Furthermore, in both cases the prevalence of personal animosities over sobriety and reason led to political mistakes that were ultimately harmful for Athens' prosperity. The tyrant-slayers' actions led to the transformation of a modest tyranny into a totalitarian governance and to Hippias' betrayal. Accordingly, Alcibiades' condemnation generated his betrayal and, subsequently, the Sicilian disaster and Athens' eventual defeat at the end of the war.[10] Others compare the tyrannicides' *erōs* with the Athenians' imperialistic *erōs* for the Sicilian enterprise.[11] Parallels are also drawn between the deterioration of the Peisistratids' tyranny after the tyrannicides' activity and the intensification of Athens' cruelty over its allies after the latter's attempts to revolt.[12] By means of these suggestive comparisons, Thucydides is believed to aim at addressing certain traditional dark spots in Athenian politics.

The digression by no means proves the unpolished state of the work; neither can it be explained by Dover's one-sided view that it exclusively reflects Thucydides' competitiveness towards other historians. Chapters 54–59 are deliberately placed by Thucydides in the middle of the Herms case and, what is more, concerning the question of how they interact with their context, Simon Hornblower has written very aptly: "[t]he answer is surely multifactorial: we need not uniquely privilege any one explanation".[13] For this reason, any effort to readdress the digression's narrative function should not have a polemical but rather a supplementary character. As Elizabeth A. Meyer notes, any new reading of the digression through the prism of its context "by no means excludes most of the previous readings – it is, indeed, to some extent dependent on them".[14] Being in full agreement with this line of thought, I thus do not aim in this paper to undermine any of the previous theories. I would rather like to unearth one fur-

---

10 This view was introduced by Schadewaldt 1919 and was followed by many scholars (see Hunter 1973; Rawlings 1981, 103–117; Orwin 1994, 125–126; Williams 1998, 246–247; Stahl 2003, 1–11; Meyer 2008). In this line of thought, de Bakker 2012, 37 discerns Thucydides' intention to highlight in the digression and its context the significant role of individuals in Athenian politics.

11 Connor 1984, 178–179. Cf. Rhodes 2006, 529. See also Wohl 1999.

12 Hunter 1973; Rood 1998, 280; Williams 1998, 246–247.

13 *COT* III, 433.

14 Meyer 2008, 15.

ther level on which, in my view, the digression is linked to its context and thereby to readdress some views hitherto noticed.

In particular, I focus on Thucydides' special emphasis on the distortive nature of the evidence offered by the witnesses and on the responsibility of the Athenian institutions for this falsification of information in the Herms episode. Thucydides' interest in the invalidity of the accusations against Alcibiades has already been addressed in previous scholarship, with the most popular theory being that in ch. 6.27–61 he juxtaposes the Athenians' unsuccessful examination of the Herms case and the stories on the tyrant-slayers with the methodological punctilio with which he approaches both issues himself. It has also been argued that the historian implicitly invites his readers to compare the Athenians' inconsiderate speculations about Alcibiades' intentions in 415 with the tyrannicides' inconsiderate judgment of Hippias' intentions in 514. These are certainly two major functions of Thucydides' emphasis on the distortive nature of witnesses and evidence in the Herms case. Still, they are not the only ones. Modern scholarship has overlooked the fact that Thucydides, by means of arresting stylistic choices, places the issue of the invalidity of the accusations against Alcibiades in an intensely institutional and rhetorical framework. In this way, as it will be demonstrated below, Thucydides invites the reader to understand the distortive way in which the story of the tyrannicides was abused by rhetoricians in law-courts and the Assembly. This means that: (a) Thucydides does not only criticise false rumours about the tyrannicides, but also castigates the institutional circumstances which nurtured such falsifications; and (b) historiography is juxtaposed with oratory.

In Sections 1 and 2 of the following discussion, I will analyse the stylistic choices with which Thucydides foregrounds the falsification of the facts in 415 and, most importantly, the responsibility of the state and orators for this falsification. I will argue that Thucydides deliberately places the tyrannicides excursus within an institutional and rhetorical framework of distortion, in order to contrast his own reliable narrative of the tyrannicides with traditional practices of their abuse in court and the Assembly. Unfortunately, in ch. 6.27–29, ch. 53, and ch. 60–61, Thucydides remains silent with regard to how the orators of 415 used Harmodius and Aristogeiton as historical *exempla* at the expense of Alcibiades. As a result, it is impossible to detect any tangible antitheses between Thucydides' treatment of the tyrant-slayers in his digression and the way Alcibiades' opponents did so. I will endeavour to fill this gap in Section 3, by reading the digression in light of the evidence from surviving 4th-century Attic oratory.

1 The institutional context of the digression: the state's responsibility for the distortion of the tyrannicides myth

The emphasis on the distortion of evidence is evident, *inter alia*, in the way Thucydides employs the verb μηνύω and its cognates throughout the passage.[15] Out of the thirteen times this verbal family occurs in the *History*,[16] this verb is found six times in the mutilation account (46%), always in a context which devalues the reliability of the witnesses and the evidence offered by them. In the opening paragraphs of the episode, Thucydides mentions the authorities' invitation to the inhabitants of the city to report without fear any information related to the case (6.27.2):

> καὶ τοὺς δράσαντας ᾔδει οὐδείς, ἀλλὰ μεγάλοις μηνύτροις δημοσίᾳ οὗτοί τε ἐζητοῦντο καὶ προσέτι ἐψηφίσαντο, καὶ εἴ τις ἄλλο τι οἶδεν ἀσέβημα γεγενημένον, μηνύειν ἀδεῶς τὸν βουλόμενον καὶ ἀστῶν καὶ ξένων καὶ δούλων.
>
> No one knew who the perpetrators were, but there was a search for them with large rewards out of public funds, and they voted in addition that whoever wished, if he knew of any other sacrilege that had occurred, was to give witness statements with impunity, citizen, foreigner, or slave.[17]

Through deliberate cross-references, Thucydides highlights the inability of the Athenian legal system to infuse the aspiring witnesses with the desired sense of security. He does so by repeatedly stressing the fact that the case was examined within an atmosphere of fear, suspicion, and insecurity. First, we read that the news of the mutilation elicited the people's fear that the sacrilege was a sinister omen for the future of the enterprise (6.27.3). In the second part of the narrative (6.53–61), Thucydides stresses the fact that the Athenians' judgment towards the testimonies of the witnesses was affected to a high degree by a general atmosphere of suspicion (6.53.2: "instead of testing the informers they found everything grounds for suspicion" οὐ δοκιμάζοντες τοὺς μηνυτάς, ἀλλὰ πάντα ὑπόπτως ἀποδεχόμενοι). Specifically, the Athenian *dēmos*, recalling the harsh

15 My analysis of the use of μηνύω and its cognates in the mutilation episode as words associated with sycophants is a detailed expansion of Harvey's (1990, 104 n. 3) short reference to this issue.

16 1.20.2; 2.42.2; 4.89.1; 6.27.2; 6.28.1; 6.53.1; 6.57.2; 6.60.2; 6.60.4; 6.61.4; 6.74.1; 8.39.3; 8.50.5.

17 I use throughout the translation of Lattimore 1998.

final period of the Peisistratids' tyranny, was afraid of a potential overthrow of democracy and thus a return to a tyranny, which is why they were occupied by fear and suspicion (6.53.3: ἐφοβεῖτο αἰεὶ καὶ πάντα ὑπόπτως ἐλάμβανεν "the people [...] were in constant fear and saw everything as suspicious", which frames the tyrannicides digression, along with 6.60.1: ὧν ἐνθυμούμενος ὁ δῆμος ὁ τῶν Ἀθηναίων [...] χαλεπὸς ἦν τότε καὶ ὑπόπτης ἐς τοὺς περὶ τῶν μυστικῶν τὴν αἰτίαν λαβόντας "taking all this to heart and recalling [...] the people of Athens were at this time bitter and suspicious of anyone who stood accused over the Mysteries", in a ring composition).[18] Suspicion against Alcibiades is also present in the closing paragraphs of the episode (6.61.4: πανταχόθεν τε περιειστήκει ὑποψία ἐς τὸν Ἀλκιβιάδην "from every direction suspicion surrounded Alcibiades"). Thucydides creates a sharp contrast between the state's invitation for everyone to testify without fear (ἀδεῶς) and the general atmosphere of fear in which the case was investigated. This antithesis foregrounds the ineffectiveness of the city to realise its goals.

The verb μηνύω occurs again in the first testimony we read, where Thucydides discretely foregrounds the self-interest that characterised the witnesses, by mentioning that they were metics and slaves (6.28.1: μηνύεται οὖν ἀπὸ μετοίκων τέ τινων καὶ ἀκολούθων).[19] He also implies that the information offered by them should not be considered as solid evidence but merely clues that Alcibiades and others were guilty for the mutilation of the Herms. For the foreigners and the servants merely testified to the sacrilegious conduct of the past (this weak evidence is also referred to by the μεμηνυμένων in 6.53.1).[20]

The verb is used in an equally snide way for the testimony which marked the fate of Alcibiades. According to Thucydides, a certain individual from among the defendants, while in prison, was convinced by one of his co-prisoners to snitch on those who were guilty for the mutilation of the Herms, including himself, in exchange for which service he would secure amnesty for himself (6.60.2–4). Thucydides draws our attention to the fact that both this witness and his advisor did not aim at contributing to actually enhancing the case, but at closing it as soon as possible (the advisor) and out of personal interest (the witness). The subsequent Historical Present (HP)[21] μηνύει (6.60.4) signals the decisive nature of this questionable testimony, the obscurity of which is

---

18 Meyer 2008, 19–20.

19 Cf. Schadewaldt 1929, 92; Rawlings 1981, 108–109, who draws a parallel between the low status of these metics and slaves and that of Aristogeiton in the excursus. Cf. Meyer 2008, 19.

20 *COT* III, 377–378.

21 For this HP see Rijksbaron 2011, 178.

explicitly noted by Thucydides in his comment that it was never discovered whether or not those accused and convicted to death were truly guilty (6.60.5).[22]

The way Thucydides uses the HP in the mutilation episode is equally enlightening with regard to the emphasis he seeks to lay on the central role of witnesses in the case. In ch. 6.27–29, ch. 53, and ch. 60–61, we meet five HP, which, as usual, mark the pivotal stages of the story-line.[23] Three out of five HP are related to the witnesses (6.28.1: μηνύεται for the metics and slaves; 6.60.2: ἀναπείθεται and 6.60.4: μηνύει for the decisive witness). The two remaining HP of these chapters are the καταλαμβάνουσι, referring to the arrival of Salaminia to Sicily, the ship which was to carry the order that Alcibiades be recalled and tried at Athens (6.53.1), and πέμπουσι, again referring to the Athenians' decision to send the Salaminia to Sicily. Thucydides uses the HP only for the main source of most developments of the case (the witnesses' false testimonies) and its main effect, the Athenians' decision to recall Alcibiades. The elements of evidence and witnesses occupy a decisive role in this cause-and-effect scheme that is delineated by the HP.

Further emphasis on the elements of evidence and witnesses is also laid by the use of some rare cognates of the verb μηνύω. First, we read the noun μήνυμα for the testimonies against Alcibiades. Out of the three times it occurs in the *History* (cf. 8.50.5), the word is found two times in the Herms episode (6.29.1: μηνύματα; 6.61.2: μήνυμα). We also read of the *hapax legomenon* μηνύτροις (6.27.2), referring to the rewards to those willing to testify.

What is the value of these observations for understanding Thucydides' goals in the digression of the tyrannicides? It has been traditionally argued that in this digression the historian wished to restore the Athenians' collective memory and thus to demonstrate that false conceptions of the past and the fear they created trapped the Athenians into convulsive mishandlings of the Herms case.[24] Indeed, Thucydides believed that the Athenians' false memories of the Peisistratids' tyranny contributed in this case to the creation of an atmosphere of fear, especially in the circles of the masses. No doubt Alcibiades' rivals also used the glorious *exemplum* of the tyrannicides in order to amplify the panic-

---

22 Meyer 2008, 20.

23 Sicking/Stork 1997, 165; Rijksbaron 2002[3]; Wårvik 2004, 99; Allan 2011, 42. On HP in Thucydides, see Lallot/Rijksbaron/Jacquinod/Buijs 2011. For the function of HP in the Herms episode, see Rijksbaron 2011, 177–194, and in Book VIII see Liotsakis 2017, 32–36.

24 Smith 1913, 102; Kinzl 1973, 506–507, with special emphasis on Thucydides' implicit response to current genealogies; Rawlings 1981, 102–103; Tsakmakis 1995, 205–208; Greenwood 2006, 51. For further bibliography see Meyer 2008, 14 n. 5.

stricken zeal of *dēmos* to defend democracy.[25] The *dēmos'* ignorance of the past rendered them vulnerable to those uplifting slogans, and this was one of the ways in which, for Thucydides, the memory of the tyrant-slayers led the Athenian people to false judgments and decisions.

However, the way Thucydides presents certain Athenians as instigating Alcibiades' conviction on the basis of untrustworthy evidence, as well as the intense atmosphere of fear and self-interest concerning both the accusers and the witnesses, transfer the focal point of interest from the masses (6.53.3; 60.1) to those Athenians who were not merely incapable of weighing the story of the tyrannicides, but were also *willing* to distort and misquote it, exactly as they did with the evidence in the process of examining the Herms case. The narrative conveys a strong impression that influential Athenians would have scrutinised the evidence and the witnesses in *any kind of* distortive fashion, out of their own narrow interests. In this way, Thucydides prepares the reader for the self-seeking and distortive spirit within which Alcibiades' rivals abused the myth of Harmodius and Aristogeiton too at his expense.

In view of this, apart from its other connections to its context mentioned by previous scholars, I discern one further way in which the digression fits well with the Herms episode: on a narrative level, the issue of the false rumours about the tyrannicides does not emerge as separate from its context or as a surprise for the reader, but as an integral part of a series of falsifications of evidence. In the process of reading so much information about the suspicious nature of the witnesses and evidence and the way they were scrutinised, the reader is invited to treat the arbitrary tales about the tyrant-slayers partly as something natural, namely as the fruit of the same political schemes.

Seen through the prism of the corrupt legal framework within which the tyrannicides were invoked, Thucydides' digression about them thus conveys the message that their story was not merely the result of misconceptions and faded memories, but that it also served as only one from among many means of a general and sophisticated distortion of evidence and facts. In this respect, the digression of the tyrannicides should not be seen as denouncing merely the inefficiency of the Athenians' collective memory, but also their intentions to falsify whatever they could and, what is more, the responsibility of the legal institutions for those schemes.

It is very important to note that Thucydides pays particular attention to the institutional framework within which evidence and witnesses were misleading-

---

25 *HCT* IV, 326. On Thucydides' emphasis on the political maneuvers of Alcibiades' enemies in these chapters, cf. Romilly 1963, 208.

ly abused. This is because, at that time, the tyrannicides story was not only circulating in private circles but also within this corrupt and thus distortive institutional framework: in court and the Assembly. So, if we wish to discern all different shades of the tyrannicides digression and unearth as many as possible messages aimed by Thucydides in composing it,[26] we cannot but read it in its legal context as well.

Before examining how reading the digression through the prism of its institutional context may lead us to new speculations about its goal-setting, let us first demonstrate the linguistic and thematic features of the Herms episode which prove Thucydides' special interest in the legal dimension of the case. To begin with, it is striking that the chapters on the mutilation are unique throughout the *History* in terms of the degree to which Thucydides penetrates the institutional mechanisms of an ancient Greek city.[27] As a result, this narrative is marked by an abundance of rare words related to the Athenians' legal life. Let us first mark out five *hapax legomena*. We have already addressed the reward offered by the authorities to those willing to testify (6.27.2: μηνύτροις), while we also find the word μετάπεμπτον, a *hapax legomenon* that refers to the Athenians' decision to recall Alcibiades from Sicily (6.29.3). The account is also spatially vivid in denoting the place where the major witness decided to testify against himself, Alcibiades, and the others (see the *hapax legomena* δεσμωτηρίῳ and ξυνδεσμωτῶν in ch. 6.60.2). We also find some rare words related to Alcibiades' apology (6.53.1: ἀπολογίαν; cf. only ch. 3.61.1) and to those accused along with him ξυνδιαβεβλημένοι (6.61.6; cf. only 6.44.1) and καταιτιαθέντας (6.60.4; cf. only ch. 3.42.3). With one further rare word, the participle οὐ δοκιμάζοντες, Thucydides zooms in on the inadequate evaluation of the evidence (6.53.2; cf. only ch. 3.38.5 referring, again, to the scrutiny of evidence and ch. 2.53.3 in a more general sense).

The historian's interest in the legal aspects of the case is also reflected by stylistic sophistication. First, Thucydides presents multiple instances of *variatio* regarding three different stages of the legal procedures through which witnesses and evidence were scrutinised: (a) the investigations (6.27.1: ἐζητοῦντο; 6.53.2: ζήτησιν ἐποιοῦντο); (b) Alcibiades' trial (6.29.1: κρίνεσθαι; 6.29.3: ἀγωνί-

26 Given that Thucydides' goal-setting in composing it is multi-dimensional. Cf. *COT* III, 433; Meyer 2008, 13–15.

27 Cf. the chapters on Pausanias' trial in Sparta (1.131–135.1), in which we do not find a similar use of vocabulary of institutional character. For a comparison between the Spartans' careful treatment of Pausanias' case and the Athenians' frivolous treatment of Alcibiades' trial, see Douglas 1966.

ζηται; 6.29.3: ἀγωνίσασθαι; 6.60.4: διὰ δίκης ἐλθεῖν); and his apology (6.53.1: ἐς ἀπολογίαν; 6.61.5: ἀπολογησομένῳ).[28] Second, the historian brings to life contemporary documentary wording; the phrase ἐψηφίσαντο ... μηνύειν ἀδεῶς τὸν βουλόμενον (6.27.2),[29] highlights the state's energetic – still ineffective – role in encouraging the inhabitants to contribute to the investigation of the case. Third, we meet the *hapax legomenon* ἐπανεῖπον (6.60.4), which is also very rare in the surviving Attic literature too, occurring only, except from here, in Ar. *Av.* 1072.[30] With this verb Thucydides records the official updating of the aforementioned decree.

Thucydides deviates from his typical indifference in legal details, undoubtedly because these events were of great significance for the very subject of his work; in his opinion, the Herms case determined the outcome of the Sicilian expedition and, to a certain degree, of the war in its entirety. However, a question still remains: why did Thucydides insist on delineating the legal framework of these events in such detail? He could have criticised the untenable nature of Alcibiades' accusers without describing the institutional circumstances under which the case unfolded.

Thucydides' aim, I believe, is to attribute the Athenians' fiasco in the Herms case to their inability to ensure that their institutional mechanisms remained untouched by personal interests; and as far as our subject is concerned, the story of the tyrannicides, the historian also wished to put the blame for the distortive use of the tyrannicides, apart from the inefficient knowledge of some part of the population, on the very institutional system of the city. As transpires from our analysis of the Herms narrative, it was the institutions too that were responsible for the climate of distortion of the truth. The investigation of the evidence was ineffective, as the truth was never discovered; the reward promised by the state to those willing to testify did not lead to the revelation of the actual events; and equally vulnerable was the city's prison system. All these aspects – the perfunctory collection of information, the corrupt public investigators of the evidence, and the perforated system of detention in official custody – are constituents of Athens' legal mechanisms; and it is these mechanisms that are presented by Thucydides as contributing to an atmosphere of suspicion and distortion, in which some Athenians found the opportunity to misuse, apart from the evidence about Alcibiades, the story of the tyrannicides as well. Be-

28 On Thucydides' special care of *variatio*, see Ros 1968.

29 *HCT* IV, 289.

30 *HCT* IV, 338.

sides, as will be demonstrated in Section 3, it was the Athenian state itself that nurtured the idolization of the tyrannicides.

2 The rhetorical context of the digression: Thucydides as a speaker against orators

The penetration into the legal context of the use of the tyrannicides in 415 is of great relevance for apprehending Thucydides' goals in his digression about them, as it opens a window towards the circumstances of communication under which the tyrant-slayers were abused during that period, in both judicial and deliberative speeches. This approach may unveil some unnoticed antitheses latent in ch. 6.27–63, namely antitheses between Thucydides' treatment of Harmodius and Aristogeiton and the way the orators involved in the Herms case treated them.

In particular, Thucydides conveys the impression that the story of the tyrannicides must have been used in a distortive way within a strict institutional framework, namely by orators in court and the Assembly. According to the historian, as soon as the first accusations against Alcibiades appeared, his political opponents took advantage of the situation and claimed not only that he had participated in all the sacrilegious activities he was accused of, but also that his aim in doing so was to overthrow democracy and impose a tyranny (6.28.2). This suggests that it was within this framework that the tyrannicides must have been employed by those demagogues as a way of protecting democracy and, subsequently, encouraging Alcibiades to be put to death.[31]

Once again, it is stylistic embellishment that foregrounds the element of rhetorical falsification of present and past events. In his first mention of Alcibiades' rivals, Thucydides writes that (6.28.2):

> καὶ αὐτὰ ὑπολαμβάνοντες οἱ μάλιστα τῷ Ἀλκιβιάδῃ ἀχθόμενοι ἐμποδὼν ὄντι σφίσι μὴ αὐτοῖς τοῦ δήμου βεβαίως προεστάναι, καὶ νομίσαντες, εἰ αὐτὸν ἐξελάσειαν, πρῶτοι ἂν

31 Undoubtedly, Alcibiades' general conduct must have already encouraged in the minds of *dēmos* the image of an aspiring tyrant, thus having led them, long before the Herms case, to associations between his political aspirations and the Peisistratids' tyranny. For Alcibiades as an aspiring tyrant in the Athenians' minds, see Seager 1967; Palmer 1982; Forde 1989, 34; Bloedow 1992a, 215; Bloedow 1992b, 147 n. 22; Gribble 1999, 37, 41, 64–65, 77, 85–86, 134–136, 140–141, 156, 189–193, 229, 268; Wohl 1999, 351ff.; Grant–Smith 2009; Larivée 2012; Harris 2016.

εἶναι, ἐμεγάλυνον καὶ ἐβόων ὡς ἐπὶ δήμου καταλύσει τά τε μυστικὰ καὶ ἡ τῶν Ἑρμῶν περικοπὴ γένοιτο καὶ οὐδὲν εἴη αὐτῶν ὅτι οὐ μετ' ἐκείνου ἐπράχθη, ἐπιλέγοντες τεκμήρια τὴν ἄλλην αὐτοῦ ἐς τὰ ἐπιτηδεύματα οὐ δημοτικὴν παρανομίαν.

Taking up the charges were those who especially resented Alcibiades for standing in the way of their assured ascendancy over the people, and in the belief that by removing him they would rise to the top they exaggerated them and raised the cry that both the Mysteries and the mutilation of the herms were connected with the overthrow of the democracy, and that none of this had been done without his complicity, adducing as evidence the undemocratic licentiousness of his conduct in general.

The verb μεγαλύνω ("to exaggerate") is very rare in Thucydides. It occurs, apart from here, only in ch. 8.81.2, in which Alcibiades endeavors to deceive the Athenians at Samos by overstating his influence on Tissaphernes. Accordingly, the verb foregrounds here the element of deceit. As for the second verb, βοάω, Thucydides typically uses it in order to delineate an atmosphere of political and diplomatic turbulence, in a context related to negotiations, either between embassies of different cities or in the assembly of a single city.[32] What is more, in four out of fifteen times it occurs,[33] the verb βοάω is used, either in simple or in compound form, with reference to Alcibiades and his political rivals in Athens,[34] a fact which in itself suggests that, for Thucydides, current debates related to Alcibiades typically generated nothing but bluster in the political life of Athens. Alcibiades' opponents are always presented as cultivating an atmosphere of fear and harming those circumstances required for sober decision-making.[35] This is so both in the Herms case as well as in ch. 8.53.2, in which they are presented as intensely complaining about Alcibiades' upcoming return to Athens.[36]

In this case, βοάω has two sentences as subjects: first, that Alcibiades participated in all the sacrilegious acts he was accused of, and, second, that his motive was to overthrow democracy (6.28.2). As mentioned above, it was within

32 On the close connection of this verb with the element of συκοφαντία in this episode, see Harvey 1990, 104 n. 3.

33 In simple form: 4.11.4; 6.28.2; 7.48.4 (twice); 8.86.2; in compound form: 1.53.3 (ἀναβοάω); 8.53.2 and 8.78 (διαβοάω); 2.92.1, 4.34.1, and 4.112.1 (ἐμβοάω); 4.28.3 (ἐπιβοάω); 1.67.1, 1.115.2, and 5.45.4 (καταβοάω).

34 5.45.4; 6.16.6; 6.28.2; 8.53.2.

35 They create an atmosphere of rage, hate and fear, elements typically, in the *History*, preventing people from sober decision-making. For anger and decision-making in Thucydides, see Liotsakis 2017 61–62. For hate and anger, see Kouskouvelis 2019, 146–151 and for fear Kouskouvelis 2019, *passim*.

36 On Thucydides' negative portraiture of Alcibiades' opponents in Book VIII, see Liotsakis 2022, forthcoming.

the framework of this second accusation that Alcibiades' accusers must have used Harmodius and Aristogeiton as *exempla* to imitate, in their efforts to rouse the Athenians against Alcibiades. The use of the verbs ἐμεγάλυνον and ἐβόων indicates that in such a context the story of the tyrannicides was employed by Alcibiades' enemies as a means of deception, in order to stoke the anger and fear of the *dēmos*.

This disorderly rhetorical atmosphere of the consultations in 415 is also retained in the second appearance of Alcibiades' rivals, once again through similar linguistic choices. Alcibiades' suggestion that he be tried before the expedition to Sicily is expressed by the *hapax* ἐπεμαρτύρετο (6.29.2). This verb brings to life the state of intense emotional stimulation, in which Alcibiades defended himself. Equally vivid are the verbs which describe the rhetorical claims of his opponents. Thucydides writes that they struggle to dissuade the Athenians from accepting Alcibiades' proposal (6.29.3):

> οἱ δ' ἐχθροὶ δεδιότες τό τε στράτευμα μὴ εὔνουν ἔχῃ, ἢν ἤδη ἀγωνίζηται, ὅ τε δῆμος μὴ μαλακίζηται θεραπεύων ὅτι δι' ἐκεῖνον οἵ τ' Ἀργεῖοι ξυνεστράτευον καὶ τῶν Μαντινέων τινές, ἀπέτρεπον καὶ ἀπέσπευδον, ἄλλους ῥήτορας ἐνιέντες οἳ ἔλεγον νῦν μὲν πλεῖν αὐτὸν καὶ μὴ κατασχεῖν τὴν ἀναγωγήν, ἐλθόντα δὲ κρίνεσθαι ἐν ἡμέραις ῥηταῖς, βουλόμενοι ἐκ μείζονος διαβολῆς, ἣν ἔμελλον ῥᾷον αὐτοῦ ἀπόντος ποριεῖν, μετάπεμπτον κομισθέντα αὐτὸν ἀγωνίσασθαι. καὶ ἔδοξε πλεῖν τὸν Ἀλκιβιάδην.

> But his enemies, fearing that he would have the army partial to him if tried right away, and that the populace would be lenient, showing favouritism because it was his doing that the Argives and some of the Mantineans made up part of the force, were opposed and put up an active resistance, bringing to bear additional speakers who urged that he sail now and not delay the departure but come back and stand trial within a specified period, wanting him to go on trial when recalled under heavier incrimination, which they expected to bring about more easily in his absence. And it was resolved that Alcibiades should sail.

Similarly to ch. 6.28.2, here too Thucydides uses language suggestive of an orator's efforts to elicit tension in the audience's minds. The pleonastic pair ἀπέτρεπον καὶ ἀπέσπευδον (which strikingly parallels the preceding rhetorical pair ἐμεγάλυνον καὶ ἐβόων in ch. 6.28.2) builds a crescendo which reflects the gradual intensification of the efforts to annihilate Alcibiades (the verb ἀποσπεύδω, also occurring in Hdt. 6.109; 7.17, means "to be zealous in preventing, dissuade earnestly").[37] Equally sophisticated is the choice of the participle ἐνιέντες ("stir-

37 LSJ *s.v.* ἀποσπεύδω.

ring up"); the verb ἐνίημι occurs only twice throughout the work (cf. 4.115.2) and only here indicates a state of rhetorical commotion.

Also significant in this respect is the use of the noun ῥήτορας for the supporters of Alcibiades' rivals. Thucydides uses this noun only three times throughout the *History*, in the other two occurrences with pejorative connotations about the Athenian rhetoricians' practice of deceiving the *dēmos* and leading them to disastrous decisions. In ch. 3.40.3, Cleon uses this noun to refer to those speakers whose purpose is to please the audience with their speeches, and thereby convince it about theses which serve their personal interest but harm the common good. Similarly, in ch. 8.8.1, Thucydides uses this noun to refer to those who had supported the Sicilian expedition, which he clearly treats with a critical eye (2.65). The fact that this noun in Thucydides is typically associated with the disastrous consequences of the Athenian orators' advices for the future of Athens indicates that its use in the Herms context, in which Thucydides openly castigates the orators opposing Alcibiades for harming Athens for the sake of their own interests,[38] is one further means for Thucydides, along with the couples ἐμεγάλυνον καὶ ἐβόων and ἐπέτρεπον καὶ ἀπέσπευδον, and the participle ἐνιέντες, to delineate a negative portrait of them.

As transpires from our analysis so far, Thucydides leads the reader through arresting verbal choices to the conclusion that the accusations against Alcibiades' alleged aspiration to overthrow democracy, and subsequently everything used in support of these accusations (including the tyrannicides' *exempla*), served as nothing less than a means of deceiving and disturbing political tranquility. And, given that Thucydides, in his digression, wished to respond to those who used the story of the tyrannicides, he is certainly targeting his account against the orators who did so.

It is striking in this respect that the very verb the historian uses for himself in the introduction to the digression betrays his wish to locate himself exactly in the institutional and rhetorical framework he delineated and within which the story of the tyrannicides was disseminated. Let us read the opening sentences of the digression (6.54.1):

38 Although in 2.65.11 Thucydides does not offer a precise list of those mistakes, most scholars rightly believe that the historian refers, among others and first of all, to Alcibiades' recall. See Finley 1942, 224; Brunt 1952, 59–60; Douglas 1966, 150; Dover in *HCT* V, 424; Pouncey 1980, 108–109; Rawlings 1981, 136; Rhodes 1988, 245; Cawkwell 1997, 77–78, with hesitation; Gribble 1999, 176–180 and 176 n. 51 with earlier bibliography. Liotsakis 2022, forthcoming.

Τὸ γὰρ Ἀριστογείτονος καὶ Ἁρμοδίου τόλμημα δι' ἐρωτικὴν ξυντυχίαν ἐπεχειρήθη, ἣν ἐγὼ ἐπὶ πλέον διηγησάμενος ἀποφανῶ οὔτε τοὺς ἄλλους οὔτε αὐτοὺς Ἀθηναίους περὶ τῶν σφετέρων τυράννων οὐδὲ περὶ τοῦ γενομένου ἀκριβὲς οὐδὲν λέγοντας.

For the exploit of Aristogeiton and Harmodius was undertaken because of a love affair, and by describing it in full I will show that neither other sources nor the Athenians themselves say anything accurate about their own tyrants or about the incident.

In Thucydides the verb ἀποφαίνω typically possesses an intense rhetorical flavor. Out of the eighteen times it occurs throughout the work,[39] in nine times (50%) it is used by orators in speeches, and mostly when an orator tries to refute his opponent's view, exactly as Thucydides does against the Athenians' memories of the tyrant-slayers. In the debate about whether or not they would annihilate the entire male population of Mytilene, Diodotus announces that he will prove that the Mytileneans committed injustices against the Athenians (3.44.2: ἀποφήνω). In Sicily, Hermocrates also explains in advance that he will share with the audience his opinion, which, he thinks, is the most profitable choice for Sicily (4.59.1: ἀποφαινόμενος). He also uses this verb in his speech in the Camarinean Assembly, explaining, again in the proem of his speech, that his aim is not merely to show that the Athenians harm the Greeks of Sicily (6.77.1: ἥκομεν ἀποφανοῦντες "we are not now come to declare").

Apart from these three cases, in which the orator does not use the verb to oppose a view, in the remaining six occurrences ἀποφαίνω is used by a speaker in his effort to refute his opponent's thesis. In the trial of the Plataeans, the Thebans open their speech by saying that they are replying to the Plataeans' accusations by demonstrating that the injustices perpetrated by the Plataeans at the expense of Greece were far greater than those committed by themselves, and thus that the Plataeans deserve to be convicted to death (3.64.5: ἀποφαίνομεν). In Camarina, Euphemus uses this verb in his effort to disprove Hermocrates' arguments (6.83.3: ἀποφαίνομεν).

On some occasions, the refutational force of the verb is also expressed linguistically, in terms of certain verbal choices. In his third speech to the Athenians, Pericles refutes their view that their power is confined to the control of their allies, explaining that they rather rule both land and sea (2.62.2). In Book III, Cleon wonders who would disagree with him and claims that the Mytilenean policy does not harm Athens' interests (3.38.1). He consequently clarifies that

39 Apart from 6.54.1: 1.133; 2.13.5; 2.13.8; 2.62.2; 3.38.1; 3.39.1; 3.44.2; 3.63.1; 3.64.5; 3.94.4; 4.3.2; 4.59.1; 4.83.5; 6.77.1; 6.83.3; 8.45.6; 8.85.2; 8.93.2.

his demonstration aims at nothing but to dissuade the Athenians from sparing the Mytileneans (3.39.1: πειρώμενος ἀποτρέπειν ὑμᾶς ἀποφανῶ).

What is more, in five out of the nine times (55.5%) it appears in a speech, the verb ἀποφαίνω has an introductory role. It is used, for example, in the proem of a speech (4.59.1) or in the introductory words of a new section of a speech (3.39.1; 3.63.1; 3.64.5; 6.77.1). In both cases, a speaker programmatically announces what he will try to prove. As transpires from the aforementioned examples, Thucydides announces his aims in the introduction to the digression by using a verb with an intense rhetorical character and refutational force. Not only has he already conveyed the impression to the reader that in the Herms case the story of the tyrannicides was used in rhetorical *agōnes*, but he also enters this rhetorical turbulence as a speaker. In light of these stylistic observations about the rhetorical and refutational force of the introductory verb ἀποφανῶ, Thucydides' intention to refute through his digression not merely the Athenians in general but demagogues in particular becomes more evident in the reader's mind. Most importantly, Thucydides' rationalism, as is reflected by the verb ἀποφανῶ, is juxtaposed with the hate, anger and fear of Alcibiades' rivals, which is reflected by the two pairs, ἐβόων καὶ ἐμεγάλυνον and ἀπέτρεπον καὶ ἀπέσπευδον, and the participle ἐνιέντες. So, on a verbal level, Thucydides implicitly juxtaposes his own sobriety and rationalism with which he treated the story of the tyrannicides with the emotional tension and spirit in which some Athenian orators hostile to Alcibiades used the same story.

What is more, Thucydides presents himself as wishing to oppose not just something that is merely believed in (as is the case in his comment on the tyrannicides' myth in ch. 1.20.2: οἴονται) but something that has been *said* (6.54.1: λέγοντας). No doubt, in Thucydides the verb λέγω is also used for rumors and information given by anonymous sources, especially when used in the third person in both singular λέγεται and plural λέγουσι(ν).[40] Moreover, Thucydides is not referring here only to the Athenians, but also to the rest of the Greeks (6.54.1: οὔτε τοὺς ἄλλους οὔτε αὐτοὺς Ἀθηναίους). The participle λέγοντας thus does not refer exclusively to the orators who abused the tyrannicides' story in the Herms' case. However, it is worth noting that Thucydides orientates his interest in the introduction to his digression towards the oral dissemination of the story of tyrannicides. Having previously delineated the rhetorical atmosphere in which the tyrannicides must have been abused at that period, Thucydides leads us through the use of the participle λέγοντας to think, *inter alia*,

40 On λέγεται, λέγει, λέγουσι(ν) and similar expressions of Thucydides for his sources: Westlake 1977; Gray 2011.

about the orators who used the example of Harmodius and Aristogeiton against Alcibiades. In this way, in the introduction to the tyrannicides digression, Thucydides is not fashioning himself as merely the historian who will restore the Athenians' collective memory but also as a speaker (ἀποφανῶ) who will refute those orators (λέγοντας) who used the story of the tyrant-slayers in oral discourse.

The present analysis approaches the tyrannicides' digression through the triple prism of "sender-message-receiver". Like every narrative, the stories circulating in Athens about Harmodius and Aristogeiton were *messages* disseminated by some *senders* to some *receivers*. The scholarly emphasis on Thucydides' interest in restoring the *message* (collective memory) and in helping the *receivers* (the Athenian people) to reach the truth marginalises the focus on Thucydides' intentions also to castigate the motives of the *senders*, including Alcibiades' rivals. This three-layer approach of the false stories about the tyrannicides is also evident in ch. 1.21. In these chapters Thucydides argues that the Greeks very often accept stories about their past carelessly, without scrutinising the validity of the stories. In support of this view, he mentions the false stories about Hipparchus' assassination by Harmodius and Aristogeiton in Athens and the false impression of many Greeks that the Spartan kings have two votes in the Spartan council. The historian clearly criticises the frivolousness with which the *receivers* (Athenians and Spartans) accept sham stories about their cities. Equally evident is his effort to restore the truth of the *message* which is distorted in such cases. Form this point of view, Thucydides juxtaposes his professionalism as a historian in his scrutiny of evidence with the amateurism and naivety of others.[41]

However, Thucydides also juxtaposes himself with the *senders* of such false messages. He invites the reader to compare him with the poets and the *logographoi*. While the historian acts out of a sincere need to unearth and disseminate the truth, the poets and the *logographoi* embellish and thus falsify the truth in order to satisfy the audience. Although Thucydides does not penetrate the reasons why and the circumstances under which the poets and the *logographoi* of his age aimed at the pleasure of their audience through the distortion of historical truth, he must have had in mind, *inter alia*, the communicative framework which the poets and *logographoi* used for their own programmes. In the poets' case, it is reasonable for us to assume that Thucydides is targeting poetic competitions and banquets, during which poets were invited to

41 Hunter 1982, 287–289; Connor 1984, 27; *COT* I, 57–58; Corcella 2006, 49–50; Nicolai 2001, 277–280; Rhodes 2006, 527–529; Thomas 2006, 88.

prove their value. They amused their listeners with attractive tales, sacrificing the truth.

As for those described as *logographoi*, it is more difficult for us to penetrate the circumstances which forced them to adorn history, since we are not clear about their identity. Some scholars argue that Thucydides is referring to his predecessors, namely to prose writers of past narratives, such as Herodotus and Hellanicus.[42] However, others offer a much more convincing alternative, namely that Thucydides defines as *logographoi* the orators who used historical *exempla* such as that of the tyrannicides in order to manipulate their audiences.[43] If the second view holds true, then one is justified to conclude that, as in the digression of 6.54–59, in ch. 1.21 as well, by referring to the *logographoi* Thucydides is targeting those orators who used the tyrannicides slogan against Alcibiades in 415.

In any case, both in ch. 1.21 and in the digression of ch. 6.54–59 Thucydides approaches the falsification of the tyrannicides story not only from the perspective of the *receivers* but also from that of the *senders*. Moreover, if in ch. 1.21 he criticises the communicative framework within which poets and prose-writers (be they historians or orators) distorted the truth, in the Herms chapters, including the tyrannicides digression, he targets the institutional framework and its communicative restrictions which allowed corrupt politicians to abuse the tyrannicides story in a distortive fashion.

3 The digression in light of 4th-century oratory

What remains is to examine how Thucydides' digression creates sharp contrasts with the practices of the Athenian orators in the use of the tyrannicides' *exemplum*. The easiest way for us to discern such potential antitheses between the digression and the Herms episode would be to compare how Thucydides treats the tyrannicides with the way that Alcibiades' rivals are presented by Thucydides as doing so in the Herms narrative. However, the Thucydidean account offers no information about how Alcibiades' enemies invoked the tyrant-slayers in their speeches. Nonetheless, the surviving works of Attic oratory of the Classical Era can be of great help in this respect. In what follows, I discuss a series of texts from 4th-century attic law-court speeches which exemplify how Athenian

42 *COT* I, 58; Corcella 2006, 49 n. 54.
43 Connor 1984, 27; Grethlein 2004; Grethlein 2013, 127–128.

orators used the tyrannicides in court. I will thereby try to fill the gap of Thucydides' silence in this respect and use my observations as a new prism through which to reconsider certain aspects of the digression's scope.[44]

Let us begin with Aeschines' speech *Against Timarchus*. During Timarchus' trial for his dishonourable sexual conduct as a male prostitute, his accuser, Aeschines, anticipates that an Athenian general would defend Timarchus by evoking glorious examples of male homosexual love, such as the one between Harmodius and Aristogeiton. According to Aeschines, the general's argument could be that the tyrannicides' love proves that love between men can greatly benefit the city, provided that it is marked by self-control, mutual devotion, faith, and strong sense of justice. Aeschines answers to this hypothetical syllogism that Timarchus did not offer himself to a lover with restraint, like Harmodius offered himself to Aristogeiton, but as a prostitute. In the distinction he makes between legitimate and dishonourable love, Aeschines introduces the tyrannicides as benefactors of Athens, recognises the noble nature of their love and presents it as the model of a modest and just love, a strong indication of a prudent soul which protects both the loved and the lover from corruption (*Tim.* 132–140).[45]

In his *Ars Rhetorica*, Aristotle offers further evidence for the view that the use of the tyrannicides as an *exemplum* was a very popular *topos* in Attic forensic oratory. He records that, in one of his speeches, Iphicrates argued that nobility lies in virtuous conduct. In support of this view, Iphicrates recalled the tyrannicides' deed, commenting that they too had nothing noble to demonstrate before their virtuous action (*Rh.* 1398a). Iphicrates means, of course, to refer to Hipparchus' assassination. Elsewhere in the *Ars Rhetorica*, Aristotle refers to the Athenian orators' ungrounded generalization that Harmodius' and Aristogeiton's love proves that male homosexual love is generally of great benefit for the city (*Rh.* 1401b; cf. above Aeschines' example in *Tim.* 132).

In his speech *Against Philippides* in 338–336, Hypereides evokes the tyrant-slayers in his efforts to sully Philippides' image.[46] He accuses him of devaluing the Athenian *dēmos* with his daily conduct, although "the people have written a law forbidding anyone from speaking ill of Harmodius and Aristogeiton or singing denigrating songs about them". Hypereides' words again prove that the

44 Harris 2016 puts a similar method into effect, by comparing Alcibiades' choice to mention his own ancestors, and not those of the entire community, with the silence of speakers in this respect in Xenophon and Demosthenes.

45 Fisher 2001, 25–36.

46 See Worthington/Cooper/Harris 2001.

institutional and legal framework of Athens discouraged the citizens from doubting the tyrannicides' virtue and contribution to democracy (fr. 15b3). Even if the Athenians did devalue the tyrannicides in private daily life (a fact suggested by the law forbidding songs against them),[47] in court or in the Assembly, then orators could hardly speak ill for them and rather used such actions as incriminating evidence or, at least, as black spots in the depictions of their opponents.[48] In 389, in the legal case about Dicaeogenes' estate, a case that is chronologically much closer to the mutilation of the Herms in 415, Isaeus touches upon the tyrannicides' origins by commenting that they were not glorified because of their noble background but thanks to their virtue (*Philip.* F15b).[49]

The aforementioned examples are particularly illuminating concerning the way that the tyrannicides were employed by Athenian orators in court and, subsequently, of how they must have been used by Alcibiades' enemies too in 415. These examples thus help us to unearth some antitheses that ancient readers, who were experienced in Athenian judicial and deliberative oratory, must plausibly have discerned between Thucydides' digression and current stereotypical rhetorical abuse of the tyrannicides. These antitheses concern the following subjects:

(a) *The tyrannicides' relationship with democracy.* Orators recognise the tyrannicides' contribution to the Athenian democracy. Aeschines calls them benefactors, while Aristotle refers to the speakers' interest in the positive results of the tyrannicides' love for the political life of Athens. Isaeus and Hypereides welcome the honours offered by the city to Harmodius and Aristogeiton and delineate a dark image of their opponents by presenting them as disrespecting or being indifferent to those honours. On the other hand, Thucydides stresses the fact that Harmodius and Aristogeiton did not contribute to the fall of tyranny. They did not kill the tyrant Hippias, but his brother Hipparchus; they did not even contribute to the weakening of tyranny, given that Hipparchus' assassination generated Hippias' fears and thus the increasing severity of his tyranny; last, it was the Alcmeonids who overthrew the Peisistratids four years after Hipparchus' death by the tyrannicides.

47 See Ehrenberg 1956, 61ff., Lambin 1979, 542ff., and Henderson 1987, 153, who read Issaeus' text in light of Aristophanes' humoristic use of the tyrannicides' skolion as a song with sexual connotations in *Ach.* 979–981, *V.* 1225, and *Lys.* 632–634. Cf. Worthington/Cooper/Harris 2001, 83.

48 Worthington/Cooper/Harris 2001, 83.

49 Wevers 1969, 16; Edwards 2007, 80.

Some Athenians did indeed believe that, since Harmodius and Aristogeiton were the tyrant-slayers, the slain was a tyrant, and Thucydides restores this false impression (cf. 1.20–21). However, Thucydides also explains that not merely *some* Athenians but the people of Athens (6.60.1: ὁ δῆμος ὁ τῶν Ἀθηναίων) knew that the Peisistratids were removed by the Alcmeonids, which means that this information is not offered as a revelation of an unknown or doubted story. In this connection, it has been rightly argued that Dover's simplistic explanation that everything in the digression serves as a restoration of the truth cannot explain why Thucydides touched upon the Alcmeonids' contribution to the fall of tyranny.

An alternative explanation would be that Thucydides wishes to castigate not what was *believed* by the Athenians but the limits of free speech in these matters which was *imposed* on them by the state. Especially in moments like 415, when democracy was or seemed to be in danger, orators could hardly dare to doubt the tyrannicides as symbols of democracy by underlining instead the Alcmeonids' activity. To mention a striking parallel to the situation of 415, after the end of the oligarchic coup of the four hundred and the restoration of democracy in 410/409, the decree of Demophantus invited every Athenian citizen to protect democracy and to invoke Harmodius and Aristogeiton.[50] Who could interrupt the Assembly at that point and try to correct the Athenians' impression of the tyrannicides by claiming that it was the Alcmeonids who had overthrown them? And who could do so during the Herms case in 415 too?

Thucydides conveys whatever message he wants to convey by overcoming the communicative restrictions imposed by the state on orators, especially in periods of a crisis of democracy. Even Demosthenes, who admits that the Alcmeonids freed Athens from tyranny (21.144), did not treat the tyrannicides' contribution to democracy and that of the Alcmeonids as two mutually exclusive events (19.280; 20.69–70).[51] Demosthenes proves that an orator could admit the Alcmeonids' service to Athenian democracy without doubting that the tyrannicides were the protectors of democracy. In both the courts and the Assembly, the tyrannicides and the Alcmeonids could only stand next to each other as protectors of democracy and they were not used as two opposing sides of different versions about the fall of tyranny. Thucydides moves beyond this compromising use of the tyrannicides and the Alcmeonids and creates a sharp contrast,

50 And. 1.96–98 and 159. See Shear 2012a, 37ff.

51 For further sources on the tyrannicides as liberators, see Shear 2012a, 38 n. 54. For the institutional cult of Harmodius and Aristogeiton, see Shear 2012a and b, with exhaustive bibliography.

which was traditionally unacceptable in all branches of Athenian oratory (forensic, deliberative, and epideictic).

(b) *The tyrannicides' ēthos.* Speakers praise the tyrannicides' choice to kill Hipparchus not only as a political action but also as an irrefutable indicator of their laudable moral qualities.[52] Aeschines foregrounds the tyrannicides' modesty and sense of justice, and presents them as models of ideal friendship and mutual fidelity. In a similar fashion, Iphicrates and Isaeus treat their deeds as signs of nobility and bravery. Subsequently, the element of homosexual love, a central feature of the tyrannicides' popular prosopography, is praised and juxtaposed with the base love shared among male prostitutes. Last but not least, speakers create strong bonds of association between the tyrannicides' homosexuality and the common interest of Athens.[53]

Orators employ the *exemplum* of Harmodius and Aristogeiton as a means of *ēthopoiia* both for themselves and against their opponents. By defending the tyrannicides as public heroes of democracy, Aeschines brings to the foreground his respect for democracy, the laws and the institutions of his country. He also fashions himself as a virtuous individual, protector of modesty, justice, bravery, self-abnegation, all of which are repeatedly represented by the tyrant-slayers in the surviving Attic law-court oratory. Conversely, as mentioned above, an orator could present his rivals as disrespecting the tyrannicides and thereby blacken their image. The goal of this *ēthopoiia* was to elicit certain affective responses in the audience (*pathopoiia*), especially sympathy for himself and indignation against his opponent.

Thucydides creates a sharp contrast with the traditional rhetorical embellishment of the tyrannicides' morality. *His* tyrannicides act out of personal interest and not for the sake of the Athenian democracy. Aristogeiton decides to help Harmodius, only because he is in love with him. Once again, this information would not have caused much surprise in an Athenian reader, given that the love of Harmodius and Aristogeiton was a basic aspect of their myth. Moreover, the Athenians associated the tyrannicides' homosexual love with the establishment of democracy (cf. above, Aeschines' speech and Aristotle's comments). However, the passages we analysed above from Aeschines and Aristotle's *Ars Rhetorica* indicate that in the law-courts and the Assembly the tyrannicides' morality, including their love, were idealised. So, the polemic information in

---

52 This practice was certainly compatible with the official attitude in Athens towards the tyrannicides. See Stewart 1997, 69–75; Wohl 1999, 355–359.

53 On the tyrannicides' love and its bonds with the Athenian democracy: Stewart 1997, 69–75; Wohl 1999, 355–359.

Thucydides' account is not to be sought in his mention of Aristogeiton's love for Harmodius, but in Thucydides' underestimation of this love.

Subsequently, by breaking the institutional and rhetorical immunity of the tyrannicides' morality, Thucydides essentially refutes Alcibiades' rivals' *ēthopoiia*. He provides an answer through his digression to the moral associations which were probably made by Alcibiades' accusers between themselves and the tyrannicides. We can imagine them saying something like the following, "We, the continuers of Harmodius and Aristogeiton and protectors of democracy, should expel Alcibiades, the aspiring tyrant". Thucydides' response to them through his digression is: "Yes, you do resemble the tyrannicides. You are as much of a fool as they were in disturbing the political order of your country for the sake of your own interests and passions".

(c) *The extent of rhetorical comments on the tyrannicides.* Equally important is the fact that in the surviving speeches there is no extensive narration of the tyrant-slayers' activity. In Aristotle's *Rhetoric*, of course, the brevity of the reference to them is due to the synoptic way in which Aristotle gathers examples of syllogisms in his work. However, in none of the aforementioned speeches does any speaker penetrate into the details of Harmodius and Aristogeiton's story. In essence, these short mentions cannot even be taken as narratives; they rather served as rhetorical fireworks. In these cases, the tyrannicides' contribution to the Athenian democracy is taken for granted and never questioned, while we discern no intentions on the orator's part to interpret and reconsider the traditional elements of the myth or to bring new ones to light.

An ancient reader who was experienced in the brevity of the rhetorical mentions of the tyrannicides could feel the difference between Thucydides' extensive narration of the tyrannicides' story and the orators' vague and fleeting comments on them. This kind of contrast is worth keeping in mind, especially because scholars have occasionally complained about the length of the digression. Thucydides endeavoured to offer to his contemporaries a narrative of the tyrannicides that was much more elaborate than what was circulated by the state and its representatives in court and the Assembly.

4 Conclusion

The present reading of the digression about the tyrannicides suggests that Thucydides, by restoring the truth about them, wished to juxtapose historiography as a literary genre, *inter alia*, with oratory. Modern scholarship has mainly focused on the contrasts which are created between Thucydides and the poets or other historians in the shaping of historical knowledge. Indeed, both in ch. 1.20–21 as well as in the digression of ch. 6.54–59, Thucydides puts on display his own exuberant agenda of methods to scrutinise sources, witnesses, and evidence as a means to compensate the frivolousness of his contemporaries. Nonetheless, his choice to employ these methods in the pursuit of truth is not only juxtaposed on an intellectual level with the inadequacy of the masses, the poets, and other historians, but also on an ethical level with the hypocrisy of Athenian orators. Thucydides does not fashion himself only as the only one who *can* find the truth, but also as the only one who is *willing* to do so. In this respect, historiography, as a literary genre, outdoes oratory on a moral level too.

By framing his tyrannicides excursus in an institutional and rhetorical context, Thucydides also stimulates readerly speculations about the advantages of historiography over oratory on a communicational level. The Thucydidean account of the Herms case and the surviving texts of 4th-century oratory make it clear that the legal system not only did not prevent but rather nurtured the distortive abuse of witnesses and evidence, including historical *exempla*. The courts and the Assembly impeded free expression of truth, which means that, although many Athenian orators knew that the tyrannicides did not overthrow tyranny, they did not feel free to express this thesis in a strict institutional framework. These communicative restrictions protected those orators who "exaggerated and raised the cry" (ἐμεγάλυνον καὶ ἐβόων) that, in sentencing Alcibiades to death, they were following the example of the tyrannicides. No one would dare to doubt the moral integrity of Harmodius' and Aristogeiton's love, especially in times when the survival of Athenian democracy was at stake. Thucydides presents himself as enjoying the luxury of escaping this suppressive communicative framework, which some orators were trapped in and others took advantage of. It is still doubtful, though, that he would have ever dared to question the tyrannicides in a court room or the Assembly in those burning moments of 415 in the carefree manner that he did in his writings.

Bibliography

Allan, R. (2011), 'The Historical Present in Thucydides: Capturing the Case of αἱρεῖ and\ λαμβάνει', in: J. Lallot/A. Rijksbaron/B. Jacquinod/M. Buijs (eds.), *The Historical Present in Thucydides. Semantics and Narrative Function (Le présent historique chez. Thucydide. Sémantique et function narrative)*, Leiden/Boston, 37–64.

Bakker, E. (2006), 'Contract and Design: Thucydides' Writing', in: A. Rengakos/A. Tsakmakis (eds.), *Brill's Companion to Thucydides*, Leiden/Boston, 109–129.

Balot, R.K./Forsdyke, S./Foster, E. (eds.) (2017), *The Oxford Handbook of Thucydides*, Oxford.

Bartlett, R.C. (2019), *Aristotle's Art of Rhetoric*, Chicago/London.
Bloedow, E.F. (1992a), 'Alcibiades "Brilliant" or "Intelligent?"', in: *Historia* 41, 139–157.
Bloedow, E.F. (1992b), 'An Alexander in the Wrong Place: Alcibiades "the Ablest of All the Sons of Athens?"', in: *SCO* 41, 191–216.
Brunt, P.A. (1952), 'Thucydides and Alcibiades', in: *REG* 65, 59–96.
Cartledge, P./Todd, S. (eds.) (1990), *Nomos. Essays in Athenian Law, Politics and Society*, Cambridge.
Cawkwell, G. (1997), *Thucydides and the Peloponnesian War*, London/New York.
Classen, J. (1881), *Thukydides*, vol. VI, Berlin.
Connor, W.R. (1984), *Thucydides*, Princeton.
Corcella, A. (2006), 'The New Genre and Its Boundaries: Poets and Logographers', in: A. Rengakos/A. Tsakmakis (eds.), *Brill's Companion to Thucydides*, Leiden/Boston, 33–56.
COT: Hornblower, S. (1991–2008), *A Commentary on Thucydides*, vols. I-III, Oxford.
Cwiklinski, L. (1877), 'Über die Entstehungsweise des Zweiten Theiles der Thukydideischen Geschichte', in: *Hermes* 12, 23–87.
de Bakker, M. (2012), 'Character Judgements in Thucydides. Between Historical Research and Literary Representation', in: A. Tsakmakis/M. Tamiolaki (eds.), *Thucydides between History and Literature*, Berlin/Boston, 23–40.
de Romilly, J. (1963), *Thucydides and Athenian Imperialism*, transl. by Philip Thody, Oxford.
Dougan, T.W. (1883), *Thucydides. Book VI*, London.
Douglas, J.S. (1966), 'Thucydides, Pausanias, and Alcibiades', in: *CJ* 61, 145–152.
Dover, K.J. (1965), *Thucydides. Book VI*, Oxford.
Dover, K.J. (1973), *Thucydides*, Oxford.
Duff, T. (ed.) (2022 forthcoming), *Alcibiades: His Ancient Reception*, Swansea.
Edmunds, L. (1975), *Chance and Intelligence in Thucydides*, Cambridge.
Edwards, M. (2007), *Isaeus*, Austin.
Ehrenberg, V. (1956), 'Das Harmodioslied', in: *WS* 69, 57–69.
Finley, J.H. (1942), *Thucydides*, Harvard.
Finley, J.H. (1967), *Three Essays on Thucydides*, Cambridge, MA.
Fisher, N. (2001), *Aeschines. Against Timarchos*, Oxford.
Forde, S. (1989), *The Ambition to Rule. Alcibiades and the Politics of Imperialism in Thucydides*, Ithaca.
Fornara, C.W. (1968), 'The "Tradition" about the Murder of Hipparchus', in: *Historia* 17, 400–424.
Freese, J.H. (1926), *Aristotle. The 'Art' of Rhetoric*, London/New York.
Grant-Smith, D. (2009), 'Alcibiades, Athens, and the Tyranny of Sicily (Thuc. 6.16)', in: *GRBS* 49, 363–389.
Gray, V.J. (2011), 'Thucydides' Source Citations: "It Is Said"', in: *CQ* 61, 75–90.
Greenwood, E. (2006), *Thucydides and the Shaping of History*, London.
Grethlein, J. (2004), '"Logographos" und Thuc. 1.21.1', in: *Prometheus* 30, 209–216.
Grethlein, J. (2013), *Experience and Teleology in Ancient Historiography: Futures Past From Herodotus to Augustine*, Cambridge.
Gribble, D. (1999), *Alcibiades and Athens: A Study in Literary Representation*, Oxford.
Grundy, G.B. (1948), *Thucydides and the History of His Age*, vols. I-II, Oxford.
Harris, E.M. (2016), 'Alcibiades, the Ancestors, Liturgies, and the Etiquette of Addressing the Athenian Assembly', in: V. Liotsakis/S. Farrington (eds.), *The Art of History. Literary Perspectives on Greek and Roman Historiography*, Berlin/Boston, 145–155.

Harvey, D. (1990), 'The sycophant and sycophancy: vexatious redefinition?', in: P. Cartledge/ P. Millett/S. Todd (eds.), *Nomos. Essays in Athenian Law, Politics and Society*, Cambridge, 103–121.
Hawthorn, G. (2014), *Thucydides on Politics. Back to the Present*, Cambridge.
HCT: Gomme, A.W./Andrewes, A./Dover, K.J. (1945–1981), *A Historical Commentary on Thucydides*, vols. I-V, Oxford.
Henderson, J. (1987), *Aristophanes. Lysistrata*, Oxford.
Hornblower, S. (2004), *Thucydides and Pindar. Historical Narrative and the World of Epinikian Poetry*, Oxford.
Hunter, V.J. (1973), 'Athens Tyrannis: A New Approach to Thucydides', in: *CJ* 69, 120–126.
Hunter, V.J. (1982), *Past and Process in Herodotus and Thucydides*, Princeton.
Jacoby, F. (1949), *Atthis, the Local Chronicles of Ancient Athens*, Oxford.
Kinzl, K.H. (1973), 'Zu Thukydides über die Peisistratidai', in: *Historia* 504–507.
Kouskouvelis, I.I. (2019), *Thucydides on Choice and Decision Making: Why War is not Inevitable*, Lanham.
Krüger, K.W. (1858), *Θουκυδίδου ξυγγραφή*, Berlin.
Lallot, J./Rijksbaron, A./Jacquinod, B./Buijs, M. (eds.) (2011), *The Historical Present in Thucydides. Semantics and Narrative Function (Le présent historique chez. Thucydide. Sémantique et function narrative)*, Leiden/Boston.
Lamb, W.R.M. (1914), *Clio Enthroned. A Study of Prose-Form in Thucydides*, Cambridge.
Lambin, G. (1979), 'Dans un rameau de myrte', in: *REG* 92, 542–551.
Larivée, A. (2012), 'Eros Tyrannos: Alcibiades as the Model of the Tyrant in Book IX of the *Republic*', in: *IJPS* 6, 1–26.
Lattimore, S. (1998), *Thucydides. The Peloponnesian War*, Indianapolis/Cambridge.
Liotsakis, V. (2017), *Redeeming Thucydides' Book VIII. Narrative Artistry in the Account of the Ionian War*, Berlin/Boston.
Liotsakis, V. (2022 forthcoming), 'Whether It Pined for Him or Loathed Him, It Should Have Wanted to Have Him: Thucydides' Judgment on Alcibiades', in: T. Duff. (ed.), *Alcibiades: His Ancient Reception*, Swansea.
Liotsakis, V./Farrington, S. (eds.) (2016), *The Art of History. Literary Perspectives on Greek and Roman Historiography*, Berlin/Boston.
Ludwig, P.W. (2002), *Eros and Polis: Desire and Community in Greek Political Theory*, Cambridge.
Luraghi, N. (ed.) (2001), *The Historian's Craft in the Age of Herodotus*, Oxford.
Marchant, E.C. (1897), *Thucydides. Book VI*, London.
McGlew, J. (2012), 'Fighting Tyranny in Fifth-Century Athens: Democratic Citizenship and the Oath of Demophantus', in: *BICS* 55(2), 91–99.
Meyer, E. (2008), 'Thucydides on Harmodius and Aristogeiton, Tyranny and History', in: *CQ* 58, 13–34.
Müller-Strübing, H. (1873), *Aristophanes und die historische Kritik: Polemische Studien zur Geschichte von Athen im fünften Jahrjundert vor Ch.*, Leipzig.
Munson, R.V. (2017), 'Thucydides and Myth: A Complex Relation to Past and Present', in: R.K. Balot/S. Forsdyke/E. Foster (eds.), *The Oxford Handbook of Thucydides*, Oxford, 257–266.
Nichols, M.P. (2015), *Thucydides and the Pursuit of Freedom*, Ithaca/London.
Nicolai, R. (2001), 'Thucydides' Archaeology: Between Epic and Oral Traditions', in: N. Luraghi (ed.), *The Historian's Craft in the Age of Herodotus*, Oxford, 263–285.

Ober, J. (1998), *Political Dissent in Democratic Athens: Intellectual Critics of Popular Rule*, Princeton.
Orwin, C. (1994), *The Humanity of Thucydides*, Princeton.
Palmer, M.J. (1982), 'Alcibiades and the Question of Tyranny in Thucydides', in: *CJPS* 15, 103–124.
Pouncey, P.R. (1980), *The Necessities of War: A Study of Thucydides' Pessimism*, New York.
Price, J.J. (2001), *Thucydides and Internal War*, Cambridge.
Proctor, D. (1980), *The Experience of Thucydides*, Warminster.
Rawllings, H.R. (1981), *The Structure of Thucydides' History*, Princeton.
Rengakos, A./Tsakmakis, A. (eds.) (2006), *Brill's Companion to Thucydides*, Leiden/Boston.
Rhodes, P.J. (1988), *Thucydides: History II*, Warminster.
Rhodes, P.J. (2006), 'Thucydides and Athenian History', in: A. Rengakos/A. Tsakmakis (eds.), *Brill's Companion to Thucydides*, Leiden/Boston, 523–546.
Rijksbaron, A. (2002), *The Syntax and Semantics of the Verb in Classical Greek: An Introduction*, Amsterdam.
Rijksbaron, A. (2011), 'The Profanation of the Mysteries and the Mutilation of the Hermae. Two Variations on Two Themes', in: J. Lallot/A. Rijksbaron/B. Jacquinod/M. Buijs (eds.), *The Historical Present in Thucydides. Semantics and Narrative Function (Le présent historique chez Thucydide. Sémantique et function narrative)*, Leiden/Boston, 177–194.
Rood, T.C.B. (1998), *Thucydides. Narrative and Explanation*, Oxford.
Rood, T.C.B. (2012), 'The Cylon Conspiracy: Thucydides and the Uses of the Past', in: A. Tsakmakis/M. Tamiolaki (eds.), *Thucydides between History and Literature*, Berlin/Boston, 119–138.
Ros, J. (1968), *Die variation als Stilprinzip des Thukydides*, Amsterdam.
Rutherford, R. (1994), 'Learning from History: Categories and Case-Histories', in: R. Osborne/S. Hornblower (eds.), *Ritual, Finance, Politics: Athenian Democratic Accounts Presented to David Lewis*, Oxford/New York, 54–68.
Scanlon, T.F. (1987), 'Thucydides and Tyranny', in: *ClAnt* 6, 289–301.
Schadewaldt, W. (1929), *Die Geschichtschreibung des Thukydides*, Berlin.
Schwartz, E. (1919), *Das Geschichtswerk des Thukydides*, Munich.
Seager, R. (1967), 'Alcibiades and the Charge of Aiming Tyranny', in: *Historia* 16, 6–18.
Shanske, D. (2006), *Thucydides and the Philosophical Origins of History*, Cambridge.
Shear, J.L. (2012a), 'Religion and the *Polis*: The Cult of the Tyrannicides at Athens', in: *Kernos* 25, 27–55.
Shear, J.L. (2012b), 'The Tyrannicides, Their Cult and the Panathenaia: A Note', in: *JHS* 132, 107–119.
Smith, C.F. (1913), *Thucydides Book VI*, edited on the basis of the Classen-Steup edition, Boston.
Stahl, H.-P. (2003), *Thucydides. Man's Place in History*, Swansea.
Stewart, A.F. (1997), *Art, Desire, and the Body in Ancient Greece*, Cambridge.
Thomas, R. (2006), 'Thucydides' Intellectual Milieu and the Plague', in: A. Rengakos/A. Tsakmakis (eds.), *Brill's Companion to Thucydides*, Leiden/Boston, 87–108.
Tsakmakis, A. (1995), *Thukydides über die Vergangenheit*, Tübingen.
Tsakmakis, A./Tamiolaki, M. (eds.) (2012), *Thucydides between History and Literature*, Berlin/Boston.
Virtanen, T. (2004), *Approaches to Cognition through Text and Discourse*, Berlin/New York.

Wårvik, B. (2004), 'What Is Foregrounded in Narrative? Hypotheses for the Cognitive Basis of Foregrounding', in: T. Virtanen (ed.), *Approaches to Cognition through Text and Discourse*, Berlin/New York, 99–122.
Westlake, H.D. (1977), 'Λέγεται in Thucydides', in: *Mnemosyne* 30, 345–362.
Wevers, R.F. (1969), *Issaeus: Chronology, Prosopography, and Social History*, Paris.
Williams, M.F. (1998), *Ethics in Thucydides. The Ancient Simplicity*, Lanham/New York/Oxford.
Wohl, V. (1999), 'The *Eros* of Alcibiades', in: *ClAnt* 18, 349–385.
Worthington, I./Cooper, C.R./Harris, E.M. (2001), *Dinarchus, Hyperides, and Lycurgus*, Austin.

David Mirhady

The Torture of Prometheus

Abstract: In this chapter, Mirhady attempts to trace the basis for the Athenian rationale for torture back to the early 5th-century. He examines both the *Prometheus Bound* and the "democratic" account of the torture of the tyrannicide Aristogeiton in the *Athenaiōn politeia*, in which not slaves, but a god and a free Athenian are tortured, both as punishment and in an attempt to elicit information. These texts prove consistent with later oratory and drama, in which Athenian democratic ideology dictates that slaves lie, unless tortured, but that if tortured (under the right conditions) tortured slaves are the surest guarantee of truth. These earlier sources reveal the flip side of this rationale: as an avatar of the free Athenian, Prometheus endures torture without revealing the sought for information, and Aristogeiton the noble proto-democrat and tyrannicide actually lies when tortured in order to spite his torturer, the tyrant Hippias.

Among the "witnesses" who "testified" in Athenian law – though the Athenians normally took pains not to refer to them as "witnesses" (*martyres*) – tortured slaves were said to provide the surest source of information for deciding a dispute. This rhetorical oddity has long puzzled scholars, but its explanation seems to lie at the heart of Athenian democratic ideology. In this paper I wish to suggest a role for historical events and then their reflection in Athenian drama in the formation of part of this construct, particularly why the Athenians were averse to the torture of their own citizens.

In 514 BC the so-called "tyrannicides", Harmodius and Aristogeiton, killed one of the tyrant Peisistratid brothers, Hipparchus, and were captured. Harmodius was killed immediately, but Aristogeiton was captured and tortured, for a long time (Arist. *Ath. Pol.* 18.3–4). According to a "democratic" telling of the story that is recorded in the *Athenaiōn Politeia*, Aristogeiton lied under torture, specifically in order to spite the tyrant Hippias and deceive him into impiously executing innocent aristocrats, as well as self-destructively killing his own friends (*Ath. Pol.* 18.5).[1] The democratic version suggests that no deaths of non-

1 The killing of the aristocrats, besides estranging Hippias from that class, was impious not because the event was connected to the Panathenaia, but because, unlike Harmodius and Aristogeiton, the aristocrats were innocent (ἀναιτίους) of killing Hipparchus. I take it that οἳ καὶ τῇ φύσει τῶν ἐπιφανῶν 18.4 = τοὺς ἀναιτίους 18.5. See also Polyaenus 1.22 and D.S. 10.17.2. Athenaeus (13.596f.) also reports that Harmodius had a lover, a *hetaira* named Leaena, who

https://doi.org/10.1515/9783110751970-011

aristocrats resulted from Aristogeiton's deception. Presumably also part of the democratic propaganda, Aristogeiton is said to have offered to inform on many more conspirators. He even shook hands with Hippias as a pledge of faith, but then melodramatically taunted him for grasping the hand that had killed his brother (*Ath. Pol.* 18.6). But for this paper what is important is that in what is explicitly described as a democratic account, Aristogeiton lied when tortured.[2]

The Athenians went on to debate competing claims about the end of the tyranny. An alternative was later supported by Herodotus (6.123) and Thucydides (6.59.3–4), according to whom the Alcmeonids and Spartans drove out the tyrant Hippias in 510 BC. Besides the "democratic" account recorded in *Ath. Pol.* 18.4–6, a stele commemorated the injustice of the tyrants (Thuc. 6.55.1) and statues were erected in their honour both before and after the Persian destruction of Athens in 480 BC (Paus. 1.8.5; 1.29.15). Beyond the physical remains, which were seen centuries later by Pausanias, as well as the early Harmodius songs (*PMG* 893–896), there was also a cult that celebrated the tyrannicides as democratic idealists.[3] In the ensuing aristocratic rivalry, Herodotus says that Cleisthenes "extended his *hetairia* to the *dēmos*" (τὸν δῆμον προσεταιρίζεται 5.66.2); the *dēmos* that "had earlier been thrust away from everything, he then adopted into his own party" (τὸν Ἀθηναίων δῆμον πρότερον ἀπωσμένον πάντων τότε (τότε πάντων *codd.*) πρὸς τὴν ἑωυτοῦ μοῖραν προσεθήκατο 5.69.2). Both the tyrannicide story and Cleisthenes' reforms suggest ideals of free and inclusive masculinity that grounded the Athenian democratic ideology and that are later clearly visible in the Periclean funeral oration (Thuc. 2.37–40).

Shortly after the establishment of the Cleisthenic democracy, during the archonship of Scamandrius, in what must have been one of its first acts, the Athenian democracy passed a decree that forbade the torture of citizens.[4] The decree seems likely to have been inspired at least partly by the torture of the tyrannicide Aristogeiton in 514 BC. We learn of the suspension of this decree in the year

---

was likewise tortured and bit off her own tongue in order to avoid betraying fellow conspirators. She is also said to have been honoured by a statue (Plut. *De garr.* 505e; Paus. 1.23.1). Rhodes 1981, 232 cites further passages. My sense is that these are later, likely post classical accretions to the "democratic" account in *Ath. Pol.*

2 *Ath. Pol.* also mentions the non-democratic view, which saw Aristogeiton inform on actual conspirators (18.5).

3 See Fornara 1970. Podlecki 1966, 117 links the cult of the tyrannicides to Themistocles. Thucydides clearly sees some parallels between the investigation of Alcibiades (cf. βασανίσαι τὸ πρᾶγμα 6.53.2) and the torture of Aristogeiton. Cf. Thuc. 6.57.4 "(Aristogeiton) was not treated gently (οὐ ῥᾳδίως διετέθη)." Other sources are cited above, n. 1.

4 Andoc. 1.43.

411 BC, on the proposal of the oligarch Peisander, when threats to their *polis* led the Athenians to agree to use torture against alleged conspirators who had been identified by informers. As it turned out, the only named conspirators escaped after recruiting guarantors, and no citizen was tortured on that occasion. The incident seems to have been an aberration in democratic norms.[5]

In *Prometheus Bound*, the god Prometheus is cast as an avatar, a divine incarnation embodying the idea of a(n elite) free man faced with tyrannical oppression. The play begins shortly after a *coup d'état*: Zeus has overthrown his father and established a new tyranny with the help of Prometheus, whom he now punishes for having allowed the *dēmos* of mortal humans to continue living by giving them fire (*PV* 7–8). In the tyranny, no one is free except Zeus (50). So this avatar not only represents an elite man but, like a Cleisthenes or an Aristogeiton, also a champion and victim on behalf of others, the underclass of mortals, and, by extension, anti-tyrannical, democratic ideology in general. The Athenian audience had to have been mindful of Athens' recent liberation from tyranny and the defeat of the Persians, whose king was likewise the only free person in the Persian Empire.[6] In the narrative arc of the Prometheus trilogy there must finally have been a reconciliation, in which Prometheus' mortals

---

5 Several of the texts that are cited in support of claims (by Bushala and Sternberg, for instance) that the Athenian democracy did torture citizens, or at least non-citizen free people, seem on reflection to be inconclusive. For instance, in Dem. 13.14 Demosthenes is saying, mockingly, that when the Parthenon was burgled, speakers in the Assembly shouted that the thieves be tortured (whether citizens or not is not said). He himself responds only that someone thieving from the Parthenon deserves death, implicitly rejecting torture. Several centuries later, Plutarch reports about the barber from Peiraeus who thought he would win glory by being the first to relay news of the Sicilian catastrophe of 413 BC in Athens and was tortured for his trouble (*De garr.* 509e; *Nic.* 30.2). If the story is true, he seems likely to have been a slave, or at best a metic, not someone who might have been sitting in the Assembly as a citizen himself. Thucydides (8.92.2) reports that the Four Hundred tortured an Argive. Since it was not the democracy, it seems rather to support the claim that avoidance of torturing citizens belonged to the democracy (cf. Lys. 6.27). Lycurgus reports on the same incident, saying that torture took place during the democracy's subsequent inquiry (βασάνων γενομένων ἀνέκρινε Lycurg. 1.112), but he does not say who was tortured. The Thirty likewise used torture indiscriminately (Lys. 13.54, 59–60). The case of the Antiphon who had been struck from the citizen roles and roughly arrested by Demosthenes is particularly interesting. The orator reports that Antiphon protested that Demosthenes had acted terribly in maltreating an unfortunate citizen (18.132: κεκραγώς, ὡς ἐν δημοκρατίᾳ δεινὰ ποιῶ τοὺς ἠτυχηκότας τῶν πολιτῶν ὑβρίζων "this malignant fellow raised a huge outcry about my scandalous and undemocratic conduct in assaulting citizens in distress"), citing exactly the principle at play in this paper. But the Areopagus exposed him as a traitor and sentenced him to a painful death (18.133; cf. Din. 1.63, Aeschin. 3.224–225).

6 Cf. Aesch. *Pers.* 234; Hdt. 7.139; Eur. *Hel.* 276.

acquired from Zeus a sense of democratic justice, somewhat as in the *Oresteia's Eumenides*, but that is only hinted at in our play.[7]

As the play opens, emphasis is put on Prometheus' kinship with the other gods, including Zeus. In this mythological construct such kinship is analogous to shared, egalitarian citizenship. It is somewhat like Herodotus' analogy of Cleisthenes' extended *hetairia*. Because of it Hephaestus and Kratos can disagree about the appropriateness of Prometheus' punishment.[8] Kratos and Bia play the role of Zeus' enthusiastic enforcers, but Hephaestus has qualms, as he says, unwillingly confining an unwilling prisoner (ἄκοντά σ' ἄκων 19). Nevertheless he does nail him to a cliff, remote from humans (ἀπανθρώπῳ πάγῳ 20), but "standing erect, sleepless, with unbent knee" (ὀρθοστάδην, ἄυπνος, οὐ κάμπτων γόνυ 32). The Suda describes wooden stocks with five apertures through which the feet, hands, and neck are inserted, and both Lysias and Demosthenes indicate that such a punishment went back to Solonian laws according to which thieves (like Prometheus) were held in such stocks for five days and nights.[9] Given what the play says about "standing erect" and "unbent knee", it seems we should not imagine Prometheus as recumbent during the play, as on the famous vase (Vat 16592), but in stocks that bind his arms, chest and feet (*PV* 53–76). He complains that, like the prisoner in stocks, he is the object of others' *Schadenfreude* (156–159).

Later in the play the focus shifts from the "penal torture" for Prometheus' supposed wrongdoing to what is called "judicial torture", the use of torment as a means of eliciting information, in this case information that will be vital to the continuation of Zeus' rule. The information has to be kept secret, of course, so it is never fully revealed in the play, but the audience knows, that Prometheus knows, that Thetis is fated to have a son greater than his father.[10] In the play the transition is marked when Hermes arrives and threatens further torments (*PV* 947–952). Prometheus responds that they are not only unjust, as the torments against him have been all along, but that they will not work. Prometheus will withstand the torture.[11] I wish to argue that, as an avatar for the Athenian citi-

7 See White 2001.

8 *PV* 14–15, 39. Cf. 290–292.

9 Ar. *Eq*. 1049. Suda, *s.v.* Πεντεσυρίγγῳ ξύλῳ (Π 976): τῇ ποδοκάκῃ. πέντε γὰρ ὀπὰς ἔχει, δι' ὧν οἱ πόδες καὶ αἱ χεῖρες καὶ ὁ τράχηλος ἐμβάλλονται. Cf. ποδοκάκκη *ap*. Dem. 24.105; Lysias 10.16. The play refers to the bonds in several ways: "constraints" (ἀνάγκαις 108), "fetters" (γυιοπέδαις 168), "bonds" (δεσμῶν 97, 113, 141, 174, 509), "adamantine torments" (ἀδαμαντοδέτοισι λύμαις 148, 426).

10 *PV* 908–910, 947–948.

11 *PV* 989–991.

zen, Prometheus demonstrates a citizen's defiance of torture, both earlier and here, as an expression of an Athenian ideology that distinguishes free from slave and democracy from tyranny.

Athenian speechwriters developed a very elaborate and consistent canon of arguments about the efficacy of "evidentiary" slave torture, when both sides in legal disputes agreed to perform the torture bilaterally.[12] Their claim was that such torture is the surest form of evidence that could ever be used. We have learned much by studying this canon, about rhetoric and evidentiary procedure, about the nature of slavery in Athens, and about Athenian attitudes surrounding the psychology of slaves. Slaves were thought in general to lie[13] on behalf of their owners[14] and to be motivated only by their immediate bodily well-being, so that torture, which compromised that well-being, was thought the only effective means to stop the lying and get truth from slaves. The slaves had to be compelled by both sides to believe that only the truth, not continued lying, would bring an end to their torment. In challenges surrounding legal disputes, both parties were to participate in the torture, each wanting the opposite result, so the slave did not just say what the torturer wanted.

In recent scholarship less attention has been devoted to the torture of free people, particularly citizens, and in fact there is little direct evidence concerning such torture.[15] For the most part we are left uninformed by Athenian oratory about the reasoning behind the Athenian refusal to torture free people more, aside from inferences we can draw from arguments in favour of the torture of slaves and comments in cases of assault and hubris about the inviolability of the body of an Athenian citizen.[16] Such comments indicate that the torture of free people, particularly citizens, was forbidden, as the torture of all people is forbidden in the civilised world today. And yet from our experience today, when arguments are repeatedly made that torture ought to be allowed in extraordinary cases, we know that there must have been counter arguments against extraordinary torture that torture is always wrong, that it is unreliable, and that there are more effective alternatives (see, e.g. Arist. *Rh.* 1377a2–5). Likewise, just as the Athenians argued so forcefully about the effectiveness of slave torture,

---

12 Canon of arguments: Headlam 1893; Thür 1977; Mirhady 1996, 2000; Gagarin 1996; Adamidis 2019.

13 Slaves lie: Eur. *Phoen.* 392.

14 Slaves are adept at lying on behalf of their masters: Hdt. 8.75; Soph. *El.* 47–48 (perjury).

15 See the brief discussions in Thür 1977, 15–25, Allen 2000, 210–213, and Sternberg 2006, 155–157. See also Lys. 4.14, 13.27; Isoc. 20.5; Dem. 21.72, 180.

16 See Isoc. 20.1; Dem. 21.179. See also Arist. *Pol.* 1311b23–26, on the dangers to government that result from anger at bodily insult. Cf. Pl. *Symp.* 182c.

they would likewise have argued both that the torture of free people was wrong and that it did not work. But for systematic evidence of this view, we must turn not to oratory but to tragedy, particularly *Prometheus Bound*, as well as the democratic narrative surrounding the torture of Aristogeiton.

As in Attic oratory, both tragedy and comedy offer passages where slaves first lie, generally to support the interests of their owners, and are then submitted to torture and reveal the truth. The most famous is the old Theban shepherd in *Oedipus the King*, who had long before first been sent out to expose the infant Oedipus but gave him instead to the Corinthian Messenger. The same slave later witnessed the road rage of the young Oedipus and the killing of King Laius. He even recognised Oedipus when the young man arrived in Thebes, overcame the Sphinx, and unknowingly married his mother Jocasta. The slave dutifully lied on behalf of his owners both about the baby and about the road-rage incident, saying that it had been a large group and not just a single man, which threw suspicion away from his new master Oedipus. When finally brought on stage the slave continues to lie until Oedipus commands that his arms be twisted back, the torture technique familiar to every schoolyard bully (Soph. *OT* 1151–1156). As soon as he is tortured the slave reveals the truth, and Oedipus' revelation, the play's *anagnōrisis*, is complete. In Euripides' *Ion*, Creusa's slave is likewise tortured and reveals everything about their poisoning plot (1215–1216). Aristophanes' *Frogs* caricatures the torture-challenge that appears so often in forensic oratory (615–674), and in Aristophanes' *Knights* the Paphlagonian slave commands his fellow slave follow him to the agora where he is also to be tortured and admit to his misdeeds (874–875).

So the attitudes about slave torture in tragedy are consistent with the argumentation concerning it in Athenian oratory, except that in the idealised conditions of drama there is no need for bilateral participation. I shall start again with a sketch of what seems to have been the Athenian expectations of free, adult-male psychology with regard to torture. First, the free generally tell the truth (*PV* 1032; Antiph. 5.50). Sophocles' *Philoctetes* illustrates the young Neoptolemus who embodies this value (Soph. *Phil.* 88). As we see with Prometheus, however, if the free do not want to speak the truth, they stay silent, and Phaedra illustrates this behaviour in Euripides' *Hippolytus*, up to a point (Eur. *Hipp.* 39–40, 271–279). Secondly, the free are motivated by virtue, not by ignoble gain (*PV* 611; cf. Aesch. *Eum.* 550). So, third, they are not (supposed to be) motivated by torture (*PV* 542). With torture, slaves are compelled to tell the truth, so if torture is applied to the free and they speak as a result, they may just as likely lie out of spite, as Aristogeiton demonstrates. The free understand the future consequences of what they say and do. They are not supposed to be compelled by torture or any other sort of compulsion. But in those circumstances when they are so motivated, their actions are likely to be unworthy of their free status and so, given the logic of tragedy, they may suffer accordingly.

Prometheus advances various arguments against his torture. Some are specific to him, such as his claim to have been instrumental to Zeus' gaining his tyranny from the Titans and his defeat of the Giants and Typhoeus.[17] Zeus owes Prometheus some consideration because of this help even if Zeus does think that Prometheus subsequently misbehaved. Other arguments are based on the idea of inviolability, the fact that because he shares kinship with the gods, Prometheus should not be physically mistreated in a manner unbecoming his status.[18] Analogously, of course, Athenian citizens, and free people in general, should not be tortured by those of equal status. The Solonian laws about the use of the stocks, which originated in a time when the free/slave distinction was not as strict as it became in the Cleisthenic democracy, were probably obsolete in the classical period.[19]

Other arguments focus on the ineffectiveness of the torture. Some of these are again specific to the mythological context: as an immortal, no matter how much he is tortured, Prometheus cannot be killed, so the torture cannot lead to his death, as it often did for slaves. Prometheus has no fear of that.[20] The implication of this argument, of course, may be that, depending on what is at stake, an Athenian citizen also ought to resist torture even to death.[21] There is a parallel here with oath-swearing: though not tortured, in Euripides' play Hippolytus abides by his oath of secrecy to what turns out to be his fatal end. As his name implies, Prometheus also has divine foreknowledge, so he knows that the torments will end. Zeus will eventually come around, and Prometheus can even anticipate that Io's descendant Heracles will eventually free him.[22]

Even aside from these arguments that are specific to Prometheus and the mythological context, there seems an implicit, analogous ideology at work that is critical of the torture of free people: the fact that it is ordered by a harsh tyrant[23] and so represents a new and by implication corrupt legal system[24] and an

---

17 *PV* 219–223.

18 *PV* 92, 119–122, 1091–1093.

19 See Ar. *Nub*. 592–593.

20 *PV* 753–754, 933, 1053.

21 I am unaware of specific examples, aside from Aristogeiton.

22 *PV* 101–102; 772–773, 998.

23 *PV* 736–737.

24 *PV* 34–35; 148–150; 402–406. See also 96–97, 312, 439–440, 942.

attitude of ingratitude.[25] Moreover, it is being carried out by lackeys. Prometheus repeatedly characterises Hermes as a slave.[26] I would like to infer that he is referring to an Athenian idea that, to a slave such as Hermes, the use of torture as a means of eliciting information makes sense, since if Hermes were himself tortured he would talk, and that is why he threatens torture. Prometheus has the character of a free citizen, however, so Hermes' reasoning does not appeal to him.[27]

When Prometheus claims that he will not become feminine, we may likewise infer that the Athenians would not suppose that Athenian citizen women were able to endure torture without revealing information. Prometheus suggests that women would raise their hands in surrender and beg for release (*PV* 1002–1006). Aristotle says that unlike a slave, a free woman could deliberate about future events (such as the consequences of perjury), but that her deliberative capacity was not sovereign.[28] So there can be challenges to have women swear oaths that are analogous to the torture-challenge, and that is how the knowledge of citizen women could be employed in court.[29] But if she were faced by great fear or by physical suffering, a women's deliberative capacity could be overwhelmed. On the other hand, as the argument between Hermes and Prometheus proceeds, the sympathies of the female chorus harden and it declares a willingness to undergo suffering with Prometheus (*PV* 1065–1070). Commentators have been struck by how the Chorus does an about-face here;[30] it had earlier urged Prometheus himself to relent (*PV* 1036–1039). But there seems to have been something about the particular words of Hermes that stiffens the Chorus' backbone. He urges them to withdraw and avoid injury from the threatened lightning. But the suggestion that they might abandon their place at Prometheus' side they take to be a serious insult, akin to an accusation of treason (*PV*

25 Gratitude entails reciprocal compassion, which would preclude such cruelty. Prometheus extends his complaint about Zeus' ingratitude to the attitude of the entire regime (*PV* 975).

26 *PV* 942 διάκονον; 953 ὑπηρέτου (983); 966 λατρείας.

27 Aristophanes, *Frogs* 615–676, describes a torture agreed upon between Aeacus and Xanthias, a slave. Thuc. 7.86.3–4 seems to follow a similar pattern of thinking: the Spartan Gylippus wants the glory of taking the captured Athenian generals to Sparta; the Syracusans fear the generals will reveal Syracusan deceit if tortured; and the Corinthians fear that Nicias will bribe his way out. Thucydides' imputation is that Spartans recognise the motivation of glory, the Syracusans (like slaves) that of torture, and the venal Corinthians that of money.

28 Arist. *Pol.* 1260a13–15 "the slave has not got the deliberative part (τὸ βουλευτικόν) at all, and the female has it, but without full authority (ἄκυρον), and the child has it, but it is incomplete (ἀτελές)".

29 See Mirhady 1991, 79–80.

30 Griffiths 1983, 273; Lloyd-Jones 2003, 656–666; Podlecki 2005, 193.

1067–1070). Certainly Prometheus does not trust them with his secret,[31] but the play suggests that women had other strengths.

Prometheus also likens Hermes to a child, as ignorant and unthinking (*PV* 955, 987). Again, the play suggests that the Athenian child is likewise to be thought vulnerable to torture in ways that the Athenian adult male is not. Specifically, the child may be susceptible to torture because the child has an undeveloped intelligence, somewhat as Aristotle says that the child has an incomplete deliberative capacity.[32] That may actually be true of Athenian thinking in general, and the fact that the Athenians referred to both a slave and a citizen child as *pais* would support this view. But there is no direct evidence that I know of for such torture. Baby Hermes who farts when forcibly questioned by Apollo is not a reliable example.[33] The point of our passage is that, as a mature adult, Prometheus has seen a thing or two – he has seen Uranus and Cronus defeated – so he knows that the torments he is suffering will not last forever. Such a long-term perspective allows the free adult male to think deliberatively, and withstand torture.

I have been emphasising distinctions from Athenian males that the play seems to make almost systematically with regard to slaves, women, and children. But we should also focus on Prometheus' own reaction to the torture, besides his obvious resentment. What might an Athenian think if he were tortured? From his perspective, Hermes charges again and again that Prometheus is being a wise guy (*PV* 944; cf. 62), that he is unreasonably bitter (*PV* 944; cf. 180, 197, 738), that he is self-willed (*PV* 964–965),[34] that he is in a sort of crazed revel (*PV* 971–972; cf. 436), that he is sick (*PV* 977; cf. 251, 386) and foolish (*PV* 999–1000), that he does not know what is good for him, and so on. Prometheus responds that there is no disgrace in being treated badly by an enemy (*PV* 1041–1042; cf. 525), that he anticipates what is coming (*PV* 925) and is not afraid (*PV* 959–960). He is, in short, of sound mind (*PV* 982–983). These responses are obviously crucial to an understanding of why the Athenians thought that the

---

31 As Odysseus initially does not entrust even the loyal slave Eumaeus with his (Hom. *Od.* 14).

32 See n. 28 above, and Golden, 1990, 8–9. Harris 1988, 45–46 argues that there was no law that forbade a child from giving testimony as a witness. But the burden seems to be on the side of those who want to argue that there was a law that allowed it. Children would then have to be susceptible to a suit for false testimony, which seems unlikely. Plato, *Leg.* 937b, who is admittedly not a good source for Athenian law, equates children with slaves as being allowed to testify only in homicide cases. In Athenian law that would require an oath to be sworn.

33 *Hom. Hymn Herm.* 294–296. Hermes is obviously not playing a servile role in the *Hymn*. Cf. 373–374.

34 Cf. *PV* 64, 436, 466, 907, 1010–1012.

torture of free Athenian adult males was not only wrong, but likely to be ineffective: to be treated badly by an enemy is not a source of disgrace, and the Athenian has an awareness of the future and not just the current pain, since that is part of being sound-minded.

Ryan Balot has recently published a compelling book on the subject of courage in the Athenian democracy,[35] but he passes over *Prometheus Bound*. Courage in the face of individual torture seems one of its most significant forms, and the fact that it so clearly distinguishes free from slave in Athenian democratic ideology underlines its importance for the Athenian context. Balot does discuss Aeschylus' *Persians* and notes that both there and in Herodotus, the Persians' military courage actually stems from their fear of the king, who rules them like a master over slaves. As the Persians move forward in battle they are whipped, so they actually fear their own king and his agents more than the enemy.[36] Balot also notes that in Herodotus Spartan courage is based on their fidelity to law: Spartans fight because their state has ordered them to do so, and they largely lack the nerve to fight outside the Peloponnesus.[37] In the Periclean funeral oration, however, emphasis is put on the link between democratic debate and courage precisely because such debate was largely absent in Sparta.[38] In Balot's highly idealised account, Athenian courage is democratic: the Athenians fight because they have participated in collective decision-making and freely chosen to go to war. Clearly Balot sees courage principally in military terms. Seen in the light of Balot's book, however, Prometheus' courage in the face of torture, which stems partly from his foreknowledge of the end of his suffering, appears somewhat like Balot's Periclean courage, which relies on knowledge-based decision-making.

As interesting as it might be to detail further how Balot's analysis of courage could be extended to the idea of the torture of Prometheus as he might be understood as a free person or citizen, I would actually like to extend the thinking of the *Prometheus Bound* in other directions, first to situations where ostensibly free characters in tragedy do not live up to Prometheus' standards, where, when faced with torture, or something very much like it, a free person acts like a slave and uses the excuse of compulsion to act badly.

---

35 Balot 2014. Allen 2000, 25–33 only discusses the penal torture of Prometheus, not the judicial torture.

36 Balot 2014, 75–81.

37 Balot 2014, 82–91.

38 See Thuc. 2.40.2–3.

In Athenian literature descriptions of slavery are closely associated with physical compulsion, particularly torture. The word ἀνάγκη is used in several passages to indicate either slavery or compulsion or torture, which underlines how closely these three ideas are associated. Of course the word ἀνάγκη is used in other contexts also, but its association with the violence of slavery is distinct.[39] Demosthenes actually makes the point most strongly: “The strongest ἀνάγκη that a free man feels is shame (αἰσχύνη) for his circumstances...; but for a slave ἀνάγκη means stripes and bodily outrage (αἰκισμός), unfit to name here” (8.11).[40] In Euripides' *Orestes* Menelaus offers the maxim that “everything that depends on ἀνάγκη is a slave”, and Aeschylus' *Eumenides* offers the flipside: the happy person who is just “willingly and without compulsion” (ἑκὼν δ' ἀνάγκας ἄτερ).[41] Aristotle even directly connects the credibility of torture to ἀνάγκη (*Rh.* 1376b32). We could collect many more passages in which ἀνάγκη is associated with slavery and torture.[42] Prometheus is likewise confronted with it, even though he is not a slave. I have discussed some of his reactions. He is resentful about it. About ἀνάγκη as compulsion, however, he is more resigned: he sees it as fated, and he has no skill to overcome it.[43] But ἀνάγκη does not make him act in a way he does not want to. It is just something he has to put up with. On the other hand, Hephaestus admits that he is acting because of ἀνάγκη, and Io says that her father Inachus drove her out of the house because of it.[44]

Agamemnon's sacrifice of Iphigenia is reported as one of the greatest evils in human history.[45] It seems enormously significant that Aeschylus' chorus says that before committing it, Agamemnon put on the yoke-strap of ἀνάγκη, and Euripides likewise has Agamemnon fall into yokes of ἀνάγκη.[46] But Aeschylus makes clear that Agamemnon had a choice; he might have given up his expedi-

---

39 See LSJ *s.v.* 3a&b.

40 Demosthenes' “shame” of the free man might be compared to Prometheus' “disgrace” (ἀεικές *PV* 1041–1042). See also Antiph. 6.25.

41 Eur. *Or.* 488. Menelaus cites this maxim in response to Tyndareus' (Spartan) argument that the laws are to be followed, which fits Balot's model. Aesch. *Eum.* 550.

42 See Hes. *Theog.* 615-616; Aesch. *Cho.* 75–81. In a passage that is more akin to *Prometheus,* Hermes (see n. above) says that Apollo used ἀνάγκη on him. As with Prometheus, it does not work on Hermes there. Cf. Hdt. 1.116.4–5; 7.135.3–136.1; and 7.172.3 on the limits on ἀνάγκη. In Soph. *OC* 655–660, Theseus overcomes the “compulsion” of fear.

43 *PV* 103–104; 514; 1050–1054.

44 *PV* 16, 671–672. Interestingly, Ocean says that kinship “compels” him to sympathise with Prometheus (289–291).

45 Lucr., *De rerum natura* 1.101.

46 Aesch. *Ag.* 218. See also Eur. *IA* 443, 511–512.

tion and disappointed the goddess Artemis.[47] Both the word ἀνάγκη and the talk of yokes and yoke straps suggest that Agamemnon takes on a servile role and that that contributes to the mistakenness of his action.[48] In Euripides' *Hecuba*, Polyxena explains that in response to ἀνάγκη she would prefer to die a free woman rather than be enslaved. Preferring life over freedom would be, for her, the act of a coward, a slavish character.[49]

If we can depart for a moment from drama, we can also see these elements at work in Herodotus. The story of Gyges and his assassination of King Candaules of Lydia offers an illustration (Hdt. 1.11.4). After Gyges watches Candaules' wife undress, she confronts him and demands that he kill Candaules and marry her. Gyges is Candaules' favourite bodyguard, so he has a somewhat servile status, but he was also able to assume the kingship, so he ought to have had some more exalted status as well. At any rate, "ἀνάγκη" is mentioned twice in the description in which Gyges is "compelled" to kill Candaules. However, he does have a choice, kill or be killed, and a noble free man might have sacrificed his own life for his king's, as Polyxena does, or a clever bodyguard might have thought out some other solution. But Gyges acts like a slave. As Herodotus says, "he chooses to survive himself." Gyges is the model of someone who acts as a result of compulsion, like a slave.

Reactions to torture, or compulsion, are just one area that seems to be illuminated by examination of the torture of Prometheus. Another seems simply the phenomenon of lying. In Athens' democratic ideology, slaves lie and free people tell the truth, or nothing at all. In Sophocles' *Trachiniae,* Deianeira warns Lichas that to be called a liar is not a good fate for a free man.[50] The suggestion is that lying is almost expected for a slave.[51] Lichas is confronted with the fact that he has divided loyalties. He lies on behalf of Heracles about the identity of Iole (453–454), Heracles' new love interest, because he wants to defend his master's interest,[52] but Deianeira is also his mistress, and thanks to the importunate messenger, Lichas is caught in his lie. Deianeira's admonition suggests that Lichas

47 *Ag.* 205–208. Cf. *Ag.* 1069–1071.

48 In Eur. *Hipp.* 282–283, the Chorus Leader asks whether Phaedra's Nurse has applied ἀνάγκη on her to discover the nature of her illness. Later (325) it becomes clear that it involves only the ritual of supplication. Cf. Soph. *OC* 1178–1180.

49 Eur. *Hec.* 346–368, 658–662.

50 Soph. *Trach.* 453–454 ἐλευθέρῳ ψευδεῖ καλεῖσθαι κὴρ πρόσεστιν οὐ καλή. See also 399 (perjury).

51 In fact the play also puts repeated emphasis on the good speech of a slave woman (*Trach.* 52–53, 62–63).

52 See also Eur. *Bacch.* 1028.

will have a bad fate, and he is dead by the end of the play. Of course, characters lie in tragedies for all kinds of reasons, but some of them are clearly connected to ἀνάγκη and their servile reaction to it.

Euripides' *Hecuba* suggests that all mortals are enslaved to something, whether money, fortune, the mob, or legal suits (*Hec.* 864–887). Slavery could metaphorically affect even free citizens. But Prometheus sets a supernatural example of fortitude, the sort of fortitude that was actually imagined of an Athenian man in the heady early days of Athens' democracy. According to democratic ideology, unlike a slave, a woman, or a child, a free adult man would act and speak correctly (particularly as a witness) not because of compulsion, but because it was the right thing to do and say. When we unpack the underlying ideology that made sense of all of this for the Athenians, however, we see that, as with any ideology, reality and ideals diverge. There were strong slaves and weak free people. Aristophanes even sees a god whimper in pain while being tortured (*Ran.* 650–655). When Athenian playwrights depict free people acting on the basis of compulsion, they seem to indicate that they act in a way beneath their status, and they suffer for it. When *Prometheus Bound* was written, sometime in the mid fifth century, the example of the tyrannicides, Aristogeiton's fortitude and cleverness in the face of torture, the decree of Scamandrius, and Cleisthenes' reforms were all currency for Athens' democratic ideologues. Prometheus' confrontation with a tyrannical Zeus and his free, adult, male resistance against torture, both penal and judicial, fit those ideals perfectly.

Bibliography

Adamidis, V. (2019), 'The Rhetorical Use of Torture in Attic Forensic Oratory', in: *Rhetorica* 37, 16–34.
Allen, D. (2000), *The World of Prometheus*, Princeton.
Balot, R.K. (2014), *Courage in the Democratic Polis: Ideology and Critique in Classical Athens*, Oxford.
Bushala, E.W. (1968), 'Torture of Non-Citizens in Homicide Investigations', in: *GRBS* 9, 61–68.
Fornara, C.W. (1970), 'The Cult of Harmodius and Aristogeiton', in: *Philologus* 114, 155–180.
Gagarin, M. (1996), 'The Torture of Slaves in Athenian Law', in: *CPh* 91, 1–18.
Golden, M. (1990), *Children and Childhood in Classical Athens,* Baltimore.
Griffiths, M. (1983), *Aeschylus*, Prometheus Bound, Cambridge.
Harris, E.M. (1988), 'The Date of Apollodorus' Speech against Timotheus and Its Implications for Athenian History and Legal Procedure', in: *AJPh* 109, 44–52.
Headlam, J.W. (1893), 'On the *proklesis eis basanon* in Attic Law', in: *CR* 7, 1–5.
Lloyd-Jones, H. (2003), 'Zeus, Prometheus, and Greek Ethics', in: *HSPh* 101, 49–72.
MacDowell, D.M. (1962), *Andocides*, On the Mysteries, Oxford.

Mirhady, D.C. (1991), 'The Oath-Challenge in Athens', in: *CQ* 41, 78–83.
Mirhady, D.C. (1996), 'Torture and Rhetoric in Athens', in: *JHS* 116, 119–131.
Mirhady, D.C. (2000), 'The Athenian Rationale for Torture', in: J. Edmondson/V. Hunter (eds.), *Law and Social Status in Classical Athens*, Oxford, 53–74.
Podlecki, A. (1966), *The Political Background of Aeschylean Tragedy,* Ann Arbor.
Podlecki, A. (2005), *Aeschylus*, Prometheus Bound, Oxford.
Rhodes, P.J. (1982), *A Commentary on the Aristotelian* Athenaion Politeia, Oxford.
Sommerstein, A. (2008), *Aeschylus, I,* Persians. Seven against Thebes. Suppliants. Prometheus Bound, Cambridge, MA.
Sternberg, R.H. (2006), *Tragedy Offstage: Sympathy and Suffering in Ancient Athens,* Austin.
Teegarden, D. (2014), *Death to Tyrants! Ancient Greek Democracy and the Struggle Against Tyranny*, Princeton.
Thür, G. (1977), *Beweisführung vor den Schwurgerichtshöfen Athens: die Proklesis zur Basanos*, Vienna.
White, S. (2001), 'Io's World: Intimations of Theodicy in *Prometheus Bound*', in: *JHS* 121, 107–140.

Margarita Sotiriou

Poet, Patron, Message: Witness-Roles and the Game of Truth in Epinician *Eidography*

Abstract: This chapter, as well as focusing on selected lyric poems of Pindar and Bacchylides, aims to examine the function of juridical phraseology in epinician poetry, while discussing the intriguing "game of truth" played out between the poet and his audience (his addressee included) as an integral part of the communicative procedure that is characteristic of the victory odes. In this fictive game, the use of juridical terminology is indicative of the poet's wish to produce an aesthetic and semantic effect and to create a feeling of "pseudo-spontaneity", which is indispensable in the "live" performance of the ode as well as in future reperformances.

1 Introduction

The epinician poetry, refined by the two great bards of the late archaic period, Pindar and Bacchylides, belongs neither to the narrative genre nor to the declamatory masterpieces of classical Athens. According to Carey, the victory song is "a complex artefact", while Kurke speaks of a "communal drama", which offers reliable information about an athletic victory which is duly celebrated in order to enhance the prowess and skill of the addressee, while at the same time promising immortality through song.[1]

The communicative process between the poet and his addressee develops on two levels. On an initial level, the poet *encodes* the message, which includes the information that is important for the performance, and transmits it to his client and his audience. On a second level, the patron, as well as the audience of the ode, equipped with the necessary tools, are encouraged to *decode* the lyric message, interpret it and thereupon evaluate its content. The lyric "message" consists of various elements of praise: tributes to the victor and his achievements, his hometown and his ancestors. The choral voice uses different rhetorical strategies, complex varieties of verbal art, creatively constructed mythical narrations in order to augment effectively the glory of the event. It has been observed that the epinician performance is in a way analogous to the legal

1 Carey 1995, 86; Kurke 1991, 257.

https://doi.org/10.1515/9783110751970-012

hearing.[2] The use of forensic and epideictic terms with their notable persuasive power, such as μάρτυς or μαρτυρία, ἀλήθεια, ἐπίδειξις, ἀπόδειξις and in many cases the swearing of an oath (ὅρκος), allows the poet to proclaim *urbi et orbi* that his praise is valid and real.[3] The ensuing feeling of "pseudo-spontaneity" is crucial for a "live performance" of a glorious occasion, synchronically as part of the actual and immediate performance of the ode, as well as diachronically in front of the secondary audiences in a future spatio-temporal frame. The aim of this chapter is, therefore, to investigate the function of juridical phraseology in the epinician poetry of Pindar and Bacchylides and how it is incorporated in specific lyric contexts. I shall focus on some of the most eloquent examples of the deployment of such juristic terms, which I shall then use as my main case study.

2 Witness, messenger and oath as aspects of epinician mannerism

In their odes Pindar and less often Bacchylides emphasise the poet's personality. Experts in this field (e.g. Lefkowitz and Carey) have already paid attention to the special use of the poetic *persona*, pointing out that what we have is not the real Pindar (as historic person) but "the *persona* projected by the poems".[4] This preliminary remark is very important for our discussion regarding especially the passages where the role of witness or messenger is taken on by the lyric poet himself.[5] The way Pindar reflects on the task of delivering a message in an epinician ode is clearly depicted in *Pyth.* 4.277–279:

> τῶν δ' Ὁμήρου καὶ τόδε συνθέμενος
> ῥῆμα πόρσυν'· *ἄγγελον ἐσλὸν* ἔφα τιμὰν μεγίσταν πράγματι παντὶ φέρειν·
> αὔξεται καὶ Μοῖσα δ' *ἀγγελίας ὀρθᾶς*.
>
> And among Homer's sayings take this to heart and cherish it: he said that in all affairs a good messenger brings the greatest honour; even the Muse is exalted by a truthful report.

2 Most 1985, 176.

3 I examine here only the oath-statements of the poet which are included in the pure encomiastic parts of an ode and not those mentioned in the mythical narration, such as in Pind. *Ol.* 7.65, where Helios asks Lachesis to swear a μέγαν ὅρκον to give him Rhodes and bids her lift up her hands (χεῖρας ἀντεῖναι).

4 See, e.g., Carey 1995, 92.

5 Similarly, cf. Braswell 1988, 379.

Pindar claims here that through the superior skill of a noble messenger even the Muse gains in honour. The importance of his view is by definition easy to apprehend because of the authority of Homer cited therein. According to the ancient commentators the poet recalls *Il.* 15.207: ἐσθλὸν καὶ τὸ τέτυκται, ὅτ' *ἄγγελος* αἴσιμα εἰδῇ ("this too is good, when a messenger knows what is right").[6] Poseidon's words to Iris suggest how the Messenger should conduct himself and, more importantly, how to impart pertinent information in the public sphere.

One of the most impressive instances regarding the poet's duty as a messenger in association with his role as a witness is that at the opening strophe of Pindar *Ol.* 4, a song which celebrates Psaumis from the Sicilian state of Kamarina[7] and his Olympic victory in the chariot-race.[8] It is a rather short ode, chorally performed (l.9) in Olympia immediately after the athletic contest was over.[9] After the invocation of Zeus as the patron of the Olympic Games, Pindar, in a first-person declaration, claims that he has personally (l.3: μ' ἔπεμψαν) been sent here by Horai, Zeus' daughters, *with* his song both as a *witness* to the greatest rewards of victory and as a *messenger* of this achievement instead of sending his song as a gift to the victor (*Ol.* 4):[10]

Ἐλατὴρ ὑπέρτατε βροντᾶς ἀκαμαντόποδος
Ζεῦ τεαὶ γὰρ Ὧραι
ὑπὸ ποικιλοφόρμιγγος ἀοιδᾶς ἑλισσόμεναί μ' ἔπεμψαν
ὑψηλοτάτων μάρτυρ' ἀέθλων
ξείνων δ' εὖ πρασσόντων
ἔσαναν αὐτίκ' ἀγγελίαν ποτὶ γλυκεῖαν ἐσλοί.
[...]
ἀλλὰ Κρόνου παῖ,
[...]
Οὐλυμπιονίκαν
δέξαι Χαρίτων δ' ἕκατι τόνδε κῶμον

6 Sch. ad Pind. *Pyth.* 4.493.

7 For a detailed overview of the political history of Kamarina as a city-state, see Hornblower 2004, 186–192.

8 Gerber 1987, 8 and *passim*.

9 Gelzer 1985, 100. The performance place of the ode has been a subject of controversial discussion. See particularly Gerber 1987, 7–9, who argues for the performance of the song during a festive procession in honour of Zeus in Kamarina. In favour of a choral performance instead of a *solo* one, see the convincing argumentation in Calame 2004, 427–431.

10 Gerber 1987, 11–12. It is not necessary to assume that the poet has been actually present in the place of the Games. The statement may as well be a rhetorical trope revealing the poet's prominence in praising lavishly the victor and his success.

χρονιώτατον φάος εὐρυσθενέων ἀρετᾶν.
[...]
οὐ ψεύδεϊ τέγξω
λόγον διάπειρά τοι βροτῶν ἔλεγχος

Driver most high of thunder with unwearied foot Zeus. On you I call because your Horai in their circling round have sent me with song on varied lyre as a witness of the loftiest games. When guest-friends are successful, good men are immediately cheered at the sweet news. [...] And so, son of Kronos [...] receive an Olympic victor and, for the sake of the Games, this celebration, longest-lasting light for achievements of great strength. [...] I shall not tinge my praise with a lie; the trial to the end is the (true) test for men.[11]

Such a statement deserves closer scrutiny, mainly for the reason that a few verses below Pindar asks Zeus to *receive* this victorious procession (l.9: δέξαι τόνδε κῶμον), "venerable light of mighty exploits".[12] Surprisingly, the poet takes on not only the role of the witness but also the role of the messenger who is responsible for the release of the relevant information. The ode is presented "enunciatively as a processional song enacted in the *hic et nunc* of its performance by a group of dancers while the speaker presents himself as both witness and messenger".[13] Pindar as μάρτυς is responsible for the truthful description of the celebrated event in the context of the first performance, while as ἄγγελος is responsible for further announcements – that is, for the diffusion of this unique event and of its posterity among a wider audience. Of course, μάρτυς does not necessarily mean that the poet has been actually present at the Games.[14] We can safely interpret this statement as a rhetorical trope for underscoring the poet's authorial excellence and his distinction in praising copiously the champion and his achievement.[15] This sign-process develops a few lines below, when Pindar insists on the truthfulness of his acclamation, thus commenting on his encomiastic mission[16] and the principles of his art, in an enunciative self-reference which links the *prooimion* to the mythic narrative of the ode (17–18 οὐ ψεύδεϊ

11 Race 1990.
12 Felson 2004, 427.
13 Felson 2004, 427.
14 Gerber 1987, 11–12.
15 Such expressions give a sense of improvisation that reminds us of the rhetorical performances of the Attic orators; see principally Thomas 1999, 117.
16 Cf. Carey 1995, 92–93: "in Pindar as distinct from other choral lyric poet's references to the poet are distributed throughout the poem".

τέγξω λόγον˙ διάπειρά τοι βροτῶν ἔλεγχος = "I will not tinge my praise with lies˙ the test till the end is the proof for the men").[17]

In *Ol.* 9 Pindar praises Epharmostos from Opus in eastern Locris. Here the poet claims to accomplish his task by delivering the message of the athletic victory all around the earth and by praising the victor's birthplace with his "fiery songs" (21–26):

ἐγὼ δέ τοι φίλαν πόλιν
μαλεραῖς ἐπιφλέγων ἀοιδαῖς,
καὶ ἀγάνορος ἵππου
θᾶσσον καὶ ναὸς ὑποπτέρου
παντᾷ ἀγγελίαν πέμψω ταύταν
εἰ σύν τινι μοιρίδιῳ παλάμᾳ
ἐξαίρετον Χαρίτων νέμομαι κᾶπον

As for me, when I shed lustre on that dear city with my blazing songs, faster than a thoroughbred horse or a winged ship I shall spread this news far and wide, if only by some fortune-driven skill I can cultivate choice flowers in the garden of the Graces.

Pindar assumes the role of the messenger who must deliver the information in every direction. The adverb παντᾷ (l.24) lays strong emphasis on the geographical diffusion of the triumph through Pindar's poetry. It is noteworthy that the poet does not speak only in a self-referential manner. He prefers to use the vivid imagery of the "blazing songs", thereby calling attention to the beauty of the present performance,[18] and then he maintains that as a messenger he delivers the news faster than any horse or ship, thereby declaring that the whole process will be completed very soon.

There is a different type of Messenger at *Ol.* 14, a short ode for Asopichos from the Boeotian state of Orchomenos. Here the essential role of the person who delivers the news of the splendid victory is played by the personified Echo. Pindar asks Echo to go down to Hades to deliver the message of Asopichos' victory to his deceased father (20–24):

μελαντειχέα νῦν δόμον
Φερσεφόνας ἔλθ', Ἀ-
-χοι, πατρὶ *κλυτὰν* φέροισ' *ἀγγελίαν*,

---

17 The mythic narration is inserted in the form of a direct speech (*oratio recta*). According to Dornseiff 1921, 121, this technique indicates Pindar's literary model and his willingness to activate his audience's awareness of the source text, in order to impart information that is essential for their understanding of the poem.

18 Cf. also Hutchinson 2004, 379.

Κλεόδαμον ὄφρ' ἰδοῖσ', υἱὸν εἴπῃς ὅτι οἱ νέαν
κόλποις παρ' εὐδόξοις Πίσας
ἐστεφάνωσε κυδίμων ἀέθλων πτεροῖσι χαίταν.

Gow now, Echo, to the black-walled house of Persephone bringing to (my)[19] father the glorious message, so that when you look on Cleodamus you may tell him that by the famed hollows of Pisa his son has crowned his hair with the wings of ennobling contests.[20]

Though the motif of sending messages between the living and the dead is very common in the Greco-Roman world,[21] this situation implies that the term ἀγγελία, relayed from the earth to the underworld, denotes the spatio-temporal diffusion of the athletic success and the wide acknowledgement of Pindar's poetic excellence (l.21).

In Bacchylides' Ode 2 for the Kean athlete Argeios, Fame is the agent of the poet and his ode.[22] In her capacity as a messenger she is invited by the poet to carry the glorious message from Isthmus to the local community of Keos. The verb ἐπιδείκνυμι (l.9), well known in attic oratory,[23] means "show", "point out", "prove" and is here in the first plural, so as to imply that the participants of this odd 'game of truth' are not only Argeios and the Kean victors of the past but also the authority of the narrator, who, as an active member of the performative event, he reaffirms the great accomplishment (1–3, 6–10):

Ἄϊξον, ὦ σεμνοδότειρα Φήμα,
ἐς Κέον ἱεράν, χαριτώνυμον φέρουσ' *ἀγγελίαν*,
[...]
ὅσ' ἐν κλεεννῷ
αὐχένι Ἰσθμοῦ ζαθέαν
λιπόντες Εὐξαντίδα νᾶ-
σον *ἐπεδείξαμεν* ἑβδομή-
κοντα σὺν στεφάνοισιν.

Come Fame, giver of glorious gifts, sped here to holy Ceos, bringing a gracious message [...] and has renewed the memory of all those good achievements that we have displayed at the neck of the famous Isthmus after we came from the beautiful island of Euxantius, winners of seventy garlands.

19 I put the word "my" in parentheses because I choose not to follow Segal's translation.

20 Segal 1995.

21 See (e.g.) Pl. *Resp.* 10.614d: ἄγγελον ἀνθρώποις γενέσθαι τῶν ἐκεῖ and Vergil's *Aen.* 547–549. Cf. also Segal 1995, 134 with further references.

22 Hubbard 2004, 73.

23 Cf. (e.g.) Lys. 1.4 and 4.14.

The personification of Fame as a messenger symbolises the wider circulation of the ode and the athletic success commemorated therein, as also is the case in Bacchylides' Ode 10. 1–2:

Φήμα, σὺ γὰρ [...] ἐποιχνεῖς
φῦλα

Fame, because you visit the tribes of men [...]

In a self-referential passage at the opening of *Pyth.* 2 and in a carefully and well-organised verbal schema (participle [φέρων] – noun [μέλος] – verb [ἔρχομαι] – noun [ἀγγελίαν]), the word ἀγγελία is employed as a pertinent appellation of the epinician song that communicates the message from Thebes to Syracuse (3–4):

ὔμμιν *τόδε* τᾶν λιπαρᾶν ἀπὸ Θηβᾶν *φέρων*
μέλος ἔρχομαι ἀγγελίαν τετραορίας ἐλελίχθονος

I come to you from gleaming Thebes bringing this song which tells of an earth-shaking four-horse team...

The simple present of the verb and of the participle denotes the *hic et nunc* of the epinician performance. It suggests a conscious literary strategy that creates a kind of pseudo-spontaneity, crucial for the vividness of the performative process.

In *Nem.* 5 the epinician song itself undertakes the role of the messenger and brings everyone the message of victory. The poet asks his "sweet song" to be the envoy (for him) and to carry the news of the Nemean triumph of Pytheas from Aegina to the whole world (2–3):

οὐκ ἀνδραντοποιός εἰμ', ὥστ' ἐλινύσοντα ἐργά-
ζεσθαι ἀγάλματ' ἐπ' αὐτᾶς βαθμίδος
ἑσταότ'· ἀλλ' ἐπὶ πάσας
ὁλκάδος ἔν τ' ἀκάτῳ, *γλυκεῖ' ἀοιδά*,
στεῖχ' ἀπ' Αἰγίνας *διαγγέλλοισ'* ὅτι [...]

I am no statue maker, to fashin delightful objects that stand idle on their bases; but on every merchant ship and every skiff, sweet song, go forth, spreading the news from Aegina.[24]

24 Felson-Parmentier 2015.

Here the lyric information is delivered through a self-confident prediction by the poet "who feels assured that his work will outlive a single performance and extend beyond a merely local audience".[25]

3 Witnesses and oaths

The epinician poet often reinforces his praise by using not only witness statements but also oaths. Such instances of oath-taking are not to be identified as real ones; they enhance the poetic argument through an explicit signal of commitment, an additional rhetorical significance and a strong dramatic force. Their fictionality "adds authority to the spoken words",[26] invests the poetic speech with the impression of a vivid and lively depiction of the 'real' performance and, in a sense, re-energises the attention and the interest of audiences in future performances. A fascinating case is *Ol.* 6 honouring Agesias from Syracuse, winner of the mule race. Here the poetic persona addresses the victor, while he "dwells on his own nature" (19–21):

τὸ καί
ἀνδρὶ κώμου δεσπότᾳ πάρεστι Συρακοσίῳ.
οὔτε δύσηρις ἐὼν οὔτ' ὦν φιλόνικος ἄγαν,
καὶ *μέγαν ὅρκον ὀμόσσαις* τοῦτό γέ οἱ σαφέως
μαρτυρήσω μελίφθογ-
γοι δ' ἐπιτρέψοντι Μοῖσαι.

This too can be said of the Syracusan master of this revel. I am not disputatious, nor overeager for victory, but I will swear a great oath and testify that this is true, and the sweetvoiced Muses will bear me out.[27]

The oath-taking reinforces the emotional tension of the moment. The poetic persona invites his audience to share common feelings. He asseverates the pertinence of Adrastus' saying concerning Amphiaraus' valour that precedes the mythical story (13–17) and, therefore, strikingly associates the past with the present. Pindar's role as a poet reaches completion. The present becomes vivid and intense; but also, in this case an element of conviction and fiction turns out to be crucial. According to Hutchinson, "the narrator's character is such, as to

25 Hubbard 2004, 72. Διαγγέλλω means "give notice by a messenger"; cf. also Eur. *Hel.* 436.
26 Fletcher 2012, 65.
27 Verity 2008.

make his judgement valid and his candour exemplary".[28] As for the directness and vibrancy of the scene Hutchinson notes further that the future tense of μαρτυρέω is often used of someone willing to bear witness at the right moment in a trial.[29] The idea of intention is in fact instrumental in making sense of Pindar's futures.[30] The oath with its emphatic quality creates further emotional effects through the use of καί. The swearing of an oath belongs to the conventions of the epinician genre and, moreover, plays a functional role in the specific context: it introduces the poetic *egō* with great forcefulness and elaborated accent on the performative ritual. It is obvious that the present endows the poem with a degree of fiction. Besides, the last clause of the passage (l.21 "the sweet-voiced Muses will bear me out") recalls also a fictive situation: here the Muses have the legal right to refer the matter to the narrator in order to be the judge of it.

A few verses below, just before the end of the poem, the poetic "I" addresses the instructor of the chorus and ask him to be "a clever messenger", perhaps "a clever interpreter" of his will, all the while keeping himself away from the boorishness, the dullness and the rusticity ascribed to the ancient Boeotians[31] (88–90):

> Αἰνέα, πρῶτον μὲν Ἥραν
> Παρθενίαν κελαδῆσαι,
> γνῶναί τ' ἔπειτ', ἀρχαῖον ὄνειδος ἀλαθέσιν
> λόγοις εἰ φεύγομεν, Βοιωτίαν ὗν.
> ἐσσὶ γὰρ *ἄγγελος ὀρθός*,
> ἠυκόμων σκυτάλα Μοι-
> σᾶν, γλυκὺς κρατὴρ ἀγαφθέγκτων ἀοιδᾶν·

Now Aeneas, exhort your companions first to proclaim Hera Parthenia, and then to see if my truthful words can deflect that ancient jibe, 'Boeotian pig'; for you are an upright envoy, a message-stick of the fair-haired Muses, a sweet mixing-bowl of loud-echoing songs.[32]

---

28 Hutchinson 2001, 384.

29 Hutchinson 2001, 385. See further *Ol.* 13.108, Aesch. *Ag.* 1505–1506, *Eum.* 576, Soph. *Ant.* 515, Pl. *Ap.* 21A. 7–8, Aeschin. 2.126. For the conception, cf. *Ol.* 4.3 and *Parth.* 2.38–39.

30 Cf. *Ol.* 8.54–59, 13.91, *Pyth.* 2.83–85, 3.107–109, *Ol.* 7.20, *Pyth.* 9.1, *Isthm.* 1.15–16, Eur. *El.* 180, *HF* 673. Additionally, see Bundy 1962, 1986, 21–22; Hummel, 1993, 228–236.

31 Pindar recalls here a Spartan tradition: messages were wrapped around sticks in order to facilitate their conveyance to the recipients. Cf. also Hutchinson 2001, 417 with further bibliography.

32 Verity 2008.

Ἄγγελος is not the poet anymore, but someone else who is also involved in the epinician procedure. The colorfulness of such a spontaneous and quite unusual request transfers the emphasis on the presence of the chorus' instructor and confirms the impression that "the effect in performance will have been arresting".[33] Such an invocation in the context of the celebration, before the audience, highlights the feeling of intimacy between the poet and his assistant and perhaps creates an illusion of informality.

In *Nem.* 7 Pindar relates Neoptolemus' story, who was killed by an unnamed assailant, while praying to Apollo in Delphi.[34] At the end of the mythical account, in addressing the island of Aegina, Pindar resembles an unknown witness, who does not speak untruthfully (49–52):

> *οὐ ψεῦδις ὁ μάρτυς* ἔργμασιν ἐπιστατεῖ
> Αἴγινα, τεῶν Διός τ' ἐκγόνων. θρασύ μοι τόδε εἰπεῖν
> φαενναῖς ἀρεταῖς ὁδὸν κυρίαν λόγων
> οἴκοθεν.
>
> It is no lying witness, Aegina, that authenticates the deeds of your and Zeus' offspring. I feel the confidence to speak of a sovereign road of words, reaching from your home, that honours your splendid achievements.[35]

The poetic identity emerges (θρασύ μοι τόδε εἰπεῖν = "I feel the confidence to speak") through the first-person (l.50: μοι) in the next sentence, while a high degree of his prominent authority is revealed (cf. below lines 60–62: σκοτεινὸν ἀπέχων ψόγον … κλέος ἐτήτυμον αἰνέσω). Obviously, the poetic *persona* presents himself to the audience as a reliable and most important self-confident witness whose mission is not simply to rehabilitate Neoptolemus' bad reputation as a murderer but mainly to augment the glory of the victor's hometown, Aegina.

Hubbard demonstrates that the Aeginetan odes of Pindar are full of imagery which praises maritime skill and power.[36] A striking example that confirms his view can be found in *I.* 5, an ode that praises Phylakidas, winner in the pancratium. Here the act of praising is endowed with a positive dynamism embodied in a vigorous image which is full of metaphoric energy (47–50):

33 Hutchinson 2001, 416.

34 It is well known that this version of Neoptolemus' myth is more favourable than the version recounted by Pindar in *Pae.* 6, where Apollo kills him because the hero has murdered Priam.

35 Verity 2008.

36 Hubbard 2001, 393.

πολλὰ μὲν ἀρτιεπὴς
γλῶσσά μοι τοξεύματ' ἔχει περὶ κείνων
κελαδέσαι· καὶ νῦν ἐν Ἄρει *μαρτυρῆσαι*
.........κεν πόλις Αἴαντος ὀρθωθεῖσα ναύταις
ἐν πολυφθόρῳ Σαλαμὶς Διὸς ὄμβρῳ
ἀναρίθμων ἀνδρῶν χαλαζάεντι φόνῳ.

My tongue, ready with words, has many arrows to sound out in their praise and in the recent war Ajax' city Salamis could testify to being saved by its sailors in Zeus' lethal rainstorm, a fall of bloody hail on numberless men.[37]

The privilege of witnessing belongs here to the narrator's tongue, in other words to his poetic φυά, his divine charisma. The objects of enthusiastic admiration are both the victor's homeland, Aegina, and the contribution of this small island of Saronic Golf to the defeat of the Persians at the sea-battle of Salamis (480 BC), when the Aeginetans, though they had suffered many losses, distinguished themselves by winning the prize for ἀριστεία.[38] As in the other passages discussed above, the use of the term μαρτυρία here is not at all conventional. It has developed to serve as a cardinal conceptual sign of encomiastic vocabulary with special significance that not only facilitates the narrator's self-advertisement but also reaffirms Aegina's maritime services in the glorious past. These nautical achievements give further μεγαλοπρέπεια to the present political and financial standing of the island and guarantee its future as a major mercantile market.

4 Oaths and ἀλάθεια

Let us now take a closer look at some cases where the swearing of an oath is directly associated with the virtue of ἀλάθεια. According to Nagy, ἀλάθεια is a panhellenic value, a value that due to its popularity offers the participants of the epinician performance a double benefit: both the addressee and the creator himself gain panhellenic fame and recognition.[39] Ἀλάθεια in epinician contexts denotes both the willingness and the ambition of the poet to make eternal the addressee's skill and bravery through his own work which is bound to become

37 Verity 2008.
38 Hdt. 8.93.1, 8.122.
39 Nagy 1991, 60.

duly established in ritualised performances all around Greece. In Bacchylides' Ode 9.82–87 we hear that:

τό γέ τοι καλὸν ἔργον
γνησίων ὕμνων τυχόν
ὑψοῦ παρὰ δαίμοσι κεῖται·
σὺν δ' *ἀλαθείᾳ* βροτῶν
κάλλιστον, εἴπερ καὶ θάνῃ τις,
λείπεται Μουσᾶν [...] ἄθυρμα.

A goodly deed that has won the strains of a true poet is laid up on high with the gods. When mortal lips give honest praise, there is a glory that survives death in song, the joy of the (glorious) Muses.[40]

Again, in Ode 13.199 Bacchylides claims that:

ἁ δ' *ἀλαθεία* φιλεῖ
νικᾶν, ὅ τε πανδαμάτωρ
χρόνος τὸ καλῶς ἐργμένον αἰὲν ἀέξει.

But truth is wont to prevail; and all-subduing time ever strengthens the repute of fine achievement.[41]

Ἀλάθεια concerns the quality of the information transmitted and how the poet and his medium are publicly revealed in both present and future. It also facilitates persuasion and makes the performative space more animated and active. Additionally, the content of the lyric message sounds significant and valid both synchronically and diachronically. When ἀλάθεια is connected with ἀγγελία or μαρτυρία, terms that invest the poetic speech with authority, both the choral identity and the influence it exerts on the formulation of the collected information become stronger.[42]

A variation of a witness-statement occurs in Pindar's *Ol.* 13. The privileged position of the independent witness is transferred now to the "regal altar of the Lycaean Zeus", an element of the local topography of the place, where the victory has been achieved. It is this religious place of Zeus' altar that assures the greatness of the victories gained in Arcadian athletic games. The word βωμός is

40 Jebb 1905.
41 Jebb 1905.
42 Rhetorical devices create effects that are similar to the authorial identification of the poetic "I" (1.49), thereby providing the poet with a vivid and powerful way to display his high artistic quality.

carefully placed between terms that recall political authority (1.107 ἀνάσσων – 1.108 ἄναξ), and this helps the narrator to highlight the political importance of the Games (49–52, 98–100, 107–109):

ἐγὼ δὲ κεῖνος ἐν κοινῷ σταλείς
μητίν τε γαρύων παλαιγόνων
πόλεμόν τ' ἐν ἡρωίαις ἀρεταῖσιν
οὐ ψεύσομ' ἀμφὶ Κορίνθῳ
[...]
Ἰσθμοῖ τά ἐν Νεμέα παύρῳ ἔπει
θήσω φανέρ' ἀθρό', *ἀλαθής τέ μοι*
ἔξορκος ἐπέσσεται ἑξηκοντάκι δὴ ἀμφοτέρωθεν
ἀδύγλωσσος βοὰ κάρυκος ἐσθλοῦ.
[...]
ὅσα τ' Ἀρκάσιν ἀνάσσων
μαρτυρήσει Λυκαίου βωμὸς ἄναξ

I am a private passenger on a public voyage, and when I speak of the talents of their forefathers and their heroic deeds in war, I shall give no false account of the people of Corinth [...] as for their victories at the Isthmus and Nemea, a short word from me will make the sum total plain; and as a true sworn witness, the excellent herald's sweet-voiced cry, uttered sixty times at both games, will add its confirmation. [...] touching those in Arcadia's valleys, the regal altar of the Lycaean will bear witness.[43]

The closing passage of Pindar's *Ol.* 2 offers an image of the poet swearing an oath truthfully. It serves as an introduction to the last encomiastic part of the poem (90–92):

ἐπί τοι
Ἀκράγαντι τανύσαις
αὐδάσομαι ἐνόρκιον λόγον ἀλαθεῖ νόῳ,
τεκεῖν μή τιν' ἑκατόν γε ἐτέων πόλιν
φίλοις ἄνδρα μᾶλλον
εὐεργέταν πραπίσιν ἀφθονέστερόν τε χέρα
Θήρωνος.

I bent my bow at Acragas, proclaiming on oath and with true understanding that no city in hundred years has given birth to a man more generous in spirit to his friends or more open-handed than Theron.[44]

43 Verity 2008.
44 Verity 2008.

In Attic drama the oath is a literary device that combines language and action.[45] In Ode 5 for Hieron from Syracuse Bacchylides adds authority to his words by pretending to take an oath; he rests his hand on the earth[46] and invites the audience to recognise his pledge.[47] The scene gives the impression that the poet was truly among the spectators of the Games, as an actual witness to the athletic triumph. The phrase is placed purposefully in the midpoint of the victory description and serves as a bridge to a detailed and powerful account of the triumph (42–45, 187–189, 195–197). Similarly, in the *narratio* the oath marks a significant transitional moment:[48]

γᾷ δ' ἐπισκήπτων πιφαύσκω
οὔπω νιν ὑπὸ προτέρων
ἵππων ἐν ἀγῶνι κατέχρανεν κόνις
πρὸς τέλος ὀρνύμενον
[...]
χρὴ δ' ἀλαθείας χάριν
αἰνεῖν, φθόνον ἀμφοτέραισιν
χερσὶν ἀπωσάμενον
[...]
πείθομαι εὐμαρέως
εὐκλέα κελεύθου γλῶσσαν
πέμπειν Ἱέρωνι.

Laying my hand on the earth I call Earth to witness: never yet in a race has he been soiled by dust from horses in front of him, as he sped to his goal [...] must give praise, for truth's sake, and thrust envy away with might and main, if any man should prosper [...] Readily am I won to send Hieron the song that tells forth his fame, without swerving from the path of justice.[49]

The same phraseology is used in Bacchylides' Ode 8. Here the oath is combined with a verb rare in Attic prose but quite common in poetic contexts. Κομπάζομαι means "boast" and the statement that the so-called poetic obligation (χρέος) "is shining with truth" serves as an artful way for the poet to underline that what he says is all true. In this case too, the phrase concerning the oath-taking is placed between those references to the hymnic task he has to complete, such as ὑμνέων and χρέος (17–21):

45 Fletcher 2012, 8.
46 Maehler 2004, 116.
47 In the Homeric texts chthonic powers are often called to witness a promise or an oath.
48 Fletcher 2012, 29.
49 Jebb 1905.

Πυθῶνά τε μηλοθύταν
ὑμνέων Νεμέαν τε καὶ Ἰσθμόν·
γᾷ δ' ἐπισκήπτων χέρα
κομπάσομαι· σὺν ἀλα-
θείᾳ δὲ πᾶν λάμπει χρέος

Singing of Pytho, where sheep are sacrificed, and of Nemea, and of the Isthmus. And laying my hand on the earth as a witness, I will make this vaunt; for only by the voice of truth can anything be set in a full light.[50]

To sum up: Segal has already pointed out that "one of the tasks of a messenger is to establish communication".[51] As for the epinician genre, this communication is successfully developed by the methodical deployment of a highly suggestive and figurative language. It is a conscious choice on the part of the poet, who aims primarily at going beyond the spatio-temporal frame of the victory and the first performance of the ode, extending to the future and involving broader audiences of different communities. The wide circulation of the victory ode is a matter that concerns not only the victor but also the poet himself. Thus, the epinician poet regularly underlines his distinct identity and his professional status, while all at once associating his task with eternal panhellenic values and axioms. The poet seems to feel assured about his own merits, as well as self-confident in the immense importance of his art and well aware of his ability to speak the truth before a panhellenic audience. He combines factual information about the athletic victory with his personal take on the event, while at the same time aspiring to transform the subjectivity of his praise into an objective poetic design with perpetual continuity and panhellenic worth.

To establish communication on multiple levels, Pindar and Bacchylides invite the audience to participate in a fictional "game of truth", in the context of which the witness- or the messenger-roles are interchanged between the poetic *persona* or part of his body (*langue*), his song, the instructor of the chorus or some elements of local topography (e.g. Zeus' altar), abstract divinities (*Phēmē* or *Ēchō*), and many more. Such a conscious poetic strategy deserves more scrutiny, principally because it helps the panegyrist to obtain more visibility, to give his judgment an additional force: the force of internal authority.

The lyric poet "delivers" his information, while simultaneously encouraging his audiences (not only the original one but also those of the future performanc-

50 Jebb 1905.
51 Segal 1998, 133.

es)[52] to play a very specific role, the role of the "savvy interpreter".[53] Thus, audiences do not remain inactive and aloof. They are invited to exercise a particular control on the poet's words, thereby taking an active part in the reading of the poetic signs. Epinician performance is therefore revealed as a unique interactive process, where the poet entrusts his audiences (present and future) with the projected goal of shaping the lyric message and all associated thoughts and feelings, asking them for attentiveness, self-responsibility, and self-control, in order to evaluate the performed words and contextualise them accordingly.

Bibliography

Braswell, B.K. (1988), *A Commentary on the Fourth Pythian Ode of Pindar*, Berlin/New York.

Bundy, E.L. (1962, 1986), *Studia Pindarica*, Berkley/Los Angeles.

Burnett, A.P. (2008), *Pindar*, Bristol.

Calame, C. (2004), 'Deictic Ambiguity and Auto-Referentiality: Some Examples', in: N. Felson (ed.), *The Poetics of Deixis in Alcman, Pindar and Other Lyric*, in: *Arethusa* 37, 415–443.

Carey, C. (1991), 'The Victory Ode in Performance: The Case for the Chorus', in: *CPh* 86, 192–200.

Carey, C. (1995), 'Pindar and the Victory Ode', in: L. Ayres (ed.), *The Passionate Intellect: Essays on the Transformation of Classical Traditions Presented to Professor I.G. Kidd*, New Brunswick, 85–103.

Dornseiff, F. (1921), *Pindars Stil*, Berlin.

Felson, N. (2004), 'The Poetics of Deixis in Alcman, Pindar, and Other Lyric', in: *Arethusa* 37.3.

Felson, N./Parmentier, R. (2015), 'The "Savvy Interpreter": Performance and Interpretation in Pindar's Victory Odes', in: *Signs and Society* 3.2, 261–305.

Fletcher, J. (2012), *Performing Oaths in Classical Greek Drama*, Oxford.

Gelzer, T. (1985), 'Μοῦσα αὐθιγενής. Bemerkungen zu einem Typ pindarischer und bakchylideischer Epinikien', in: *MH* 42, 95–120.

Gerber, D. (1987), 'Pindar's Olympian Four: A Commentary', in: *QUCC* 25, 7–24.

Hutchinson, G. (2003), *Greek Lyric Poetry: A Commentary on Selected Larger Pieces: Alcman, Stesichorus, Sappho, Alcaeus, Ibycus, Anacreon, Simonides, Bacchylides, Pindar, Sophocles, Euripides*, Oxford.

Hubbard, T. (2001), 'Pindar and Athens after the Persian Wars', in: D. Papenfuss/V.M. Strocka (eds.), *"Gab es das Griechische Wunder?" Griechenland zwischen dem Ende des 6. und der Mitte des 5. Jahrhunderts v.Chr.*, Mainz am Rhein, 387–397.

52 Cf. Spelmann 2018, 228: "Pindar's reputation reflexively celebrated within his work must also matter to those who attend the first performance of his poems as well as to his second audiences".

53 The term belongs to Felson/Parmentier (2015). Note especially the title of their thought-provoking paper: "The 'Savvy Interpreter': Performance and Interpretation in Pindar's Victory Odes".

Hubbard, T. (2004), 'The Dissemination of Epinician Lyric: Pan-Hellenism, Reperformance, Written Texts', in: C. Mackie (ed.), *Oral Performance and its Context*, Leiden/Boston, 71–93.
Hummel, P. (1993), *Le syntaxe de Pindare*, Louvain/Paris.
Jebb, R. (1905), *Bacchylides: The Poems and the Fragments Edited with Introduction, Notes and Prose Translation*, Cambridge.
Jong, I. de (1997), 'Homer and Narratology', in: I. Morris/B. Powell (eds.), *Narrators, Narratees, and Narratives in Ancient Greek Literature*, Leiden, 213–232.
Jong, I. de (2004), 'Pindar and Bacchylides', in: I. de Jong/R. Nünlist/A. Bowie (eds.), *Narrators, Narratees, and Narratives in Ancient Greek Literature*, Leiden, 213–232.
Kurke, L. (1991), *The Traffic in Praise: Pindar and the Poetics of Social Economy*, Ithaca, NY.
Mader, W. (1988), *Die Psaumis-Oden Pindars (O. 4 und O. 5). Ein Kommentar*, Innsbruck.
Maehler, H. (2004), *Bacchylides: A Selection*, Cambridge.
Most, G. (1985), *The Measures of Praise: Structure and Function in Pindar's Second Pythian and Seventh Nemean Odes*, Göttingen.
Nagy, G. (1991), *Pindar's Homer: The Lyric Possession of an Epic Past*, Baltimore/London.
Nisetich, F. (1989), *Pindar and Homer*, Baltimore.
Race, W.H. (1990), *Style and Rhetoric in Pindar's Odes*, Atlanta.
Segal, C. (1998), *Aglaia: The Poetry of Alcman, Sappho, Pindar, Bacchylides, and Corinna*, Lanham/Boulder/New York/Oxford.
Sommerstein, H.A./Bayliss, J.A. (2013), *Oath and State in Ancient Greece*, Berlin/Boston.
Spelmann, H. (2018), *Pindar and the Poetics of Permanence*, Oxford.

Part IV: The Cultural Workings of Witnesses and Evidence

Smaro Nikolaidou

Information and Decision in Sophocles' *Trachiniae* and Euripides' *Medea* and *Ino*

Abstract: In my article "Information and decision in Sophocles' *Trachiniae* and Euripides' *Medea* and *Ino*", I argue that in Sophocles' *Trachiniae* and Euripides' *Medea* and *Ino*, produced, in all probability, before the Peloponnesian War, there is awareness about love and conjugal fidelity. It is expressed through the theme of female jealousy tragically combined with kin killing, which is organised by carefully using witnesses and evidence. In the fragmentary *Ino,* in particular, there is a clear reference to sophistic ideas about monogamy and polygamy spoken out by Ino's husband, Athamas. Perhaps, the well-known decree of 413 BC about bigamy (if existed) was preceded by a period of ideological mediation on marriage relationship, which found some shocking expressions in all three tragedies discussed in the article.

Marriage in classical Athens was monogamous, which protected the wife's position and influence in her household. The only example of polygamy (precisely bigamy) is dated in the Peloponnesian War, somewhere around 413 BC, after the Athenian disaster in Sicily, when Athens temporarily changed the law and permitted a man two wives in order for the city to be repopulated.[1] However, in Sophocles' *Trachiniae* and Euripides' *Medea* and *Ino*, which were performed before the War,[2] there is awareness (or/and anxiety) about monogamous marriage; and it is expressed through the theme of female jealousy, tragically combined with kin killing.

---

1 Diog. Laert. 2.26 (Arist. *On Good Birth* fr. 93 Rose) Φησὶ δ' Ἀριστοτέλης δύο γυναῖκας αὐτὸν (Σωκράτην) ἀγαγέσθαι· προτέραν μὲν Ξανθίππην, ἐξ ἧς αὐτῷ γενέσθαι Λαμπροκλέα· δευτέραν δὲ Μυρτώ, τὴν Ἀριστείδου τοῦ δικαίου θυγατέρα, ἣν καὶ ἄπροικον λαβεῖν, ἐξ ἧς γενέσθαι Σωφρονίσκον καὶ Μενέξενον. οἱ δὲ προτέραν γῆμαι τὴν Μυρτώ φασιν· ἔνιοι δὲ καὶ ἀμφοτέρας σχεῖν ὁμοῦ, ὧν ἐστι Σάτυρός τε καὶ Ἱερώνυμος ὁ Ῥόδιος. φασὶ γὰρ βουληθέντας Ἀθηναίους διὰ τὸ λειπανδρεῖν συναυξῆσαι τὸ πλῆθος, ψηφίσασθαι γαμεῖν μὲν ἀστὴν μίαν, παιδοποιεῖσθαι δὲ καὶ ἐξ ἑτέρας· ὅθεν τοῦτο ποιῆσαι καὶ Σωκράτην. On the date of the decree and its content, Harrison 1968–1971, vol. I, 16–17; Ogden 1996, 72–75. On the interpretation of the decree and its "legitimate" reproductive arrangements, see Lape 2010, 263–273.

2 Sophocles' *Trachiniae* remains undated, but was probably written between 440 and 430 BC; for problems of dating the play, see Hoey 1979. For the date of Euripides' *Ino*, see the next footnote.

https://doi.org/10.1515/9783110751970-013

I will begin with Euripides' fragmentary *Ino*, which was surely performed before 425 BC, according to a reference in Aristophanes' *Acharnians* produced in 425 BC.[3] From the play itself twenty five book fragments and one papyric text are saved, which I will deliberately use, in accordance with the aim of my paper. The plot is given by Hyginus' *Fabula* 4, which remains our only source for the hypothesis of the play:

> Athamas in Thessalia rex, cum Inonem uxorem, ex qua duos filios <susceperat>, perisse putaret, duxit Nymphae filiam Themistonem uxorem; ex ea geminos filios procreavit. postea resciit Inonem in Parnaso esse, quam bacchationis causa eo pervenisse; misit qui eam adducerent; quam adductam celavit. resciit Themisto eam inventam esse, sed quae esset nesciebat. coepit velle filios ejus necare; rei consciam, quam captivam esse credebat ipsam Inonem sumpsit, et ei dixit ut filios suos candidis vestimentis operiret, Inonis filios nigris. Ino suos candidis, Themistonis pullis operuit; tunc Themisto decepta suos filios occidit; id ubi resciit, ipsa se necavit. Athamas autem in venatione per insaniam Learchum majorem filium suum interfecit; at Ino cum minore filio Melicerte in mare se dejecit et dea est facta.

> King Athamas of Thessaly thought that his wife, Ino, by whom he had fathered two sons, was dead. So, he married Themisto, the daughter of a Nymph, and had twin sons by her. Later, he learned that Ino was on Mount Parnassus; she had gone there to celebrate the Bacchic mysteries. He sent men to bring her back, and when they had, he kept her out of view. Themisto learned that they had found a woman but did not know who she was. Themisto planned to kill Ino's sons and took as her accomplice Ino herself (who, she thought, was just a captive girl), and told her to dress her sons in white and Ino's in black. Misled in this fashion, Themisto killed her own sons. When she realised her error, she committed suicide. As for Athamas, in a fit of madness he killed his elder son, Learchus, while hunting. Ino threw herself into the sea along with her younger son, Melicertes, and was made a goddess.[4]

If Hyginus' narrative is not mistaken, the dramatic space would have been Thessaly. In his monologic, in all likelihood, prologue (in the typical Euripidean manner), Athamas would have first reverted back to Ino's fleeing to Cithaeron and his subsequent marriage to Themisto. He would then explain his undertaking to bring Ino home after finding her in Cithaeron, as well as the choice to

---

3 In his *Acharnians* 432–434, Aristophanes parodies the rags in which Euripides' Ino was costumed by representing the poet himself, when Dicaeopolis approaches him and begs for a rag, ordering a serve as such : ὦ παῖ, δὸς αὐτῷ Τηλέφου ῥακώματα·/κεῖται δ' ἄνωθεν τῶν Θυεστίων ῥακῶν/ μεταξὺ τῶν Ἰνοῦς ("Slave! Give him the tatters of Telephus; they are on top of Thestes' rags, in between them and those of Ino").

4 Text from Marshall 2002; translation by Smith/Trzaskoma 2007.

place her among the servants of the palace and concealing her identity from Themisto. The fragment 398 εὕδουσα δ' Ἰνοῦς συμφορὰ πολὺν χρόνον/νῦν ὄμμ' ἐγείρει (*TrGF* 5.1 Kannicht) could have summarised the new –and difficult– situation by using the wording of sleep metaphorically: Ino's new situation is a trouble which was asleep for a long of time and now opens its eyes.

One scene – probably from the first episode – would have shown the grim prospects of Ino's return to her former home. The heroine, addressing the chorus of women, would have expressed her inability to renounce her former ways and resume a role in the palace of Athamas: fr. 399 φίλαι γυναῖκες, πῶς ἂν ἐξ ἀρχῆς δόμους / Ἀθάμαντος οἰκήσαιμι τῶν πεπραγμένων/δράσασα μηδέν; In a dialogue between her and Athamas, Ino would probably have responded negatively to the erotic appetite of her former spouse, who in fact wanted her to be his secret second wife (frr. 400, 401). In fr. 400 Ino cries for women's hearts by cursing Aphrodite (Eros/Love) as a disease: ὦ θνητὰ πράγματ', ὦ γυναικεῖαι φρένες· / ὅσον νόσημα τὴν Κύπριν κεκτήμεθα.[5] In fr. 401 she loudly protests women's unhappiness against that of men and argues that female sex is left far behind in good times, and yet further in bad: φεῦ, ὅσῳ τὸ θῆλυ δυστυχέστερον γένος / πέφυκεν ἀνδρῶν· ἔν τε τοῖσι γὰρ καλοῖς / πολλῷ λέλειπται κἀπὶ τοῖς αἰσχροῖς πλέον.

The crucial passage for my paper is fr. 402, where Ino's vigorous protests maybe answered with elements of sophistic ideas about monogamy and polygamy propounded by Athamas. In the saved lines, laws in force are accused for their monogamic content:

> νόμοι γυναικῶν οὐ καλῶς κεῖνται πέρι·
> χρῆν γὰρ τὸν εὐτυχοῦνθ' ὅτι πλείστας ἔχειν
> {γυναῖκας, εἴπερ τροφὴ δόμοις παρῆν},
> ὡς τὴν κακὴν μὲν ἐξέβαλλε δωμάτων,
> τὴν δ' οὖσαν ἐσθλὴν ἡδέως ἐσῴζετο.
> νῦν δ' εἰς μίαν βλέπουσι, κίνδυνον μέγαν
> ῥίπτοντες· οὐ γὰρ τῶν τρόπων πειρώμενοι
> νύμφας ἐς οἴκους ἑρματίζονται βροτοί

Laws are not well made concerning wives: the prosperous man should be having as many as possible {if his house could maintain them}, so he could throw the bad one out of his home and be pleased at keeping the one who actually is good. Now, however, they look to

---

5 Love is described as a disease in lyric poetry, e.g. Archil. fr. 193 West δύστηνος ἔγκειμαι πόθῳ,/ἄψυχος, χαλεπῇσι θεῶν ὀδύνῃσιν ἕκητι/πεπαρμένος δι' ὀστέων; cf. the well known Sappho fr. 31.5–15 Lobel/Page (= 192.5–16 Voigt), where there is an outburst of emotions expressed with symptoms of love on the lover's body.

one wife, and risk much on the throw; for people take wives into their houses like ballast, with no experience of their ways.[6]

Having been unwillingly transferred from Cithaeron by Athamas and become Themisto's secret servant, Ino suffers misfortune (frr. 406, 407). But, as it seems, Ino was sympathetic to Themisto. Some fragments refer to the unhappiness Ino – in all probability – feels and to Themisto, the queen, consoling her for it with moderate *sententiae* (frr. 418, 408, 409). Debates would have then ensued between the two women, based on the general disadvantaged state of women as well as the demands of marriage. In fr. 414 Themisto would urge Ino to spare noble men but disdain the bad ones as they deserve: φειδώμεθ' ἀνδρῶν εὐγενῶν, φειδώμεθα,/κακοὺς δ' ἀποπτύωμεν, ὥσπερ ἄξιοι.[7]

At the culminating point of the play, Ino, as Themisto's trusted servant, participates in Themisto's crime against Athamas, but she secretly changes the garments of the potential victims, saving her own children from the murder that was being plotted against them by the jealous Themisto who commits the last tragic filicide. The papyric fragment, which is recently discussed by Finglass,[8] points safely to the murder and Ino's subsequent *thrēnos*. Therefore, Euripides' Ino combines the role of a tragic heroine – probably the central one – with that of a witness: as Themisto's devoted servant, Ino plans her own plot after having been informed by her mistress (and rival) Themisto. But, unfortunately, Ino's exceptional paradigm belongs to a lost play.

In the preserved *Trachiniae* and *Medea*, however, we can clearly see the development of their plot through witnesses and evidence, which are crucial for the dramatic heroines to be informed and make their catastrophic decisions.[9] In Sophocles' *Trachiniae*, Heracles' wife, Deianeira, attempts to deter him from loving his young captive, Iole, but unwillingly causes his death.[10] In the beginning of the play, Heracles has been away for fifteen months in order to perform a labour. He has not sent any news during all this time. The duration of his absence is mentioned in the end of the prologue by his concerned wife, who further states that her actual problem is the lack of information about her hus-

6 Translation by Collard/Cropp 2008.

7 Cf. Pind. *Pyth.* 8.95 sq. The fragment is cited by Stobaeus 4.41.19 as exemplary of fluidness of human welfare (ὅτι ἀβέβαιος ἡ τῶν ἀνθρώπων εὐπραξία).

8 Finglass 2014 and 2016.

9 See Hall 2009, for the *Trachiniae*.

10 For the play, see the commentaries by Easterling 1982 and Davies 1991. For items concerning my analysis, see Segal 1981, 60–108.

band's fate (40–48).[11] She is mainly worried about a tablet, which was left by Heracles before his departure. With respect to the content of said tablet, Deianeira only mentions that it causes her distress and a need to pray to the gods. For this reason, she seeks the help of her son, Hyllus, who comes right on time. However, the news he brings, that Heracles was on a quest at the town of Eurytus, is insufficient (74–75). As a result, Hyllus promises his mother that he will make sure to learn the whole truth (86–91). The chorus, entering the orchestra, prays to Helios to reveal the whereabouts of Heracles (94–102).

In the first episode, Deianeira justifies her distress by giving more details about the content of the tablet (156–174): No one can explain why, in the case of this labour, Heracles wrote in the tablet that a fifteen-month period of absence would be a limit beyond which he would either be dead or achieve eternal bliss.[12] In order to support this, Deianeira reveals the existence of a relevant prediction given by the oracle at Dodona, on which the order of Heracles' tablet was based.[13] The Messenger, who enters the scene and announces the good news that Heracles is alive (180–183), could bring relief immediately. Deianeira, however, inquires as to the identity of the person who gave the information to the messenger (187) and, when she hears the name of Lichas (189–190), who is a herald of Heracles, she wonders why Lichas had not already rushed to bring such good news himself (192). The joy caused by the facile excuse given by the Messenger is only temporary (200–224).[14]

Immediately after that, Deianeira announces Lichas' arrival (225–228), who enters the scene (229) accompanying a group of women (241). After being assured than Heracles is alive and that he will return (230–240), Deianeira pays attention to the captive women (242–243). She is informed that they come from the city of Eurytus where Heracles had launched a campaign (244–245). After

---

11 For Deianeira in the role of witness and spectator, see Allen-Hornblower 2016, 94–170 (esp. 98–107).

12 Probably, the tablet is a metaphorical expression of memory. See Aeschylus' *PV* 789 ἣν ἐγγράφου σὺ μνήμοσιν δέλτοις φρενῶν, *Supp.* 179 αἰνῶ φυλάξαι τἄμ' ἔπη δελτουμένας, *Eum.* 275 δελτογράφῳ δὲ πάντ' ἐπωπᾷ φρενί; cf. Soph. *Phil.* 1325 ... καὶ γράφου φρενῶν ἔσω.

13 The oracle at Dodona was the holy place of Zeus, Heracles' father; Plato mentions it as the place where prophecies were first uttered (*Phdr.* 275b: ἐν τῷ τοῦ Διὸς τοῦ Δωδωναίου ἱερῷ δρυὸς λόγους ἔφησαν μαντικοὺς πρώτους γενέσθαι). It is worth noticing that, apart from an invocation by the chorus (209 Ἀπόλλω προστάταν), neither Apollo nor his holy oracle at Delphi are referred to in the play. For the role of prophecy in the *Trachiniae*, see Bowman 1999.

14 Verses 205–224 belong to the famous first stasimon of the play, where the chorus express their happiness for Heracles' return with wedding ritual cries culminating in bacchic ecstatic dance: ἀνωλολυξάτω δόμος/ἐφεστίοις ἀλαλαγαῖς/ὁ μελλόνυμφος ... (205–207); ἰδού μ' ἀναταράσσει, εὐοῖ/ὁ κισσὸς ἄρτι Βακχίαν/ὑποστρέφων ἅμιλλαν (216–220).

hearing from Lichas the details of Heracles' triumph (248–290),[15] she expresses interest and pity regarding the condition of the women (293–306) and notices Iole's presence (307).[16] The witnessing procedure is now shifting to the young girl. Concerned about the liquidity of happiness, Deianeira distinguishes Iole among the captive women thanks to her gentleness and purity, and asks to know who she is (308–313). Lichas answers her questions with evasiveness (314–328; e.g. 317 οὐκ οἶδα· καὶ γὰρ οὐδ' ἀνιστόρουν μακράν). Iole remains silent and exits without saying a word, together with the other captive women and Lichas (329–334).[17]

Deianeira learns the truth from the Messenger, who watched the previous scene in silence. Now, the Messenger breaks his silence and stops Deianeira, who was leaving, promising to disclose to her the identity of the captive women (335–341; e.g. 338 τούτων – ἔχω γὰρ πάντ' – ἐπιστήμων ἐγώ). What follows is a scene which is typical for the importance of testimony in finding the truth (342–496). The Messenger calls Lichas a liar (346–348) and reveals that the real motive for the campaign of Heracles was his love for king Iphitus' daughter, namely Iole (351–382). A wailing chorus encourages Deianeira to request an explanation from Lichas (385–388), who, fortunately, reappears almost automatically (391–392). A scene of a proper judicial interrogation of the herald follows, which is carried out in the presence of the Messenger, who is ready to check Lichas' honesty (395–435).[18] The details are typical. Deianeira asks Lichas to swear to speak the truth (398) and he invokes Zeus as his witness (399).[19] However, the information is elicited with difficulty (400–407). After threatening Lichas that he will be punished by Deianeira if it is proven that Lichas is dishonest (408–415), the messenger challenges him to confirm Iole's identity (416–420). Lichas alleges that he conveyed rumours (421–426), but the Messenger confirms that he had heard him confirming Iole's identity under oath (427–433). Deianeira intervenes in the interrogation, requesting that Lichas respect her and tell her the truth (436–469): It is not the truth itself that aggrieves her – she is used to Heracles' affairs and she likes Iole – but not knowing the truth. Lichas complies immediately and confirms everything the Messenger had said about Iole (472–478), adding that he had not concealed the truth because Heracles had demanded so, but due to the pity he felt for Deianeira herself (479–489).

15 For the role of this (lying) story by Lichas, see Davies 1984; Halleran 1986; Heiden 1988.
16 For Iole's reception, Beck 1953.
17 For Iole's silence, Hourmouziades 1984, 202–208; Marshall 2012, 194.
18 For this encounter, see Payne 2000, 409–412.
19 Throughout the play it is Zeus who rules the destiny of his son Heracles; see also n. 13.

Then Deianeira decides to use the love potion which the Centaur Nessus had given her in secret when he was dying by Heracles' arrow. In order for the decision to be executed, the chorus must keep all this in strict confidence (490–496, 553–587). At first, Deianeira establishes her decision on an ideological foundation, condemning, like a prosecutor, Heracles' choice as polygamy (536–551). Heracles will share his bed with two women (539–540: καὶ νῦν δύ' οὖσαι μίμνομεν μιᾶς ὑπὸ/χλαίνης ὑπαγκάλισμα...). He will hold the title of husband, yet he will actually be Iole's husband (550–551: ταῦτ' οὖν φοβοῦμαι μὴ πόσις μὲν Ἡρακλῆς/ἐμὸς καλῆται, τῆς νεωτέρας δ' ἀνήρ). She (Deianeira) is aware of Heracles' affairs (543–544: ἐγὼ δὲ θυμοῦσθαι μὲν οὐκ ἐπίσταμαι/νοσοῦντι κείνῳ πολλὰ τῇδε τῇ νόσῳ), but she cannot tolerate sharing the conjugal bed in her knowledge (545–546: τὸ δ' αὖ ξυνοικεῖν τῇδ' ὁμοῦ τίς ἂν γυνὴ/δύναιτο, κοινωνοῦσα τῶν αὐτῶν γάμων;). She does not doubt that Iole has already been Heracles' sexual partner (536: κόρην γάρ, οἶμαι δ' οὐκέτ', ἀλλ' ἐζευγμένην, 538 λωβητὸν ἐμπόλημα τῆς ἐμῆς φρενός) and that she will win his sexual love since she is younger and more beautiful (547: ὁρῶ γὰρ ἥβην τὴν μὲν ἕρπουσαν πρόσω).[20]

Later, Deianeira delivers the robe and has Lichas carry it to Heracles as a welcoming gift, indicating meticulously all the relevant details 594–632).[21] She places particular emphasis in the seal, a token within the circle of a seal, which evidences that the gift for Heracles is from her; and which Heracles will easily recognise (615: σφραγῖδος ἕρκει τῷδ' ἐπὸν μαθήσεται).[22] And, as long as she expects her order to be carried out, the first signs of the action of the potion, which Deianeira watches foaming dangerously, cause her distress (663–722).[23] The chorus tries to subdue her concern giving her hope, but Deianeira feels certain for her mistake (723–730). The real results of the potion will be made known later by her son Hyllus, who enters the scene cursing his mother (734–737). The cause is told in a straightforward manner: You killed your husband and my father (739–740). Hearing this, Deianeira looks for a ray of hope in the identity of the person who informed her son: "who told you this?" (744: πῶς εἶπας, ὦ παῖ; τοῦ παρ' ἀνθρώπων μαθών;). Confirming that he saw what happened with his own eyes (746–747: αὐτὸς βαρεῖαν ξυμφορὰν ἐν ὄμμασιν/πατρὸς

---

20 For the idea that in the *Trachiniae* Heracles is in a sense polygamous, see Heiden 2012, 144. Cf. Segal 1994.

21 Krappe 1939. For the (dark) role of the hidden *peplos*, see Segal 1981, 96; Marshall 2012, 194.

22 Cf. Eur. *IA* 155, where Agamemnon orders the Old Man to preserve the seal which he bears on the tablet (σφραγῖδα φύλασσ', ἣν ἐπὶ δέλτῳ/τῇδε κομίζεις).

23 Deianeira here acts as a messenger reciting the terrible signs of the potion; Goldhill 2012, 138.

δεδορκὼς κοὐ κατὰ γλῶσσαν κλυών), Hyllus announces in horror the action of the potion and describes the condition of his moribund father (749–812).[24]

The following act is about Deianeira's suicide. It is completely her own decision. The chorus comments on the silent departure of Deianeira as a possible admission of her guilt (813–814), which was attributed to her by her son as prosecutor (815–820).[25] In the following (third) *stasimon* (821–861), the chorus clearly finds that the pronouncement is confirmed and soon after that lamenting cries are heard from the house (862–867). The old nurse, who immediately gets out (871–872) in a raving state (876–897), confirms Deianeira's death twice (881: ταύτην διηίστωσεν <ἄμφηκες ξίφος>, 891 αὐτὴ πρὸς αὑτῆς χειροποιεῖται τάδε). Being an eye-witness (896–897: ... μᾶλλον δ' εἰ παροῦσα πλησία/ἔλευσσες οἷ' ἔδρασε, κάρτ' ἂν ᾤκτισας), she describes reliably the details of her mistress' suicide on Heracles' conjugal bed (899–946).[26] In fact, almost all the dramatic characters become messengers in this Sophoclean tragedy; and the *didaskein* wording used (64, 671, 681, 934, 1110, 1245) is noteworthy.[27]

The last scene which is interesting for my theme is that of the end of the play (983 ff.). Heracles is carried, moribund, and, amidst his writhing, he asks his son to promise to him under oath that he will marry Iole (1221–1229). The unexpected – and enigmatic – demand of Heracles causes confusion to the boy (1230–1231).[28] However, he is compelled to agree (1232–1247) and gives an oath before the gods invoked by Heracles as witnesses (1248–1251).[29] The play ends with an enigmatic choice which now has the features of endogamy: "Let no other espouse her who hath lain at my side, but do thou" (1225–1226: μηδ' ἄλλος ἀνδρῶν τοῖς ἐμοῖς πλευροῖς ὁμοῦ/κλιθεῖσαν αὐτὴν ἀντὶ σοῦ λάβῃ ποτέ).[30] Besides, Deianeira had also acknowledged Iole's gentleness before (308–309: ἄνανδρος, ἢ τεκνοῦσσα; πρὸς μὲν γὰρ φύσιν/πάντων ἄπειρος τῶνδε, γενναία δέ τις).

Now, I come to Euripides' *Medea*.[31] As it is generally accepted, the filicide committed by Medea in the tragedy of the same name is an element introduced

---

24 For Hyllus acting here as a messenger, see Goldhill 2012, 181.

25 For Deianeira's guilt, see Carawan 2000.

26 For the nurse as a messenger of Deianeira's suicide, see Barrett 2002, 76–81; Goldhill 2012, 143.

27 Goldhill 2012, 40–41.

28 Mackinnon 1971; Hoey 1977; Holt 1989.

29 For rituality implied in this scene, see Pozzi 1999.

30 For the *Trachiniae* as a mediation on items of gender and marriage, see Wohl 1998, 17–56; Ormand 1999, 36–59; Patterson 2012.

31 See the commentaries by Allan 2002; Mastronarde 2002; Mossman 2011.

by Euripides.[32] However, the enigmatic character of this play lies in the fact that Medea, who knowingly committed this heinous act, does not cause repulsion to the audience. The character who becomes repulsive is Jason.[33] The arguments put forward by Jason regarding his decision to marry the daughter of the king of Corinth (where he lives in exile together with Medea and his children) render his infidelity sufficient to create emotions of extreme vengefulness in Medea's psyche. The fact that Medea has not decided to commit filicide from the beginning of the play but she does so as the plot progresses (790–797), namely after the middle of the play, is crucial in the interpretation of this tragedy. It is, then, reasonable to watch how Medea is led to take the decision to knowingly commit filicide.[34]

In the beginning of the play, Jason has already committed adultery and Medea is aware of the fact. It is announced during the prologue by the Nurse both as the framework in which the events of the play will be incorporated and as a fact which all the heroes must face.[35] The Nurse declares Jason's decision a betrayal against Medea and his children (16–18) and justifies Medea's reaction: She saw her denouncing the old oaths of marital fidelity (21: βοᾷ μὲν ὅρκους, ἀνακαλεῖ δὲ δεξιάς) invoking the gods as witnesses (22: καὶ θεοὺς μαρτύρεται);[36] she lies still and silent on the ground, mourning the relatives whom she herself betrayed because of Jason (24–35). The Nurse is afraid that Medea's condition will lead to grim events: She does not want to see her children (36); her sadness due to the offence she suffered (38) could make her murder all those who harmed her (39–42).[37]

The arrival of the Paedagogus, who accompanies Medea's children, is related to the communication of new data of reality (evidence), of which Medea is not aware (62). With great hesitation (63–64) and with the reservation that it is a product of indirect information (67: ἤκουσά του λέγοντος, 72–73: ὁ μέντοι μῦθος εἰ σαφὴς ὅδε/οὐκ οἶδα), the Paedagogus gives in to the Nurse's pleas (65–66) and announces King Creon's decision to banish Medea and her children from his kingdom (70–72). For the sake of plot advancement, the Paedagogus and the Nurse agree to keep this information secret from Medea (80–81). The Nurse, however, goes a step further and takes a stand against the situation which has

32 See McDermott 1989, 9–24.

33 Mossman 2011. Cf. Rabinowitz 1993, 125–154; Segal 1996; Roisman 2014. In a different direction (towards a greater understanding of Jason), Morwood 2014.

34 Segal 1996, 16–27; Hall 2010, 21–23.

35 Ruffell 2014.

36 For the importance of oath-breaking in the play, Stewart 1978 and Boedeker 1991.

37 For how the language of pity evokes pathos in the play, see the analysis by Pucci 1980.

been shaped. Addressing the children themselves (who are watching in silence) denounces their father's act (82–84) and, addressing the Paedagogus (89–95), she asks him to keep the children away from their mother. The Nurse now brings Medea's look toward her children more clearly in her memory and ascertains the fierceness of a bull which is ready to act (92–93).

Medea's two melic anapaests (96–97), which are immediately heard from the interior of the house, introduce a lyrical action which will confirm the gravity of the emotional condition of the heroine. During such action, Medea will be heard, unseen, from the interior of the house; the Nurse, at first, and then the chorus, while entering and taking position at the orchestra, will reply to Medea's expression of mourning. The Nurse reacts with a concern greater than before to Medea's first mourning anapaests (98–110): As she arranges for the children to enter the house, she advises them not to go near their raging mother. The following (four) lyrical anapaests of Medea are also mourning, including curses for the children and their father. The Nurse, who thinks that the curse of Medea against her children is inexplicable, is now expressing her fear about their fate more clearly (115–118) and greets the chorus of Corinthian women with a brief description: "There is no more house" (138 οὐκ εἰσὶ δόμοι). Medea's third lyrical interference (144–147) continues to be mourning, possibly invoking Zeus, Gaia (Earth) and Light, before whom she wishes for her own death. The chorus repeats the invocation immediately (148) and tries to console Medea by assuring her that Zeus will provide assistance (158–159).[38] For this reason, Medea's fourth lyrical insertion (160–168) does not include any expressions of mourning: Invoking, with rather too much self-confidence, Themis and Artemis, Medea complains about Jason's infidelity against her marital vows and wishes for his and his new bride's deaths;[39] she also declares (under oath) her remorse for what she did to her own relatives. After Medea's wish, the Nurse is almost certain that the heroine's wrath will not stop at a small incident (171–172) and invokes Themis and Zeus as *tamias* (ταμίαν) of the oaths (168–172) in order to certify her certainty. Immediately after that, the Nurse communicates to Medea the encouragement of the chorus (185–203), who had incited Medea to get out of the

38 Kovacs 1993 argues that the numerous evocations of the gods suggest "a divine governance of the universe" in the play. Cf. Hall 2014, on the complexity of divine and Medea's human and superhuman aspects in the play.

39 See Garstand 2006, for the idea that the oaths referred to here by Medea are not specified to concrete marital vows, but they are left open to variant interpretations by the audience throughout the play.

house (172–184), confirming that the women of Corinth are sworn allies in her suffering (204–212).[40]

When Medea appears (in the first episode), she has stopped the previous expressions of mourning and exhibits rational composure contrary to her previous suffering (214–230).[41] However, since she is not aware of the decision on her exile, she only confronts the fact of Jason's infidelity. Although a barbarian,[42] she knows well all the conventions of Greek marriage. With ideological clarity, she complains about the social dominance of men and the corresponding weakness of women in marital and public matters (231–251), and completes the picture of her personal unhappiness with the argument of the absolute loneliness caused by her barbaric origin and the absence of her relatives, whom she herself killed for Jason's sake (252–258). With the same clarity she also states her determination to find a way to take revenge (259–264), proclaiming that wronging a woman in her marriage can make her the most bloodthirsty creature (265–266). Medea asks the chorus to keep this in confidence and be silent (263: σιγᾶν); and she ensures such confidence in a straightforward manner (267: δράσω τάδ'). The (more extensive) continuation of the episode includes the confrontation between Medea and Creon.[43] The King enters the scene and announces his decision to Medea in person. Consequently, the information of the Paedagogus becomes a reality and Medea, who is directly affected, faces exile – both her own and of her children–, having in front of her the very person who gave the relevant order. Since there is no room for misrepresentation or misinterpretation of the information, Medea reacts by using her well-known cunning and, by skilfully modifying her behaviour, which even include humble pleas and invocation of Zeus under oath (324–347), she manages to trick Creon and convince him to grant her permission to stay one more day (340). Despite the fact that he thinks that this is a mistake, Creon gives in (348–356), by making a "rational" assessment, which will be proven tragically ironic: which dreadful deed could Medea do in one day? (346).

Having been left alone on stage, Medea is now mocking Creon's naiveté, who trusted her, and she is thinking of action, making the chorus a partaker of her thoughts (364–409). Her vengefulness wants the king, his daughter and

---

40 For the chorus' *philia* towards Medea, see Schein 1990, 65–66. On the various aspects of the chorus' identity explored in the play, see Swift 2013, 133–144.

41 Williamson 1990, 16–17, interprets this difference as a symbolic as well as literal expression of Medea's movement from her private space of the inside of her home into the public space of the city. For Medea's first exit, see Reckford 1968.

42 For the theme of Medea's ethnicity, see Allan 2002, ch. 3; Mastronarde 2002, 22–26.

43 Lusching, 2007, 131–134.

Jason dead (374–375) by any means (setting the bridal chamber on fire or murder by a sharp sword or poison). The obstacle is her own fate, because she must not become a laughing stock to her enemies. In any case, she will conduct a contest of courage (403) as the grand-daughter of Helios (406), having the goddess of darkness, Hecate, whom she worships at the inner chambers of her house, as her accomplice (395–397).[44]

The well-known *agōn* between Medea and Jason in the second episode (446–626) does not promote the plot. However, Jason's arguments, which highlight his opportunistic character, shed light on the real dramatic content of the situation caused by his choice.[45] Jason explains that he does not prefer the king's daughter over Medea sexually (555–556, 593–594), but he wants to integrate his children in the royal family of the children born by Creousa (562–565) and to ensure prosperity for all (559–560, 565), without excluding Medea (565: εὐδαιμονοῖμεν, 595–596: σῶσαι θέλων/σέ). In other words, he is creating a new conjugal relationship from which he does not exclude elements of bigamy, at least in the level of real amorous passion.[46] Medea's position with respect to this claim is absolute. She is monogamous (489). Her children belong to only one house (one marital status), her own, the house that now Jason destroys; his new wife will now rule the home (694).

In the following (third) episode, King Aegeus' "accidental" visit (663–763) will unexpectedly offer Medea the solution she was seeking. Aegeus' promise that Athens will receive Medea willingly and will offer her sanctuary in her exile (719–730) is actually the honorary escape that Medea wanted.[47] For this reason, Medea seals this promise in an official manner, obliging Aegeus to take an oath before the Gods, among whom Earth and Helios prevail (731–756). Immediately after this, Medea takes action, certain of her triumph (767: καλλίνικοι), for which she invokes Zeus, his daughter, Dike, and the light of Helios. Her movements are now specific and seem different to those previously contemplated. She summons Jason (774–775) and asks him that her children be excluded from the exile (780) pretending regret (776–778). She does not actually intend to leave her children in that hostile land (781–782), but she needs them to carry bridal poisonous gifts to the new bride, which will kill both her and her father

44 According to Lusching 2007, 192, this oath "reveals a new Medea".

45 See Lloyd 1992, 41–43; Lusching 2007, 37–62. For a wider reading of the "agonistic" spirit of the play, Rush 1985, 34–118.

46 Cf. Eur. *Andr.*; Vester 2009.

47 In his *Poetics* (1461b20), Aristotle considers Aegeus' visit as an example of the 'irrational' (τὸ ἄλογον), implying thus the idea that this episode is unnecessary for the plot of the play. For its central position, however, see Buttrey 1958; Dunkle 1969.

(783–789). Exactly at this point, while Medea concludes the development of her plan, the idea to also kill her children enters her mind as a momentary lapse of reason resulting from an extreme vengeful passion (790: ἐνταῦθα μέντοι τόνδ' ἀπαλλάσσω λόγον). Medea's first response to her lapse of reason is to cry (791: ᾤμωξα δ' οἷον ἔργον ἔστ' ἐργαστέον). Yet she instantly turns her demented idea into a rational process, and incorporates it into her plan (792–793: τοὐντεῦθεν ἡμῖν· τέκνα γὰρ κατακτενῶ/τἄμ'· οὔτις ἔστιν ὅστις ἐξαιρήσεται). She knows that filicide is an unholy deed (795–796: ἔξειμι γαίας, φιλτάτων παίδων φόνον/ φεύγουσα καὶ τλᾶσ' ἔργον ἀνοσιώτατον), but she cannot tolerate the hostile offence she suffered (797: οὐ γὰρ γελᾶσθαι τλητὸν ἐξ ἐχθρῶν, φίλαι). Jason's childlessness is prevalent among Medea's criteria. He will lose the children he already has and will not have any more children with his new bride (803–805: οὔτ' ἐξ ἐμοῦ γὰρ παῖδας ὄψεταί ποτε / ζῶντας τὸ λοιπὸν οὔτε τῆς νεοζύγου/ νύμφης τεκνώσει παῖδ'...), who must suffer a wretched death by Medea's poisons (805–806: ... ἐπεὶ κακὴν κακῶς/θανεῖν σφ' ἀνάγκη τοῖς ἐμοῖσι φαρμάκοις). The murder of Jason's children will be a mortal blow to him (817: οὕτω γὰρ ἂν μάλιστα δηχθείη πόσις).

The plan will be executed according to Medea's wishes. In the following (fourth) episode, Jason has not understood anything of the false change in Medea's behaviour. Medea even seems willing to participate in the new marriage (887–888: καὶ συγγαμεῖν σοι, καὶ παρεστάναι λέχει/νύμφην τε κηδεύουσαν ἥδεσθαι σέθεν) according to Jason's wishes (886: ᾗ χρῆν μετεῖναι τῶνδε τῶν βουλευμάτων).[48] However, she thinks that exile is more useful to her than staying in the kingdom, because Jason will not have any problems arising from the hostility of the royal family against her in the future (934–937); but the children must be raised by their father (939), who must request that they be exempted from exile (940, 943). Following the ritualistic delivery of the deadly veils to the children (969–975) after being informed that they were exempted from exile and the royal bride had accepted her gifts willingly (1001–1004), Medea enters a state of confusion which can be easily seen by the chorus, probably due to her facial expression (1005: τί συγχυθεῖσ' ἕστηκας ἡνίκ' εὐτυχεῖς;). Facing now the act of filicide, which she must commit immediately according to her plan, Medea pronounces a shocking monologue (1021–1080), which places the final seal of her criteria.[49] Her children will be happy in Hades (1073), but not in Jason's

48 See Lusching 2007, 172.

49 For Medea's divided self in her monologue, Foley 1989. Diggle 1984 proposes the excision of the last – much quoted – twenty-five lines of Medea's monologue (1056–1080). Despite

Corinth, where they will suffer from the *hybris* of her enemies (1060–1061); their father is the only person liable, because he took away the happiness they used to have (1073–1074). For Medea, the house created by Jason and herself was the only happy home. Jason could accept all of them in the new house which he would create with the king's daughter, not excluding Medea. Insisting on monogamy, however, Medea cannot gift her children to the new house in which they are actually unwanted.[50]

For this reason, in the final scene of the play, Medea will not allow Jason to touch the dead bodies of his children (1320, 1401–1404). She will bury them herself in the sanctuary of Hera Akraia, where she will ensure a new house for them and initiate a celebration in their honour (1378–1388). Riding the chariot of Helios, Medea foretells that unfaithful Jason (1392) will die, hit by a mouldy relic, the ship Argo (1387); however, his real punishment is the bitter end of his marriage to Medea (1388: πικρὰς τελευτὰς τῶν ἐμῶν γάμων ἰδών).[51] Jason cries that Medea's murder of their children has destroyed him with childlessness (1326 ... κἄμ' ἄπαιδ' ἀπώλεσας) and makes his final prey to Zeus as a witness of his suffering (1405–1414).[52] But Medea will remain unpunished; the Nurse foretold her victory (*kallinikos*) in the prologue: no man who clashes with her will easily sing for his victory (44–45: δεινὴ γάρ· οὔτοι ῥᾳδίως γε συμβαλὼν/ἔχθραν τις αὐτῇ καλλίνικον ἄισεται).[53]

One might think that the institution of the decree of 413 BC was preceded by a period of ideological mediation on monogamous marriage, which is manifested in all three tragedies discussed above. In all of them, a wife, after having received the information of her husband's infidelity, makes her catastrophic decision by using witnesses and evidence; and she does so in order to express loyalty and responsibility to her marriage, which she desires to be monoga-

---

recognising Diggle's right, Kovacs 1986 argues for the genuineness of the most of the passage with strong stylistic criteria. See also Stanton 1987, on the two last lines of the monologue.

50 For childlessness as a curse linked with Medea's children, see Ferguson 1972, 251–253.

51 The ending scene of the play has been given several interpretations, for which see Cowherd 1983. Already in antiquity, Aristotle criticised the *deus ex machina* chariot scene at the end of the *Medea* as a resolution (*lysis*) which is unadequate to the *mythos* of the play (*Poet.* 1454a37–b2 καὶ τὰς λύσεις τῶν μύθων ἐξ αὐτοῦ δεῖ τοῦ μύθου συμβαίνειν, καὶ μὴ ὥσπερ ἐν τῇ Μηδείᾳ ἀπὸ μηχανῆς); see Worthington 1990.

52 Mastronarde 2002 *ad* 1404 thinks that Medea leaves the scenic space after line 1404; Levett 2009 argues that Medea remains on stage (as *kallinikos* ?) while Jason makes his prey to Zeus. Cf. Rutherford 2014, who thinks that the image of Jason's defeat makes strong contrast to Medea's divine appearance on the chariot of Helios, confirming her noble *physis* (406 γεγῶσαν ἐσθλοῦ πατρὸς Ἡλίου τ' ἄπο).

53 Hanson 1965.

mous. Particularly, Euripides' *Medea*, performed on the eve of the Peloponnesian War, is an extreme example. By choosing dramatically the version of filicide, ironically expressed through a barbarian woman, who, however, had been conformed to the conventions of her Greek marriage before her husband's infidelity, the tragic poet created the unique model of a child-murdering heroine, giving the most tragic expression to the emotions of the female psyche, who needs exclusivity in her love, though.[54] On the other hand, the decree itself (if existed) does make a distinction between *gamein* and *paidopoieisthai*,[55] which means that it is caused by the special conditions created by the extension of the War; it does not actually legitimate bigamy or/and disproves the monogamous Athenian marriage.[56] From this point of view, the ancient information that Euripides himself enjoyed bigamy (*Vita* 69–77) may be thought as an anecdotological one,[57] for which the reception of his *paidoktonos* Medea could be greatly responsible.

Abbreviations

TrGF 5.1: Kannicht, R. (2004), *Tragicorum Graecorum Fragmenta: Euripides*, vol. I, Göttingen.

Bibliography

Allan, W. (2002), *Euripides: Medea*, London.
Allen-Hornblower, E. (2016), *From Agent to Spectator: Witnessing the Aftermath in Ancient Greek Epic and Tragedy*, Berlin/Boston.
Barlow, S. (1995), 'Euripides' *Medea*: A Subversive Play?', in: *Bulletin of the Institute of Classical Studies Supplement* 66, 36–45.
Barrett, J. (2002), *Staged Narrative: Poetics and the Messenger in Greek Tragedy*, Berkeley/Los Angeles/London.
Beck, A. (1953), 'Der Empfang Ioles', in: *Hermes* 81, 10–21.
Boedeker, D. (1991), 'Euripides' *Medea* and the Vanity of ΛΟΓΟΙ', in: *CPh* 86, 95–112.

54 For the subversive spirit of the play, see Barlow 1995. Cf. also the description by Segal 1996, 27 ff. (esp. 38–44), for Medea's subversive heroic status. For Euripides' tension to expose the ironies of the Athenian social conventions, see Patterson 1990, 67. See also the legal study by Burn 2010.

55 For the text, see n. 1.

56 Patterson 1991, 70 n. 56.

57 For the anecdotological character of the Euripides *Vita*, see Lefkowitz 1979, esp. 204–210.

Bowman, L. (1999), 'Prophecy and Authority in the *Trachiniae*', in: *AJPh* 120, 335–350.
Burn, A. (2010), "A Thoroughly Modern Medea': The Fear of Female Insubordination in Euripides' *Medea* and Contemporary Legislative', in: H. Bartel/A. Simon (eds.), *Unbinding Medea: Interdisciplinary Approaches to a Classical Myth from Antiquity to the 21st Century*, New York, 263–280.
Buttrey, T. (1958), 'Accident and Design in Euripides' *Medea*', in: *AJPh* 79, 3–6.
Carawan, E. (2000), 'Deianeira's Guilt', in: *TAPhA* 130, 189–237.
Collard, C./Cropp, M. (2008), *Euripides: Fragments, Aegeus ... Meleager*, Cambridge, MA.
Cowherd, C. (1983), 'The Ending of the *Medea*', in: *CW* 76, 129–135.
Davies, M. (1984), 'Lichas' Lying Tale: Sophocles *Trachiniae* 260ff.', in: *CQ* 34, 480–483.
Davies, M. (1991), *Sophocles: Trachiniae*, Oxford.
Diggle, J. (1984), *Euripidis Fabulae* I, Oxford.
Dunkle, R. (1969), 'The Aegeus Episode and the Theme of Euripides' *Medea*', in: *TAPhA* 100, 97–107.
Easterling, P. (1982), *Sophocles: Trachiniae*, Cambridge.
Ferguson, J. (1972), *A Companion to Greek Tragedy*, Austin.
Finglass, P. (2014), 'A New Fragment of Euripides' *Ino*', in: *ZPE* 189, 65–82.
Finglass, P. (2016), 'Mistaken Identity in Euripides' *Ino*', in: P. Kyriakou/A. Rengakos (eds.), *Wisdom and Folly in Euripides*, Berlin/Boston, 299–318.
Foley, H. (1989), 'Medea's Divided Self', in: *ClAnt* 80, 61–85.
Garstand, B. (2006), 'The Oaths in Euripides' *Medea*', in: *Arctos* 40, 47–53.
Goldhill, S. (2012), *Sophocles and the Language of Tragedy*, Oxford.
Hall, E. (2009), 'Deianeira Deliberates: Precipitate Decision-Making and *Trachiniae*', in: S. Goldhill/E. Hall (eds.), *Sophocles and the Greek Tragic Tradition*, Cambridge, 69–89.
Hall, E. (2010), 'Medea and the Mind of the Murderer', in: H. Bartel/A. Simon (eds.), *Unbinding Medea: Interdisciplinary Approaches to a Classical Myth from Antiquity to the 21st Century*, New York, 16–24.
Hall, E. (2014), 'Divine and Human in Euripides' *Medea*', in: D. Stuttard (ed.), *Looking at* Medea*: Essays and a translation of Euripides' tragedy*, London/New Delhi/New York/Sydney, 139–156.
Halleran, M. (1986), 'Lichas' Lies and Sophoclean Innovation', in: *GRBS*, 239–247.
Hanson, J.O.D. (1965), 'The Secret of Medea's Success', in: *G&R* 12, 54–61.
Harrison, A. (1968–1971), *The Law of Athens*, vols. I-II, Oxford.
Heiden, B. (1988), 'Lichas' Rhetoric of Justice in Sophocles' *Trachiniae*', in: *Hermes* 116, 13–23.
Heiden, B. (2012), '*Trachiniae*', in: A. Markantonatos (ed.), *Brill's Companion to Sophocles*, Leiden/Boston, 129–148.
Hoey, T. (1977), 'Ambiguity in the Exodos of Sophocles' *Trachiniae*', in: *Arethusa* 10, 269–294.
Hoey, T. (1979), 'The Date of the *Trachiniae*', in: *Phoenix* 33, 210–232.
Holt, P. (1989), 'The End of the *Trachiniae* and the Fate of Herakles', in: *JHS* 109, 69–80.
Hourmouziades, N. (1984), *Όροι και Μετασχηματισμοί στην Αρχαία Ελληνική Τραγωδία*, Athens.
Kovacs, D. (1986), 'On Medea's Great Monologue (E. *Med.* 1021–80)', in: *CQ* 36, 343–352.
Kovacs, D. (1993), 'Zeus in Euripides' *Medea*", in: *AJPh* 114, 45–70.
Krappe, A. (1939), 'La robe de Déjanire', in: *REG* 52, 565–572.
Lape, S. (2010), *Race and Citizen Identity in the Classical Athenian Democracy*, Cambridge.
Lefkowitz, M. (1979), 'The Euripides Vita', in: *GRBS* 20, 187–210.
Levett, B. (2009), 'Medea's Exit', in: R. Cousland/J. Hume (eds.), *The Plays and Fragments. Essays in Honour of Martin Cropp*, Leiden, 157–168.

Lloyd, M. (1992), *The Agon in Euripides*, Oxford.
Lobel, E./Page, D. (1995), *Sappho and Alcaeus: Poetarum Lesbiorum Fragmenta*, Oxford.
Lusching, C. (2007), *Granddaughter of the Sun: A Study of Euripides'* Medea, Leiden/Boston.
Mackinnon, K. (1971), 'Heracles' Intention in His Second Request of Hyllus: *Trach.* 1216–1251', in: *CQ* 21, 33–41.
Marshall, C.W. (2012), 'Sophocles *Didaskalos*', in: K. Ormand (ed.), *A Companion to Sophocles*, Oxford, 187–203.
Marshall, P. (2002), *Hyginus: Fabulae. Editio altera,* Munich/Leipzig.
Mastronarde, D. (2002), *Euripides: Medea*, Cambridge.
McDermott, E. (1989), *Euripides'* Medea: *The Incarnation of Disorder*, Philadelphia.
Morwood, J. (2014), 'Re-Evaluating Jason', in: D. Stuttard (ed.), *Looking at* Medea: *Essays and a Translation of Euripides' Tragedy*, London/New Delhi/New York/Sydney, 83–88.
Mossman, J. (2011), *Euripides: Medea*, Warminster.
Ogden, D. (1996), *Greek Bastardy in the Classical and the Hellenistic Periods*, Oxford.
Ormand, K. (1999), *Exchange and the Maiden: Marriage in Sophoclean Tragedy*, Austin.
Patterson, C. (1990), 'Those Athenian Bastards', in: *ClAnt* 9, 40–73.
Patterson, C. (1991), 'Marriage and the Married Woman in Athenian Law', in: S. Pomeroy (ed.), *Women's History and Ancient History*, Chapel Hill/London, 48–72.
Patterson, C. (2012), 'Marriage in Sophocles: A Problem for Social History', in: K. Ormand (ed.), *A Companion to Sophocles*, Oxford, 381–394.
Payne, M. (2000), 'Three Double Messenger Scenes in Sophocles', in: *Mnemosyne* 53, 403–418.
Pozzi, D. (1999), 'Hyllus' Coming of Age in Sophocles' *Trachiniae*', in: M. Padilla (ed.), *Rites of Passage in Ancient Greek Literature, Religion, Society*, Lewisburg, 29–41.
Pucci, P. (1980), *The Violence of Pity in Euripides'* Medea, Ithaca/New York.
Rabinowitz, N. (1993), *Anxiety Veiled: Euripides and the Traffic in Women*, Ithaca/London.
Reckford, K. (1968), 'Medea's First Exit', in: *TAPhA* 99, 329–359.
Roisman, H. (2014), 'Medea's Vengeance', in: D. Stuttard (ed.), *Looking at* Medea: *Essays and a Translation of Euripides' Tragedy*, London/New Delhi/New York/Sydney, 111–122.
Ruffell, I. (2014), 'The Nurse's Tale', in: D. Stuttard (ed.), *Looking at* Medea: *Essays and a Translation of Euripides' Tragedy*, London/New Delhi/New York/Sydney, 65–82.
Rush, R. (1985), *The "Agon" and the Audience: A Study of Euripides'* Medea, Heracles *and* Ion, Stanford.
Rutherford, R. (2014), 'The Final Scene', in: D. Stuttard (ed.), *Looking at* Medea: *Essays and a Translation of Euripides' Tragedy*, London/New Delhi/New York/Sydney, 89–98.
Schein, S. (1990), 'Philia in Euripides' *Medea*', in: M. Griffith/D. Mastronarde (eds.), *Cabinet of the Muses: Essays on Classical and Comparative Literature in Honor of Thomas G. Rosenmeyer*, Berkeley, 57–73.
Segal, C. (1981), *Tragedy and Civilization: An Interpretation of Sophocles*, Cambridge, MA.
Segal, C. (1994), 'Bride or Concubine? Iole and Heracles' Motives in the *Trachiniae*', in: *ICS* 19, 61–64.
Segal, C. (1996), 'Euripides' *Medea*: Vengeance, Reversal and Closure', in: *Pallas* 45, 15–44.
Smith, S./Trzaskoma, S. (2007), *Apollodorus'* Library *and Hyginus'* Fabulae: *Two Handbooks of Greek Mythology*, Indianapolis/Cambridge.
Stanton, G. (1987), 'The End of Medea's Monologue: Euripides *Medea* 1078–80', in: *RhM* 130, 97–106.
Stewart, F. (1978), 'Medea's Right Hand: Promises and Revenge', in: *TAPhA* 108, 69–74.

Swift, L. (2013), 'Conflicting Identities in the Euripidean Chorus", in: R. Gagné/M. Hopman (eds.), *Choral Mediations in Greek Tragedy*, Cambridge, 130–154.
Vester, C. (2009), 'Bigamy and Bastardy, Wives and Concubines: Civic Identity in *Andromache*', in: R. Cousland/J. Hume (eds.), *The Plays and Fragments. Essays in Honour of Martin Cropp*, Leiden, 293–305.
Voigt, E.-M. (1971), *Sappho and Alcaeus*: *Fragmenta*, Amsterdam.
West, M. (1980), *Delectus ex Iambis et Elegis Graecis*, Oxford.
Williamson, M. (1990), 'A Woman's Place in Euripides' *Medea*', in: A. Powell (ed.), *Euripides, Women and Sexuality*, London/New York, 16–31.
Wohl, V. (1998), *Intimate Commerce*: *Exchange, Gender, and Subjectivity in Greek Tragedy*, Austin.
Worthington, I. (1990), 'The Ending of Euripides' *Medea*', in: *Hermes* 118, 502–505.

Rosalia Hatzilambrou

Scandals as Evidence in Attic Forensic Oratory: The Case of Aeschines' *Against Timarchus*

Abstract: This chapter explores the point that scandals could be offered in place of testimony and could function as evidence, when other testimony was weak or absent. The case study is provided by Aeschines' *Against Timarchus.* The core of this chapter lies on the narration by Aeschines of the alleged affair between Timarchus and the public slave Pittalacus (§§53–64). Hatzilambrou argues that the narration of this scandalous story compensates for Aeschines' lack of factual evidence, mainly regarding his claim that Timarchus had prostituted himself, and contributed to the success of the action that Aeschines brought against Timarchus. Attention is paid to the tactics employed with reference to the narration of "Pittalacus' episode", whose importance for the narrative and argumentative strategy in Aeschines' speech is highlighted.

1 Introduction

According to the *Oxford English Dictionary*, a scandal is defined "as an action or event regarded as morally or legally wrong and causing general public outrage". Scandals involve a blatant breach of social, moral norms, and legal requirements, which usually arise from greed, lust, or the abuse of power. Moreover, scandals have the advantage of attracting the interest of the audience, since they are normally titillating and satisfying. They allow their audience vicariously to experience another life, as it were, while leaving the audience reassured that it is better off in its mundane, non-scandalous life. Thus, scandalous stories allow their audience to feel superior, despise the transgressor and express its outrage over the shocking and unacceptable behaviour. What is certain is that scandalous stories have a strong impact upon their audience and therefore that the inclusion of scandalous stories in a narrative may help achieve various interwoven rhetorical goals. This also applies to the forensic context of classical Athens. Here, in this chapter, I would like to explore the point that scandals could be offered in place of testimony and could still function as evidence, when other testimony was weak or absent. Of course, the effectiveness of this rhetorical tactic depended on various factors, such as construction, content,

https://doi.org/10.1515/9783110751970-014

plausibility, the position of the scandal within a larger narrative and how the scandal was presented, which should always take account of the interests and concerns of the Athenian society.

In this chapter I offer further evidence for my preliminary conclusions, which are two: first, that the narration of scandalous stories could compensate for the lack of factual evidence and could thus contribute to the success of a legal action; and, second, that Attic orators realised the potential persuasive power of skilled construction and presentation within their narrative of scandalous stories, which could function, and in some speeches do so, as pieces of evidence. One of these, I will argue, is Aeschines' *Against Timarchus*, which will provide my case study to illustrate the thesis of the chapter.

The factual background of the speech is well known. Timarchus and Demosthenes charged Aeschines with treason for partiality towards Philip on the occasion of the second Athenian Embassy in 346 BC to Pella, whose purpose was to ratify the peace agreed by the same envoys in the preceding year. Aeschines' response was to retaliate against Timarchus later in the same year.[1] The process started with a proclamation (*epangelia*, §§32, 81) to the effect that Athenian laws forbade Timarchus from speaking before the people as a fully competent citizen because his life had hitherto been disgraceful (*aischrōs bebiōkōs*).[2] The consequence was a trial. The whole procedure is called by Aeschines "scrutiny of public speakers" (*dokimasia rhētorōn*, §28; also §32).[3] Such a task was not easy for Aeschines and he could easily have jeopardised his own career.[4] The political situation was, at the very least, unstable and unpredictable after the settling of matters after the Sacred War and the harsh punishment inflicted on Phocis.[5] Furthermore, Timarchus enjoyed the support of Demosthenes, of two

1 On the dating of the trial: Harris 1985, 376–380; Fisher 2001, 6–8.

2 See §§3, 28, 38, 180, 188.

3 On the *dokimasia rhētoron*: MacDowell 2005; Gagliardi 2005.

4 It is highly probable that the usual penalty for a prosecutor who dropped the prosecution or failed to secure one-fifth of the dicastic vote also applied to a trial triggered by "a scrutiny of the orators", see Harrison 1971, 205.

5 See Harris 1995, in particular 95–106, who describes the political climate as unfavourable to Aeschines. Kapparis 2018, 189–190, 205, 252–253, on the other hand argues that Aeschines seized the initiative and scored an unexpected victory in court, since at this particular period the political scene favoured Aeschines and those who advocated a peaceful accommodation with Philip. In a political trial, of course, the political climate certainly counts. However, since there is only a single reference to the political contest behind the current trial, which pops up in cursory form in the predictable boasting of Demosthenes (§174), if the political setting had been favourable to Aeschines' policy, then Aeschines would have referred more to the current political scene. The absence of such a discussion from the speech suggests, at the very least,

prominent politicians, the brothers Hegesander and Hegesippus,[6] and of the unnamed general whom Aeschines attacks in §§132–140.[7] However, despite all this support, the judges convicted Timarchus, sentencing him to complete and permanent disenfranchisement (*atimia*).[8] According to Ps. Plutarch and the first *hypothesis* to the speech, after the trial Timarchus hanged himself.[9]

2 A scandal as evidence in Aeschines 1: The Pittalacus' episode

Aeschines lists four grounds of disgraceful living in §§28–30. According to these, the law does not allow anyone to address the people who a) beats his father or his mother, or fails to support them materially or to provide a home for them, or b) did not go on the military campaigns for which he was called up, or has thrown away his shield, or c) has prostituted himself or acted as an escort, or d) has consumed his ancestral property and whatever else he has been inherited.[10] Aeschines bases his charge against Timarchus on the third and fourth of these criteria. That is, he claims, that his opponent should be excluded from Athenian public life because he had prostituted himself and had dissipated his inherited property. Furthermore, Aeschines makes allegations against Timarchus that approximate to the first heading, namely the maltreatment of par-

that the political climate was so fluid and unpredictable, that Aeschines himself was not feeling confident and tried to avoid the matter.

6 On Hegesippus and Hegesander see Davies 2011.

7 On the possible identification of the "general" with either of men named Diopeithes of Sounion (see §63), both belonging to the influential *genos* of the Salaminians, see Fisher 2001, 200–201. The substantial difficulties faced by Aeschines in pressing this charge are neatly presented by Fisher 2021, 45–70.

8 Dem. 19.257, 284, 285, 287.

9 Ps.-Plut. *Lives of the Ten Orators, Mor.* 840ff.; *Scholia* Aeschin. 1 Arg. 1.5 (ed. Dilts). MacDowell 2000, 205, and Fisher 2001, 22 n. 71, is probably right that this information may be a dramatic exaggeration of what Demosthenes asserts at 19.2, 285, who simply claimed that "Aeschines destroyed him". See also Roisman/Worthington 2015, 188–189.

10 The list of actions which defined disgraceful living in the text of the law may not be necessarily limited to those mentioned by Aeschines. The orator may have chosen to limit himself to these four, because he could then direct accusations against Timarchus on three of these grounds, while the fourth, the defective military record, may have been mentioned to underline the importance of all the cases of wrong-doing that he mentions as serious public offences.

ents,[11] although he makes no reference to Timarchus' military record, presumably because he did not find anything reprehensible there.

However, it was easy to put a plausible case that a wealthy young man, like Timarchus, who had inherited and run through his late father's estate at an early age (§42; also §§97–101, 103, 105), had needed subsequently to support himself through prostitution. Elsewhere, I have argued that Aeschines decided to include in his indictment against Timarchus the charge that he prostituted himself because it added coherence to Aeschines' construction of a certain rhetorical identity for Timarchus, which consisted of an addiction to the most shameful desires, that is to the consumption of fish, to expensive dinners, to flute-girls and *hetairai* and to gambling (§42).[12] But what about hard evidence? Indeed, most of the actual evidence Aeschines provides concerns Timarchus' squandering of his patrimony (§100), although he presents none in support of his claim that Timarchus had prostituted himself. There were no witnesses to any exchange of money, no formal lovers came forward to testify. Apart from offering the expected justification for the absence of evidence with respect to private acts (§§74–75), Aeschines tries to convert rumour and gossip into factual evidence (§§44, 48, 53, 55, 130),[13] personified and deified as the goddess Phēmē (§§127–130),[14] referring also to physical appearance (§26), insinuation and laughter (§§81–84).[15] One of his most effective tactics to conceal a lack of evidence, however, is his narration of the alleged affair between Timarchus and the *dēmosion oiketēn tēs poleōs*, the public slave Pittalacus.[16]

The status of Pittalacus at the time of the events narrated, that is in 361/0, about fifteen years before the legal action against Timarchus and the subse-

11 See §§103–104 on Timarchus' maltreatment of his aged and blind paternal uncle, Arignotus, and §99 on the sale of a plot of land his mother begged him to keep for her burial place.

12 See Hatzilambrou 2019.

13 On the effective use of gossip in Attic oratory and on the attack against Timarchus in Aeschines 1, see Hunter 1990, esp. 309–310. In this speech, Aeschines implies, for tactical reasons, that his action against Timarchus merely consolidates and presents in official form the gossip surrounding Timarchus' lifestyle. On the function of gossip in Attic forensic oratory see also Eidinow 2016, 191–209.

14 See Serafim 2020, 34–36, 74.

15 On the function of laughter in Attic oratory see Spatharas 2006, 374–387, esp. 381–382. On the use of laughter as an effective tool in Aeschines' attack against Timarchus, see also Kamen 2018, 49–56.

16 On public slaves, see Jacob 1928; Lewis 1990, 254–258; Fisher 1993, 55–57; Hunter 2006; Kamen 2013, 19–31, esp. 25–27. On *oiketēs*, see Wrenhaven 2012, 17–19. The term is used for public slaves with the perception of the slave as a possession not only of an individual family, but collectively of the *dēmos*.

quent trial, "has created a nightmare for generations of scholars", in Vlassopoulos' words.[17] Some scholars have argued that at the time of the trial, Pittalacus was no longer a public slave and in fact was a freedman (and so a metic).[18] Others have suggested that he was still a public slave,[19] or that he was actually the slave of Hegesander,[20] Timarchus' political companion and alleged lover, although many scholars agree that Aeschines is deliberately ambiguous about Pittalacus' status.[21] Determining Pittalacus' real status is a significant matter for the study of the institution of public slavery, but what is important for the effectiveness of Aeschines' narrative is that Pittalacus unambiguously remains a slave throughout. Three times within the eleven paragraphs of the Pittalacus' episode (§§53–64) Aeschines expressly states that Pittalacus was a public slave,[22] thus making quite sure that the judges had fully grasped that at the time of the events Pittalacus was a slave and that Timarchus was fully aware of this.

The Pittalacus episode (§§53–64) is part of the Hegesander narrative, which occupies the last part of the section of the speech devoted to Timarchus' lovers and his willing self-*hetairēsis* (§§40–70). Hegesander is the last named alleged lover of Timarchus who treated him as a prostitute. Pittalacus is the lover mentioned just before Hegesander in the list of Timarchus' many alleged notorious affairs. However, the lack of testimony would certainly have become evident and would have threatened Aeschines' credibility. It was at this point that Aeschines cleverly places the short account on Timarchus' alleged affair with Pittalacus, which emerges as an enormous scandal.

One cannot be certain of what is true in the Pittalacus' episode. Since Aeschines had to find ways to compensate for the embarrassing lack of evidence, he may have fabricated much of this episode or/and exaggerated gossip concerning the matter, in order to create a scandalous story, whose narration could then make up for an absence of testimony. The substantial gap of about fifteen years between the events narrated and the trial itself left room for both lapses of memory on the part of the judges and the fabrication of events to the advantage

17 Vlassopoulos 2007, 35.

18 See Jakob 1928, 160–162; Fisher 2001, 190–191; *idem* 2004, 66–67; Vlassopoulos 2009, 352.

19 See Cohen 2000, 130–141, 168–169; Hunter 2006, 1–8; Ismard 2015, 112–115 and 243–244.

20 See Silver 2013.

21 Todd 1993, 193–194; Fisher 2004 and *idem* 2008, 133–136 argues that Aeschines presents Pittalacus as a slave only when it is rhetorically useful to do so.

22 Twice in §54 and once in §62 Pittalacus is designated as *anthrōpos dēmosios oiketēs tēs poleōs* ("public slave-fellow, a servant of the city"). Translation of the passages from Aeschines 1 is from Fisher 2001. On the connotations regarding the status of someone referred to as *anthrōpos*, see Fisher 2001, 190.

of Aeschines. More specifically, I assume that while Aeschines was doing his research before composing the speech, or even before submitting the indictment, he came across the information that Pittalacus was an associate of Timarchus, probably in connection with his gambling activity (§§42, 53). In order to participate in such activities, Timarchus was probably often to be seen hanging around Pittalacus' house, which perhaps served as a private gambling club and where Pittalacus kept all his gambling equipment (§§57, 59). On the other hand, perhaps Aeschines received the information that one day about fifteen years in the past Pittalacus took refuge at an altar in the *agora*, accusing Hegesander and his group of having beaten him and having destroyed the tools of his job. This incident at the heart of the civic life of Athens provided Aeschines with a great opportunity to compose a scandalous story involving his political enemy, and to argue that the whole city had witnessed it. Thus, not only does Aeschines manage to substitute actual court evidence for this scandal. He also manages implicitly to claim that he is providing impeccable evidence given by a large number of most honourable witnesses, the Athenian citizens.

The Pittalacus' incident in the Agora may have arisen from some gambling dispute. The rather similar story in Demosthenes 54 (*Against Conon*)[23] indicates that nocturnal violence (*paroinia*) as a form of bullying or motivated by revenge was not uncommon and was considered an acceptable form of male violence.[24] Timarchus may not have been at the centre of the real events at all, which may have mainly involved his friends, Hegesippus and Hegesander. Perhaps for this reason, Aeschines is eager to stress that Timarchus had met Pittalacus and had become his lover *before* Hegesander arrived in Athens from the Hellespont (§55). Fisher has persuasively argued that at the heart of the story there may have been some territorial dispute over gaming activities around the shrine in Phaleron controlled by the Salaminian, the *genos* to which Hegesander belonged.[25] However, such a story, true or not, would not have suited Aeschines' rhetorical needs. He needed Timarchus to be the protagonist of the story and the public incident at the altar had to be the outcome of an outrageous sexual affair between Pittalacus, a slave, and Timarchus, a young wealthy citizen, in essence a story of disgusting lust and greed.[26]

23 Dem. 54.5, 8, 14.

24 See Fisher 1998, 75–77; Fisher 2001, 198–199.

25 Fisher 2001, 357–362.

26 On the uses of disgust, a dominant emotion elicited in the *Against Timarchus*, see Spatharas 2016.

Aeschines does not leave room for his listeners to question his presentation of Pittalacus' relations with Timarchus as anything other than a sexual affair. His omniscient, third-person narration adds to the persuasive power of the narrative. Timarchus' reputation helped Aeschines in making such a presentation appear at least feasible. For this reason, Aeschines often points to Timarchus as a target of gossip (§§ 81, 86, 125–131, 157), and Demosthenes also admits that Timarchus' sexual past was the subject of rumors (Dem. 19.233). Timarchus' youth and exceptionally good looks, tactically reiterated many times in the speech with special reference to his body (§§41, 42, 75, 126), understandably attracted admirers from all social strata. But the intentional shocker is that Timarchus, instead of objecting, actually accepted or even invited the disgraceful advances on the part of social inferiors, in order to satisfy his addiction to every kind of shameful desire. Even more shocking was Aeschines' presentation of Pittalacus' affair with Timarchus as an extreme form of the submission of a young free Athenian to the desires of a slave. Timarchus allegedly became Pittalacus' kept man[27] and lived for a prolonged period in the slave's house, alongside birds and the slave's other possessions (§59). Timarchus, therefore, voluntarily endured the actions, termed *hamartēmata* and *hubreis* in the plural only here in the whole speech, that Pittalacus perpetrated on his body and which Aeschines refuses to describe. Instead, Aeschines appeals to the most powerful god of all, Olympian Zeus, thereby employing the strongest possible version of the rhetorical trope of *prodiorthōsis*,[28] which allows the imagination free play to envisage what went on behind Pittalacus' closed door.[29] Furthermore, Hegesander's request to Pittalacus for permission to take Timarchus to his own house aptly stresses Timarchus' subordination to Pittalacus (§57).[30]

---

27 §54: ἀνέλαβεν αὐτὸν καὶ ἔσχε παρ' ἑαυτῷ ("[Pittalacus] took him up and kept him [Timarchus] at his house").
28 On this trope see Lanham ²1991, 42; Rowe 1997, 142.
29 §55: καὶ τοιαῦτα ἁμαρτήματα καὶ τοιαύτας ὕβρεις ἐγὼ ἀκήκοα γεγονέναι ὑπὸ τοῦ ἀνθρώπου τούτου εἰς τὸ σῶμα τὸ Τιμάρχου, οἵας ἐγὼ μὰ τὸν Δία τὸν Ὀλύμπιον οὐκ ἂν τολμήσαιμι πρὸς ὑμᾶς εἰπεῖν ἃ γὰρ οὑτοσὶ ἔργῳ πράττων οὐκ ᾐσχύνετο, ταῦτ' ἐγὼ λόγῳ σαφῶς ἐν ὑμῖν εἰπὼν οὐκ ἂν δεξαίμην ζῆν ("The sort of offences, the sort of acts of hubris, that I hear were committed by that person against the body of Timarchus were such that that I could not possibly bring myself, by Olympian Zeus, to utter to you; the things that the defendant was not ashamed to do in action, I would not be prepared to speak clearly about in words to you and continue living").
30 §56: πρῶτον μὲν οὖν τῷ Πιτταλάκῳ διελέχθη (*sc.* Hegesander) δεόμενος παραδοῦναι τοῦτον (*sc.* Timarchus) ("First of all, he spoke to Pittalacus, asking him to hand Timarchus over to him".)

The particularly shocking aspect of the matter is that Timarchus, in allowing a slave to exploit him sexually, has freely chosen to commit *hubris* against his own body,[31] in that he has allowed, in a manner unworthy of a citizen, another man (in fact, a slave) to abuse his body. Deliberate infliction of dishonour was a paradigmatic antidemocratic offence,[32] a crime in Attic law, actionable also in regard to slaves,[33] and thus one of the most effective rhetorical means of arousing anger in the audience.[34] The most scandalous aspect of Timarchus' behaviour is that his willing sexual enslavement has allowed a reversal of status of a type unacceptable in Athens. In Aeschines' presentation of matters, Timarchus has voluntarily destroyed the antithesis between slave and citizen, so fundamental for classical antiquity. In a society in which the identity of the citizen was formulated through a polar opposition to the image of the slave,[35] Timarchus' alleged behaviour was profoundly offensive and certainly evoked feelings of anger and disgust in the judges.

Aeschines claims that Timarchus' *hetairēsis* to Pittalacus is common knowledge, on the grounds that Timarchus himself displayed his shamelessness in the crowded Agora just before a meeting of the Assembly (§§60–61). According to Aeschines' narrative, after Timarchus has abandoned Pittalacus for Hegesander, Pittalacus, in the grip of jealousy and anger,[36] continues to visit them and becomes a nuisance. Timarchus, Hegesander and some of their gambling companions therefore burst into Pittalacus' house at a night, smash his gambling equipment, kill his birds, tie Pittalacus himself to the pillar and whip him so hard, that his screams are heard by the neighbours.[37] Aeschines' slanted

31 Repeatedly declared at §§29, 108, 116, 185, 188.

32 See Fisher 2005; further Halperin 1990, 88–112; Lape 2008, 145–146.

33 See §§15–17. Indeed, Pittalacus resorted to this legal procedure to achieve some redress and restoration of his honour (§62). On the problems surrounding the provision in Attic law on *hubris*, see Fisher 1995, esp. 62–84.

34 On the meaning and the rhetorical use of *hubris* in this speech, see Fisher, 2005, 67–89, who shows how Aeschines presented *hubris* as an overarching fault of Timarchus' character revealed in erotic humiliating acts, adultery with the wives of free men when holding office on Andros (§108), and in the ruthless beating of the defenseless Pittalacus.

35 See, for instance, Cartledge 2001, 133–166.

36 The persuasiveness of the narrative is enhanced by the image of the jilted Pittalacus, who bears some resemblance to the familiar to the audience stock-type of the "locked-out lover" of the New Comedy; see, for instance, Hunter 1985, 64. On vocabulary of the Pittalacus' episode belonging to the register of comedy, as for instance the term *triskakodaimōn* (§59), see Rubinstein 2012, 156–157.

37 On corporal punishment, especially whipping, commonly inflicted on slaves, but prohibited for Athenian citizens in classical Athens, and its ideological significance, see, for instance,

description of this violent incident, which emphasises the social inferiority and powerlessness of Pittalacus, is designed to emphasize Timarchus' degradation[38]. Timarchus' ensuing alleged conduct reaches levels of utmost civic humiliation. The next morning, after Pittalacus, half-naked in order to display his wounds,[39] has taken refuge at the altar of the Mother of Gods in the Agora,[40] Timarchus is the only one of the group that has attacked Pittalacus who managed to mollify him. Timarchus urges him to leave the altar and does so by begging, touching Pittalacus' chin,[41] and promising to do anything that might satisfy him. Aeschines, of course, implies that Timarchus reminds Pittalacus of previous intimacy and renews his offer of sexual services, although the truth may have been totally different. For instance, in reality Hegesander may have promised Pittalacus to help him gain his freedom.

The altar episode is the culminating point of the Pittalacus' section and one of the most memorable scenes of the speech. It is highly visible in an already vivid narrative, in a technique which Greek rhetorical theory terms *enargeia*.[42] Certainly, the more vivid a narrative is, the more persuasive it becomes and, naturally, the greater the sense the judges have that they are witnessing a real

Hunter 1994, 154–184; Fisher 2006, 334–336; Wrenhaven 2012, 63–71; Lewis 2018, 40–41, 45. In particular on the *kiōn*, the pillar used for the corporal punishment of slaves, see Fisher 2001, 197.

38 And not primarily to generate anger towards Timarchus through creating pity for Pittalacus. However, it is not clear what emotions Aeschines wanted his audience to feel towards Pittalacus. See Rubinstein 2012, 156–158. Furthermore, see Fisher 2001, 189–190, who detects a pronounced switch towards sympathy for Pittalacus towards the end of this account.

39 On the rhetorical "display" of wounded bodies in Attic oratory cf. Spatharas 2019, 97–103. See also Naiden 2006, 36.

40 The shrine including the altar of the Mother of the Gods referred to in the text lay on the west side of the Agora. Many going up to the Pnyx for an assembly, as they crossed the Agora, would have passed the shrine. On the location of this altar, see Wycherley 1957, 150–160; Fisher 2001, 197–198. On the cult of the Phrygian Mother Cybele in Classical Athens, see Parker 1996, 188–194. Slaves are more often reported to seek asylum in the temple of Theseus or in the shrine of the Furies in Athens. Thus Fisher 2001, 198, has argued that Pittalacus was asserting that he was not a slave by deliberately choosing a different central altar. Certainly, the choice of the altar could have been deliberate and may also have expressed the contention on the part of Pittalacus that as a state slave he could not be maltreated by private citizens, since there is evidence that seeking refuge at the Theseion or the shrine of the Furies was a type of legal recourse open to slaves who were maltreated by their masters and who thus demanded to be sold to another master. On this legal resort for slaves, see Fisher 1993, 64–65.

41 On this classic gesture of supplication, which expresses supplication and affection for beloved, or supplication for favours, see McNiven 1982, 90; Naiden 2006, 47–49.

42 On *enargeia* cf. D.H. *Lysias* 7, and see Webb 2009, *passim*, esp. 87–106.

event also becomes. When such a narrative is reinforced by performance, that is, by tone and gesture, as scholars confidently believe was the case with Aeschines' speeches, its effect on the audience becomes even more powerful and effective.[43] The altar scene is very powerful indeed, since Aeschines presents a scandalous scene of supplication, in which the pitiable suppliant is Timarchus and the object of his supplication is Pittalacus, the slave, who in turn piteously supplicates the Athenian *dēmos*.[44] To make matters even worse for Timarchus, Aeschines' narration of the scene at the altar consciously recalls the episode in the first book of the *Iliad*, in which Thetis touches Zeus' knees with her left hand, while taking hold of him under the chin with her right (*Il*. 1.498–502):

> εὗρεν δ' εὐρύοπα Κρονίδην ἄτερ ἥμενον ἄλλων
> ἀκροτάτῃ κορυφῇ πολυδειράδος Οὐλύμποιο·
> καί ῥα πάροιθ' αὐτοῖο καθέζετο, καὶ λάβε γούνων
> σκαιῇ, δεξιτερῇ δ' ἄρ' ὑπ' ἀνθερεῶνος ἑλοῦσα
> λισσομένη προσέειπε Δία Κρονίωνα ἄνακτα·
>
> She found Kronos' broad-browed son apart from the others
> sitting upon the highest peak of rugged Olympos.
> She came and sat beside him with her left hand embracing
> his knees, but took him underneath the chin with her right hand
> and spoke in supplication to lord Zeus, son of Kronos.[45]

Indeed, Aeschines carefully places an invocation to Zeus (*ma Dia* ["by Zeus"], §61) in the sentence, in which he mentions that Timarchus' touches Pittalacus' chin (*hupogeneiazōn*);[46] This is (in my view) a clear attempt by Aeschines to cause the judges to recall this parallel scene in the *Iliad* and so to provoke their anger against Timarchus, who supplicates a slave in exactly the same way in which the immortals beg favour of lord Zeus.

In Gould's view, physical contact with parts of the body of the object of supplication is the most complete and strongest form of supplication. In this

---

43 On tactics regarding Aeschines' performance in his prosecution of Timarchus, see Carey 2017, 275–282. On Aeschines' strong performance as an orator, see also Easterling 1999, 154–166.

44 See also Gottesman 2014, 128, 165–166, who terms this scene "a publicity stunt from a marginal person" (p. 128).

45 The translation is by Lattimore 1951.

46 An indication of how memorable the altar scene is in the *Against Timarchus* is given by the glossing of its key verb, *hupogeneiazein*, by Ps. Herodianus in *Philetaerus* 39, with special reference to this particular passage, and by Hesychius (and the majority of Greek lexicographers after him) as *hupogeneiazōn*, that is, in the form attested in Aeschines' text.

ritual, the suppliant comes forward and adopts a posture of inferiority towards the object of his supplication, which is comparable to that of a slave.[47] The suppliant normally directs his or her gestures towards knees, chin, and hands. It has been persuasively argued that these parts of the body were thought of as the seat of physical strength and sexual power.[48] If this was indeed the case, Timarchus' alleged touching of Pittalacus' chin may have had strong sexual connotations, which aptly served Aeschines' rhetorical goal, that is, to present Timarchus as the paid lover of even a public slave. The memorable detail with which Aeschines furnishes his narrative, such as, for instance, the touching of the chin, is crucial to its success. An opponent was unlikely to challenge the accuracy of such details, since such a challenge would alienate the judges panel and waste valuable time needed to address other, more crucial, aspects of the case.

That the Pittalacus' episode occupies a central position in Aeschines' plan is suggested by the fact that it includes allusions to various important points in both narrative and argumentative sections of the rest of the speech. First of all, Aeschines makes the metaphorical allegation that Pittalacus has acted as the *chorēgos* for Timarchus' disgusting behaviour (§54),[49] thus making a sly allusion to the poor liturgic record of Timarchus and his father, although they both belonged to the liturgic class (§§97–105). This allusion is particularly effective with respect to the composition of the scandalous story and the sketching of Timarchus' attitude and habits, since it stresses that Timarchus not only spent all his wealth on the satisfaction of base pleasures, but has also drawn in a slave, to act as the sponsor of his shameless desires. Thus, Timarchus shows that he prefers temporary personal financial gain, obtained through his own degradation, to the good-will of the gods, whose festivals he would otherwise have helped fund, and to the permanent relationship of gratitude that binds liturgists to the Athenian *dēmos*.[50]

Moreover, the image of Timarchus kneeling in supplication of Pittalacus contrasts powerfully with the image, in which the language of supplication is emphatically employed, of Timarchus' mother, who pleads in vain with her son for a burial plot (§99).[51] Indeed, the thought crosses one's mind that Aeschines

47 Cf. Eur. *Hec.* 249.

48 On the religious and social institution of supplication in general; see Gould 1973; Naiden 2006. See in particular Gould 1973, 75–77, 94, 96–97 for the argument of this paragraph.

49 ἀλλ' εἰ λήψεται χορηγὸν τῇ βδελυρίᾳ τῇ ἑαυτοῦ, τοῦτο μόνον ἐσκέψατο ("if he was going to acquire a financial sponsor for his foul debauchery, that was the only thing he looked for").

50 See also Fisher 2001, 192; Spatharas 2016, 133. Cf. also §11.

51 §99: τὸ δ' Ἀλωπεκῆσι χωρίον, ὃ ἦν ἄπωθεν τοῦ τείχους ἕνδεκα ἢ δώδεκα στάδια, ἱκετευούσης καὶ ἀντιβολούσης τῆς μητρός, ὡς ἐγὼ πυνθάνομαι, ἐᾶσαι καὶ μὴ ἀποδόσθαι, ἀλλ' εἰ μή τι

may actually have fabricated the highly unusual scene of a slave supplicating at the altar of the Mother of Gods (§60).[52] The scene of the half-naked Pittalacus, who, crouched at the altar, displays his injuries, mirrors the offensive display of Timarchus' body, which, ruined by drink and debauchery, reflects his moral condition, as he speaks at the Assembly. (§26).[53] The spirit of two Solonian laws cited in §§138–139, one forbidding slaves to exercise in *gymnasia*, and the other forbidding them to become the lovers of freeborn boys, conflicts with Timarchus' willing sexual subordination to a public slave. The judges, aware that Timarchus had allegedly sold himself to Pittalacus, whose sex slave he became, may have viewed with some irony the sale of the dozen slaves inherited by Timarchus (§§97, 99) and the accusation levelled at him that he had made the sycophantic accusation that an Athenian citizen, Philotades, had been one of his slaves, thereby managing to extort two thousand drachmas (§114).

Finally, and perhaps more importantly, Timarchus' affair with Pittalacus, characterised by submission on the part of a citizen to a slave, echoes and enhances the metaphorical use of the language of slavery and enslavement to describe Timarchus' addiction to sex, gambling and overeating (§42).[54] The skilled construction of the (rhetorical) identity of Timarchus as a man permanently addicted to shameful desires is a prime strategy in the speech, which, in my view, ensured the success of Aeschines' action against Timarchus.

ἄλλο, ἐνταφῆναί γ' ὑπολιπεῖν αὐτῇ, τούτου τοῦ χωρίου ἀπέσχετο, ἀλλὰ καὶ τοῦτ' ἀπέδοτο δισχιλίων δραχμῶν, "the piece of land at Alopeke, which was eleven or twelve stades from the city-wall, his mother supplicated and begged him to let alone, as I have heard, and not sell; let him leave that, if nothing else, for her to be buried in. He did not keep his hands off even that land, but sold that too for two thousand drachmai". Cf. also §24 the orator's reference to the honour of old age (*timan to gēras*).

52 Since slaves were said to seek refuge more often at the Theseion or at the shrine of the Furies. See n. 39.

53 On this incident as narrated by Aeschines see also Fisher 2001, 153–155; Spatharas 2016, 134–135; O'Connell 2017, 74–79.

54 ἀλλ' ἔπραξε ταῦτα *δουλεύων* ταῖς αἰσχίσταις ἡδοναῖς, ὀψοφαγίᾳ καὶ πολυτελείᾳ δείπνων καὶ αὐλητρίσι καὶ ἑταίραις καὶ κύβοις καὶ τοῖς ἄλλοις, ὑφ' ὧν οὐδενὸς χρὴ κρατεῖσθαι τὸν γενναῖον καὶ ἐλεύθερον, "no, he did these things *because he was a slave* to the most shameful pleasures, fish-eating, extravagant dining, girl-pipers and escort-girls, dicing, and the other activities none of which ought to get the better of any man who is well-born and free". See Hatzilambrou 2019, 50 and n. 20; also Lewis 2018, 59–67.

3 Conclusion

The short Pittalacus' episode within the narrative of the speech *Against Timarchus* is certainly a good scandalous story. It involves a status reversal that was unacceptable in Athenian society and associated social anxieties concerning civic identity. Moreover, it included an event allegedly played out in public and witnessed by many Athenian citizens. The content of the episode, its place within a larger context, the vividness with which it is presented and Aeschines' no doubt highly professional delivery must have made this scandalous story completely plausible. So Aeschines achieved his goal. Scandals, however, take on a life of their own. The evidence of the facts is then of little importance. The judges probably failed to notice that no witnesses were called to substantiate the core of this scandalous story. Glaucon (§§65–[66]) probably testified only about the security of Pittalacus' freedom from Hegesander, when the latter was attempting to make Pittalacus his slave.[55] Aeschines cautiously avoids making any reference that he himself had witnessed anything of this episode. Finally, suspiciously enough, Aeschines fails to summon Pittalacus himself to testify. Aeschines does not even use the procedure known as *proklēsis eis basanon*,[56] which he could have done, if Pittalacus was still a slave at the time. Aeschines offered no comment as to why he does not do this, although he summons other alleged lovers of Timarchus, namely Misgolas and Hegesander, (§§45–50, 67–69), who predictably refuse to testify.

Timarchus' relationship to Pittalacus is singled out for special mention as the cause of Timarchus' wicked life in the *hypothesis* of Libanius to Dem. 19:[57]

> ἡ δὲ κίνησις τῆς ἔχθρας λέγεται διὰ Τίμαρχον τὸν φίλον Δημοσθένους, ὃν ἠτίμωσεν Αἰσχίνης κατηγορήσας ὡς κακοῦ βίου, διότι πρὸς Πιττάλακον τὸν ὀρνιθίαν, φησίν, εἰσῄει εὔμορφος ὢν ἐπὶ τῷ θεᾶσθαι τὰς μάχας τῶν ὀρνίθων, διαφθειρόμενον καὶ διαφθείροντα.

> The motivation of Demosthenes' hatred is said to be Aeschines' successful disfranchisement of Timarchus, a friend of Demosthenes. Aeschines accused Timarchus of leading a wicked life, because (as he claimed) this good-looking man Timarchus went to Pittalacus the bird-dealer's house to watch cock-fights, a man who is both corrupted and a corrupter.

---

55 See also Fisher 2001, 362.

56 See for instance Thür 1977; Gagarin 1996.

57 See also I. Tzetzes *Chiliades* 6.55–56, where Pittalacus is mentioned for the same cause together with Misgolas. Translation of the text of Libanius is from Gibson 2003.

I firmly believe that the Pittalacus' episode made a similarly strong impact on contemporary Athenians, including, of course, the judges of the case. It seems that Aeschines' scandalous narrative concerning Pittalacus became a real *scandalon* against Timarchus, that is, "a snare or trap laid of an enemy", which, of course, is the original meaning of the word.[58]

Bibliography

Carey, C. (2017), 'Style, Persona and Performance in Aeschines' Prosecution of Timarchus', in: S. Papaioannou/A. Serafim/B. da Vela (eds.), *The Theatre of Justice*, Leiden, 275–282.

Cartledge, P. (²2001), *The Greeks. A Portrait of Self and Others*, Oxford.

Cohen, E. (2000), *The Athenian Nation*, Princeton.

Davies, J. (2011), 'Hegesippos of Sounion: an Underrated Politician', in: S.D. Lambert (ed.), *Sociable Man: Essays on Ancient Greek Social Behaviour in Honour of Nick Fisher*, Swansea, 11–24.

Easterling, P. (1999), 'Actors and Voices: Reading between the Lines in Aeschines and Demosthenes', in: S. Goldhill/R. Osborne (eds.), *Performance Culture and Athenian Democracy*, Cambridge, 154–166.

Eidinow, E. (2016), *Envy, Poison, and Death. Women on Trial in Classical Athens*, Oxford.

Fisher, N. (1993), *Slavery in Classical Greece*, London.

Fisher, N. (1995), 'Hybris, Status and Slavery', in: A. Powell (ed.), *The Greek World*, London/New York, 44–84.

Fisher, N. (1998), 'Violence, Masculinity and the Law in Classical Athens', in: L. Foxhall/J. Salmon (eds.), *When Men Were Men: Masculinity, Power and Identity in Classical Antiquity*, London/New York, 68–97.

Fisher, N. (2001), *Aeschines against Timarchos*, Oxford.

Fisher, N. (2004), 'The Perils of Pittalakos: Settings of Cock Fighting and Dicing in Classical Athens', in: S. Bell/G. Davies (eds.), *Games and Festivals in Classical Antiquity*, Oxford, 65–78.

Fisher, N. (2005), 'Body-Abuse: the Rhetoric of *Hybris* in Aeschines' *Against Timarchos*', in: J.M. Bertrand (ed.), *La violence dans les mondes grec et romain*, Paris, 67–89.

Fisher, N. (2006), 'Citizens, Foreigners and Slaves in Greek Society', in: K.H. Kinzl (ed.), *A Companion to the Classical Greek World*, Malden, 327–349.

Fisher, N. (2008), '"Independent" Slaves in Classical Athens and the Ideology of Slavery', in: C. Katsari/E. Dal Lago (eds.), *From Captivity to Freedom. Themes in Ancient and Modern Slavery*, Leicester, 121–146.

Fisher, N. (2021), 'Creating a Cultural Community: Aeschines, Timarchus and Demosthenes', in: A. Michalopoulos/A. Serafim/F. Beneventano della Corte/A. Vatri (eds.), *The Rhetoric of Unity and Division in Ancient Literature*, Berlin/Boston, 45–70.

Gagarin, M. (1996), 'The Torture of Slave in Athenian Law', in: *CPh* 91, 1–18.

58 See *LSJ*⁹ s.v. *skandalon*.

Galiardi, L. (2005), 'The Athenian Procedure of Dokimasia of Orators. A Response to Douglas M. MacDowell', in: R. Wallace/M. Gagarin (eds.), *Symposion 2001: Vorträge zur griechischen und hellenistischen Rechtsgeschichte*, Vienna, 89–97.
Gibson, C. (2003), *Libanius Hypotheses to the Orations of Demosthenes,* at *http://www.stoa.org/projects/demos/article_libanius?page=1*
Gottesman, A. (2014), *Politics and the Street in Democratic Athens*, Cambridge.
Gould, J. (1973), 'Hiketeia', in: *JHS*, 74–103.
Halperin, D.M. (1990), *One Hundred Years of Homosexuality: and Other Essays on Greek Love*, New York.
Harris, E.M. (1985), 'The Date and the Trial of Timarchus', in: *Hermes* 113, 376–380.
Harris, E.M. (1995), *Aeschines and Athenian Politics*, Oxford.
Harrison, A.R.W. (1971), *The Law of Athens*, vol. II, Oxford.
Hatzilambrou, R. (2019), 'Constructing the Identity of Timarchus in Aeschines 1', in: J. Filonik/B. Griffith-Williams/J. Kucharski (eds.), *The Making of Identities in Athenian Oratory*, London/New York, 47–62.
Hunter, R.L. (1985), *The New Comedy of Greece and Rome*, Cambridge.
Hunter, V. (1990), 'Gossip and the Politics of Reputation in Classical Athens', in: *Phoenix* 44, 299–325.
Hunter, V. (1994), *Policing Athens. Social Control in the Attic Lawsuits, 420-320 B.C.*, Princeton.
Hunter, V. (2006), 'Pittalacus and Eucles: Slaves in the Public Service of Athens', in: *Mouseion* 6, 1–13.
Ismard, P. (2015), *La démocratie contre les experts: les esclaves publics en Grèce ancienne*, Paris.
Jacob, O. (1928), *Les esclaves publics à Athènes*, Liège.
Kamen, D. (2013), *Status in Classical Athens*, Princeton.
Kamen, D. (2018), 'The Consequences of Laughter in Aeschines' *Against Timarchos*', in: *Archimède* 5, 49–56.
Kapparis, K. (2018), *Prostitution in the Ancient Greek World*, Berlin/Boston.
Lanham, R.A. ([2]1991), *A Handlist of Rhetorical Terms*, Berkeley.
Lape, S. (2006), 'The Psychology of Prostitution in Aeschines' Speech *Against Timarchus*', in: C.A. Faraone/L.K. McClure (eds.), *Prostitutes and Courtesans in the Ancient World*, Madison, 139–160.
Lattimore, R. (1951), *The Iliad of Homer*, Chicago/London.
Lewis, D. (1990), 'Public Property in the City', in: O. Murray/S. Price (eds.), *The Greek City from Homer to Alexander*, Oxford, 245–263.
Lewis, D.M. (2018), *Greek Slave Systems in their Mediterranean Context c.800–146 B.C.*, Oxford.
MacDowell, D.M. (2000), *Demosthenes, On the False Embassy (Oration 19)*, Oxford.
MacDowell, D.M. (2005), 'The Athenian Procedure of *Dokimasia* of Orators', in: R. Wallace/M. Gagarin (eds.), *Symposion 2001: Vorträge zur griechischen und hellenistischen Rechtsgeschichte*, Vienna, 80–87.
McNiven, T.J. (1982), *Gestures in Attic Vase Painting: Use and Meaning, 550-450 B.C.* (diss.). University of Michigan.
Naiden, F.S. (2006), *Ancient Supplication*, Oxford.
O' Connell, P.A. (2017), *The Rhetoric of Seeing in Attic Forensic Oratory*, Austin.
Parker, R.C.T. (1996), *Athenian Religion: A History*, Oxford.

Roisman, J./Worthington, I. (2015), *Lives of the Attic Orators: Texts from Pseudo-Plutarch, Photius, and the Suda*, Oxford.
Rowe, G.O. (1997), 'Style', in: S.E. Porter (ed.), *Handbook of Classical Rhetoric in the Hellenistic Period, 330 B.C. – A.D. 400*, Leiden, 121–157.
Rubinstein, L. (2012), 'Evoking Anger through Pity', in: A. Chaniotis/P. Ducrey (eds.), *Unveiling Emotions II*, Stuttgart, 136–165.
Serafim, A. (2020), *Religious Discourse in Attic Oratory and Politics*, London/New York.
Silver, M. (2013), 'Pittalacus the Slave and the Mother of the Gods: Between the Lines of Aeschines 1.54–66', in: *Marburger Beiträge zur Antiken Handels-, Wirtschafts-und Sozialgeschichte* 31, 97–119.
Spatharas, D. (2006), 'Persuasive ΓΕΛΩΣ: Public Speaking and the Use of Laughter', in: *Mnemosyne* 59, 374–387.
Spatharas, D. (2016), 'Sex, Politics and Disgust in Aeschines' *Against Timarchos*', in: D. Lateiner/D. Spatharas (eds.), *The Ancient Emotion of Disgust*, Oxford, 125–140.
Spatharas, D. (2019), *Emotions, Persuasion and Public Discourse in Classical Athens. Ancient Emotions II*, Berlin/Boston.
Thür, G. (1977), *Beweisführung von den Schwurgerichtshöfen Athens. Die Proklesis zur Basanos*, Vienna.
Todd, S.C. (1995), *The Shape of Athenian Law*, Oxford.
Vlassopoulos, K. (2007), 'Free Spaces: Identity, Experience and Democracy in Classical Athens', in: *CQ* 57, 33–52.
Vlassopoulos, K. (2009), 'Slavery, Freedom and Citizenship in Classical Athens: Beyond a Legalistic Approach', in: *European Historical Review* 16, 347–364.
Webb, R. (2009), *Ekphrasis, Imagination and Persuasion in Ancient Rhetorical Theory and Practice*, Farnham/Burlington.
Wrehhaven, K.L. (2012), *Reconstructing the Slave. The Image of the Slave in Ancient Greece*, London.
Wycherley, R.E. (1957), *The Athenian Agora III: Literary and Epigraphical Testimonia*, Princeton.

Notes on Editors and Contributors

Edward M. Harris is Emeritus Professor of Ancient History at Durham University and Honorary Professorial Fellow at the University of Edinburgh.

Rosalia Hatzilambrou is Assistant Professor of Ancient Greek Literature at the National and Kapodistrian University of Athens.

Asako Kurihara is Professor of Classics at Osaka University.

Vasileios Liotsakis is Assistant Professor of Ancient Greek Literature in the Department of Philology at the University of the Peloponnese.

Andreas Markantonatos is Professor of Greek in the Department of Philology at the University of the Peloponnese.

David Mirhady is Professor of Classics in the Humanities Department at Simon Fraser University.

Smaro Nikolaidou is Lecturer of Ancient Greek Literature at Democritus University of Thrace.

Ioannis N. Perisynakis is Emeritus Professor of Ancient Greek Literature in the Department of Philology at the University of Ioannina.

Pasquale Massimo Pinto is Professor of Classics in the Department of Humanities at the Aldo Moro University of Bari.

Noboru Sato is Associate Professor of Classics at Kobe University.

Andreas Serafim is a Research Fellow at the Research Centre for Greek and Latin Literature of the Academy of Athens.

Margarita Sotiriou is Assistant Professor of Ancient Greek Literature in the Department of Philology at the University of the Peloponnese.

Robert Sullivan is Professor of the Humanities in the Communication Studies Department at Ithaca College.

Guy Westwood is Lecturer in Classics at Lady Margaret Hall at the University of Oxford.

General Index

https://doi.org/10.1515/9783110751970-016

Index Locorum

https://doi.org/10.1515/9783110751970-017